Becoming. Architectures for a planet in transition

Becoming. Architectures for a planet in transition

A collection of original contributions for the UIA World Congress of Architects 2026 Barcelona

Edited by Pau Bajet, Mariona Benedito, Maria Giramé, Tomeu Ramis, Carmen Torres and Pau Sarquella

PUENTE EDITORES

PARK BOOKS

Contents

Becoming Hyper-conscious

Becoming Attuned

Seven Visions of Becoming

Biographies and Project Credits

The UIA World Congress of Architects 2026 Barcelona

Founded in 1948, the UIA works to unify architects, influence public policy, ensure dialogue with global decision-making bodies, and advance architecture in the service of society. For seventy years, the UIA World Congresses have provided a platform for professional reflection and international dialogue on the major challenges shaping our built environment. Since 2020, the Congress host city has also been designated as the UNESCO–UIA World Capital of Architecture, affirming architecture as a discipline of public interest and inviting citizens to take part in this global conversation.

With nearly seventy per cent of humanity projected to live in urban areas by 2050, the way we govern, plan and design will determine whether cities deepen inequality or become engines of wellbeing, inclusion and resilience. This transformation calls for a collaborative effort, and for platforms for exchange. Barcelona offers a compelling context for this exchange. Throughout its history, the city has demonstrated how planning and design can serve broader social, cultural and environmental objectives. We can critically learn from Barcelona's complexity – by engaging in site-specific design investigations and discussions that provoke and inspire. Through the Congress, and as World Capital of Architecture 2026, Barcelona invites us to reconsider the relationships between cities and nature, heritage and innovation, local identity and global responsibility.

The theme, 'Becoming. Architectures for a planet in transition', builds on shared international frameworks and calls for institutional commitment to integrated, inclusive and interdisciplinary urban development. Architecture cannot act in isolation. Responsible urban environments require political will, professional integrity, interdisciplinary collaboration and meaningful participation, placing human dignity, cultural diversity, environmental balance and long-term collective value at the heart of decision-making.

As we gather in Barcelona for the World Congress of Architects, we reaffirm our shared responsibility to shape the built environment in the public interest. Architecture is not only about constructing buildings. It is about shaping the conditions for life – both for today and for generations to come.

Regina Gonthier
President
International Union of Architects (UIA)
March 2026

The UIA World Congress of Architects 2026 Barcelona convenes at a critical juncture for the architectural profession. The accelerating environmental, social, economic and technological transformations that are reshaping the conditions of life on our planet compel a renewed and rigorous examination of architecture's role and its responsibilities towards the public good. Within this context, the curatorial framework 'Becoming. Architectures for a planet in transition' advances a perspective that conceives architecture not as a static discipline, but as a dynamic, continuously evolving practice capable of adapting, transforming and envisioning alternatives in response to emerging global challenges.

Barcelona, the host city of the Congress, offers an exceptional setting for fostering such a debate. Its urban trajectory, defined by innovation, civic engagement and a long-standing commitment to high-quality, equitable public space, today intersects with a vibrant culture of experimentation that positions the city as a contemporary laboratory of urban inquiry. From sustainable mobility initiatives to renaturalisation strategies, from heritage rehabilitation to new models of metropolitan governance and public housing, Barcelona has become a fertile ground for testing forward-looking approaches to urban life.

This publication presents the collective work of the six curators who, within the framework of the UIA's Scientific Committee, articulated the conceptual narrative of the Congress. Their proposal invites a critical exploration of the multiple ways in which architecture may respond to a planet undergoing profound transition: by embracing complexity, attending to ecological systems, acknowledging cultural pluralities, integrating emerging technologies and advancing transformations that are both just and sustainable. 'Becoming' encapsulates this ethos: it foregrounds temporality, process, openness and the imaginative capacity to project that which is not yet realised.

The Congress brings together architects, scholars, students and institutions from around the world, establishing a platform for the exchange of ideas, methodologies and projects aimed at rethinking the future and calling for collective action. Architects must play an active role in shaping cities that foster coexistence and shared wellbeing; ours is a discipline that must anticipate, propose and contribute meaningfully to the construction of a more equitable and resilient world.

The book serves as the written and visual synthesis of the 'becoming' process that underpins the Congress, an endeavour which, like the city of Barcelona, looks to the future with responsibility, awareness and a steadfast commitment to advancing a more balanced and habitable planet.

Marta Vall-llossera Ferran
President, UIA World Congress of Architects
2026 Barcelona

Guim Costa Calsamiglia
Director, UIA World Congress of Architects
2026 Barcelona

Becoming activates time as a projective design tool. In the face of global matters of concern – climate change, biodiversity loss, growing inequality – it rejects isolated analysis and paralysis and instead stimulates speculation and imagination. Becoming looks into the future by exploring spatial practices that foster individual and collective, human and more-than-human rights of appropriation and transformation. Through nuanced interplays of permanence and change, it cares for short-term urgencies while foreseeing long-term horizons, seeking to catalyse joyous yet open-ended prospects. The practice of becoming is inherently transcalar, recognising that situated, local actions reverberate across planetary networks. Rooted in a deep awareness of pre-existing physical and cultural landscapes, it opposes the notion of tabula rasa by curating attentive transitions of spatial change through material, political, ecological and poetic interrelations.

Spatial change is not neutral – it is neither impartial nor harmless. Moving beyond the depletion of laissez-faire paradigms, Becoming articulates a series of challenges that embrace a multiplicity of purposes. Six thematic research lines frame these explorations, inviting intersecting and evolving inquiries into what it means to design for a planet in transition.

Becoming More-than-human
How can architecture embrace biodiversity and trans-species coexistence?

Becoming Circular
Within post-extractivist proximity policies, which cycles can be spatially produced?

Becoming Embodied
How can agency be embedded in the transitions from matter to construction?

Becoming Interdependent
How can we design politics of space that activate interpersonal relationships?

Becoming Hyper-conscious
What actions can arise from a deeper awareness of global and local interplays?

Becoming Attuned
What forms of meaning and poetics can we engage with in our everyday practice?

A grounded design laboratory

In addition to bringing together architectural practices from across the globe as a platform for dissemination and exchange, Becoming operates as a collective device for knowledge production that initiated a constellation of commissioned investigations. These unfold through the six thematic lines not as analytical exercises, but as design-driven forms of inquiry, where spatial speculation becomes a critical and prospective mode of research.

Twelve international teams developed the year-long Research by Design projects featured in this book in real-world contexts, through the construction of mock-ups, speculative visions and critical cartographies. In parallel, twelve architectural practices led intensive one-week Emerging Workshops, under the title 'A Wicked Laboratory', with 180 international participants, mobilising the territory of Barcelona into a situated research site.

These long- and short-term investigations are grounded in earthy, vivid and often fractured realities – in an unstable design laboratory that resists the illusion of experimental research in clean and predictable conditions. Instead, they operate within uncertainty, ambiguity and conflict, prioritising relevance over verification and transdisciplinarity over specialisation.

Further resonance and critical interpretation of both the design investigations and the curatorial framework are provided by twelve invited Critical Antagonists. From different disciplines and positions, they contribute to the book through a series of interviews and essays that intersect, challenge and expand awareness of Becoming.

<u>A post-industrial seafront congress</u>

This publication gathers the architectural investigations and critical writings produced for the UIA World Congress of Architects 2026 Barcelona. At the time of writing in April 2026, we are looking forward to the coming together of thousands of visitors and 270 international speakers, across eight stages and more than a hundred sessions, as well as the 4,000-square-metre central exhibition. Set along the Mediterranean seafront – at sites such as the former turbine hall of the Tres Xemeneies (Three Chimneys) building, the International Barcelona Convention Centre (CCIB) and other civic venues – the Congress expands beyond a traditional conference format to allow architecture to be experienced in alternative ways.

The six plenary roundtables at the beginning and end of each day confront the ideas of the core contributors and participants of the Congress (and therefore of this book), reflecting diverse ways of understanding each Becoming. Between the plenary events, the wide range of lectures, debates, interviews and conversations encourage friction and exchange among participants to destabilise predictable speech and provide a space for unexpected dialogues and findings, visualised in this book at the end of each chapter.

The Three Chimneys site is host to informal discussions, performances, book presentations and celebratory events. This post-industrial landmark

is also the site for the central exhibition, which translates the investigations undertaken in spatial terms – as built artefacts, performative installations, original drawings, and a wide range of audiovisual work.

Open participation

A third of the talks presented at the Congress were selected through an international Open Call launched a year before the event. From 1,544 submissions representing 88 countries, 90 contributions were selected in three different categories. For the Critical Design category, an international jury formed by Carlos Facio, Catherine Mosbach, Kersten Geers and Xu Tian Tian selected 32 mostly realised architecture and landscape design projects. Likewise, the Critical Image international jury formed by Giovanna Borasi, Maxime Delvaux, Louise Lemoine and Urtzi Grau nominated a cohort of 28 visual projects and proposals encompassing photographic narratives, documentaries, digital collage, archival research, data visualisation and hybrid media.

The Critical Essay category was developed through a two-stage anonymous peer-review process, following standard academic procedures. In the first phase, an extensive team of 81 academics selected 122 essay proposals. In the second phase, 42 evaluators contributed to selecting 63 accepted essays. An international jury formed by Keller Easterling, Lydia Kallipoliti, Marina Otero Verzier, Philip Ursprung, Samia Henni and Raquel Rolnik conducted a final cross-evaluation to select the 30 essays whose authors were invited to give oral presentations of their work at the Congress. The same jury also singled out the 'Seven Visions of Becoming' essays included in this book, collectively reflecting a significant contribution to renewed awareness of political empowerment, ecological intelligence, and spatial and material experimentation across diverse geographies and scales.

Under the title 'Catalysts of Resilience', the UIA International Student Competition invited students worldwide to explore architecture's capacity to engage vulnerable territories through time. Rather than proposing fixed solutions, participants developed strategies for gradual

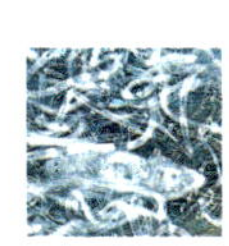

transformation, addressing ecological, social and political challenges across diverse contexts. The 587 submissions revealed a remarkable range of approaches, from landscape-based interventions to adaptive urban frameworks, all grounded in existing conditions. Further information about the competition and the winning entries can be found towards the end of this book. Aligned with the ethos of Becoming, these projects demonstrate how architectural thinking can activate latent potentials and operate as a catalyst for long-term resilience, connecting immediate action with open-ended futures.

The Congress, and by extension this book, reflect a high level of density and multiplicity. Each visitor or reader is invited to navigate their content freely, resisting the deceptive temptation of believing that it can all be absorbed. Becoming ultimately positions architecture not as a discipline of control and determinism, but as a transdisciplinary form of situated practice moving towards intersubjective, non-anthropocentric transformation. In the midst of an expansive and diffuse disciplinary field crossed by social, technological and environmental shifts, this approach suggests a sense of collective orientation towards open-ended futures with a simple yet radical programme: fostering delightful and unforeseen ways of living in common.

Pau Bajet, Mariona Benedito, Maria Giramé,
Tomeu Ramis, Pau Sarquella and Carmen Torres
Curators of the UIA World Congress
of Architects 2026 Barcelona

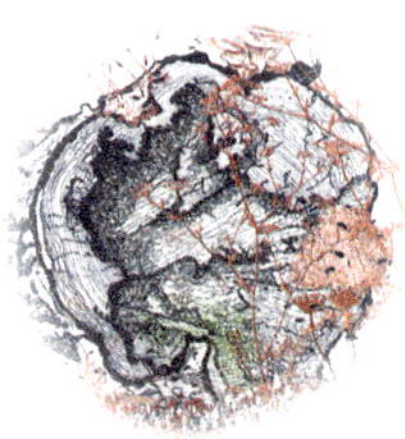

Water
Water
Deserted Oil Field
CO2
CO2
Deserted Gas Field
CO2 Storage Station
Geo-thermal Station
Burj Khalifa (2010)

volcano
buried vestiges
FRACTURES

Becoming More-than-human

'We are not autonomous beings.
We are compost.'

Donna Haraway, *Staying with the Trouble*, 2016

How can architecture embrace ecological coexistence?

The construction of inhabited environments has historically been governed by the anthropocentric paradigm that positions humans as the sole agents in shaping the built environment, marginalising the agency of other living and non-living beings.

Rooted in the Western nature–culture divide, this hierarchy has legitimised extractivist practices that intensified after the Industrial Revolution, culminating in the ecological crisis described as the Capitalocene. In this context, environmental conservatism grounded in idealised notions of nature would only aggravate this disjunction.

'Becoming More-than-human' emerges as a critical framework that acknowledges planetary crises as intrinsic to contemporary ecological systems and calls for the reimagining of inhabited environments as complex, hybrid, multispecies ecosystems. It reframes architecture, across all its scales, as a mediator of adaptive resilience and transformation, foregrounding symbiosis, extended practices of care and regenerative soil, water and energy cycles.

Mark Wigley

ARCHITECTS GONE WILD

Inviting the largest international gathering of architects to think about 'Becoming More-than-human' challenges the very idea of architecture and the traditional figure of the architect. It calls for a dramatic transformation of both buildings and designers. The health of humans is completely entangled with that of the estimated billions of other species on Earth, along with the planet they all share and co-produce. What lies beyond the human, or beyond our conventional understanding of the human, is the very basis of survival, of life itself. Even the most selfish defence of human life must embrace rather than exclude, subordinate and control what is beyond human. Paradoxically, the best defence of humanity is to be less defensive. Yet architecture keeps getting in the way, rigidly resisting cohabitation and co-evolution. A whole new set of skills is needed to undo architecture and reopen it to other species and other futures.

The architectural animal

Vitruvius established the basis for architecture as a discipline and eventually a profession by portraying it as the exclusion of the more-than-human. He famously told a story of the origin of architecture when the first shelter was formed in a forest. For Vitruvius, architecture marks the superiority of the human species by sheltering it from other species, weather, variations, disease, irrationality and surprise. Living, twisting, entangled interacting forms of organic life gave way to lifeless static geometry. Pulsations gave way to permanence. Dead wood and mud eventually gave way to stone. The 'beasts' that made the first shelters and lived within them – inventing language, culture and technology – were no longer animals and 'subjected all other creatures to their power'. Architecture is not made by humans. On the contrary, it makes humans.

For millennia before the calls for so-called 'human-centred-design' started in the late 1950s, architecture has always put humans at the centre. More precisely, it manufactured and sustained a certain narrow idea of 'the' human, a creature that is no longer an animal. Symptomatically, actual humans don't appear in architectural narratives and drawings, just idealised figures without any of the diversity and fluctuations between childhood and old age, illness, disability, loneliness, agitation, curiosity, joy, fatigue, sleep, confusion and stress. These idealised humans don't sleep, shit, kiss, menstruate, laugh, leak, talk, yawn, smell or love. They don't even have phones or watch TV. Architecture defines itself as sheltering the human but seems to be as afraid of humans as it is of all the things that buildings keep outside. The multiplicity, fluidity, unpredictability and mystery of human life is as excluded as any other species. Becoming More-than-human might include finally embracing the animality of humans in all the ever-changing diversity of their genetic, microbial, chemical, electrical, liquid, emotional, sexual and psychological complications.

It certainly means confronting human violence towards the non-human and the vast majority of humans treated as other-than-human. The UIA was explicitly formed as a collaborative response to the inhumanity of humans. Just a few months after peace was declared in 1945, the Paris-based Hungarian architect Pierre Vago – in close contact with a global network of designers before the war as editor of *L'Architecture d'Aujourd'hui* – imagined an international union of architects devoted to the postwar reconstruction of the built environment and mentality of society. When the organisation was formally launched at the first congress in Lausanne in 1948, the attendees from 27 countries signed a joint declaration committing their 'collaboration' to the defence of human society. This declaration – made in the same year as the Universal Declaration of Human Rights – remains the opening statement of the UIA's official articles and bylaws:

> ...making their contribution to a better understanding between men and peoples by continually striving for the fulfilment of their aspirations for material and spiritual well-being; in collaboration with the other professional and cultural international organizations, they have resolved to contribute to the progress of human society and to the strengthening of peace.[1]

1. 'Preamble Adopted in Lausanne, 1948', *UIA Articles and Bylaws*, 2024, p. 5. https://www.uia-architectes.org/wp-content/uploads/2025/01/UIA-Articles-Bylaws-2024-EGA.pdf

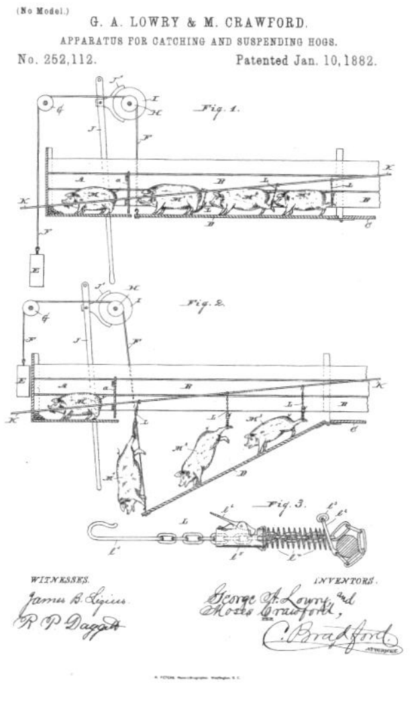

An 1882 patent drawing of apparatus for catching and suspending hogs, illustrated in Sigfried Giedion's *Mechanization Takes Command*, 1948.

Not by chance, 1948 was also the year Sigfried Giedion ended his remarkable book *Mechanization Takes Command* by saying 'It is time for us to become human again.'[2] As the most influential historian and promoter of modern architecture, and secretary of the Congrès Internationaux d'Architecture Moderne (CIAM) since its founding in 1928, Giedion was critiquing himself and his colleagues. He argued that the industrialised machinery on which they had modelled buildings had actually unbalanced, alienated and destroyed humans – realising nineteenth-century fears that machines are a new form of organic life that distorts and enslaves humanity. In an unspoken yet unambiguous reference to the Holocaust, the book is full of animals being constrained, monitored, analysed, dissected, slaughtered and transported. Not just frogs, pigeons, seagulls, horses, chickens and hogs, but humans whose movements are tested in time-motion laboratories or suspended in mechanised farm equipment, factories, kitchens, bathrooms and patent furniture. Life only appears in being controlled or extinguished. Plants, for example, only appear in industrialised reaping, binding, threshing, cleaning and bagging. Insects (80 per cent of all animal life) are missing, along with microbes (by far the majority inhabitants of the planet), as they have been from the more than seventy-five years of UIA meetings. Architects gather in praise of human life, unconsciously understood as the death of others.

2. Sigfried Giedion, *Mechanization Takes Command: A Contribution to Anonymous History*, Oxford University Press, 1948, p. 723.

Toxicities of design

If the UIA is the house of architects, it has been an all-too-clean human-centric shelter – despite occasional appeals to the environment. One paragraph of the declaration signed at the 1981 congress in Warsaw on 'Architecture, Man, Environment' called for architects to 'extend' their responsibility to the natural environment given its 'catastrophic' contamination by the built environment.[3] But only because this toxicity threatens human well-being. The rest of the eleven-page statement only speaks about how to improve urban human life. Subsequent congresses declared collective commitment to sustainability. Yet only in 2022 was the UIA's opening statement of its core defence of humanity amended to include the defence of ecosystems:

> Within its responsibilities and scope of action … the UIA shall advocate for human dignity and the eradication of all forms of violence, discrimination, and inequity, and promote environmental and climate conditions that allow life in ecosystem balance and the well-being of humanity.[4]

3. 'The Warsaw Declaration of Architects of the World', International Union of Architects (UIA), 1981. https://www.uia-architectes.org/wp-content/uploads/2024/03/DeclarationVarsovie1981.pdf

4. 'Addendum to the Preamble, Adopted in Madrid, 2022', *UIA Articles and Bylaws*, 2024, p. 5.

This finally echoed the long history of calls to think of architecture in terms of ecosystems going back to figures like Patrick Geddes at the end of the nineteenth century that were repeated by activists in defence of the planet in the 1960s and 1970s.[5] It is now hard to find architects who think overwise. Almost every design project seems to promise some sensitivity to ecosystems. The UIA belatedly affirmed the shared sense that each building needs to minimise its multiple footprints for the good of both humans and the planet. Yet just four years later, the UIA congress now invites architects to consider Becoming More-than-human. It is no longer a matter of offering self-interested care to the wider living environment. Rather it is about tuning into the myriad of entanglements that blur the limits of the so-called human, buildings and environment. The very idea of the client and of shelter is transformed when bodies and buildings are understood as intertwined sets of porous membranes that enable continuous heterogeneous flows and interactions of species, molecules, DNA, data and environmental gradients.

5. Geddes argued that architecture is not just suspended within multiple nested ecosystems, impacting them and impacted by them. It is itself a natural evolving ecosystem: 'Even the modern city is but the most complex evolutionary expression and development of the life of nature.' Patrick Geddes, 'Civics: As Applied Sociology', *The Sociological Review*, 1, January 1904, p. 137.

The ancient ongoing architectural attempt to shelter humans from the environment in a prophylactic bubble paradoxically turns out to be a form of entanglement that dramatically harms both human and environment. The division between culture and nature, human and non-human, that is made by architecture according to Vitruvius, is a toxic fiction.

On the one hand, there is no corner of the planet untouched by the human species. The built environment has no limit. Humans are a biological, geological, hydrological and atmospheric force. Buildings don't simply defend against weather. They co-produce it. They don't simply offer separation from soil. They transform it. And so on.

On the other hand, every human is already an environment. Each is made and sustained by a community of more than 100 trillion

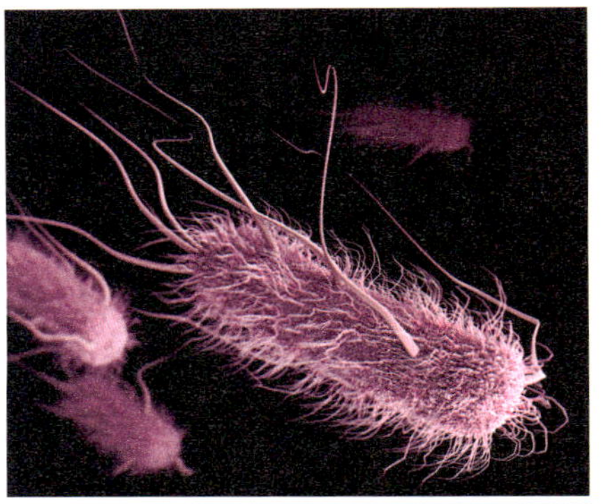

Computer-generated image of a group of *E.coli* bacteria based on electron microscopic imagery by Allisa Eckert of the Centers for Disease Control and Prevention (CDC).

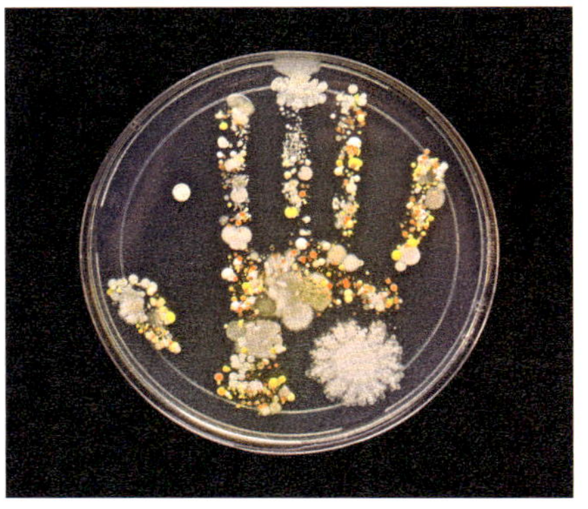

Bacterial handprint of an eight-year-old child after playing outside, by Tasha Sturm.

microbes in unique combinations of thousands of species. Humans only touch the world via the microbes that cover their every exterior and interior surface, from the outer surface of eyeballs to the innermost fold of intestines. This diverse coalition of microbes is directly connected to the brain, part of every thought and emotion. Humans are microbial creatures suspended in a world filled with and manufactured by microbes. Every building element is made, maintained and occupied by bacteria and fungi. When making supposedly human-centric spaces, architects unwittingly curate specific microbial communities that can both nurture and threaten humans.[6]

6. Beatriz Colomina and Mark Wigley, *We the Bacteria: Notes Toward Biotic Architecture*, Lars Müller, 2025.

In other words, humans have always been beyond human, as have the buildings that supposedly defend and represent them. 'Becoming More-than-human' is a manifesto for urgent change, to realise the deepest ethical, intellectual, technical and aesthetic ambitions of architects. But it is also simply an affirmation that humans have never simply been humans and buildings have never been what they appear to be. Bodies and buildings breathe, sweat, flex and contaminate. They incubate, host and depend on multiple forms of life. Most architects speak of their love and care for nature yet are disinterested in the living nature of buildings themselves. In fact, they are experts at repressing it.

To embrace the more-than-human is to invert the conventional understanding of architecture, welcoming what it normally excludes and paying attention to what is always overlooked. It means more than just extending professional care to realms beyond the human, a gesture that could anyway easily become some new form of colonisation. More importantly, it means allowing professional expertise to form coalitions with those realms, becoming somehow part of them. At the very least, it means imagining the architect as an animal coexisting and collaborating with countless other life forms. Not imposing patterns on others, no matter how well intentioned, but embracing the difference, intelligence and collaboration of others. Cultivating design that allows itself to form unexpected relationships. Design as a form of living together. Not diminishing professional expertise but increasing it – empowering the multidimensional transscalar architectural brain by risking it.

Hybrid creatures

What kind of creature would architects operating beyond the conventional limits of architecture be? Are the realms beyond the human also by definition beyond architecture?

Following Vitruvius again, architecture never simply houses humans. It is part of the species, as biological as any other body part. If the first works of architecture were not made by humans but made humans, this remains true with every building. Humans are remade with each act of building, becoming human through building. Neither the organism nor its shells are static. Buildings are not objects. They are verbs. Or said differently, architecture is the becoming human of humans. Strictly speaking, the architect, or whatever is responsible for architecture, has always been by definition something other than human. Paradoxically, there is something irreducibly wild about the architectural animal that presides over the constant activity of domestication. Perhaps the other-than-human attributes of architects could just as easily be reverse-engineered to untether humans and the countless species constrained by them. This sustained ethics of rewilding would start when architects stop domesticating themselves.

It is worth remembering that Patrick Geddes was a bacteriologist before turning to urbanism. He challenged Darwin by showing that seemingly incompatible micro-organisms often host each other to their mutual advantage, raising the possibility that each macro-organism is sustained by countless such permanent collaborations, that evolution is driven more by partnerships than competition.

Patrick Geddes, 1879.

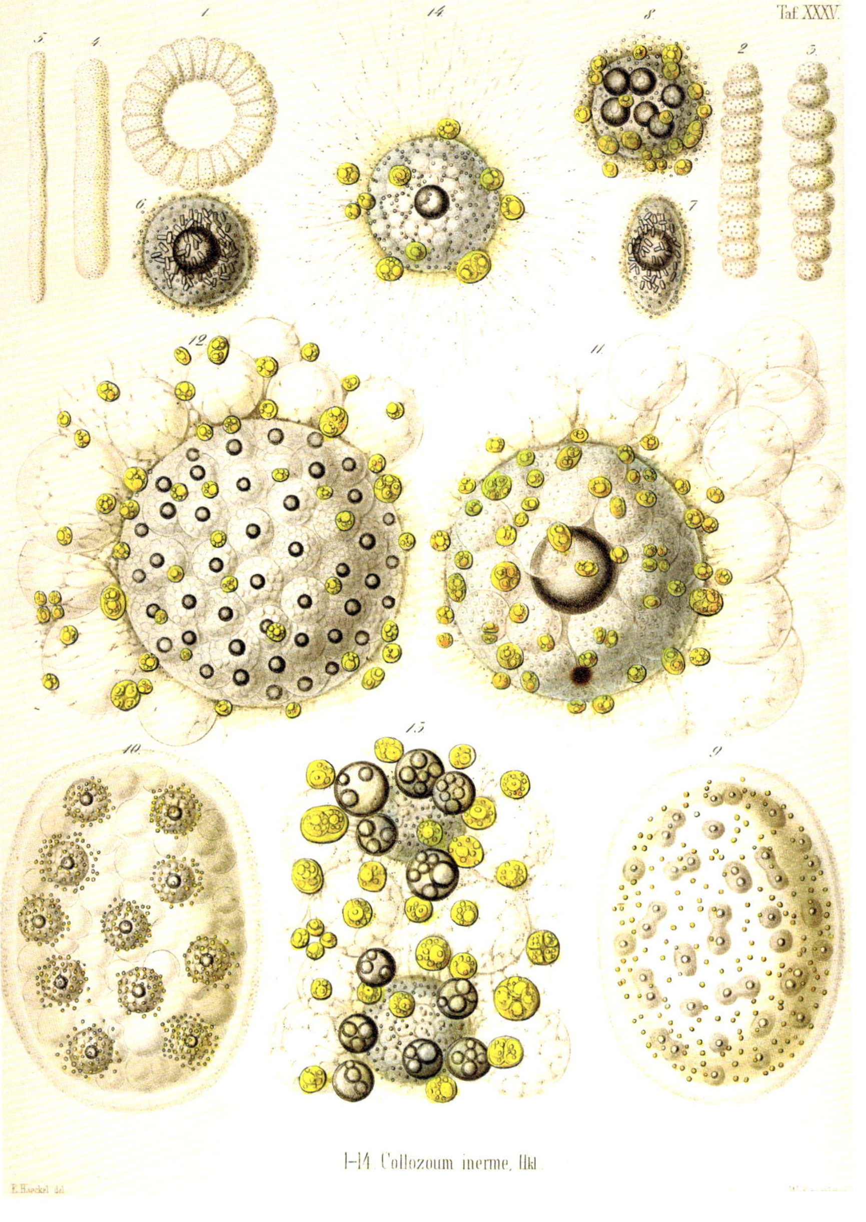

Ernst Haeckel, *Collozoum inerme*, from his monograph *Die Radiolarien*, 1862, showing the 'mutual interdependence' of species living within each other that Patrick Geddes analysed.

Geddes went on to argue that something similar was true with and between buildings, cities, territories and planet.[7] Humans were not the centre of any universe. On the contrary they had created a precarious niche through collaborations with countless more-than-human agents. This remains true, even if the currently occupied built environment now weighs more than the entire planetary biomass, and is the single biggest contributor to climate change and biodiversity reduction. Indeed, the human niche has never been more precarious. To think Becoming More-than-human is to rethink the idea of collaboration on which the UIA was founded. It is not about a single form of collaboration between human and more-than-human agencies. At the very least, it is a diversification and multiplication of heterogeneous forms of agency.

7. Patrick Geddes, *Cities in Evolution: An Introduction to the Town Planning Movement and the Study of Cities*, Williams and Norgate, 1915.

Imagine that the four 'research by design' practices exhibited at the UIA congress under the theme Becoming More-than-human form a coalition – combining the 1,200 trillion microbes of 4+3+2+3 designers: Dirk Sijmons and the KK+N+S team + Eva Franch i Gilabert (FAST) and TAKK + DESIGN EARTH + Simulaa. Isn't that the effect of asking each to carry out a year-long design research project and showing it in the same place through the same curatorial frame? Don't we at least momentarily unconsciously combine what we see in any exhibition or hear in any congress? Each studio is independently brilliant and expansive but likely even more so if combined. Like any strong musical group, they would agree a lot and disagree even more. Their coalition would combine expert knowledge of lichens, sediments, minerals and infrastructural systems. It would think at local, regional, national and planetary scales and across different time scales. It would be articulate in genetic evolution, fluid dynamics, chemistry, interspecies entanglements, soil and politics. It would visualise patterns with more dimensions, complexity and nuance. It would both imagine and realise alternative futures with speculative fiction and geo-engineering from furniture to flood plains. It would stimulate others to think and act differently, whether in galleries, magazines, schools, conferences, community groups, governments, streets, landscapes or territories.

These are not just imagined attributes of some future architectural supergroup. These are the new skills of an ever-increasing number of designers, teachers, curators, historians and theorists today. This is what is on show in Barcelona. The daunting set of disciplines that Vitruvius insisted architects need to have a working knowledge of (geometry, astronomy, history, medicine, law, philosophy, music) turns out to have been just the tip of the transdisciplinary iceberg. Perhaps the very point of a UIA congress is simply to visualise new kinds of architectural community. It can gather, entangle, cross-contaminate and diversify forms of intelligence rather than regressively use singular voices and ideas to synchronise architects.

Listening to architects today as they speak with their newly hybrid voices in schools, publications, competitions, exhibitions, congresses, books and building departments, there is every reason for optimism in the face of the pervasive inequities and stupidities shaping and shaped by the built environment. New kinds of architectural brain are emerging and connecting, thinking together beyond human for the benefit of both human and more-than-human. New forms of collaborative intelligence, politics and design with more-than-human partners. New roles for architects, new sites, new clients, new materials. The very concept of shelter is being transformed, along with ethics, aesthetics and technologies. The architectural animal is untethered and untethering others. Gone wild. At last.

Dirk Sijmons (KK+N+S)

SEA-LEVEL RISE? LAND-LEVEL RISE!

The Moon, our goddess of gravity, drives the tides and sediment flows. Although sediment is fixed by nature, human assistance in the form of trailing suction hopper dredgers and 'hard' defence systems remains essential.

We cannot summarise our message more succinctly than in the title of our project. Climate change and its accompanying sea-level rise are phenomena that low-lying deltas such as the Netherlands will face for many generations to come. This reality compels us to reconsider the resilience of our current flood-protection strategy. Our research-by-design project explores the possibility of harnessing natural processes – both abiotic and biotic – to help vulnerable parts of the country rise in tandem with the sea. This new chapter in rethinking flood safety goes hand in hand with a less hubristic way of relating to nature.

An ecological turn for our Promethean prosthesis?

It is common knowledge that a quarter of the Netherlands lies below sea level. Without protection, almost half would be flooded regularly – a vulnerability that is significantly increased by global warming.

This is the cumulative result of a thousand years of land reclamation: the loss of some seven metres of peat through agriculture, the creation of polders and drained lakes, and the building of towns and cities. The impacts of these interventions on our natural environment have been controlled or mitigated by ingenious technical measures: dikes, sluices, weirs, river embankments, and fine-tuning the groundwater levels. A major keystone in the twentieth century was the closure of estuaries in the southwest as part of the celebrated Delta Works flood-defence system, a strategy that pursued the shortest possible sealed coastline as the best possible solution.

The result of this unrelenting Promethean endeavour to reclaim land from the sea has been the gradual transformation of the Netherlands into a finely tuned water machine: a vast – but for most inhabitants invisible – prosthesis that makes life within this artificial condition possible. It requires periodic maintenance, carried out by the water boards, our oldest public institutions dating back to the thirteenth century. The monitoring of this civil-engineering infrastructure, its dikes, levees and waterworks, is codified in protocols and laws. For now, the system

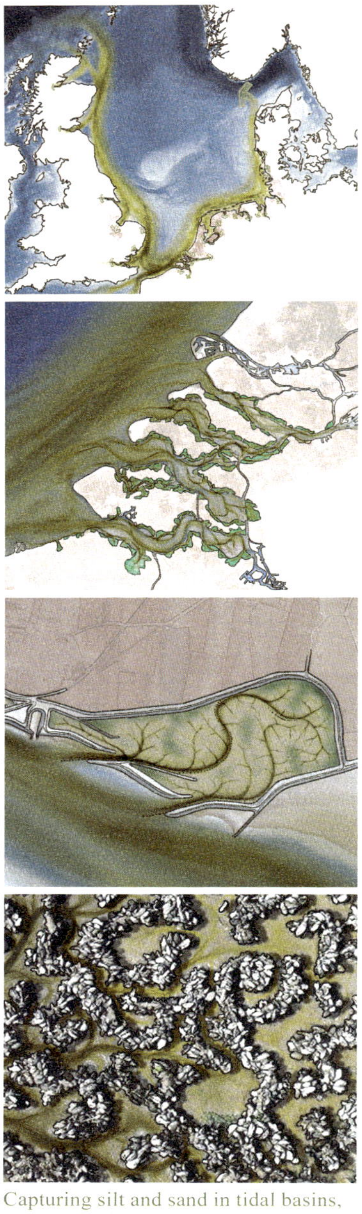

Capturing silt and sand in tidal basins, a principle that works at every scale – from the Delta and islands of Zeeland to a polder or mussel bed.

The silt-succession series stabilising the newly accreted land and boosting the sedimentation process.
From top to bottom: The intertidal zone, a rich table for waterfowl such as foraging Oystercatchers; low salt marsh, with *Spartina anglica* (common cordgrass); middle salt marsh, with *Salicornia europaea* (marsh samphire) in autumn colours and *Halimone portulacoides* (sea purslane); and high salt marsh, with *Limonium vulgare* (sea lavender).

performs remarkably well. Our civil engineers still feel confident that they can manage a two-metre rise with this traditional set of technical defence mechanisms. Water safety is institutionalised and delegated to specialists, and is therefore taken for granted by most of us. But global warming is irreversible, so what if accelerated Arctic ice-melt leads to a five-metre sea-level rise by the year 2200 as extreme scenarios forecast? Will this Promethean, modernist way of thinking still serve us?

If – and when – this scenario will materialise is, of course, highly uncertain. What we have learned from the history of climate projections is that with every scientific update from the Intergovernmental Panel on Climate Change (IPCC), the water seems to get higher, and sooner. We also know from our history of water management that the time span between identifying a strategy and completing the accompanying works measures in decades rather than years. So, although it is a long-term problem, we can't bet on a lucky break. Proactive, urgent research into alternative strategies is therefore essential.

Nature-based solutions leverage natural systems to simultaneously address pressing environmental, social and economic challenges, moving beyond traditional 'grey' infrastructure and single-purpose interventions to provide multiple, integrated benefits. In recent decades there has been a growing awareness that our heavy-handed treatment of the delta not only impoverishes the estuarine ecosystem but may also undermine long-term flood safety. The sectoral civil-engineering approach has been criticised, and alternatives have emerged. The first major turning point came in 1976, when the decision was made to equip the Oosterschelde estuary with a storm-surge barrier instead of sealing it off entirely. In the 1980s, successful nature-development projects along our major rivers – after near-disasters in 1993 and 1995 – inspired the Room for the River programme, which acknowledged that our hydraulic zeal had forced the rivers into a corset that was far too tight. This shift yielded major ecological gains. The Sand Engine, a pilot project to strengthen our sandy coast with an artificial dune of some twenty million cubic metres of sand, revealed that sea currents would themselves pick up the sand and deposit it at the coastline's weak points. Dams that had closed off inland seas and estuaries are being fitted with openings to partially restore fish migration, helping to revitalise the degraded ecosystems behind them.

Artist's impression of a sea-defence landscape in 2125, the cumulative result of a century of sedimentation.

A new step

We are now taking a new step in this research-by-design process. In 2025, we were part of a team of ecologists, coastal geomorphologists, civil engineers and landscape architects tasked with exploring how natural forces might help the land rise alongside the inevitably rising sea. The aim of the proposal, presented at the National Delta Congress 2025,[1] is not to elevate the entire country inch by inch, but to create water-defence landscapes at strategic locations that are gradually shaped by harnessing the immense force of tides and their sediment flows. Even with today's near-absence of riverine sediment, this may still be possible by choreographing the tidal silt stream in such a way that it is lured back into currently sealed tidal basins, depositing its loads of sediment in carefully prepared areas.

1. M. Steenstra, B. van Wesenbeeck, B. van Maren, B. Kolen, L. van Nieuwenhuijze, P, Schengenga and A. J. F. Hoitink, *Meegroeien met zeespiegelstijging: Onderzoek naar nature-based strategieën om Nederland te beschermen tegen de effecten van zeespiegelstijging*, Ministerie van Infrastructuur & Waterstaat, 2025.

These interventions would literally and figuratively reshape the delta landscape. Tide after tide, millimetre by millimetre, the land would grow alongside the rising sea, with new layers fixed by the vegetation of salt marshes, and drifting sands accumulating in living dunes. A living proof of the power of the combination of abiotic and biotic forces is the drowned land of Saeftinghe, a never-reclaimed salt marsh near the Belgian border that silted up to the highest land along the Westerschelde estuary.

Reawakening the natural forces that thrive on the gradient where fresh- and saltwater meet, where land is periodically flooded and exposed – in short, restoring the intrinsic dynamics of estuaries – would help to stabilise and secure this gradual rise of the land. Reviving the resilient ecosystem of the sea, land and intertidal zone so that it no longer needs to be protected like a greenhouse plant, may ultimately help protect us. The roles are reversed in this unexpected plot twist. The abiotic forces of silt and tidal energy, and the natural succession they set in motion,

Beneath the silt layers, a variety of bio-builders are at work: lugworms, clam worms and mussels, with sometimes thousands per square metre. *Far right*: The Hedwigepolder, currently the highest ground along the Westerschelde estuary.

are the protagonists of this story. Flood safety and biodiversity advance hand in hand, but this does not happen automatically: the inventive ways in which landscape engineering converts these combined natural forces into water-defence landscapes play Oscar-worthy supporting roles. Nature-based engineering proves to be civil engineering at an advanced level.

Time lapse of the Sand Engine, an artificial dune that served as a pilot to observe how the coastal stream erodes, transports and deposits sand on the weak parts of the coast, from its completion in 2011 onwards. The highly dynamic environment is now also popular with kite surfers.

The toolbox

Nature-based engineering has a well-stocked toolbox: removing certain dams; restoring tidal basins; allowing mudflats and salt marshes to accrete; creating forelands in front of existing dikes attenuating the waves; reactivating peat formation behind the dikes where possible; positioning large sand motors at strategic points; and, last but not least, when necessary, giving nature a helping hand with our fleet of hopper dredgers. Our pragmatic approach means we do not hesitate to rely on ‘hard’ civil-engineering measures when there is no soft alternative.

Spatially, this strategy rewinds parts of our hydraulic-engineering history while applying methods of land-making that are partly ancient and partly highly innovative. Indeed, this may require sacrificing some previously reclaimed land: a strategic withdrawal to gain long-term safety. But it also saves the water boards one in every three rounds of dike reinforcement, resulting in a multi-billion-euro cost reduction. Moreover, modelling shows that these nature-strengthened dikes offer two-layered protection. In the event of a disaster, the number of casualties will be lower, as these water-defence landscapes may flood but cannot fail.

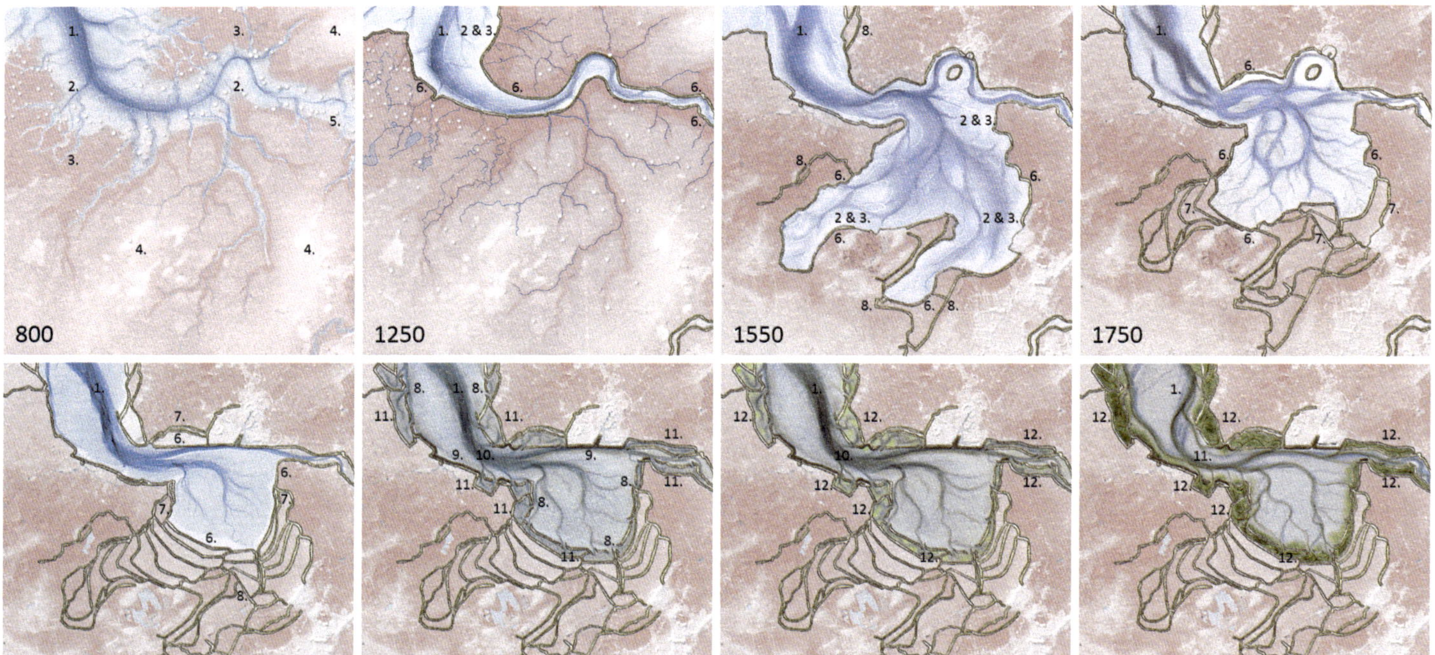

Time travel showing the genesis of the landscape of the Dollard (Ems estuary) from the year 800 – the period when human influence began to reshape the topography – into the future (2200). 1. River Ems; 2. Intertidal area; 3. Salt marsh; 4. Peat bogs; 5. Mounds; 6. Sea dike; 7. Former sea dike; 8. Opening in dike; 9. Dike enhancement; 10. Sediment flow; 11. Start of land-level rise; 12. Continued land level rise.

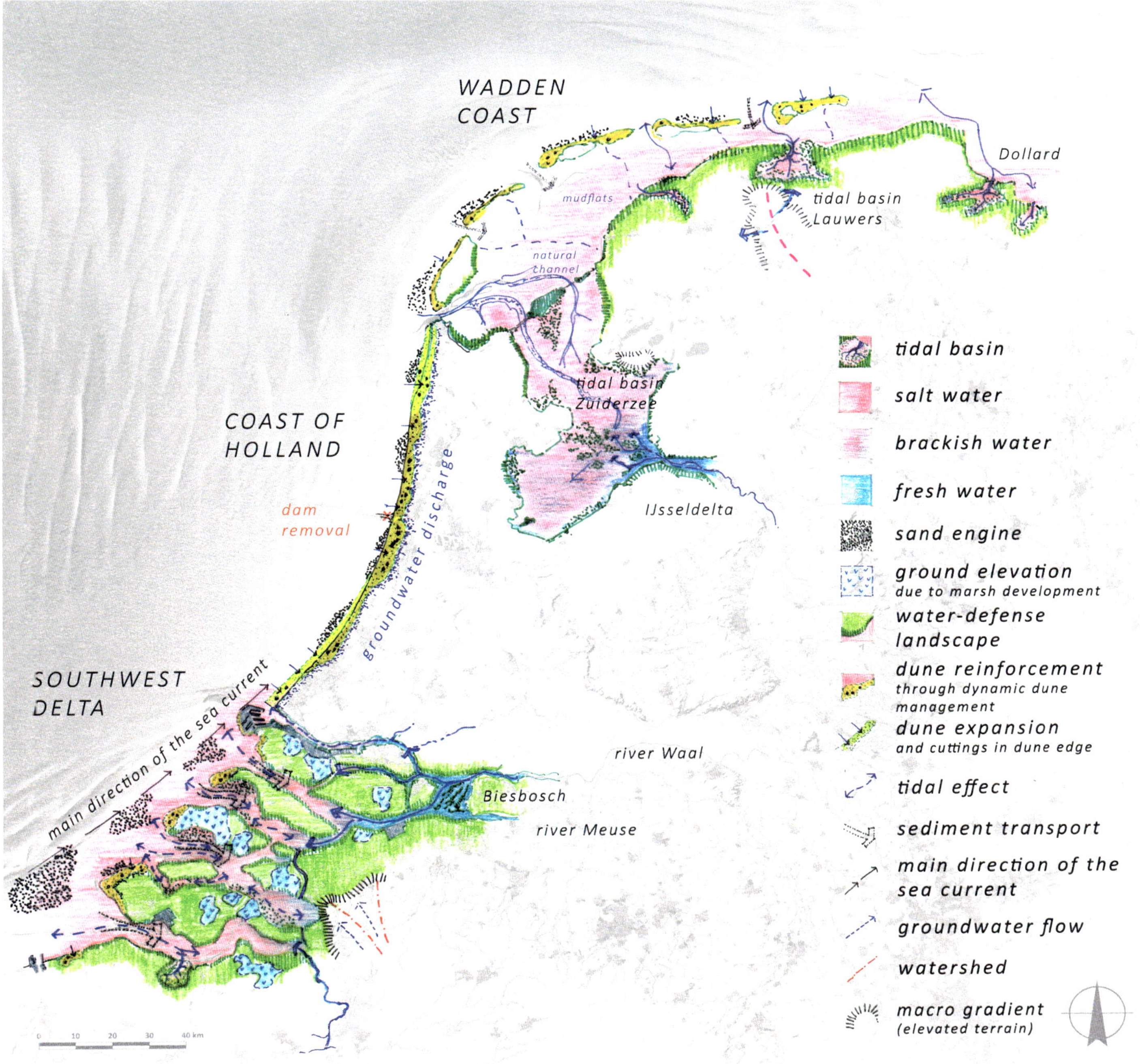

Overview of the potential interventions at the scale of the Rhine-Meuse-Scheldt-Ems Delta. The (opened-up) tidal basins are shown in pink.

Dirk Sijmons (KK+N+S)

The lowering of a dike in 1992 to reintroduce river dynamics, a pilot project stemming from H+N+S Landscape Architects' 'Ooievaar' plan, created a floodplain that has shown spectacular ecological development ever since.

The locations where the Land Level Rise strategy can be deployed are selected with care. Here a completely fictitious – salt seepage affected – agricultural landscape situated along one of the estuarine branches.

The first intervention is the construction of a setback dike, several hundred metres landward of the existing sea defence – a new and stronger barrier. Once completed, one or two carefully designed openings restore access for life-giving sediment.

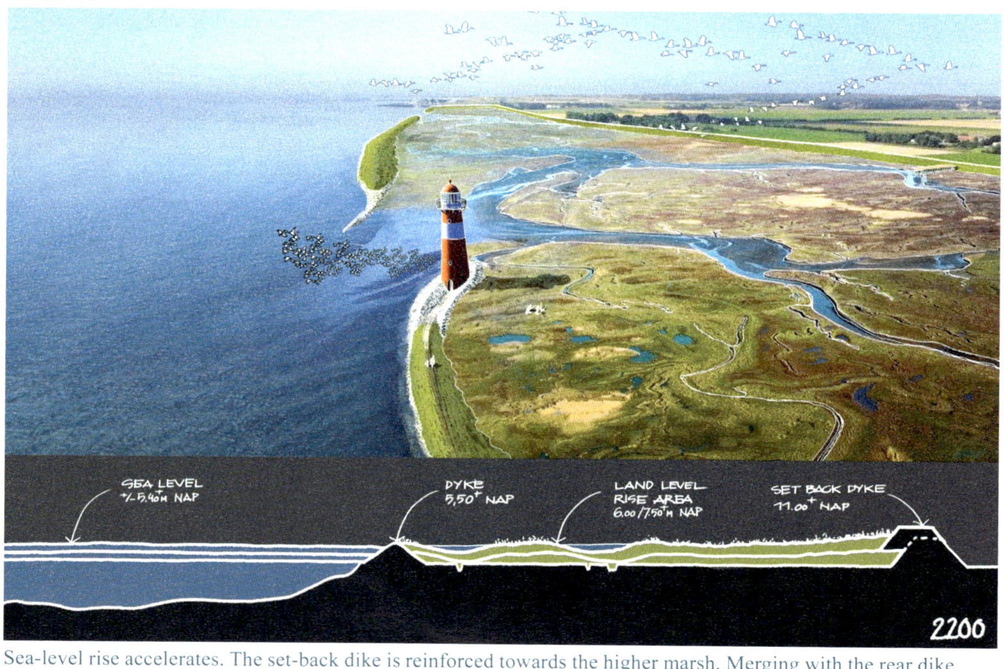

Sea-level rise accelerates. The set-back dike is reinforced towards the higher marsh. Merging with the rear dike, the elevated salt marsh forms a robust, unyielding sea defence. Life-giving sediment is elevated to life-protecting: occasional washing-over claims fewer lives than a breach. Situation around 2200.

Becoming More-than-human?

The exciting prospect that we might theoretically grow alongside a rising sea lies far from the instinctive logic of most people, who often display the Dutch Pavlovian reaction that any threat of flooding must be countered simply by raising the dikes. It requires a cultural shift in thinking about flood safety over an inhumanly long-time horizon: a form of timefulness. Perhaps even more, it calls for a shift in the way we think about nature – transcending the idea of humans as the crown of creation and recognising our embeddedness within the web of life. We not only need to solve a flood-protection problem; we must also halt the destructive erosion of our biosphere. The non-human actors that have inhabited the delta for millions of years may well help us to continue to live here, side by side, shoulder to shoulder, if we may use this anthropomorphic comparison.

We see our flood safety culture, and achieving the right balance with nature, as a never-ending learning (by doing) curve in which the delta itself is our 1:1 laboratory.

Emerging Workshop 1/12

DESIGN EARTH (Rania Ghosn and El Hadi Jazairy)

BRAVA!

DESIGN EARTH, *Elephant in the Room*, 2021. Awakened in the Hall of African Mammals, a matriarch elephant taxidermy breaks out of the American Museum of Natural History in New York to sound a climate alarm – devouring the icons of white male capitalist supremacy and setting a divest-and-decolonise countdown.

DESIGN EARTH, *Whale Song*, 'Elephant in the Room' series, 2022. Hope – the stranded blue whale made into a mascot at London's Natural History Museum – breaks from her cables and swallows the legacies of whaling, fossil fuels and philanthropy, including the Crystal Palace, turning her final 'whale fall' into a living chorus that feeds ecosystems and demands a choice on climate.

DESIGN EARTH, *The Way of Dinosaurs*, 'Elephant in the Room' series, 2023. From Gold Rush quarry pits and the Bone Wars to the Carnegie Museum of Natural History in Pittsburgh, Dippy the dinosaur links fossil hunting to fossil-fuel capitalism, showing how Manifest Destiny, steel and philanthropy built a still world of specimens – and why a future beyond 'fossil fools' means leaving both bones and carbon buried deep.

The Museu de Ciències Naturals de Barcelona is a prominent institution preserving over 130 years of natural history heritage. One of its most emblematic pieces is 'Brava', a 20-metre-long skeleton of a whale beached on the Costa Brava in 1862. Since the 1950s, Costa Brava tourism has taken over from fishing as the principal economy, fundamentally changing the region's relationship with the sea and marine life. Increased tourism, maritime traffic and the expansion of marine infrastructure such as ports, pipelines and desalination plants, pose significant threats to cetaceans, leading to habitat degradation, population decline and mortality.

How might stories help us to make sense of and navigate the unprecedented destruction humanity is now facing? In what ways could the narrative aura of 'charismatic' figures such as Brava be leveraged to recount environmental histories and speculate on climate futures? The Brava! workshop is part of DESIGN EARTH's ongoing 'Elephant in the Room' fable series, which addresses the elephant in the room

DESIGN EARTH, *800-Pound Gorilla*, 'Elephant in the Room' series, 2024. Bushman, a western lowland gorilla, is captured in Cameroon and taken to Chicago – from the jungle to Lincoln Park Zoo, and finally to his taxidermied afterlife at the Field Museum of Natural History, revealing how colonial exchange, industrial slaughter, racialised urban planning and the climate crisis are woven into the same 'City Beautiful' narrative, and what it might take to break the glass cage.

– the climate crisis – by animating enchanting characters from natural history museums.[1] The methodology draws on Donna Haraway's SF – sf: science fiction, speculative fabulation, string figures, speculative feminism, science fact, so far,[2] a storytelling practice that braids fact and fiction, to imagine ways of living together on a damaged planet.

1. DESIGN EARTH, Elephant in the Room: www.youtube.com/@DESIGNEARTH-l1d. See also Rania Ghosn and El Hadi Jazairy, 'Elephant in the Room', *Journal of Architectural Education*, 75(2), 2021, pp. 264–74. https://design-earth.org/publications/elephant-in-the-room--jae/

2. Donna J. Haraway, *Staying with the Trouble: Making Kin in the Chthulucene*, Duke University Press, 2016, p. 2.

DESIGN EARTH, *A Pas de Loup*, 'Elephant in the Room' series, 2025. Through wolves and dogs – wild kin and trained enforcers – the piece traces how power 'mounts' its narratives in museum specimens, national monuments and the political pageantry of Washington DC's National Mall – and asks what happens when the howl returns.

Workshop participants curate a media archive of Brava to explore ecological themes across museum, city, region and planetary scales. They then assemble some of these fragments in an animated form, so the speculative afterlives of Brava may speak – in fantastic images, rhyming verse, colourful imagery, and with some poignant humour – of the Mediterranean coast and of marine life. The workshop thus positions architecture and exhibition design as critical media for public environmental imagination, asking how design might render planetary scales legible while exposing the moral stakes of contemporary life on Earth.

Emerging Workshop 2/12

Simulaa (Andre Bonnice and Anna Jankovic)

ADDITIONS AND ADAPTATIONS

Simulaa, House for Lichen, detail view, 2024. An architectural concept for a dwelling in rural Victoria, Australia, the house is designed to foster lichen, acting as a barometer for a healthy ecosystem where humans and non-humans can cohabit.

A persistent misconception is that architecture is impervious to the natural world, standing apart from the ecological forces and systems that support life. In reality, no building is sealed off; every artefact is interconnected with climatic conditions, plant growth, microbial life and the passage of time. This is evident in instances where architecture yields to these other conditions. In the nineteenth century, botanists recorded more than four hundred species thriving among the ruins of the Colosseum in Rome. Its perceived state of decay had inversely supported the renewal of a biodiverse ecosystem, generating

Simulaa, iNaturalist observation logs, Victoria, Australia, 2025.
Extracts from iNaturalist field logs – geo-tagged photographic observations of non-human life, which contribute to a citizen-scientists-led environmental monitoring database.

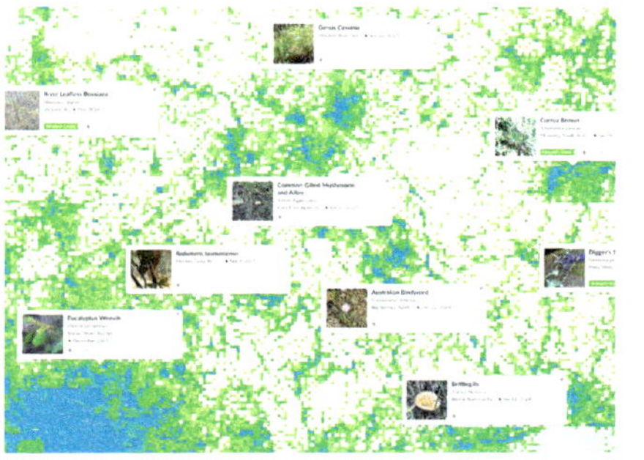

Simulaa, Object tracking in *An Interior View of the Colosseum, Rome*, original painting by John Warwick Smith, Yale Center for British Art, undated, digital edit 2025.

microclimates and habitats for non-humans. In an age of climate and ecological transition, architecture must resist the impulse to dominate or control these dynamics and instead act as a mediator, recognising interdependence and giving form to relationships of coexistence.

In support of this, the Gaia hypothesis articulated by American microbiologist Lynn Margulis and British chemist James Lovelock in the 1970s[1] posits the Earth as a self-regulating system sustained through relationships of codependency, a conception that unsettles the anthropocentric frame of modernity. Similarly, and around the same time, Belgian ecologist Paul Duvigneaud depicted energy and matter circulating across scales in a series of diagrams that brought both natural and industrial systems into the same frame.[2] These notions insist that survival is contingent on the collective process of negotiation between multiple actors. For architecture, this prompts a shift in the role of the designer, from author of discrete objects to facilitator of co-beneficial exchanges.

1. James E. Lovelock and Lynn Margulis, 'Atmospheric Homeostasis by and for the Biosphere: The Gaia Hypothesis', *Tellus*, 26(1–2), 1974, pp. 2–10.

2. Paul Duvigneaud, *La synthèse écologique: populations, communautés, écosystèmes, biosphère, noosphère*, Doin, 1980, pp. 60–206, especially the diagram series depicting exchanges between natural and industrial/urban systems.

Simulaa, *Strata Signals* installation, 'Deep Time Real Time' exhibition, RMIT Design Hub Gallery, Melbourne, Australia, 2025.
Thermographic imagery in collaboration with the Clean Air Task Force, identifying instances of illegal methane emissions.

Copernicus satellite data imagery from *Strata Signals*, 2019–25.
Vegetation health and density detected through multispectral reflectance patterns of the Grampians, Australia.

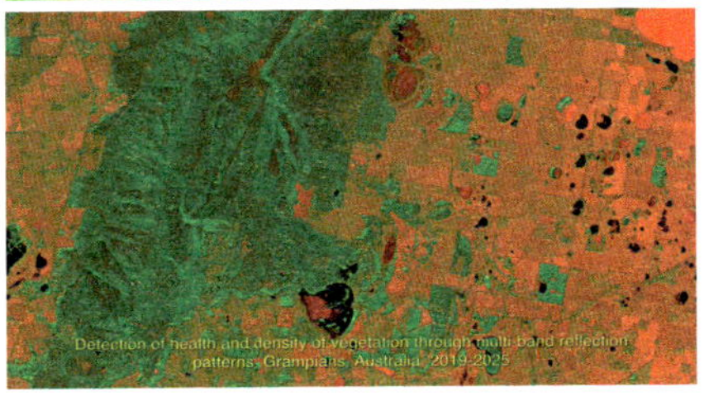

This approach requires distinct modes of observation and representation to make these conditions visible, not as endpoints but in support of speculation, deriving architecture from within a wider field of environmental considerations. Likewise, they have the potential to bring architecture into dialogue with forms of knowledge traditionally outside the discipline.

Organised through acts of sensing and making across Barcelona, the 'Additions and Adaptations' workshop experiments with tools and techniques – through video, environmental monitoring and geolocated biodiversity mapping – to reveal and document overlooked and emergent conditions. These and other technologies, although not new, are being redeployed for environmental stewardship. In focus, the workshop views Barcelona through the habitation of lichen, and their role as excellent bioindicators of environmental health, and the conditions that support life. From sensing, the workshop shifts to speculation through interventions that test how architecture and infrastructure can be in service of both human and non-human life. Adapting everyday anthropocentric functions and utilities, they retain water in dry conditions, provide shade for bryophytes, create surfaces for lichens to anchor, offer perches for birds or crevices for insects, mediating and enhancing conditions of mutual benefit.

Manifesto for Sedimentary Futures is a research project developed as part of 'Water Parliaments: Projective Ecosocial Architectures' for the Catalan Pavilion at the 2025 Venice Architecture Biennale. Curated by Eva Franch i Gilabert (FAST) and architects TAKK (Mireia Luzárraga and Alejandro Muiño), the project was commissioned, produced and organised by the Institut Ramon Llull through an international competition, the brief and content for which were developed in collaboration with the curators of UIA 2026 Barcelona with the support of the Col·legi Oficial d'Arquitectes de Catalunya (COAC).

'Water Parliaments' frames the water crisis as an ecosocial, cultural and political condition, positioning architecture as a medium for critical speculation and collective agency. Within this context, Manifesto for Sedimentary Futures foregrounds sediments, long immobilised by hydraulic infrastructures and agricultural regimes, as material and political actors.

Research by Design 2/12

Eva Franch i Gilabert (FAST) and TAKK
(Mireia Luzárraga and Alejandro Muiño)

MANIFESTO FOR SEDIMENTARY FUTURES: PRACTICES OF CARE AND MORE-THAN-HUMAN COEXISTENCE

Flowing towards the sea, rivers carry organic and inorganic materials that are deposited across floodplains and water bodies. These sediments, formed through processes of erosion, are essential to the constitution of wetlands, deltas and estuaries – ecosystems of extraordinary productivity and biodiversity. Their physical and chemical properties configure aquatic and terrestrial habitats, while the nutrients they contain sustain primary productivity and soil fertility in riparian and coastal zones. At the same time, sediments function as significant carbon sinks, storing organic matter for millennia and contributing decisively to the global carbon cycle.

Eva Franch i Gilabert, Mireia Luzárraga and Alejandro Muiño, Film still from *Catalonia in Venice – Water Parliaments: Projective Ecosocial Architectures*, Venice Architecture Biennale, 2025.Microscopic view of zooplankton used to feed endangered species in the fish hospital in the Parc Natural del Delta de l'Ebre.

Human intervention in river systems has not only disrupted their natural dynamics but has also compromised the delicate equilibria of the ecologies that depend upon them. The proliferation of dams and reservoirs – justified in the name of urban supply, intensive irrigation or hydroelectric production – has interrupted sediment flows towards river mouths. This appropriation of fluvial dynamics, designed to sustain an extractive and productivist model, structurally weakens deltaic and coastal ecosystems, depriving them of the materials and nutrients that ensure their productivity and resilience.

The pressure of climate change – sea-level rise combined with the reduction of sediment supply – accelerates coastal erosion and the regression of deltas. The result is a progressive loss of territory to the sea, with severe consequences for biodiversity and for the human communities that inhabit these landscapes.

Eva Franch i Gilabert, Mireia Luzárraga and Alejandro Muiño, Film still from *Catalonia in Venice – Water Parliaments: Projective Ecosocial Architectures*, Venice Architecture Biennale, 2025. Renaturalised landscape in the Ebre Delta.

In the coming years, the socioecological survival of deltas across the world will demand a collective effort, requiring architects, engineers, scientists and activists to collaborate in repairing ecosystems and addressing the multiple crises derived from climate change. In relation to sediment flows, interventions are already being explored: controlled flushing of reservoirs to mobilise trapped materials, the construction of bypass tunnels to allow sediment passage downstream, or the artificial replenishment of gravel and sand in fluvial stretches.

Though still incipient, such strategies will become increasingly relevant in a world where ecological crises compel us to intervene to safeguard the survival of multiple species. This requires a consensus across disciplines that avoids reproducing inequalities or systematically privileging human needs over those of other forms of life.

Manifesto for Sedimentary Futures acknowledges the centrality of sediments and places them at the core of attention and care.

The Ebre

As it descends from the Pyrenees to the Mediterranean, the Ebre river[1] carries clays, silts, sands, organic fragments, pollutants, spores and eggs. Over millennia, these sediments built the Ebre Delta, southwest of the Province of Tarragona in Catalonia: around 330 square kilometres of land where rice fields coexist with wetlands and coastal lagoons that rank among the most important marsh habitats in the western Mediterranean.

1. We use Ebre, rather than the Spanish Ebro, to follow the Catalan toponym used in the river's delta, the territorial perspective from which this text is written. The name ultimately derives from the ancient Iberus, but adopting Ebre acknowledges the linguistic landscape of the region and its historical suppression, both territorially and linguistically.

Hundreds of dams in the basin now store a large share of the annual runoff; structures such as Mequinenza, Riba-roja and Flix have reduced the suspended sediment load reaching the lower Ebre by 67 per cent, from nearly 28 million tonnes per year to just 9 million.[2] As a consequence, coastal retreat is accelerating, deltaic elevations are falling relative to sea level, and a substantial share of the emerged delta is projected to sink below mean sea level by 2100 if sediment inputs are not restored.

2. Albert Rovira and Carles Ibáñez, 'Sediment Management Options for the Lower Ebro River and its Delta', *Journal of Soils and Sediments*, 7, 2007, pp. 285–95. See also the technical presentation by the authors available at: https://sednet.org/download/A-09%20Rovira.pdf

This deficit compromises the delta's ability to sustain habitats and to counter both subsidence and sea-level rise. The ecological consequences are already visible: more than a hundred species present in the delta are listed on the International Union for Conservation of Nature (IUCN) Red List,[3] and projections estimate that by 2100 up to 70 per cent of wetland bird habitats could be lost.[4] Simultaneously, marine intrusion may flood more than 20,000 hectares of agricultural and natural land, irreversibly transforming the ecological and social configuration of the territory.[5] The architecture of the river, its material continuity, has been radically interrupted.

3. IUCN Red List: https://www.iucnredlist.org

4. Ministerio para la Transición Ecológica y el Reto Demográfico (MITECO), 'Plan para la Protección del Delta del Ebro', 2021. https://www.miteco.gob.es/content/dam/miteco/images/es/planparalaprotecciondeldeltadelebro_jmg_signedfe_tcm30-522381.pdf

5. Ana Genua-Olmedo, Stijn Temmerman, Carles Ibáñez and Carles Alcaraz, 'Evaluating Adaptation Options to Sea Level Rise and Benefits to Agriculture: The Ebro Delta Showcase', *Science of The Total Environment*, 806, Part 2, 2022, 150624.

Eva Franch i Gilabert, Mireia Luzárraga and Alejandro Muiño, Film still from *Catalonia in Venice – Water Parliaments: Projective Ecosocial Architectures*, Venice Architecture Biennale, 2025. The European eel's decline is systemic. Now critically endangered, its migration is obstructed by dams and damaged by turbines, while pollution, parasites and changing ocean conditions further threaten its survival by disrupting larval drift routes and reducing reproductive success.

Agents and riparian realities

The Ebre river is governed and inhabited by a dense assemblage of human and non-human agents. At basin scale, the Confederación Hidrográfica del Ebro (CHE), a Spanish state river-basin authority, is responsible for hydrological planning, water concessions and reservoir management, including in the Catalan stretch of the Ebre. The Agència Catalana de l'Aigua (ACA) oversees water policy and ecological status in Catalan basins and has challenged some ecological flow proposals for the Ebre on the grounds that they do not adequately protect wetlands in the delta. Coordination between these bodies, together with Spanish and Catalan administrations, is a stated requirement of the Integrated Plan for the Protection of the Ebro Delta, which seeks joint management of water, sediments and habitats.

Eva Franch i Gilabert, Mireia Luzárraga and Alejandro Muiño, Film still from *Catalonia in Venice – Water Parliaments: Projective Ecosocial Architectures*, Venice Architecture Biennale, 2025. Future laboratories: research gatherings of local agents in the Ebre Delta.

At delta scale, the Ebro Delta Natural Park (Parc Natural del Delta de l'Ebre), created in 1983 at the request of local residents, aims to balance ecological conservation with agricultural, fishing and tourism activities. It manages protected wetlands, supports restoration projects and mediates conflicts over land use, hunting, bird conservation and water quality. Wetland restoration in abandoned rice fields has focused on renaturalising hydrology, improving water quality and creating habitats for endangered species such as the Spanish toothcarp.

Irrigation communities such as the Comunitat General de Regants del Canal de la Dreta de l'Ebre and the Comunitat de Regants Sindicat Agrícola de l'Ebre are public-law corporations tasked with distributing irrigation water over tens of thousands of hectares of agricultural land. Their decisions on flow timing, volume and drainage directly influence salinisation, nutrient cycles, wetland inundation and, crucially, whether sediments circulate through canals or are flushed directly to the sea. Historically, these networks played a key role in delivering fine sediments from the river into rice fields and marshes, generating vertical accretion that helped offset subsidence. Today, hydropower companies, nuclear plants, aquaculture enterprises, tourist operators and environmental NGOs add further layers of negotiation to this governance landscape.

Non-human agents are equally decisive. Sediments, trapped behind dams, transported as suspended load, resuspended by storms or recirculated through irrigation, materially condition whether marshes accrete or drown. Marsh vegetation, rice plants and halophytes stabilise soils and generate organic accretion, partially compensating low mineral inputs. Dramatically endangered species without any protection – eels, hundreds of migratory birds, zooplankton communities, benthic invertebrates and even the black fly, whose outbreaks in the Ebro region have become a public-health nuisance – articulate the delta as a multispecies habitat and a contested space of coexistence.

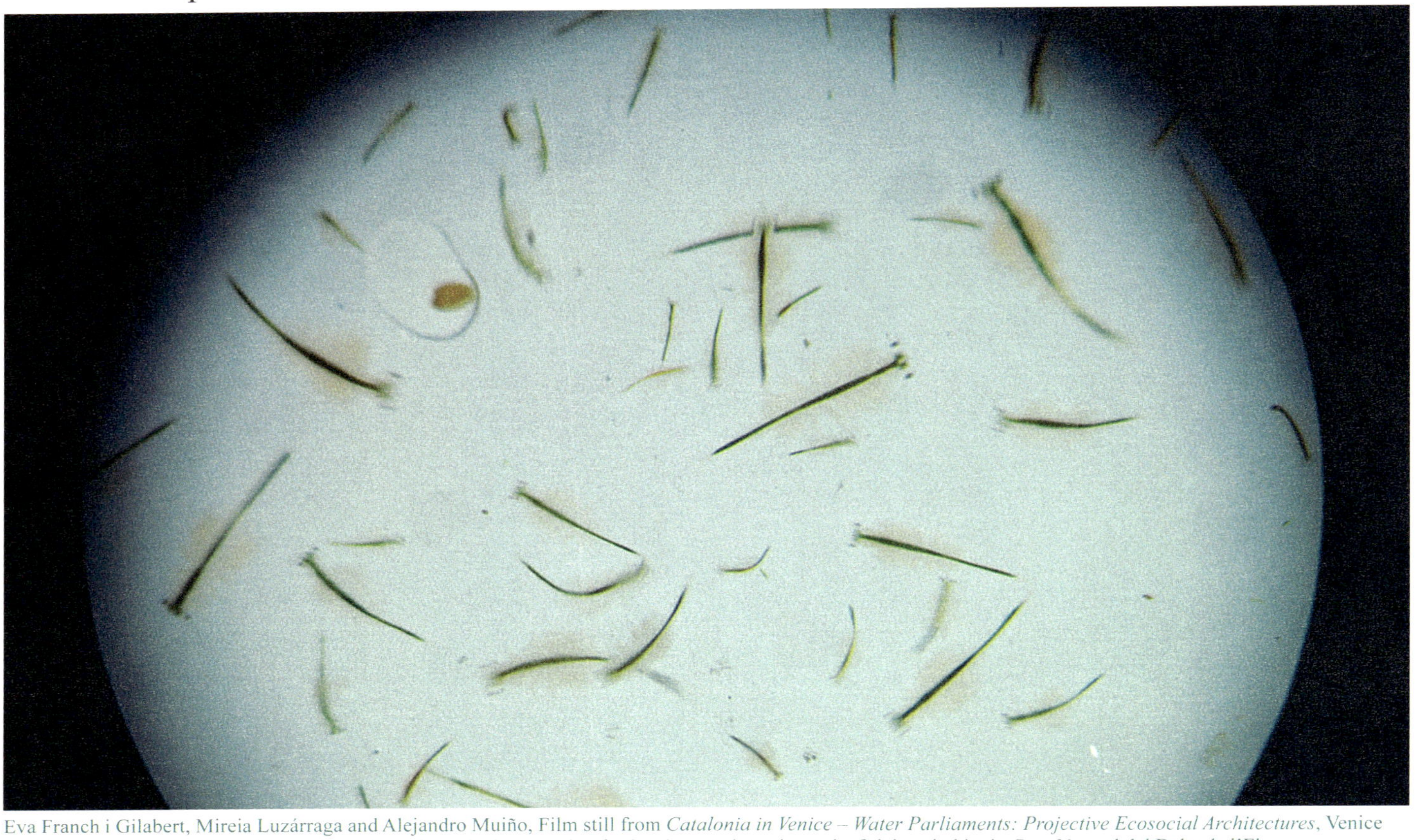

Eva Franch i Gilabert, Mireia Luzárraga and Alejandro Muiño, Film still from *Catalonia in Venice – Water Parliaments: Projective Ecosocial Architectures*, Venice Architecture Biennale, 2025. Microscopic view of zooplankton used to feed endangered species at the fish hospital in the Parc Natural del Delta de l'Ebre.

A walking manifesto

Against this backdrop, Manifesto for Sedimentary Futures proposes a new kind of architectural practice where sediments are no longer just inert background matter, but protagonists and political subjects – a living 'sedimentary commons' where materials, stories and species are brought together to negotiate shared futures. Future habitability in the delta depends on recentring sediments as active agents and on cultivating practices of care, monitoring and redistribution. Rather than relying solely on defensive infrastructures such as dikes and seawalls, our work calls for ecological engineering approaches, such as controlled flushing, sediment bypass systems and the reuse of irrigation networks, infrastructures of care and multispecies practices of repair to restore sediment flux. The Manifesto for Sedimentary Futures proposal translates these technical scenarios into spatial, sensorial and cultural devices, enabling the architecture to act as a visible, audible and discussable sediment form.

We propose a sedimentary ritual ground, not a monument.
An open, process-based commons for shared ritual, maintenance and sediment care.

We assemble a constellation of agencies,
a necessary alternative to the heroic figure.

We build with altars of evidence. Sediment 'altars' hold samples – a distributed archive of extraction and loss.

We make water legible, revealing flows, rhythms and thresholds.

We practise filtration as care rather than purification,
sustaining traces, residues and sedimentary memory.

We host species as active participants in multispecies habitats.

We name sediments as ecological and political actors, situating sediment not as waste, but as agent, archive, leverage and responsibility.

We do not celebrate permanence. We commit to flows, vulnerability, reciprocity and shared responsibility.

We inaugurate an annual ritual: the Sediment March.
Once a year, communities along the Ebre collect sediments from a chosen reach, or from sediment islands, and carry them on foot, by boat or through collective journeys.

We move sediment towards urgency. We bring it to strategic places in the delta where it is desperately needed, facing dramatic losses intensified by climate change and reduced sedimentation.

We choose the bag as our unit of transformation, remembering Ursula K. Le Guin's bag[6] as a primordial technology of care and gathering: a reminder that big change is also made of countless small acts.

6. In her 1986 essay 'The Carrier Bag Theory of Fiction'.
See Ursula K. Le Guin, *The Carrier Bag Theory of Fiction*, Ignota Books, 2019.

We believe architecture is an ethics of care, a practice devoted to the often-invisible infrastructures that sustain shared life.

We offer a space of ongoing repair, attention and contestation.
Not a finished object claiming timelessness, but a responsive ground.

We insist that sediments are the ground of the future.
Material, cultural and political grounds for more-than-human futures – recognised, carried and cared-for together.

A conversation between Bas Smets and the Congress curators on Becoming More-than-human and architecture's capacity to shape microclimates

INVENTING POSSIBILITIES

CURATORS The idea of becoming frames time as an operative design tool instead of a passive condition. Landscape projects do not unfold within a single linear timeframe, but engage multiple temporalities simultaneously. Which of these temporalities most strongly inform your work, and how are they translated into design decisions?

BAS SMETS I connect it to something that intrigued me from a young age. When I began studying architecture in Leuven in Belgium, I realised that everything around us is designed; buildings, cars, as well as the clothes we wear, nothing is simply natural. At some point, you understand that almost every aspect of reality has been shaped by others, and once something is designed, it could also have been different. What seems fixed becomes unstable, and reality shifts into probability.

That is my notion of time: not as a linear sequence, but as a present condition that will inevitably change. In those moments of instability, you can intervene, you can hack into the cracks. Things begin to shift, sometimes very fast.

C Contemporary practice is shaped by a tension between climatic urgency and the long-term rhythms of ecological transformation. How does your work reconcile immediate action with processes that unfold over time?

BS Our way of working is closely tied to our main agents of transformation: plants. To plant is to enter cycles of growth, seasons and ecological succession. Responding to urgency means initiating processes that continue to evolve over time.

The climate crisis will not be solved by one grand gesture; it requires a million small actions. Working with plants, and understanding more deeply how they function, is one concrete way to act. Each intervention may seem modest, but together they generate long-term change.

Recent research has reshaped how we understand vegetation. Suzanne Simard's work on underground root networks[1] and Stefano Mancuso's research on plant communication[2] expand our imagination of landscapes. We no longer look to rigid nineteenth-century typologies; trees in rows, ornamental gardens, fixed compositions. Instead, we can design landscapes that mobilise the adaptive intelligence and resilience of plant communities.

1. Suzanne Simard, *Finding the Mother Tree: Uncovering the Wisdom and Intelligence of the Forest*, Allen Lane, 2021.

2. Stefano Mancuso, *The Revolutionary Genius of Plants: A New Understanding of Plant Intelligence and Behavior*, Atria Books, 2018.

This transforms how we see the city. It becomes a second nature, a space for nature to emerge. We read it as a constellation of microclimates: buildings modify wind, sunlight, humidity and heat, streets affect permeability and soil. A neighbourhood functions like an artificial microclimate. Once these conditions are understood, species can be introduced accordingly. Design shifts from static composition to adaptive thinking. What we have already built becomes an opportunity for ecological transformation.

C So the bigger the problem becomes, the smaller the solutions need to be?

BS Yes. The solution is in addressing the problem differently, not in finding the big solution to the big problem. The bigger the problem, the more we need small solutions.

C If the response to large problems lies in small, precise interventions, microclimates become a key strategy. They challenge the idea of uniform comfort and introduce climatic variation into urban space. How do you understand this shift in the way we define comfort?

BS Comfort in public space is measured differently from comfort inside a building. In public space, we use the Universal Thermal Climate Index, which considers humidity, wind, radiation and reflection, not only temperature.

For our project at the Luma Parc des Ateliers in Arles, southern France, we designed wind-shaped hills that on one side provide cooling shade in summer while benefitting from the refreshing wind. In winter, the opposite side shields you from this cold wind while exposing you directly to the sun. The asymmetrical forms of these hills create a double climatic effect. For our project for the public space around Notre-Dame in Paris, we proposed a thin layer of reused rainwater to run down on to the parvis on hot days. The cooling effect comes not from the water itself, but from evaporation, which lowers the air temperature.

These are forms of knowledge that modernity largely set aside and that we are now reactivating through research. By studying humidity, wind and solar exposure, and by applying new botanical insights, we can create plant communities capable of thriving in harsh conditions.

What interests me is inventing new urban ecologies; landscapes that do not impose uniform comfort, but cultivate differentiated, adaptive climates within the city.

C Notre-Dame shows how even the most protected heritage can evolve. How can this approach extend to the broader urban fabric? What possibilities exist within what has already been built to rethink its climatic performance?

BS Notre-Dame is exemplary because intervening around such an important monument makes transformation conceivable elsewhere. It not only addresses a specific site; it reshapes the collective imagination of a new alliance between heritage and ecology.

But there are many other contexts where similar strategies can unfold. Last year, for instance, we worked in Athens, in the historic centre of Plaka around the Acropolis, an area that overheats dramatically in summer. Planting trees is impossible because archaeological layers lie just beneath the surface and the streets are extremely narrow. Instead, we proposed introducing climbing plants to create vegetal ceilings above the streets, generating shade without touching the ground. There is also a precedent in Jerez de la Frontera, in Spain, where streets are covered with grape vines. It forms a natural canopy; simple, inexpensive, and up to ten degrees cooler.

We need built examples that embody this shift. Otherwise, it remains abstract. Landscape is experienced through the body and change begins there.

Critical Antagonist

C Extending this logic of microclimates beyond public space, how might buildings themselves become climatic ecosystems? How can vegetation become integrated into architectural energy cycles, redefining comfort as something heterogeneous and adaptive rather than mechanically controlled?

BS When we worked on our 'Building Biospheres' proposal for the 2025 Venice Architecture Biennale, we understood the Belgian Pavilion primarily as a shelter, a roof that protects from rain and provides minimal comfort. Rather than treating it as a conventional building, we began to see it as a microclimate.

Its indoor space stands in permanent shade, an understorey condition, with an ideal temperature of twenty to twenty-two degrees, essentially subtropical. So we introduced plants suited for that climate and asked ourselves how they could participate in producing the indoor environment themselves.

It is paradoxical: the first human shelters were made of branches and leaves, directly shaping microclimates from the biosphere. Over time, we replaced this with sealed, mechanically controlled interiors, standardised at twenty degrees. We have, in effect, re-created a subtropical climate everywhere on this planet.

Yet we originate from the biosphere. We feed on it, we breathe through it, plants generate the air that sustains us. Still, we spend most of our lives detached from these living systems.

Can we imagine a new relationship between architecture and nature? Can architecture not only be a way of survival for humans, but also for plants and animals? That is what I wanted to bring to Venice: seeing architecture as a possibility for life, not as an object.

C So the pavilion becomes an ecological device, and also a kind of research prototype. How do you understand this relationship between plants, architecture and experimentation?

BAS SMETS Working with Stefano Mancuso and Ghent University, we measured sap flow to understand how much water the trees evaporated. We also measured the contraction and expansion of the trunks. This data allowed us to better understand what the trees need to grow in this artificial climate. We connected these measurements to three main actions: irrigation, lighting and ventilation. The trees themselves actively produced their environment. As they grew, they increased photosynthesis and evapotranspiration, lowering the temperature and gradually stabilising their own environment.

It was an experiment that we conducted over twelve months, first in Ghent and then in Venice. After the biennale, the plant installation was reinstalled in Belgium to continue the experiment. I see every project as research. The more we understand how buildings and plants can cohabit, the more this knowledge can be extended, to create more generous spaces with less control; spaces where life, even insects, are part of the equation. I prefer a city that is shared with different life forms.

C If plants reposition architecture within the biosphere, they also bring us back to the question of water, which is becoming increasingly unstable due to climate change. As heavy rainfall and prolonged drought intensify, how can landscape design rethink water not as something to evacuate or control, but as a structuring element of living urban environments?

BS The paradox is that the city is actually an extraordinary machine for harvesting rainwater: roofs and streets are impermeable, so they collect it efficiently. Yet over the past decades, we have treated this water as waste, channelling it away as quickly as possible, pushing it downhill. The consequence is twofold: flooding at the lowest points, and groundwater tables that no longer recharge. Even trees that have stood for a century suddenly lose access to water. The infrastructure to collect rainwater already exists. What is missing is the vision and the will to keep it within the city.

In Brussels, we developed a simple principle for a new manual for the design of public space: the first two metres along the façade accommodate services; the next two metres become a water-retaining layer, with soil above. Rainwater from the roofs flows into this zone, and the street functions like a dry valley, storing water beneath its surface. The idea is straightforward: stop discarding water. Every drop should remain part of the urban ecosystem.

C Your practice relates to this broader shift towards nature-based strategies, but these approaches operate over long-term horizons, depend on governance and redistribute risk. How do you position your practice in relation to this paradigm shift?

BS Nature-based solutions seem logical. You use the force of nature instead of going against it. Ecology is an understanding of a complex transformative force. Nature is not only something to preserve, but also a design tool. A better understanding of ecology will give us new solutions. If you don't work with the force of nature, these solutions will always be overrun by it.

C If design means working with the force of nature, the challenge intensifies when that force becomes unstable. Dirk Sijmons and his team's work on the Netherlands North Sea engages long-term processes like tides and sedimentation, yet sea-level rise may accelerate beyond them. In such uncertainty, how should design position itself between gradual adaptation and abrupt change?

BS We are entering uncharted territory, because nobody can tell you how much sea level will rise. Ice caps could melt much faster than expected. The system could shift abruptly. The more we measure, the more uncertainty surfaces.

In that sense, Dirk Sijmons's study is very interesting because it explores what would happen under different hypotheses. At Harvard, with my students, we work with four scenarios for my studio Biospheric Urbanism: plus two, plus three, plus four, plus five degrees. It is better to study them now than to face them unprepared.

C If ecological transformation unfolds at this scale, it is not only environmental but cultural. Eva Franch i Gilabert (FAST) and TAKK suggest that rituals and shared imaginaries can help societies navigate transition. How can these collective narratives enable people to confront and internalise disruptive change?

BS For many people, these changes represent profound disruption, not only to daily habits, but also to beliefs. Rituals can help prepare people for the transformations ahead and construct collective narratives. It is not enough to have the right technical answer if inhabitants do not believe in it or feel part of it.

When we speak about rising temperatures, two, three, four degrees more, we speak about a fundamental transformation of life. We must prepare for multiple scenarios. This awareness generates a different political reality, and that political shift makes drastic transformation possible.

C The workshop research projects Additions and Adaptations by Simulaa and DESIGN EARTH's Brava! similarly question architecture's ability to control environmental processes, instead foregrounding vulnerability and ecological entanglement. What do these approaches reveal about the limits of architectural agency today, and how might vulnerability become an operative condition for design?

BS We often forget that we cannot fully control environmental processes, as we are part of this environment. Presenting this as a vulnerability is an opening of consciousness. This vulnerability demands a responsibility. We share one planet with all these life forms. The atoms that compose us have been recycled time and again through different forms of life. Understanding that our expansion affects other life forms changes the way we think about architecture and landscape architecture.

C If 'Becoming More-than-human' means overcoming the separation between nature and culture that has shaped modernity, what kind of architectural practice does this demand today?

BAS SMETS

For me, 'more-than-human' is inseparable from becoming more human. We originate from nature, we breathe it, eat it, depend on it, yet we continue to position ourselves as if it were external. To become more human means recognising continuity rather than separation, understanding that we are participants, not observers. In that shift, the divide between human and more-than-human, and between architecture and landscape, begins to dissolve.

In 2016, at Bozar in Brussels, I curated the exhibition 'The Invention of Landscape'. Its invention not its discovery. Landscape is not simply found; it is imagined. In sixteenth-century painting, Renaissance artists like Joachim Patinir inverted the relationship between figure and background, allowing landscape to take centre stage.

Similarly, in landscape architecture, the brief is never enough. One must reorganise a site through imagination, understanding what it wants to become. The most compelling projects dissolve figure and ground, constructing new possibilities.

Imagination always precedes transformation.

Curators

TOWARDS AN INSURGENT ECOLOGY OF ARCHITECTURAL PRACTICE

Interspecies alliances
Atmospheric materiality
Microclimatic interactions
Territorial metabolism
Hydrocommons
Soil ecologies
Food ecologies

To engage with the proposition of 'Becoming More-than-human' is to confront the collapse of the conceptual architecture that has sustained the discipline for centuries. Architecture, as an instrument of Western modernity, has long enacted a fiction: that humans alone possess intentionality and agency, and that the world exists as a passive resource awaiting optimisation, extraction or management. As has been argued, the division between nature and culture was never a discovery but a performance that sustained the illusion of human sovereignty while relegating all other beings, forces and material processes to the background.[1]

1. Bruno Latour, *We Have Never Been Modern*, trans Catherine Porter, Harvard University Press, 1991.

Yet the world resists this ontological construction. Climate systems destabilise, microbial ecologies proliferate, hydrological cycles shift, and vegetal and geological processes continuously reorganise the conditions of life. What has been termed the Capitalocene reveals the extent to which these transformations are not external crises but consequences of a worldview that separated humans from the environments they inhabit.[2] In response, architecture can no longer position itself as an external agent acting upon a passive world. It must instead locate itself within what has been described as the mesh: a dense entanglement of relations in which no entity exists independently.[3]

2. Jason W. Moore, *Capitalism in the Web of Life: Ecology and the Accumulation of Capital*, Verso, 2015.
3. Timothy Morton, *The Ecological Thought*, Harvard University Press, 2010.

This recognition demands an ethical reorientation. The theory of symbiogenesis[4] reframes life as a process of co-evolution and mutual dependency, while an ethics of care situates maintenance, attention and responsibility as fundamental conditions for the persistence of shared worlds.[5] The call to 'stay with the trouble'[6] reinforces this shift, proposing practices that do not seek to resolve complexity but to inhabit it. Within this framework, architecture is no longer a discipline of domination but a practice of mediation, operating between species, materials, infrastructures and atmospheres, and engaging with the temporalities of ecological change.

4. Lynn Margulis, *Symbiotic Planet: A New Look at Evolution*, Basic Books, 1998.
5. Maria Puig de la Bellacasa, *Matters of Care: Speculative Ethics in More than Human Worlds*, University of Minnesota Press, 2017.
6. Donna Haraway, *Staying with the Trouble: Making Kin in the Chthulucene*, Duke University Press, 2016.

From this perspective, architecture is embedded within dynamic territorial processes, where land and water form a shifting interface shaped by ecological and multispecies interactions. Coastal areas, rivers and wetlands become spaces of constant negotiation, where environmental and political forces intersect. Water emerges as both commons and agent, calling for adaptive, integrated design strategies. (1, 2, 3, 4, 5, 6)

This condition redefines the ground as a living, evolving medium rather than an inert support, shaped by practices of care, cultivation and maintenance. Landscape is approached as a process of transformation, working with soil, topography, water and vegetation as active design materials. (7) Within this framework, design combines precision with openness, establishing conditions that evolve through growth, seasons and use, operating within a tension between control and abandonment. Emphasis is placed

(1) Dirk Sijmons/H+N+S Landscape Architecture, Room for the River, Nijmegen, The Netherlands, 2007–16.

(2) Kate Orff / SCAPE, Living Breakwaters, Staten Island, New York, 2023.

(3) aldayjover, The Water Park, Zaragoza, Spain, 2004–08.

(4) Taller Capital, Pooling Xolox, San Lucas Xolox, Mexico, 2025.

(5) Turenscape, Tianjin Qiaoyuan Wetland Park, Tianjin, China, 2008.

(6) Eva Franch i Gilabert and TAKK, *Water Parliaments: Projective Ecosocial Architectures*, Venice Architecture Biennale, Italy, 2025.

(7) 51N4E, Skanderbeg Square, Tirana, Albania, 2017.

on the sensory and atmospheric experience of space, understanding landscape as an ongoing process rather than a fixed outcome. (8, 9, 10)

In parallel, architecture extends these logics towards more open and indeterminate relationships with nature, where built form engages light, weather and environmental conditions as part of its spatial definition. (11, 12)

Within these interdependencies, coexistence becomes a central concern. Architecture increasingly operates as a mediator within multispecies environments, where vegetation, animals, micro-organisms and human communities co-produce space. Design shifts from control towards collaboration, engaging living systems as active participants in the formation of habitats and infrastructures. This perspective also extends to invisible ecological dimensions, microbial life, air and atmospheric conditions, which challenge ideals of sterility and enclosure, revealing architecture

(8) mosbach paysagistes, Lost in Transition, Ulsan, South Korea, 2020.

(10) junya.ishigami+associates, Art Biotop Water Garden, Tochigi, Japan, 2019.

(9) Petra Blaisse/Inside Outside, Living Soil section, The Netherlands, 2020–25.

(11) junya.ishigami+associates, Zaishui Art Museum, Rizhao, China, 2023.

(12) Gustavo Utrabo, YOU MAY HAVE NOTICED, I AM NOT THERE ALONE, Santo André, Bahia, Brazil, 2025.

as a living medium intertwined with biological and environmental processes. (13, 14, 15, 16, 17)

At the territorial scale, landscape systems and spatial organisations are understood as long-term ecological and political frameworks that structure environments and collective life over time. Rather than serving as neutral supports, they distribute risks and responsibilities, foregrounding care as a design ethic grounded in maintenance, repair and sustained engagement with fragile ecologies and communities. (18, 19, 20, 21) In this context, architecture operates as a long-term practice that responds to environmental vulnerability, social inequality and local cultures through stewardship and collaboration, reframing territorial design as a shared responsibility towards human and more-than-human inhabitants. (22, 23)

At the same time, climate and energy are redefined as operative materials of design. Atmospheric conditions, temperature, humidity and radiation

(13) Beatriz Colomina and Mark Wigley, *We The Bacteria*, 2025.

(14) Beatriz Colomina and Mark Wigley, *The Other Side of the Hill*, Venice Architecture Biennale, Italy, 2025.

(15) Elii and Husos arquitecturas, Building for Infinito Delicias, Madrid, Spain, 2025.

(16) Lydia Kallipoliti, Areti Markopoulou and Post-Spectacular Office, *The Metabolic Home*, Venice Architecture Biennale, Italy, 2025.

(18) Michel Desvinge, Parc aux Angéliques, Bordeaux, France, 2018.

(17) Simulaa, House for Lichen, Central Victoria, Australia, 2023–.

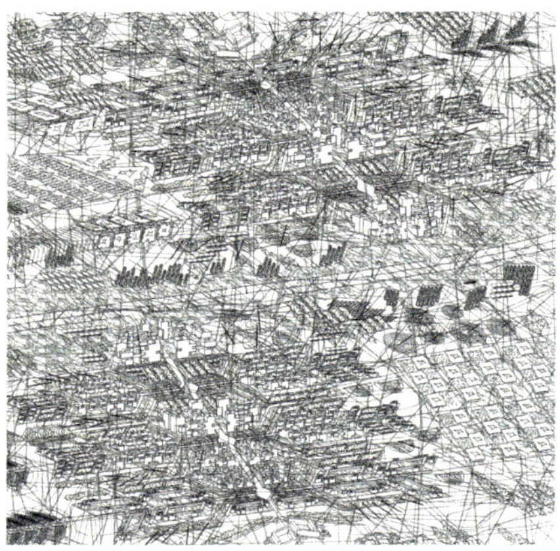
(19) Charles Waldheim, *Rapeseed Town Species-Town* vignette, China, 2022.

shape spatial experience while energy is understood as a set of flows linking bodies, buildings and territories. Architecture becomes an interface within larger climatic systems, integrating environmental performance with cultural and sensory dimensions, and redefining relationships between comfort, sustainability and space. (24, 25, 26)

Through a lens of radical ecology, architecture is approached as a transdisciplinary and critical field that reveals hidden ecological and social relations, negotiating power through material, spatial and narrative practices. Rather than focusing on problem-solving, this approach engages with living systems as political terrains, making visible the entanglements between bodies, infrastructures, environments and governance. Design operates here as a form of inquiry and storytelling, expanding architectural practice into modes of representation, speculation and collective awareness that address questions of justice, environmental

(20) Studio Associato Bernardo Secchi Paola Viganò, Zac La Courrouze, Rennes, France, 2003–.

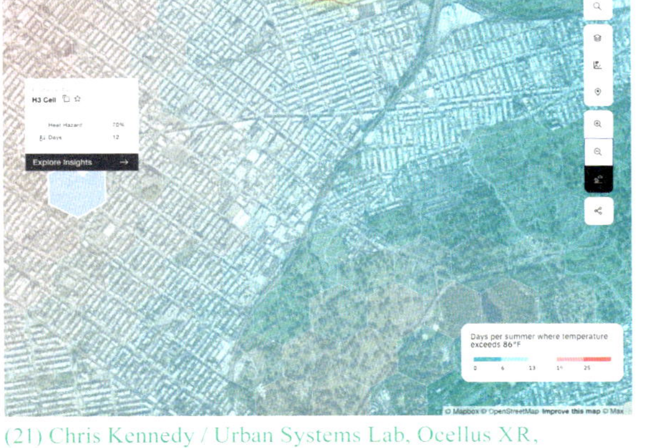

(21) Chris Kennedy / Urban Systems Lab, Ocellus XR, New York City, 2022.

(22) Al Borde, Esperanza_dos, Puerto Cabuyal, Ecuador, 2012.

(23) Boonserm Premthada / Bangkok Project Studio, Elephant World Brick Observation Tower, Surin, Thailand, 2020.

(24) Bureau Bas Smets, Luma Parc des Ateliers, Arles, France, 2024.

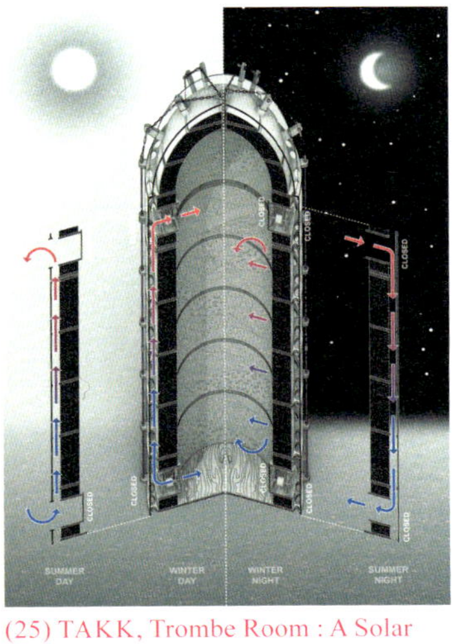

(25) TAKK, Trombe Room : A Solar Mass Chamber, Biennale d'Architecture et de paysage de la Région Île-de-France, Versailles, France, 2025.

transformation and more-than-human coexistence. (27, 28)

Across these interconnected domains, architecture assumes an explicitly political role where engaging more-than-human ecologies entails addressing power, inequality and environmental responsibility. Design emerges as a critical and collaborative practice that reveals hidden relations, negotiates contested territories and operates within uncertainty, not by offering definitive solutions but by constructing frameworks for coexistence and shared responsibility. In this sense, Becoming More-than-human calls for architecture to relinquish its autonomy and engage with the interdependent systems that sustain life, situating itself within networks of care, metabolism and atmospheric exchange to respond to the complexities of a planet in transition.

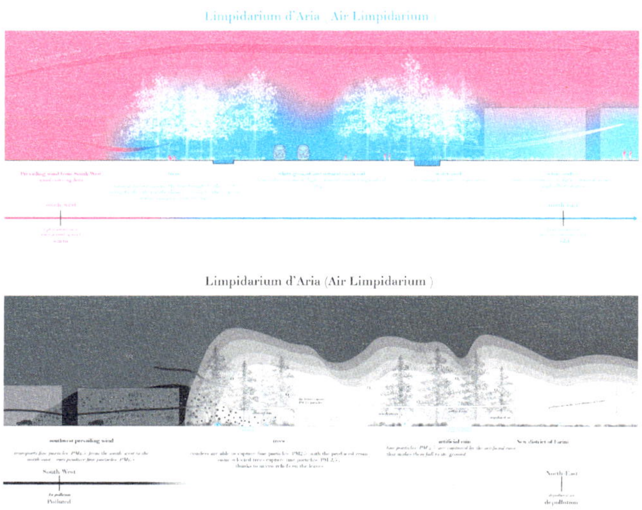

(26) Philippe Rahm, Climatic Agents, Farini, Milan, Italy, 2019.

(27) Andrés Jaque / Office for Political Innovation, Reggio School, El Encinar de los Reyes, Madrid, Spain, 2022.

(28) DESIGN EARTH, *After Oil*, Kuwait Pavilion, Venice Architecture Biennale, Italy, 2016.

Becoming Circular

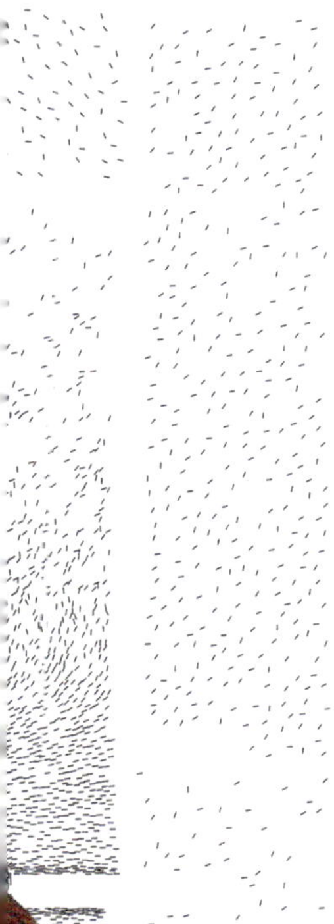

'It's a matter of never demolishing, substracting or replacing things, but of always adding, transforming and utilising them.'

Frédéric Druot, Anne Lacaton and Jean-Philippe Vassal, 'Attitude', in *Plus*: *Large-scale Housing Development*, 2007

Within post-extractivist proximity policies, which cycles can be spatially produced?

Our built environments, trapped in the accelerated dynamics of late capitalism – whether in the form of dense metropolises or endless suburban sprawl – have exhausted their capacity for unlimited growth. Alternative means of production must therefore be explored that replace profit-driven high-speed, high-consumption systems with proximity policies more aligned with decarbonisation and post-extractivism.

'Becoming Circular' promotes material circularity, energy-flow recirculation and spatial reprogramming, offering a pathway towards a more regenerative and low-carbon built environment. It suggests rethinking spatial practice and exploring aesthetic imaginaries and methods that integrate reclaimed components, upcycled waste streams, design for future disassembly, organic and metabolic constructive materials, passive atmospheric strategies and thermodynamic interactions that redefine comfort levels and reactivate uses and functions as alternatives to indiscriminate demolition.

Sana Frini

FORM(S) FOLLOW(S) FUNCTION(S), BEHAVIOUR(S) AND BELONGING(S): TOWARDS A CIRCULAR ARCHITECTURE IN THE ERA OF POST-EXTRACTIVISM / ECO-LOCALISM

The late-nineteenth-century functionalist maxim ‘Form Follows Function’, popularised by Louis Sullivan and later embraced as one of the major pillars of the modernist movement, reshaped the architecture of the twentieth century by insisting that a building’s form should emerge from its purpose. A bank should look stable, a school should feel open and light-filled, a factory should prioritise efficiency, etc.[1]

1. Louis Sullivan, *Kindergarten Chats and Other Writings* [1901], Courier Corporation, 1979, p. 340.

Emerging from a post-industrial drive for efficiency, from the search for human-adapted architectural solutions, and from the abundance of coal extraction, Sullivan’s principle rejected ornamental historicism in favour of industrial materials, programmatic clarity and simplified – often geometric – forms in which function, and more specifically human needs, became the central determinant of architectural expression. Later, Le Corbusier’s ‘Machine for living’ aligned itself with the same discourse of progress, crystallising the abundance of fossil-fuel energy into a rational, human-centred shelter seemingly freed from social and environmental constraints.[2]

2. Le Corbusier, *Vers une architecture*, Les Éditions G. Crès et Cie, 1923, p. 73.

From functionalism to the fossil logic of form

Functionalism, however, was never neutral; it was materially and energetically grounded. Coal enabled steel; steel enabled spans; spans enabled open plans; open plans enabled new social arrangements. Oil enabled plastics; plastics enabled insulation; insulation enabled sealed environments; sealed environments enabled climatic independence from surrounding ecosystems and their non-human agents. Cheap petroleum further enabled central heating, air conditioning and mechanical ventilation; these systems enabled regulated interiors; regulated interiors enabled the detachment of buildings from local climates and seasonal rhythms. The ideology of modernism – transparency, universality, repetition – mirrored the logic of industrial production and extractive economies. Architecture became an expression of linear growth: extraction, production, consumption and disposal.

Recontextualised within our twenty-first-century Anthropocene – an era marked by climate change, extreme weather, resource depletion, water scarcity, biodiversity loss and planetary excess – Sullivan’s maxim reveals its limits. Form following function is no longer sufficient. The urgency of ecological crisis, technological

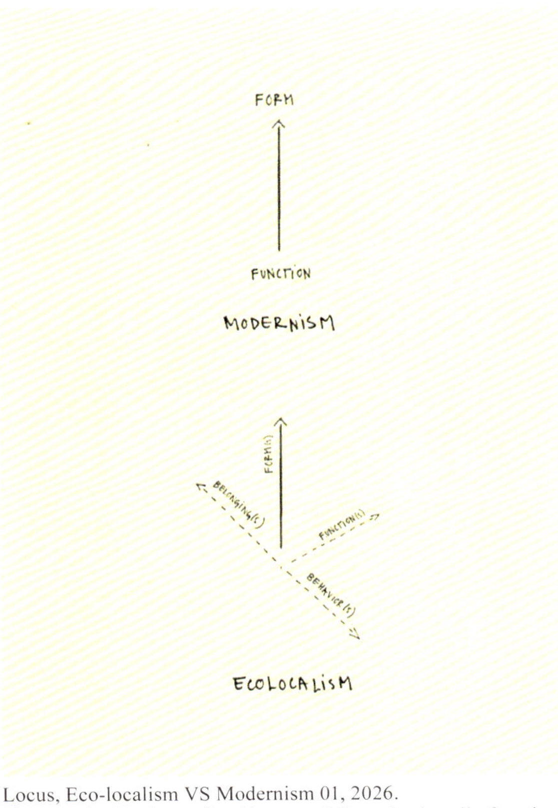

Locus, Eco-localism VS Modernism 01, 2026.
If the modernist form of architecture followed primarily function, the eco-localist one(s) will Follow(s) Function(s), Behaviour(s) and Belonging(s).

entanglement, fossil energies, geopolitical complexities and widening social inequities demands new frameworks that understand architecture not as an isolated object, but as relational, dynamic and embedded within both human and non-human systems. Through this lens, architectural form is no longer only a response to function(s), but also to behaviour(s) – of users, ecosystems, climates, materials and temporal processes – and to belonging(s) – to communities, species, landscapes and local material resources. Function(s), behaviour(s) and belonging(s) become plural, interdependent and evolving across linked ecosystems. In the era of post-extractivism, these dimensions must be rooted in an urgent transformative condition: circularity.

Wind catchers and domes, Yazd, Iran, 2020. Minor Asian climatic devices used to cool a house by extracting shaded cool air from the lower/subterranean layers of the earth through clay chimneys (by a combination of conduction, convection and radiation).

Becoming circular, belonging again

To become circular means expanding architecture beyond shelter and aesthetics to include material stewardship, adaptability, regeneration and long-term responsibility. It requires shifting from linear lifecycles to cyclical metabolisms. Buildings are no longer endpoints of extracted matter; they become temporary assemblies within continuous material flows.

A rereading of architectural history through the lens of energy cycles reveals that functionalism was tied to coal, and modernism to oil. Yet even more revealing is the pre-industrial world of vernacular architecture, when energy systems were intimately linked to the four elements – air, fire, water and earth. Construction was constrained by climate, local material availability and renewable cycles. Settlements were oriented towards sun and wind, thermal mass moderated temperature, water was harvested and reused, and materials decomposed and returned to the soil. These practices were not labelled sustainable – they were simply necessary in a time when humans were part of an entangled ecosystem rather than its centre. Modern architecture, propelled by industrial abundance, progressively detached itself from these elemental dependencies. Mechanical ventilation replaced cross-ventilation; artificial lighting replaced orientation; synthetic materials replaced local craft.

Humans moved from a peripheral position within ecosystems to the centre of architectural production, while ecosystems became externalities. Circularity, therefore, is not an invention of contemporary environmental discourse. It is a reintegration – a remembering – of the cyclical behaviour inherent to ecosystems. It is the acceptance of dependence over dominance, and the recognition that architecture is not outside nature, but contained within it.

C. Aala, R. Bianco, D. Dulaj, F. Leone, M. Morgia, L. Pomella, D. Scalia and G. Solis, Sassi di Matera, Italy, 2025.
Elise Wipff, Vegetated Patio, Seville, Spain, 2025.
Sacha De Amorim, Patio, Granada, Spain, 2025.

Vernacular architecture integrates climate-responsive strategies through material, form and natural elements. The Sassi di Matera exemplify thermal mass and topographic adaptation, with dwellings carved into insulating tuff that stabilises indoor temperatures and organises the town along canyon slopes, where roofs become pathways and homes extend into terraces and hanging gardens. In Seville, a patio house demonstrates cooling by radiation, using vegetation to create shaded canopies that reduce heat gain, while in Granada a house illustrates cooling by evaporation, incorporating water to lower ambient temperatures. Together, these examples show how architecture works with local environments to achieve passive climatic comfort. From Philippe Rahm and Sana Frini, *4°C Entre Toi Et Moi*, Actar, 2025.

Today, functionalism is not obsolete, but rather in need of evolution within a post-extractivist and eco-local context. Architecture today must commit to a situated practice. Sustainability must operate as a structural logic, not as a superficial adjective or certification. Designing bioclimatically means designing with climate rather than against it: orienting, shading, ventilating, storing heat, harvesting water. It means understanding solar and atmospheric behaviour as formal generators. Form no longer follows only programmatic function, but also thermal, hydric and energetic performance. Smart technologies – sensors, adaptive systems, energy monitoring – remain relevant, but with a shifted purpose. Rather than compensating for passive design failures through energy overconsumption, technology should optimise and support low-impact strategies. The question is not one of greater technical complexity, but of deeper ecological intelligence. User experience expands towards a broader understanding of comfort that includes cultural belonging, material identity and environmental awareness. The building becomes a mediator between the individual and the ecosystem. Function remains important, but alongside context, impact and durability.

Circular architecture introduces an additional temporal dimension that classical functionalism rarely considered: the future life of the building. How will it be disassembled? How will it be repaired? How will it adapt? What will happen to its materials when it no longer fulfils its original function? Design for disassembly, modular systems, reversible joints and material passports are not merely technical strategies; they are ethical positions that acknowledge architecture's participation in a longer material narrative. A steel beam today may become a column tomorrow. A brick may be reused in another settlement. A timber panel may one day biodegrade and nourish soil.

In this context, behaviour(s) become(s) a central driver of design. Buildings are no longer static containers; they are dynamic systems interacting with occupants and environments. Behaviour(s) include(s) energy consumption patterns, spatial appropriation, maintenance practices and community engagement. A circular building must anticipate and guide these behaviours towards regenerative cycles. Belonging(s) also transform(s) architectural meaning. Belonging implies that materials come from somewhere – forests, quarries, soils – and that their extraction affects communities and ecologies. It implies that design reflects cultural narratives and local knowledge. Eco-localism does not reject globalisation outright, but it does resist homogenisation. Belonging revalues proximity, craft and climatic specificity. In this sense, circular architecture challenges the universalising tendencies of high modernism. The glass curtainwall that performs identically in New York, Dubai or Shanghai disregards local climatic behaviour. Eco-local circularity demands adaptation. In arid regions, material mass and shading dominate. In humid tropics, porosity and ventilation prevail. In cold climates, density and insulation become forefront.

Andrés Jaque / Office for Political Innovation, *Le Trianon de Boue*, and Colectivo C733, *Wind Catcher*, Cour des Fontaines, Biennale d'Architecture et de Paysage d'Île-de-France, Versailles, 2025. Exhibition curated by Sana Frini and Philippe Rahm.
Conceived as full-scale climatic devices, the pavilions mobilise water, air and radiation to generate microclimates through evaporation, shading and thermal exchange. Rather than enclosing space, they organise it through atmospheric behaviour, positioning climate as a primary generator of form. In doing so, they embody a shift from form as a response to programmatic function alone towards form shaped by environmental behaviour(s) and situated belonging(s), embedding architecture within local ecological cycles rather than abstract, universal models inherited from extractive modernity.

> Form follows function – yes.
> But function now includes ecological performance.
> Form follows behaviour – the behaviour of wind, water, sun, users and time.
> Form follows belonging – to place, to culture, to material cycles.

We live in an era of shifting paradigms. The Anthropocene is beginning to compel architecture to redefine the definition of success. We can no longer assess efficiency through structural span or economic output alone. Success must be measured in carbon reduction, biodiversity integration, social resilience and material circularity. Post-extractivism implies a gradual decoupling from the practice of endless resource extraction. It does not mean an immediate cessation of material use, but rather a reorganisation of value systems. Waste becomes resource. Demolition becomes urban mining. Construction becomes assembly. This paradigm shift also transforms aesthetics. The visible reuse of materials, patina of ageing and expression of joinery for adaptability produce a new architectural language. Imperfection becomes narrative. Ageing becomes beauty. Temporality becomes visible rather than concealed.

In circular eco-local architecture, buildings are conceived as part of larger metabolic territories. They harvest rainwater and release it slowly. They integrate vegetation and support pollinators. They reduce heat-island effects. They produce energy and share it. They become infrastructural nodes rather than isolated monuments. Ultimately, the evolution from 'Form Follows Function' to 'Form Follows Function(s), Behaviour(s) and Belonging(s)' signals a philosophical shift: from singularity to multiplicity, from control to reciprocity, from extraction to stewardship. Architecture is never neutral; it is always embedded in energy systems, material economies and cultural narratives.

Building against extraction

'Becoming Circular' offers a contemporary illustration of circularity not as a technical protocol of sustainability, but as a political and material repositioning of architecture itself. As one of the major thematic topics of the UIA World Congress of Architects 2026 Barcelona, under the broader scope of 'Becoming', it frames architecture as a transformative discipline capable of responding to ecological, social, political and cultural transitions. Against the tabula rasa logics inherited from the fossil-fuel and extractivist era, it advocates working with what already exists: treating time as a design tool, territory as a complex relational field, and matter as something to be reorganised rather than endlessly replaced. Across four invited practices – H arquitectes, BAUKUNST and the Structural Xploration Lab (SXL), Nicolas Dorval-Bory Architectes, and HOLES (Mio Tsuneyama with Fuminori Nousaku) – circularity is framed not as environmental performance measured after the fact, but as a refusal of depletion embedded in the act of building itself. Rather than producing through accumulation, these practices build through calibration: extending the life of materials, reactivating latent capacities, and situating architecture within renewable territorial cycles. What emerges is a post-extractivist ethic grounded in restraint – dry assembly, reversible details, local resources, low-transformation materials, and forms of construction that preserve the future availability of matter.

It is therefore no surprise to find H arquitectes among the protagonists of Becoming Circular. Their work demonstrates how circularity can be embedded directly in architectural form, construction and environmental performance without being reduced to a technological supplement. Rather than treating sustainability as an added layer, H arquitectes develop a materially coherent architecture in which structure, enclosure and climate operate as a single system. Their projects are grounded in contextual materiality, constructive simplicity and climatic responsiveness, allowing individual elements to perform multiple roles while reducing unnecessary layers, technical complexity and resource consumption. Their Clos Pachem Winery in Tarragona, Spain (completed in 2019), for example, makes this logic explicit: its brick vaults simultaneously act as structure, enclosure and passive climatic device, using porosity, thermal mass and ventilation flow to respond to Mediterranean conditions with minimal mechanical dependence.

In this sense, form follows not only programmatic function, but also the behaviours of air, heat, humidity and light. More radically, their work proposes an eco-local construction culture that resists the extractivist violence of globalised supply chains. By privileging regionally available materials, reversible details and low-transformation assemblies, H arquitectes do not simply reduce impact, they preserve material availability and embed the building within the ecological and constructive cycles of its territory. In their Becoming Circular proposal, 'Flows and Proportions', circularity is less the afterlife of materials than the tectonic intelligence that prevents their exhaustion. By linking the proportions of a building to the natural flow energies, they prevail upon their proportional methods and analytical tools to produce a form that aligns with the contextual natural flows instead of fighting against them. Form, in this expanded sense, follows function, behaviour and belonging.

If H arquitectes locate circularity in the constructive intelligence of the building, BAUKUNST and the Structural Xploration Lab radicalise the question by shifting attention to the afterlife of the city itself. In their work, the built environment becomes an 'urban mine': a material reserve whose residues – demolition debris, infrastructural fragments, industrial remains – can be reactivated within new forms of construction. Circularity here is not embedded primarily in reversibility or low-tech restraint, but in the recirculation of matter already expelled from the urban cycle. Their research reframes waste as latent value and the project as an act of recovery, displacement and reassembly rather than fabrication. This position is clearly articulated in their Spolia project, where fragments of asphalt and concrete recovered from the city are assembled into new structural walls with minimal transformation. What matters is not simply reuse as an ecological gesture, but a redefinition of architectural value itself: the discarded becomes structurally and conceptually operative. In contrast to H arquitectes, who organise matter so that it remains available, BAUKUNST and the Structural Xploration Lab begin from matter already lost to extractivist processes and pull it back into circulation. The building is no longer a final object, but a provisional arrangement of recovered resources – a temporary repository of matter held in suspension.

A different but equally radical position emerges in the work of Nicolas Dorval-Bory, where circularity is approached through reduction rather than recirculation. His projects challenge extractivist construction not by reintroducing urban waste into new systems, but by drastically lowering the threshold of intervention itself. Working with rubble, reclaimed elements, raw material and low-value matter, Dorval-Bory develops an architecture of material directness in which the project often appears as an essential gesture rather than a complex assembly. In this sense, circularity is not organised through systems of material recovery, but through a radical economy of means that limits transformation, minimises extractive violence, and allows the inherent capacities of available matter to shape form. His 'Mechanics of Cold' proposal extends this logic into the climatic realm, treating coolness not as a mechanical service but as a spatial and material resource to be produced, conserved and distributed through both vernacular and technological means.

This refusal becomes more radical in the work of Mio Tsuneyama and Fuminori Nousaku, whose projects often begin by questioning the need to build unnecessarily. Their architecture starts from what is already there – existing structures, residual conditions, latent spatial capacities – and operates through minimal intervention, subtraction, redistribution and recalibration rather than material addition. Here, circularity is not simply a question of reuse, nor even of constructive reversibility, but of refusing unnecessary production altogether. Form does not precede use, it follows the behaviours already embedded in a place: inherited patterns of inhabitation, residual constructive logics, and the overlooked capacities of existing matter to continue otherwise. Architecture becomes less an act of fabrication than an act of attention – a precise editing of what already belongs. In this sense, Tsuneyama and Nousaku's work expands the logic of circularity towards a post-extractivist ethics of belonging, where the project extends the life of matter by reinforcing its relation to use, memory and site rather than by imposing a new object. If H arquitectes preserve matter through constructive intelligence, BAUKUNST and the Structural Xploration Lab through recirculation, and Dorval-Bory through reduction, Tsuneyama and Nousaku push the argument furthest: circularity as the suspension of extraction through the radical continuity of what already exists.

Becoming Circular foregrounds the relevance of a new architectural era. If Le Corbusier's modernist machine for living sought to rationalise life through industrial logic, the eco-local architecture of the post-extractivist circular era seeks to harmonise life within ecological limits. It is less about control and more about reciprocity; less about permanence and more about adaptability; less about domination and more about coexistence. If the nineteenth and twentieth centuries were defined by extraction and acceleration, the twenty-first must be defined by regeneration and reconnection. Architecture, as both cultural artefact and material practice, stands at the centre of this transition.

> Form still matters. Function still matters.
> But today, architecture must also listen – to climate,
> to community, to cycles, to time.

Only then can it truly belong.

Research by Design 3/12

H arquitectes

FLOWS AND PROPORTIONS: RELATIONSHIPS BETWEEN THE DIRECTION OF SPACE AND ITS DEGREE OF CIRCULARITY

There is a direct relationship between the proportions of spaces and the energy required for their construction and use. Our aim is to investigate the link between the 'direction' of spaces – and the flows that coexist within them – and their degree of circularity.

Flows

When the organisation of spaces and matter follows the direction of natural phenomena, buildings and the materials used tend to require less energy. When architecture synchronises with the direction of major natural flows, it can easily take advantage of the planet's intrinsic energy, which already mobilises a lot of energy and matter. On the contrary, when architecture does not follow these flows, the 'frictions' of going against them start to appear, making the use of external (extra) energy unavoidable. An analogy would be the difference between sailing downstream where the water's kinetic energy helps you advance, and sailing upstream, against the current, where the water pushes you back and you can only move forward by applying more energy than the river itself.

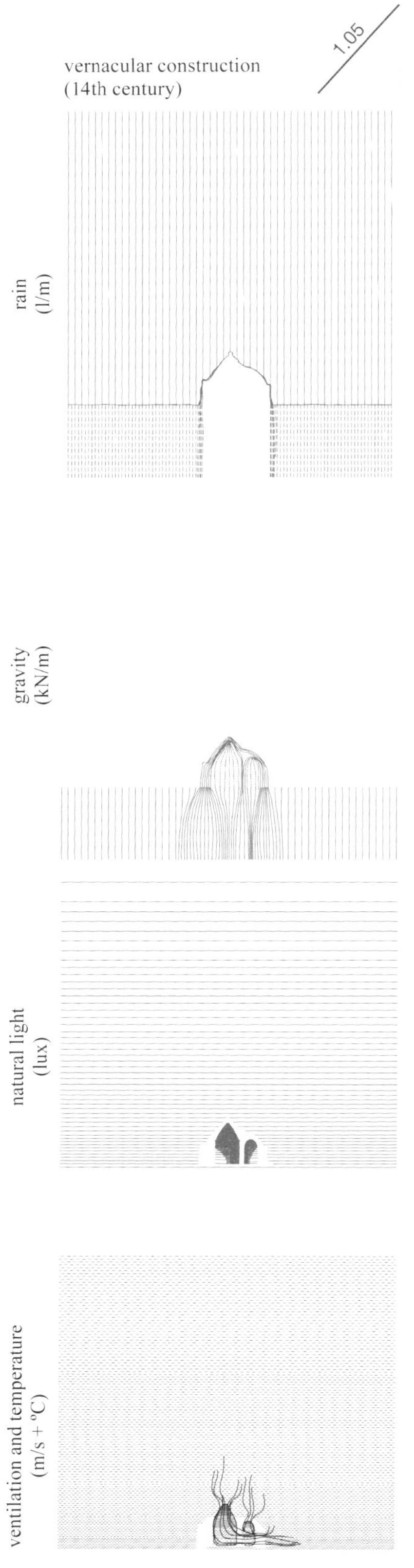

Direction

Major natural phenomena that shape architecture include gravitational load paths, the movement of warm air through stratification or pressure changes, evaporation, rain, solar radiation and indirect daylight. All of these are planetary-scale phenomena with a predominantly vertical direction.

The organisation of our planet is subject to solar radiation and gravity, with a clearly vertical natural component. Therefore, when its spaces and physical matter are organised in accordance with this directionality, architecture tends to be more efficient and circular as it prioritises and allows these major natural forces to flow through it. On the other hand, if the spaces or the materials interfere or extend the transit of these flows, solutions that require additional energy are often needed. A very clear example is rain – a natural flow with an unequivocally vertical vector – which needs to be redirected or channelled to create habitable spaces. If such deviations retain a predominantly vertical component – for example, a steep roof – it can be built with low-embodied-energy materials such as straw, timber, stone or earth. Where a roof's geometry becomes more horizontal, the materials must be more impermeable and require higher embodied energy: for example, ceramic tiles or metal solutions in steel, copper or zinc, and, ultimately, flat roofs where materials are entirely synthetic. The less the original vertical direction is altered, the simpler, more natural and more circular the solution can be. The more we deflect the rain horizontally, the more anthropic and impactful the solution becomes.

popular construction
(18th century)
1.23

Villa Rotonda, Vicenza
Andrea Palladio (1570)
1.74

Casa Milà, Barcelona
Antoni Gaudí (1910)
1.45

Highfield House Apartments,
Baltimore, Maryland, USA
Mies van der Rohe
(1964)
0.31

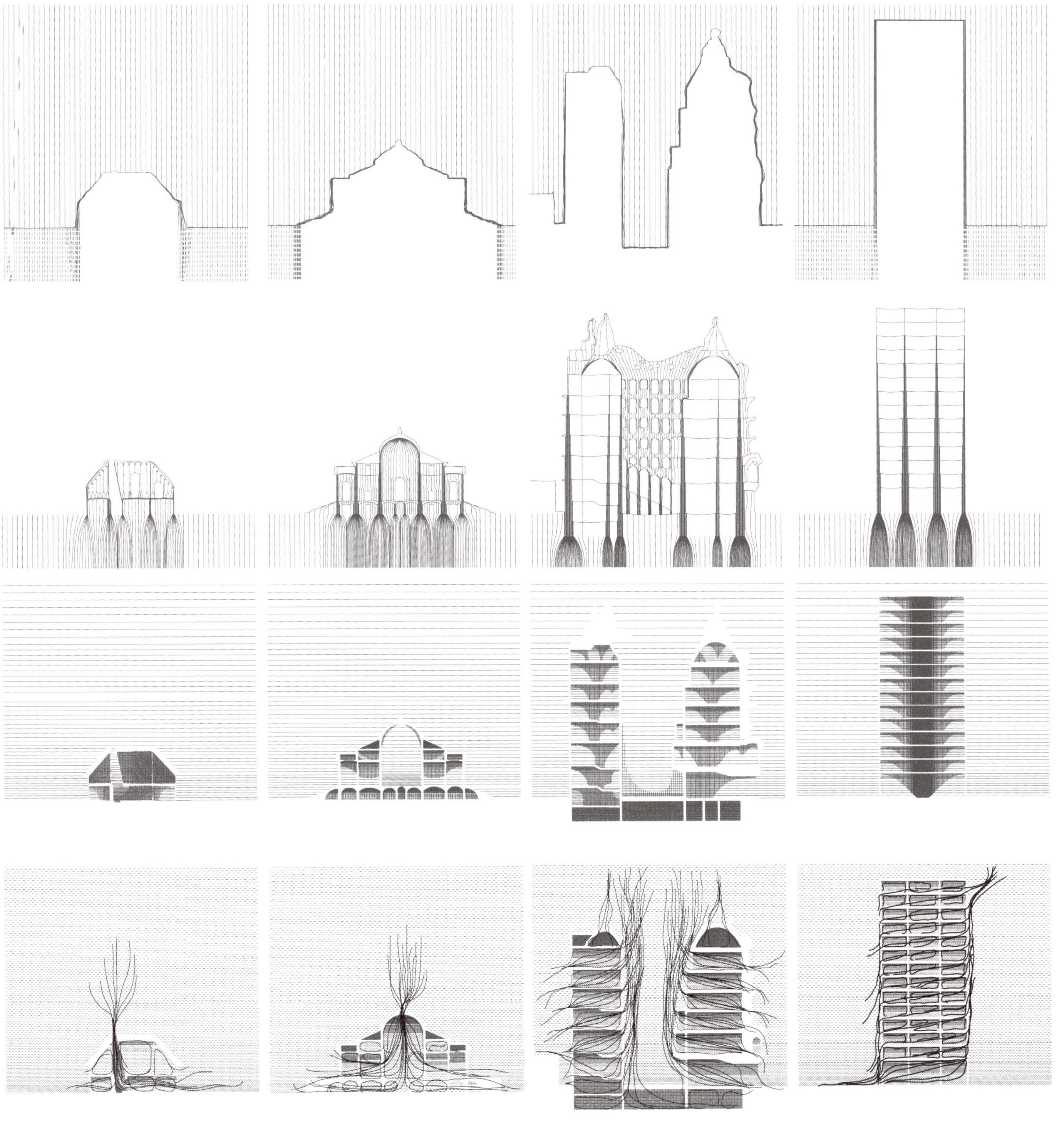

Lleieltat Santsenca civic centre, Barcelona (2017)
H arquitectes

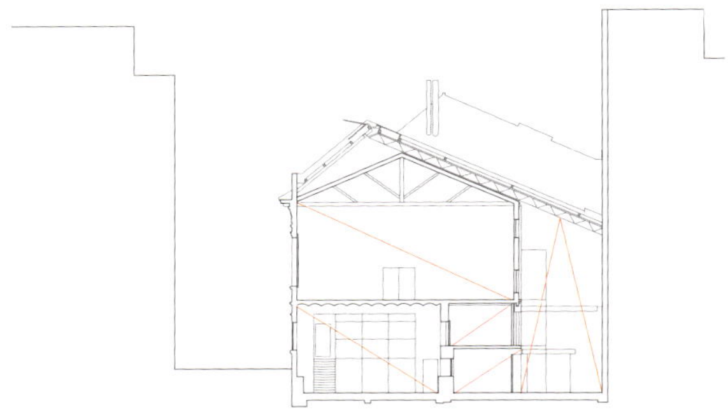

Esdevé space, Granollers, Barcelona (2025)
H arquitectes

House on Francesc Macià street, Granollers, Barcelona (2021)
H arquitectes

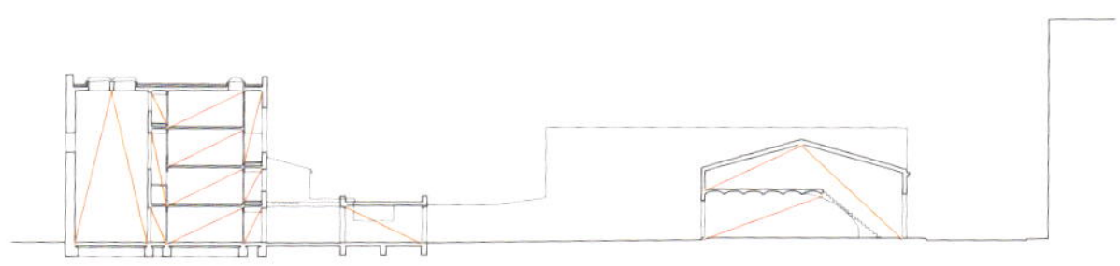

The same can be said of load paths. To build space we need structures that redirect gravitational flow. If this path maintains a degree of verticality, as in load-bearing masonry with short spans, or in pure compression structures like arches, vaults or domes, we can still use highly circular materials such as timber, earth, stone or ceramics. Again, the more a structure forces gravitational loads to travel horizontally over a long distance, the more antagonistic it is to gravity's direction. As a result, the construction systems and materials used (such as steel or reinforced concrete) must be more engineered and artificial, requiring significantly more energy for extraction, manufacturing, transportation, assembly and eventual dismantling. These spatial configurations and proportions struggle to close their material cycles.

This relationship between spatial proportion and degree of circularity is also evident in natural light. Its predominantly vertical component allows vertically proportioned spaces such as those with high ceilings, tall windows, skylights or atria to distribute daylight more evenly and effectively than horizontally proportioned ones, which almost always result in the need for significant supplementary artificial lighting at lower levels.

It also appears in the movement of air, which rises and stratifies as it warms. Vertically proportioned spaces promote this natural upward movement and self-organisation of temperature, becoming a natural driver of ventilation. In contrast, horizontally proportioned spaces obstruct this flow and generally require mechanical ventilation systems.

House on Major de Sarrià Street, Barcelona (2023)
H arquitectes

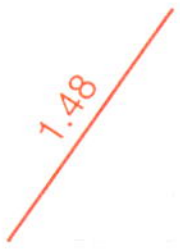

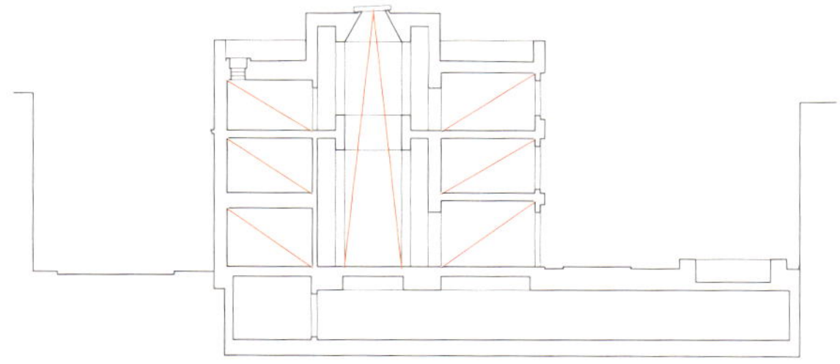

Rehabilitation of Vapor Cortés (Prodis headquarters), Terrassa, Barcelona (2024)
H arquitectes

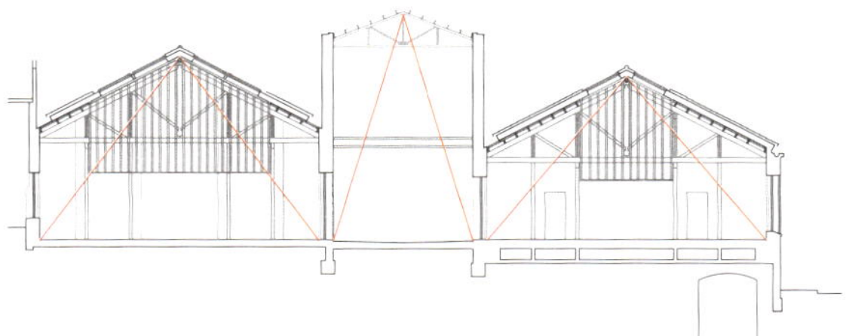

Social housing in Gavà, Barcelona (2019)
H arquitectes

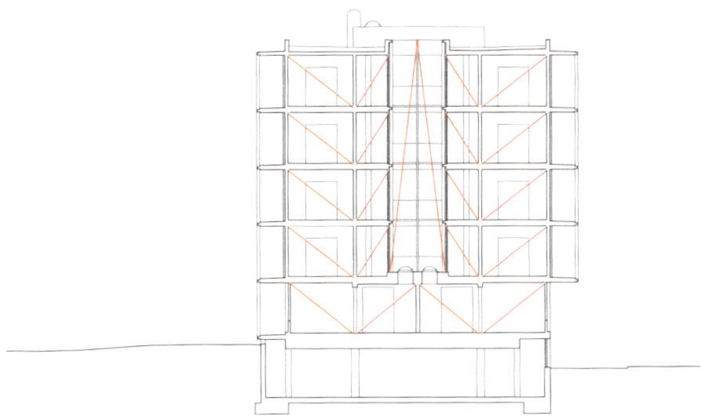

Proportions

There is, therefore, a geometric relationship between the effort required to redirect natural flows and the environmental impact of architecture, as well as a relationship between the proportions of spaces and their intrinsic natural quality. To observe how spatial proportions shift according to the energy intensity of the technologies employed, we graphed and calculated the average vector of these proportions in a selection of vernacular, traditional and modern buildings. Those with an average vector greater than 1 can be considered circular, while averages below 1 require a lot of energy. Architectural history therefore reflects the spatial consequences of these technological and cultural transformations.

Redirecting natural vertical flows is perhaps the most primordial act of architecture – the art of creating space. Sometimes spaces need to accommodate the transit of these natural phenomena; at other times they must do the opposite – shift, temper or slow them down. Reorganising these invisible flows means designing the physical directions, dimensions and proportions of architecture – designing environmental experience through matter, and making the invisible visible to reveal the natural qualities of space.

Historically, before the use of fossil fuels, one had to be extremely careful when deciding whether to favour, redirect or block these flows, and where to invest effort and the little energy available. The shape of spaces was the result of a defensive strategy within the limits imposed by available energy and resources. Architecture was inevitably circular and therefore organised into typologies and directions aligned with natural flows to ensure proper load descent and optimal natural lighting and ventilation. The quality of spaces depended primarily on their proportions.

Today, natural flows are reorganised and domesticated more than ever, but no longer through proportions or architectural attributes; instead, energy is injected into materials and spaces to artificially transform them. It is used to give spaces the form that satisfies new human goals – economic, social or cultural. The rules that shape architecture are no longer set by the planet, but by the market, regulations or trends. The natural quality and proportions of spaces have been drastically diminished. Instead of a defensive strategy of adapting to the environmental constraints of our surroundings, we now apply an invasive strategy of domination powered by energy that transforms, blurs and destabilises everything.

These imbalances compel our discipline to pause and reconsider what architecture really is. Perhaps we have reached a moment in history when architecture no longer needs to be so de-

Existing conventional housing
based on horizontal proportions

0.23

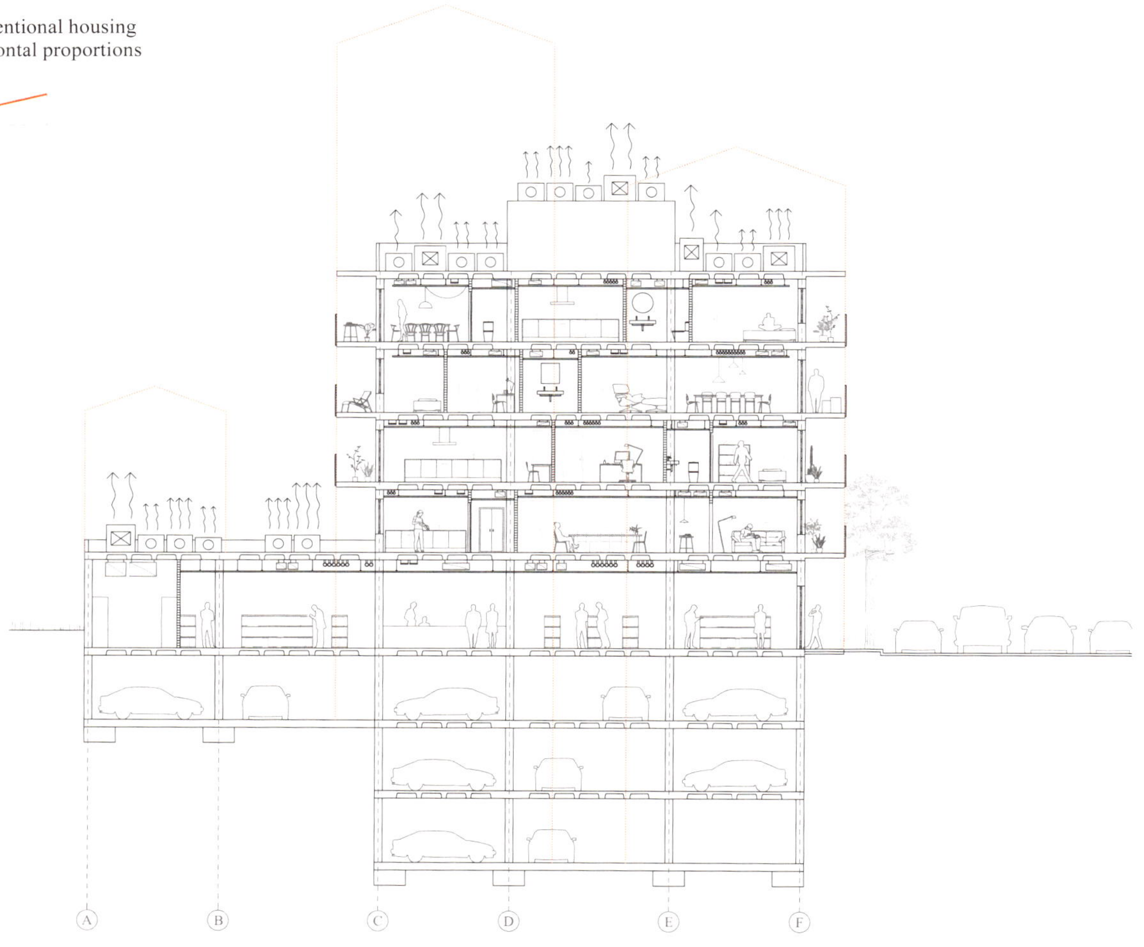

Becoming

Circular

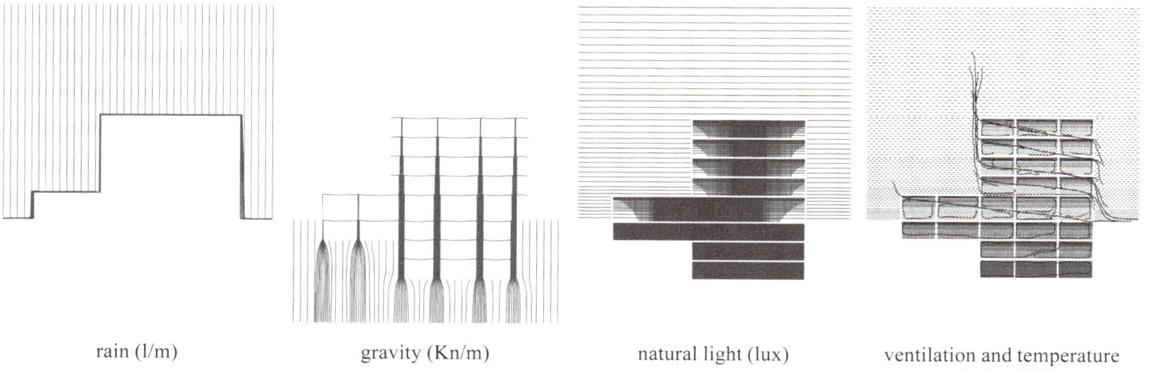

rain (l/m)

gravity (Kn/m)

natural light (lux)

ventilation and temperature (m/s + °C)

fensive nor so invasive. Perhaps it is no longer necessary to fight ‘against’ these natural phenomena but rather the opposite – to design radically ‘in favour’ of them. It is the moment to redefine our connection with the planet and move beyond the notion of domestic, safe and purely utilitarian space to explore the concept of disproportion. Our practice pursues a new verticality, an increasingly natural scale of architecture.

Another scale

Most architecture built in the last hundred years contradicts the direction of natural flows, exhibiting deeply artificial proportions and behaviours. This enormous amount of obsolete pre-existing fabric will need to be transformed, with new spatial conceptions and proportions more aligned with the planet. This is likely the greatest challenge ahead.

We envision a progressive process of vertical ‘disproportion’ applied to existing buildings: spaces redesigned more in section than in plan, where selective deconstruction allows increased heights, reduced building depths, improved natural light and ventilation, and a new relationship with gravity, climate and rain. An architecture that frees itself from ancestral fears and exposes itself to the environment, embracing the conditions and dimensions of natural phenomena to create less domesticated spaces – a transition towards a new architectural scale that is less anthropomorphic and increasingly proportioned to the planet.

Transformation proposal based on vertical proportions

Research by Design

H arquitectes

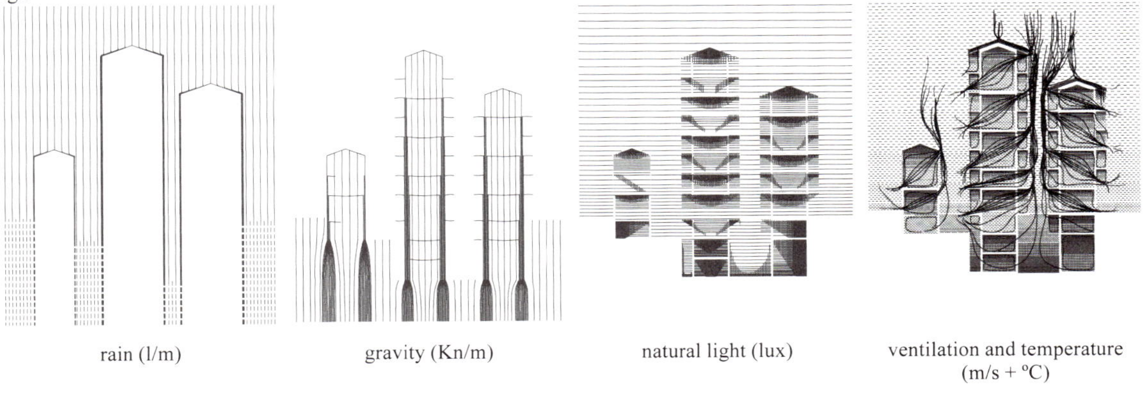

HOLES (Mio Tsuneyama and Fuminori Nousaku)

MAKING KNOTS, WEAVING SHED

Textile crafts developed as extensions of household labour, producing essential items such as clothing and bedding that protect the body from the environment. In many societies across the world, this work was primarily carried out by women. The Japanese scholar Sadako Fukui writes in her book *Kasuri* (2002)[1] that women often worked on needlework late at night after men and children had gone to sleep, in addition to daytime farmwork and housework.

1. Sadako Fukui, *Kasuri: Cultural History of Objects and Humans, Vol. 105*, Hosei University Press, 2002.

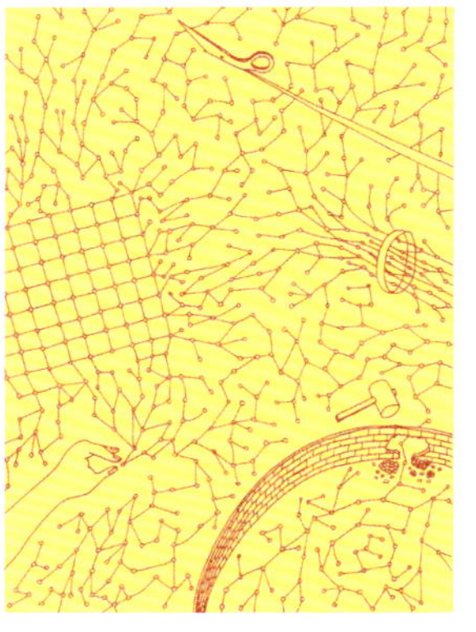

HOLES, *Urban Fungus: Architecture is a Complex Mesh*, conceptual drawing, 2024.

Beyond needlework, a long tradition of textile downcycling existed. Adult kimonos were remade into children's garments; fabrics were reinforced and repaired through patchwork or *sashiko* stitching; scraps became rugs; and the final remnants were used as cleaning rags before being returned to the earth. Despite the ingenuity and sustainability of these practices, they have long been dismissed as mere 'handicraft'.

In *The Four Elements of Architecture* (1851),[2] German architect Gottfried Semper argued that architecture originated in the use of woven textiles in early huts, identifying hearth, foundation, enclosure and roof as its four elements, with enclosure derived from textile-based structures such as woven fences – a logic that still underlies spatial partitions and wall systems today.

2. Gottfried Semper, *The Four Elements of Architecture and Other Writings*, trans. Harry F. Mallgrave and Wolfgang Herrmann, Cambridge University Press, 1989.

If the hut marks the beginning of architecture, this also suggests alternative architectural possibilities. Cloth – familiar as everyday clothing yet materially 'weak' – offers a way to rethink dominant notions of strength and construction. At the same time, textiles carry histories of labour and exploitation, while their biodegradability reminds us that they ultimately return to the earth through the action of other organisms, such as fungi.

HOLES, Study models for Making Knots, Weaving Shed, using the traditional Japanese technique of *sakiami*, 2026.

In the Making Knots, Weaving Shed workshop, participants build a hut from discarded cloth, weaving it into structural form through knotting, braiding and interlacing. By working with supple, thread-based materials unlike conventional building components, we explore how minimal architectural structures can emerge from weakness and flexibility. The aim is to imagine architectural applications for thin, low-waste materials that readily decompose.

Although fashion is enjoyed daily, the apparel industry is the world's second most polluting industry after oil, driven in part by the enormous volume of discarded garments. Inspired by *sakiami*, a traditional Japanese technique of shredding old cloth into new thread, the workshop investigates whether used clothing can be transformed into architectural enclosures. Held in the Turbine Hall – the former Tres Xemeneies (Three Chimneys) industrial space designed to concentrate energy for power generation – the workshop becomes a modest act of community building, cultivating new sensitivities towards the overlooked, the vulnerable and the weak.

Emerging Workshop 4/12 Nicolas Dorval-Bory Architectes (Nicolas Dorval-Bory and Hugo Taillardat)

THE COOLEST SUMMER OF THE REST OF OUR LIVES

Nicolas Dorval-Bory Architectes, Cooled stone prototype (thermography), FAIRE, Pavillon de l'Arsenal, Paris, 2024.
A 330-kilogramme limestone block cooled by a 150-Watt recycled refrigeration unit, creating a localised cool microclimate through mineral heat absorption.

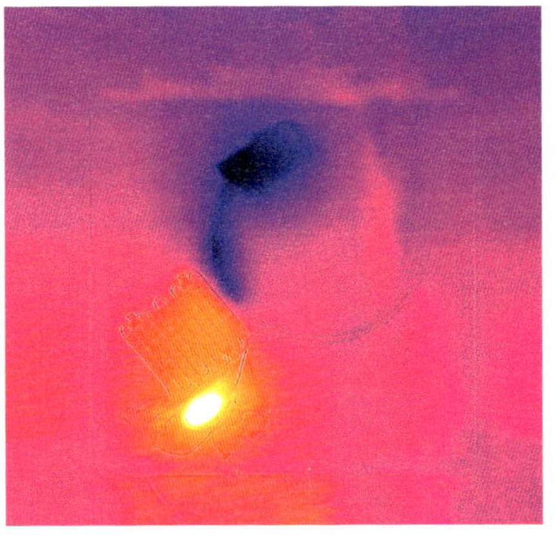

Building on our Mechanics of Cold research project at the Pavillon de l'Arsenal in Paris, and at the École nationale supérieure d'architecture Versailles, the workshop explores the spatial and architectural potential of cold as a pretext to imagine an unexpected, comfortable and economical climatic future within a particular built environment. Contrary to the image of the red and blue taps of our plumbing systems, cold is not the symmetrical opposite of heat. It is an absence of energy: thermodynamics shows that only heat exists and dissipates irreversibly. Heating is heating, while cooling is moving heat, generating a thermal surplus elsewhere.

Nicolas Dorval-Bory Architectes, Cooled stone prototype (thermography), FAIRE, Pavillon de l'Arsenal, Paris, 2024.
The prototype assembles a reused refrigeration system (compressor+evaporator), dismantled and arranged on a plasterboard support, together with a limestone rock. After a few hours, frost forms at the start of the coil and on the rock.

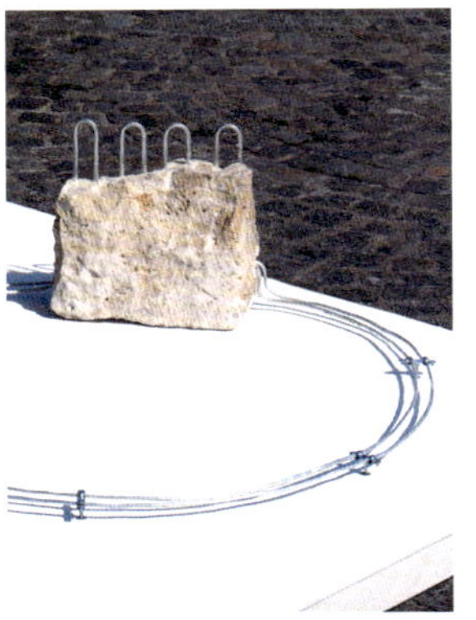

Fortunately, the average temperature of the Earth's surface is around 15°C, which means that a faint thermal input is sufficient to reach the comfort zone of approximately 20 to 25°C. On average, heating alone would therefore be enough to live. But we do not live in averages, and the significant thermal amplitudes across regions and seasons – further intensified each year by climate change – force us to artificially stabilise our environment. While heating has been technically mastered thanks to abundant energy and improved insulation, cooling is becoming the major challenge, particularly in urban contexts, where all activity dissipates energy.

Architecture must therefore select, store or displace calories in order to maintain a zone of comfort. Unlike heating, the principles of cooling are extremely varied, low-intensity and delicate, ranging from the microscopic scale (the Peltier effect, for example) to the cosmic scale (geothermal cooling or radiative cooling). They can be implemented as active or passive devices, or even be found and revealed in existing situations. Cooling strategies thus require precision, contextual awareness, and an ability to work with subtle gradients rather than absolute control.

Frigidarium, Pompeii, Ancient Rome, 1st century BCE.
Engraving from around 1831 depicting a frigidarium (cold-water room), which served as the final step in the bathing sequence of Roman thermae. These often north-facing, thick-walled architectural structures had minimal openings to reduce solar heat gain, and were cooled by imported snow or ice.

Our research engages with the physical and thermodynamic principles of cold, as well as with devices for its production, conservation and diffusion, both vernacular and technological. Barcelona and its surroundings provide a rich climatic, material and cultural context in which to identify latent resources for coolness and to test how architecture can mediate thermal conditions through form, materiality and use.

Occupying the Turbine Hall (formerly the Tres Xemeneies [Three Chimneys] power plant) – a place originally dedicated to combustion and energy production – this exploration inverts its original logic, transforming it into a terrain for rethinking comfort, energy and domestic practices through cooling.

Perhaps by experiencing the hottest summer ever known, we will invent rituals and techniques to forever remember the coolest summer of the rest of our lives.

Spolia is part of the 'Mineral: Architectures of Urban Mining' urban innovation challenge developed during 2025 and 2026 in collaboration with the World Capital of Architecture and the Barcelona City Council through the Manager's Office for the Chief Architect, the BIT Habitat foundation and BIMSA (Barcelona d'Infraestructures Municipals), together with DIBA (Diputació de Barcelona), the Mies van der Rohe Foundation, and the UIA World Congress of Architects 2026 Barcelona. Based on the curatorial framework of the Congress, 'Becoming. Architectures for a planet in transition', the challenge explored urban mining as a design and production strategy, focusing on the potential reuse of the thousands of tons of mineral waste (asphalt, concrete, granite, paving and earthwork) generated every year in the renovation of public works in Barcelona's streets. From the international open call, creative technologists collective BAUKUNST and the Structural Xploration Lab at EPFL in Lausanne were selected to develop a research-driven process exploring different decarbonised material systems – testing and producing a mock-up for the congress, followed by a pilot intervention in public space, as well as presenting a series of long-term visions that expand the potential of the project in the future.

BAUKUNST and the Structural Xploration Lab (SXL), EPFL

SPOLIA: REVALUING URBAN MATTER

Spolia proposes a circular construction system that reuses urban mineral waste as structural elements. Using simple, low-tech methods and drawing on a primitive architectural grammar of walls and floors, it produces modular, prefabricated components that preserve material identity, allow reversible assembly and scale across architectural and infrastructural applications for low-carbon, resource-conscious building.

The project operates within a post-extractivist framework that views the city not as a consumer of resources but as a mine in reverse. By reusing materials extracted from public works within their original territory, the proposed construction method reduces dependence on virgin resources, shortens supply chains and minimises the environmental footprint of building activities. It supports a circular spatial logic in which waste becomes resource and construction is reimagined as territorial regeneration rather than depletion. Mineral waste recovered from urban infrastructure becomes a vector of social and territorial memory rather than a neutral input. By preserving the heterogeneity of construction waste, its embedded narratives are revealed and translated into new architectural interpretations. Rather than dissolving material identity through homogenisation, reuse is aligned with the fundamental elements of architecture. By valorising reclaimed materials, the system embraces a contemporary culture of Spolia, where traces of the past form the foundation for renewed architectural expression.

Resource and process

The proposal develops an original construction method that directly reuses mineral waste from urban works, including composite materials such as concrete and asphalt, without transformation. Aiming for an economy of means based on the simplest possible approach, the project employs these raw materials without any specific processing. The proposed dismantling and storage methods for mineral urban waste require no industrial adaptation, relying instead on existing infrastructures such as concrete and asphalt recycling centres or urban deposits. Existing mineral waste and the current stock of reusable components can also be integrated into the system. Building on the PhD research of Maxence Grangeot at EPFL (Re:bble Prefa), dismantled waste elements are assembled in a masonry-like pattern and encased in concrete to create prefabricated structural elements – load-bearing walls and slabs – in a controlled workshop environment. Large waste pieces are arranged in the formwork according to masonry principles and a peripheral reinforcement cage is installed within the mould. Recycled concrete is poured between the elements while larger rubble pieces remain partially exposed. Connections are designed for sling attachments, facilitating lifting, transportation and on-site assembly.

To manufacture the slabs, grooves are sawn lengthwise to insert rebars, which are then grouted. For retaining walls, the process is similar and includes a reinforced-concrete base. After hardening of the recycled concrete, the precast elements are demoulded, tilted, washed and prepared for transport and installation. Each component consists of approximately 80 per cent waste and 20 per cent recycled concrete. Their dimensions are designed for transportability, with a maximum width of 2.4 metres, a thickness between 16 and 28 centimetres, and one rough side opposite a smooth one. The system is a prefabricated, modular and reversible solution that is both structurally viable and replicable, opening new pathways for circular and low-carbon construction.

<u>Elements of architecture</u>

Spolia takes the fundamental architectural load-bearing elements – vertical walls and horizontal slabs – as its starting point. These components then unfold into a more comprehensive construction system. Together, they form a structural framework that accommodates various assembly methods and architectural applications. Far from being simple reused fragments, the elements are defined by their structural roles and correspond to two primary logics: compression for the walls and bending for the slabs.

Elements working in compression typically only require additional reinforcement for transport and handling, whereas elements subjected to bending are reinforced in grooved assemblies to resist tensile forces. The prefabricated system relies on reversible connections, allowing the elements to be dismantled and reused elsewhere – extending their service life and enhancing sustainability. These visible connections,

Maxence Grangeot/Structural Xploration Lab (SXL), EPFL, Re:bble Prefa, 2025.
Top to bottom:
Materials.
Dismantling.
Storage.

composed primarily of nuts and bolts, provide a robust and efficient solution that aligns with existing prefabrication industry standards.

Structure and infrastructure

The modular and reversible logic of the system allows it to adapt across scales and contexts. Its simplicity of implementation combined with the breadth of possible applications makes it capable of addressing the challenge of reusing mineral waste on a large scale – from infrastructure to architecture. At the territorial scale, the proposal engages with topography, road and rail networks, and the maritime environment of Barcelona. The side-by-side arrangement of walls enables the creation of various infrastructural forms, including retaining walls for terrain stabilisation, noise barriers along transport routes or breakwaters along coastlines. At the architectural scale, the system is well suited to the prefabrication sector. It introduces a new grammar of building components – walls and slabs – supported by a simple, modular assembly principle that allows for the efficient and flexible construction of multistorey structures. This versatile approach facilitates rapid assembly, adapts to diverse programmatic needs, and supports innovative architectural solutions. The prototype developed for UIA 2026 Barcelona proposes the implementation of these initial elements in the form of a pavilion on the Tres Xemeneies site.

Top to bottom:
Components.
Precast.
Prefabricated.

BAUKUNST and the Structural Xploration Lab (SXL), EPFL, with Olivier Campagne, Spolia: Infrastructure, Barcelona, 2026.
Side-by-side walls enable diverse infrastructural applications, such as retaining walls for terrain stabilisation, and noise barriers along transport routes or coastal breakwaters.

BAUKUNST and the Structural Xploration Lab (SXL), EPFL, with Olivier Campagne, Spolia: Public space, Barcelona, 2026.
Performative artefacts improve public spaces by enhancing both environmental comfort and social interaction.

BAUKUNST and the Structural Xploration Lab (SXL), EPFL, with Olivier Campagne and Simone Marcolin, Spolia, Barcelona, 2026.
Post-tensioned prefabricated floor plates can be integrated into standard building systems to create adaptable surfaces and easily demountable construction.

BAUKUNST and the Structural Xploration Lab (SXL), EPFL, with Olivier Campagne, Spolia: Prototype, Barcelona, 2026.
Load-bearing prefabricated wall assemblies enable efficient and flexible erection of multistorey structures.

A conversation between Matthias Schuler and the Congress curators on Becoming Circular and the carbon implications of building reuse

THE CARBON LOGIC OF REUSE

CURATORS The Congress situates circularity within a post-extractivist horizon, acknowledging planetary resource limits while the built environment continues to expand globally. From your perspective as a climate engineer, how do you interpret circularity today?

MATTHIAS SCHULER For me, circularity starts with a very basic awareness: we are dealing with limited resources, particularly when it comes to land and materials. We have already consumed a large part of the planet's green and undeveloped areas, even though these areas are essential for maintaining a balanced carbon cycle. Natural systems – forests, oceans, soils – can absorb around seven billion tons of carbon per year. If we translate that into global per-capita terms, this corresponds to roughly one ton of carbon per person annually.

Today, we are very far from this balance. In the United States, emissions are around fifteen to twenty tons per person per year; in Europe, around ten; in Switzerland, roughly four, with a clear ambition to move closer to one. At the same time, large parts of Africa are at around 0.2 tons per person. This immediately raises a global question. We cannot simply assume that the development model of industrialised countries can be replicated everywhere.

DECA architecture, Christou Lada Street 3 – Kaleidoscopic Pragmatism, Athens, Greece, 2024. A typical example of 1960s and 1970s buildings in Athens that require major upgrading if they are to be used for another fifty to a hundred years but can't be rebuilt due to high carbon emissions and material resource consumption.

Transsolar, illustration of Christou Lada Street 3. The 27-metre deep floorplan with only south- and north-facing windows demanded additional daylight in the centre of the building, which was realised by activating a historical ventilation shaft as a light pipe fed by a heliostat system on the roof, creating a kaleidoscopic effect that gives all floors of the building a special identity. Illustration by Edith Maier-Neretin.

From this perspective, circularity is inseparable from land use. Densification and working with what already exists are not just urban strategies; they are planetary necessities. The same applies to materials. Many key resources are already largely consumed. Copper is a good example: around 80 per cent of global reserves have already been extracted. What remains is harder to access and requires much more energy. Cities therefore have to be understood as future material stocks hidden in urban mines. Materials embedded in existing buildings – cables, steel, structural elements – are not waste; they are resources that are already there.

Energy, however, is different. The planet receives far more solar energy than humanity could ever consume. The limitation is not energy itself, but carbon. Fossil fuels are abundant, but their use destabilises the climate. Once energy production becomes renewable and carbon-neutral, embodied carbon and material cycles inevitably move to the centre of the discussion, which can already be seen in countries with low carbon footprints for energy, such as Denmark.

C Over the last decades, environmental design has shifted from a focus on energy efficiency towards carbon accountability. Where do the most decisive carbon choices lie today?

MS When we started Transsolar, more than thirty years ago, reducing energy demand was clearly the main objective. Heating dominated the discussion, and improving insulation and system efficiency were the primary strategies. Today, carbon has become the central metric, largely because energy systems themselves are changing. Many European countries aim to become carbon-neutral in energy production within the next two decades. Once energy is produced without carbon emissions, operational energy consumption becomes much less relevant from a climate perspective.

At that point, embodied carbon becomes dominant. In countries with low-carbon electricity, up to 80 per cent of a building's total carbon footprint over its lifetime can come from construction materials. This changes priorities fundamentally. Material optimisation and efficient systems still matter, but the most radical and effective carbon decision is often whether to build new at all.

In many cases, around 60 per cent of a building's carbon footprint is already embodied in its existing structure. Demolishing it means losing that investment and adding new emissions through demolition, transport and reconstruction. Reuse and upgrading therefore become central strategies. Decisions about materials and systems only make sense within a broader approach that prioritises keeping buildings and structures in use for as long as possible.

C How do legislation and financial mechanisms influence decisions around reuse and demolition, and how do they help distinguish genuine sustainability from greenwashing?

MS Regulation is crucial because it creates binding conditions. In several European countries, carbon accounting is already part of the building permit process. If a project exceeds a defined carbon threshold over its lifecycle – including construction, operation and demolition – it simply does not receive approval. Sustainability is no longer an added quality; it becomes a prerequisite.

This logic is now extending into finance. European taxonomy regulations require banks to assess the environmental performance of investments. If a project does not meet certain criteria, financing can be refused. Since most investors depend on banks, this has immediate consequences. Reuse and upgrading of existing buildings suddenly become economically viable, not only environmentally desirable.

These mechanisms also expose greenwashing. A building may appear sustainable through certain visible measures, but when its full carbon footprint is calculated, it often performs far worse than a reused building with more modest technical standards. Carbon accounting shifts the discussion from appearance to actual performance.

C A central proposition of the Congress is that time is not merely a backdrop to architecture, but an operative design variable. How does this temporal perspective affect the way you approach performance, comfort and the capacity of buildings to evolve?

MS Time fundamentally changes how we design and evaluate buildings. In the past, buildings were often designed using steady-state calculations, sized for extreme conditions. This led to oversized systems that operated inefficiently for most of their lifespan. Today, dynamic simulations allow us to consider daily and seasonal fluctuations, thermal mass, and the interaction between structure and climate over time.

We also work with future climate data. Meteorological institutes already provide datasets for 2040, 2050 or 2060, and we use these to test buildings against future scenarios. This shifts the focus from optimisation to adaptation. Buildings should not be demolished when conditions change; they should be able to adapt.

While working on a project for a university building in Singapore, a large part of the space height – around a third of the volume – was occupied by mechanical systems. The initial idea was to demolish it. Instead, we proposed to remove ceilings and significantly reduce technical systems. This allowed us to recover very generous spaces that would no longer be possible in a new university building. Spatial quality and daylight access improved, and at the same time the building could operate with simpler systems as thermal mass and stratification supported the climate concept.

Erik L'Heureux, Renovation of the School of Design and Environment buildings 1 & 3, National University of Singapore, 2023. Upgrading the existing building resulted in significantly increased room heights – originally designed to accommodate bulky, now-obsolete air-conditioning ductwork – allowing for much better daylight penetration and saving 60 per cent of embedded carbon compared to a new construction.

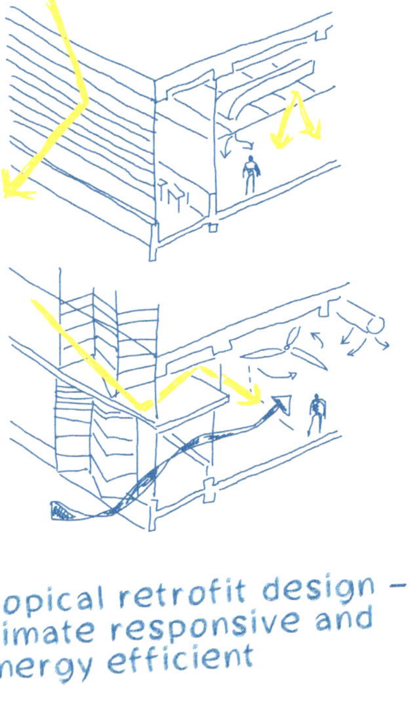

Transsolar, illustration of the School of Design and Environment buildings 1 & 3, National University of Singapore.
Removing ceilings and reducing the technical systems recovered generous spaces that would no longer be possible in a new university building. Illustration by Edith Maier-Neretin.

This highlights an architectural issue that is often underestimated. Section and free room height are long-term resources. Buildings should be able to function, at least to a certain degree, with natural light and ventilation, rather than being fully dependent on active systems.

C So comfort becomes less about a fixed target, and more about a range that people and buildings can manage over time?

MATTHIAS SCHULER For a long time, thermal comfort was defined through fixed indoor temperatures and humidity levels that had to be maintained at all times. These definitions leave little room for seasonal variation or for differences in use. From a climatic point of view, this is not

Serie Architects and Multiply Architects, School of Design and Environment, National University of Singapore, 2023.
The large overhangs protect the balcony area and create open cross-ventilated spaces which are partially used as teaching areas. The proof of concept convinced the client that this concept works, and it was eventually adopted during the refurbishment of the School of Architecture too, in place of a total rebuild.

Transsolar, illustration of the School of Design and Environment, National University of Singapore.
The breathing building concept for the new school meets the client's mandate for net-zero energy consumption, which was established at the start of the design process. To achieve a 75 per cent reduction in energy consumption compared to standard designs in Singapore, the design team employed innovative passive-active hybrid conditioning systems for adaptive comfort, with elevated air speed, and developed façades with reduced loads but visual and physical connections to the outside. Illustration by Edith Maier-Neretin.

necessary. People are able to adapt to a certain range of conditions, and buildings can support this adaptation.

This also relates to how people can interact with buildings. If everything is controlled through a central system, users lose the possibility to respond themselves. Operable windows, shading, increased air movement or simple controls allow people to adjust conditions locally and, remarkably, increase occupant acceptance of higher temperatures and humidity level. This does not replace technical systems, but it changes their role. Instead of enforcing a single condition everywhere, systems can support a broader range of acceptable situations.

C This question of adaptation does not stop at the building itself. You often point out that buildings cannot compensate for an overheated environment. When we talk about cooling and adaptation, where do the limits of building-based solutions appear in relation to the urban context?

MS Buildings cannot be understood in isolation. If the surrounding environment becomes too hot, cooling buildings efficiently becomes extremely difficult. Exterior temperatures, radiation and air movement directly affect indoor conditions.

As cities become denser and more people spend time outdoors, these effects become more pronounced. If streets and public spaces reach very high temperatures, buildings are constantly exposed to heat, and cooling systems have to work against that background. In such situations, technical solutions quickly reach their limits. This is why strategies at the urban scale – shading, vegetation, surface materials and proportions – are a necessary part of adaptation to reduce urban heat islands.

C Within the 'Becoming Circular' track, the two Research by Design projects, by H arquitectes, and BAUKUNST and the Structural Xploration Lab, explore circularity through spatial and energetic flows on the one hand, and through structural reuse and urban mineral waste on the other. How do you read these approaches from an engineering perspective?

MS They address different questions and should be discussed on different terms.

The research on flows and proportions touches on something fundamental. Proportion, section and verticality are clearly related to climate, and the idea that buildings should work with light, air and thermal effects rather than relying entirely on technical systems is something I support. We also share the ambition that buildings should be able to function, at least to a certain degree, with natural light and ventilation if energy becomes scarce.

At the same time, some aspects require closer examination. Wind plays a major role in many climates and is not always sufficiently considered, as it behaves very differently from gravity-driven flows. Daylight performance also depends strongly on depth and proportion. These ideas can work very well at the scale of individual buildings or small ensembles, but they are not universally transferable without limits.

The research on structural reuse raises another set of questions. From an engineering perspective, many things are technically possible, and reusing elements can preserve the identity of existing structures. In practice, however, the main obstacles are not conceptual but practical: standards, liability, logistics and regulations. Structural systems require long-term guarantees, and without changes in codes and responsibility frameworks, it is difficult to generalise these approaches. Reusing entire buildings with their proven structural concept remains the most effective strategy in terms of carbon reduction.

C The Congress takes place amid resource conflicts, political fragmentation, and growing resistance to climate policy. How does this global context reshape what you consider realistic or necessary in climate engineering?

MATTHIAS SCHULER

Climate change is a global problem, but it is perceived very differently depending on context. As long as people are not directly affected, there is a strong tendency to postpone action. This applies to individuals, but also to politics, which often operates on short time horizons, while climate strategies require long-term commitments and continuity over decades.

Kazuyo Sejima + Ryue Nishizawa / SANAA, Zollverein School of Management and Design, Essen, Germany, 2006.
A perfect example of a holistic concept reflecting the local identity of the Ruhr region, where they dug for coal for a hundred years until 1985. The mining water used to heat the building is the last reminder of this local culture.

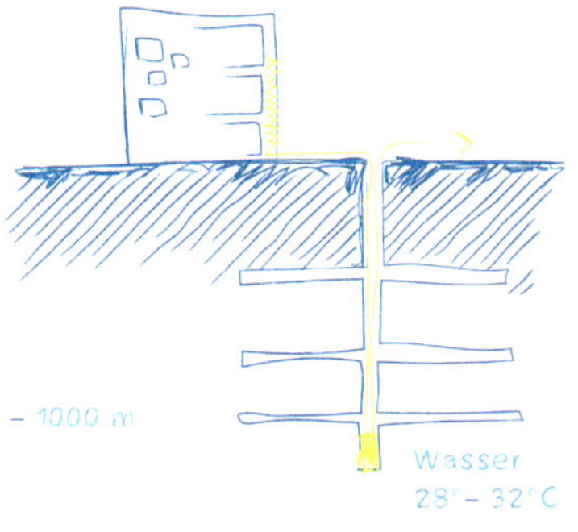

Transsolar, illustration of the Zollverein School of Management and Design.
Even though coal excavation has ceased, the mines in the region were legally forced to to operate pumping stations to a depth of 1,000 metres to prevent the 30°C mine water from rising and flooding the tunnels. As part of more recent controlled flooding strategies, the pumps must continue to maintain water levels 300 metres below ground to prevent re-lifting of the 20-metre sunken area. Illustration by Edith Maier-Neretin.

There are clear differences between regions. In Europe, sustainability is often framed as a societal responsibility and translated into regulations. In the United States, action tends to happen when economic pressure appears. At the same time, global inequalities shape the debate: regions that contribute little to emissions are often those most exposed to climate impacts, while still seeking to improve basic living conditions.

In this situation, the role of architects and engineers is to develop and share references – to demonstrate, through built work and research, what is possible. The exchange of knowledge through practice and forums such as the UIA Congress helps establish these references.

The critical point is to avoid presenting sustainability as a purely technical challenge. It is a societal approach that involves values, habits and political choices.

Curators

AFTERLIVES AND ECONOMIES OF TRANSFORMATION

Material cycles

Spatial cycles

Carbon policies

Energy cycles

Fifty years after the publication of *The Limits to Growth* in 1972,[1] the finite nature of the Earth's resources remains an unresolved condition of architectural production. While the dominant political and economic model continues to reward expansion, extraction and short-term return, the built environment keeps consuming land, matter and energy at a planetary scale. In this context, circularity cannot be understood simply as an environmental correction, nor can it be captured by a business-as-usual rhetoric of greenwashing that merely produces further obsolescence. It reorganises the relation between matter, use, climate and time, shifting architecture away from linear models of extraction, construction and disposal towards longer cycles of assembly, inhabitation, transformation and return. 'Becoming Circular' therefore understands the built environment not as a series of finished objects, but as a field of stocks, supports, atmospheres and infrastructures that must remain in circulation for longer.[2]

1. Donella H. Meadows, Dennis L. Meadows, Jørgen Randers and William W. Behrens III, *The Limits to Growth: A Report for the Club of Rome's Project on the Predicament of Mankind*, Universe Books, 1972.

2. United Nations Environment Programme, *Building Materials and the Climate: Constructing a New Future*, 2023, section 2.4. The report frames decarbonisation through a 'whole life-cycle approach', considering the environmental impacts of material choices before extraction and throughout the building life cycle, and understanding end-of-use as a potential 'bank' of resources for reuse.

(1) Anupama Kundoo, Wall House, Auroville, India, 2000.

One line of work engages circularity through material cycles by returning architecture to renewable, low-processed and territorially grounded matter. These approaches reactivate material cultures rooted in earth, timber, fibres, stone, brick and other materials whose extraction, transformation and decay remain legible and low-waste. (1, 2, 3, 4, 5) Circularity operates through proximity to resource, craft and site while keeping construction open to repair, adaptation and eventual reintegration into new cycles of use. In some cases, even fragments and debris from traditional materials are reworked into new elements through low-tech and materially continuous processes,

(2) Carles Oliver and Xim Moyá, 6 social housing units at 21 Ses Monges St, Santa Eugènia, Mallorca, Spain, 2023.

(3) Natura Futura, Las Tejedoras community centre, Chongón, Equador, 2025.

(4) Sana Frini / Locus, Visitor Centre, Lake Texcoco Ecological Park, Texcoco, Mexico, 2023.

(5) Worofila, Labo x Fou training centre, Sebikotane, Senegal, 2025.

pushing performance without severing ties to local construction cultures. (6, 7)

A further approach to material cycles is pioneered through cultures of practice that open paths for reuse before the necessary structures are in place. Here, circularity becomes a technical matter of components and assemblies as well as a collective framework through which material stewardship produces social value, cooperative organisation, knowledge transfer and shared agency. (8, 9)

Elsewhere, material cycles are addressed through salvage, reassembly and design for future disassembly. In these terms, the city is understood as a material reservoir: buildings are surveyed, catalogued and dismantled. Their components are then stored, matched and recirculated through new supply chains instead of being sent to waste. (10, 11, 12) In other cases, structure itself is treated as an active material resource: slabs, columns

(6) Solano Benítez, Gabinete de Arquitectura, Asunción, Paraguay, 1993.

(7) Amateur Architecture Studio, Ningbo Museum, Ningbo, China, 2008.

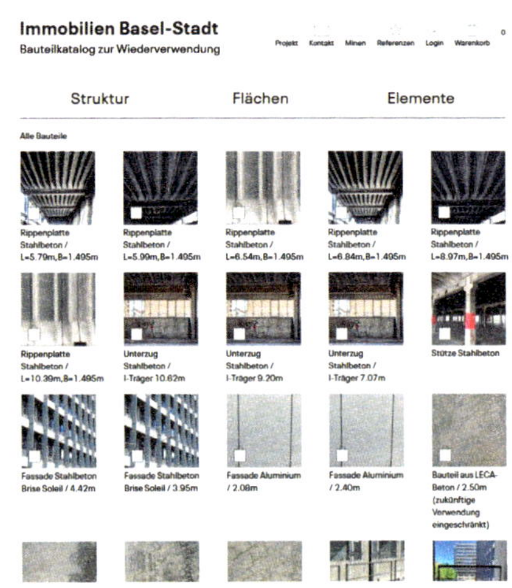

(12) Zirkular, Catalogue of components for the city of Basel, Switzerland, 2023.

(8) Barbara Buser, *Pionierin der Nachhaltigkeit*, 2026. Directed by Gabriele Schärer, produced by Sulaco Film, Maat Film, Swiss Public Television SRF.

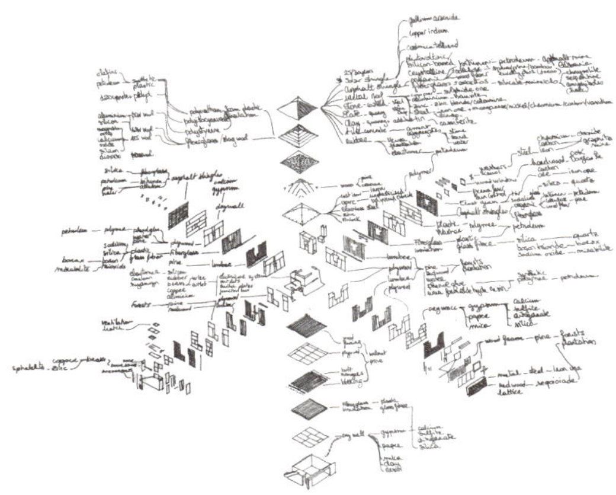

(10) Charlotte-Maltherre Barthes, *Scales of Extraction After Morphosis*, 2020.

(9) Curro Claret, T300, 'More than this' exhibition, Sala Vinçon, Barcelona, Spain, 2014. Chairs produced in the La Troballa workshop managed by Arrels Fundació.

(11) Rotor, Unloading on the site of RotorDC, Brussels, Belgium, 2024.

(13) Maxence Grangeot/Structural Xploration Lab (SXL), EPFL, Re:bble In Situ, Lausanne, Switzerland, 2023.

and concrete remnants are cut, reconfigured and reassembled into new constructions. (13, 14) Some proposals work directly with demolition debris, recomposing mineral remnants into new architectural matter; others focus on inventories, protocols and reversible systems to explore how reuse might turn from an exceptional gesture into an ordinary practice. (15, 16)

Circularity also unfolds through spatial cycles. It is grounded in the capacity of existing spaces to continue hosting life through adaptation, subtraction, recalibration and reuse. In this sense, the most radical circular gesture is to 'never demolish'.[3] (17) Working with what is already there, extending the life of structures, recovering latent capacities and transforming inherited environments through precise intervention becomes a way of treating the existing as an active spatial resource. (18, 19) Here, architecture appears as a careful negotiation with traces, memories, additions and ordinary uses

(14) Søren Pihlmann, Thoravej 29, Copenhagen, Denmark, 2025.

(15) BAUKUNST, School building, Unterstrass, Zurich, Switzerland, 2023.

(16) PARABASE, Elementa housing development, Walkeweg, Basel, Switzerland, 2023.

(17) Lacaton & Vassal, Transformation of 530 occupied dwellings, Bordeaux, France, 2017.

accumulated over time. Reuse is involves more than material persistence. It depends on the capacity of architecture to remain in use by absorbing change and retaining previous lives. (20, 21)

3. 'Never demolish' is a recurring principle in the work and public discourse of Anne Lacaton and Jean-Philippe Vassal, associated with strategies of transformation, adaptive reuse, and the extension of the life of existing buildings.

Another field of circularity approaches the concept through energy cycles. Attention shifts from static form to the movement of heat, air, humidity, light and gravity. Here, environmental performance depends not only on technical devices, but on how matter and space are proportioned in relation to thermodynamic flows. Some practices conceive architecture as part of larger climatic systems across both buildings and cities. (22, 23) In other cases, environmental behaviour is embedded in the section, mass, porosity and constructive logic of the building itself, so that what is latent in matter and space becomes an active source of climatic performance. (24, 25) Others explore how passive

(18) HOLES (Mio Tsuneyama and Fuminori Nousaku), Holes in the House, Tokyo, Japan, 2017.

(19) BURR Studio, Halo, Madrid, Spain, 2023.

(20) Flores & Prats, Sala Beckett, Barcelona, Spain, 2017.

(21) SO? Architecture and Ideas, The Pool public hall, Istanbul, Turkey, 2023.

(22) Transsolar / TVK Trévelo and VigerKohler Architectes Urbanistes, Redevelopment of Place de la République, Paris, France, 2013.

(23) Onsitestudio, baukuh, dotdotdot, (Ab)Normal, SCE Project, Starching, Montana Ambiente, STAIN Engineering, Studio Mistretta and Atmos Lab, Nuova BEIC (European Library of Information and Culture), Milan, Italy, 2026.

strategies, thermal exchange and coolness can reorganise form, atmosphere and spatial composition at the scale of the building. (26, 27) Energy is no longer treated as a background layer of technical service, but as an active design driver that reshapes comfort and inhabitation.

But these shifts cannot remain isolated experiments. Carbon policies define the conditions under which circularity can move from scattered initiatives to an operative architectural and urban transition. If demolition remains financially simpler, legally safer and institutionally normalised, circular design will remain marginal. Before such shifts become policy, they are often first made visible by practices that expose the hidden costs of extraction, waste, territorial depletion and environmental injustice, turning material flows into a field of public and political attention. (28, 29) For circularity to become a common practice, a series of immaterial instruments needs to be

(24) H arquitectes, Civic centre Cristalleries Planell, Barcelona, Spain, 2016.

(25) Jo Taillieu Architecten, Paddenbroek Education Centre, Pajottegem, Belgium, 2021.

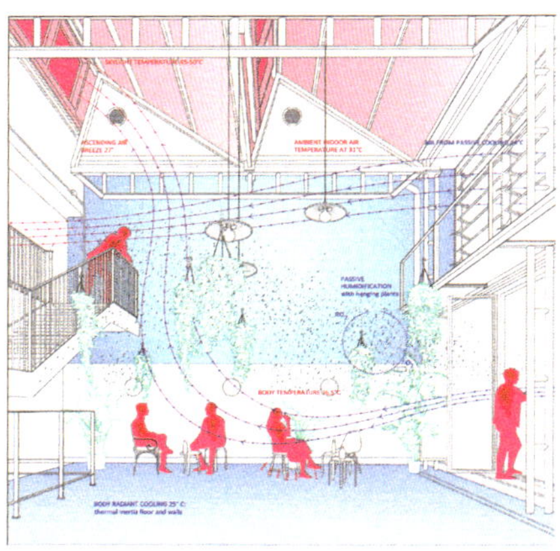

(26) TAAs – totem arquitectos asociados, Carabanchel Housing, Madrid, Spain, 2022.

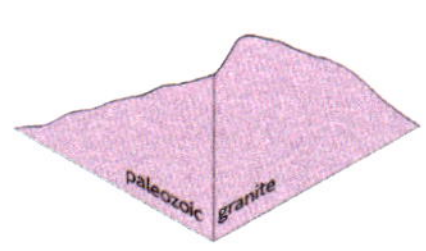

(27) Nicolas Dorval-Bory, *A house in the Sun*, Chicago Architecture Biennial, 2025.

developed in parallel: bold carbon regulations, incentivising mechanisms and urban permits, as well as responsible forms of procurement and finance. Said otherwise, circularity appears as a matter of housing politics, economic frameworks and institutional capacity. (30, 31, 32).

Through these practices, circularity has been portrayed as a form of reorganising architectural flows across interdependent cycles. Materials cease to appear as obsolescent substances and begin to be understood as resources held in temporary processes; buildings are treated less as final objects than as spaces subject to reoccupation and change; energy is no longer a background service but an active spatial driver; and policy becomes one of the conditions that shape what architecture can preserve, transform and avoid. This understanding seeks to sustain a situated and conscious architectural culture: an approach that values temporal continuity and imperfect juxtaposition,

(28) Lara Almarcegui, *Construction Rubble*, Secession, Vienna, Austria, 2010.

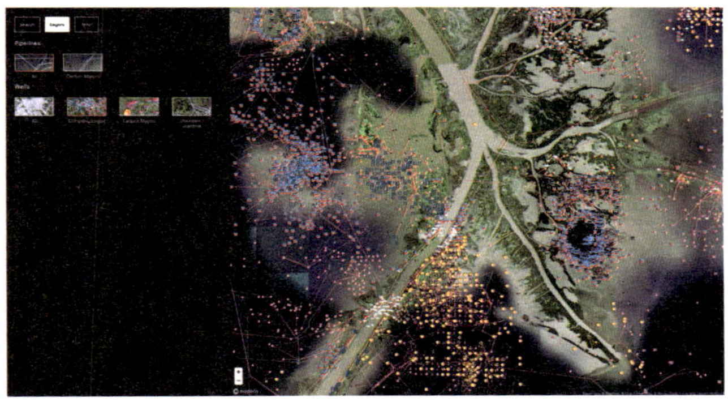

(29) Imani Jacqueline Brown, Follow the Oil, Louisiana, 2023.

(30) HouseEurope!, Campaign graphic for the European Citizens' Initiative – Power to Renovation by HouseEurope!, 2024.

(31) Ann Pettifor, *The Global Casino: How Wall Street Gambles with People and the Planet*, 2026.

(32) Iñaqui Carnicero, *Law on High-Quality of Architecture*, Ministerio de Vivienda y Agenda Urbana, Spain 2022.

embracing the finitude of locally resourced materials. In short, against current models dependent on extraction and short-term return, circularity points towards an architecture grounded in continuity, stewardship and the longer duration of matter.

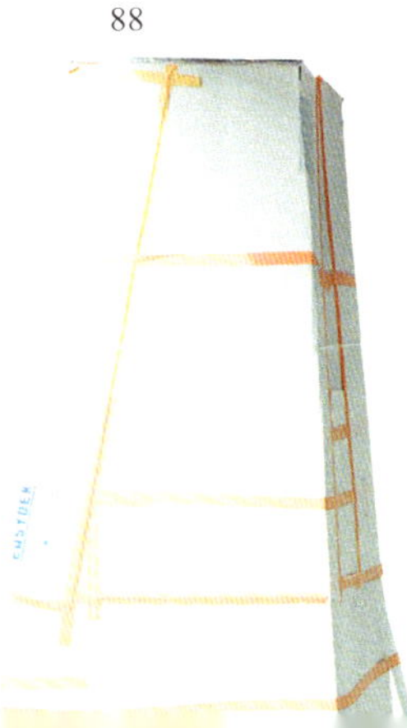

Garraf Massif
Collserola
slates
limestone
silts
technosols
city of
Barcelona
sandstone &
consolidated clays
sands & clays
silts
paleozoic

Becoming Embodied

'We need to have a much more material, much more mundane, much more immanent, much more realistic, much more embodied definition of the material world if we wish to compose a common world.'

Bruno Latour, 'An Attempt at a "Compositionist Manifesto"', 2010

How can values be embedded in the transition from matter to construction?

A deeper, rawer, more realistic notion of the material world, with its multiple conflicts and fortunes, opens up a fertile ground of material embodiment. 'Becoming Embodied' aims to explore the agency of materials by incorporating political, economic, ecological and poetic relationships inherent in contemporary spatial practice and its technologies of construction.

The way in which we now extract, process, transport, use and reuse flows and exchanges of matter is embedded in our commitment to social equity, gender perspective, decolonisation, decarbonisation and energy transition. At the same time, this material transit can reveal the potential of alternative tectonic approaches: everyday gestures of beautiful, unexpected poetics of construction to curate intensified coexistence.

These material and spatial transitions spring from a deep awareness of becoming: rather than perceiving the built environment as homogeneous in time, we aim to emphasise their stratification and adaptability, enhancing their varying longevity and agency in shaping our cities and territories.

Philip Ursprung

GRAVITY AND GRACE: AESTHETICS OF EMBODIMENT

'Grace is the law of the descending movement.'
Simone Weil, *Gravity and Grace*, 1947[1]

In a sunny week in October, shortly after the pandemic, I travelled with my students to Nisyros, a small Greek volcanic island not far from the Turkish coast. On long walks with the architect Lydia Xynogala we learned how geology and the healing forces of thermal springs shaped life on the island. While heading towards the crater where fumaroles still steam from the most recent eruptions in the late nineteenth century, we crossed a field littered with stones, obviously the result of that volcanic activity. An almost perfectly spherical stone the size of a small football caught my eye. I picked it up. Most likely it was a so-called lava bomb, formed when molten lava is hurled through the air and shaped into a sphere like a snowball, and then solidifies as it rolls down the slope of the crater. Everyone was fascinated. Some wanted to play soccer with it, but one student interrupted them: 'Be careful, it might break!' She carried it with her throughout the hike like a pet. Later, she took it home with her and wrote an essay about it.[2]

1. Simone Weil, *Gravity and Grace* [1947], trans. Emma Crawford and Mario von der Ruhr, Routledge, 2002, p. 4.
2. Vanessa Grünig, 'Die Bombe', unpublished manuscript, Department of Architecture, ETH Zürich, 2022.

This sympathy for a stone ball is typical of a shift of attention and a broader penchant that has been noticeable for some time in architecture. It is a penchant to both the yield to gravity, the pull towards the terrain and even into the depths of the ground, and to embodiment, materiality and specificity. It is an interest in the relation between architecture and the deep history of the Earth. In the classrooms of architecture schools, it can be perceived where drawings show trees with extensive root systems and foundations of houses resting in meticulously depicted layers of soil. Models and plans are accompanied by stones, chunks of clay, wood, sand, salt crystals, wires, moss, screws and other objects. There is prevalence for solid materials and 1:1 scale details.

During our travels, students are attracted not only to volcanoes but also to quarries, moors, primeval forests, mines and landfills. The reading list features books such as Jane Bennett's *Vibrant Matter* (2010), in which the author argues for an understanding of matter as animated and vital.[3] The students are orientated by the writings of Bruno Latour, for instance his notion that humans, animals, things and affects are all 'actants' in a generalised symmetry, which questions the hierarchy of humans over non-humans, and animated over non-animated matter.[4] It allows them to change their perspective and see the world from the viewpoint of a stone ball. They are inspired by the combination of critique and faith, analysis and poetry in the writings of Simone Weil.

3. Jane Bennett, *Vibrant Matter: A Political Ecology of Things*, Duke University Press, 2010.
4. Bruno Latour, *Reassembling the Social: An Introduction to the Actor-Network-Theory*, Oxford University Press, 2005.

Architecture as a continuation of Earth's crust

Buildings that seem to merge with the Earth, taking on its colours, materials and texture as if architecture were a kind of extension of its crust, are changing the architectural canon. The thermal baths in Vals, designed by Peter Zumthor and located far from Switzerland's city centres in a shady valley in the Alps, were listed as a historic monument just two years after their opening and are still current 30 years later. On the other hand, the world's tallest building, the Burj Khalifa in Dubai designed by SOM, already seemed anachronistic when it was completed, a relic from the past. The modest round buildings coated with clay, designed by Yasmeen Lari in the early 2010s following the Pakistan floods, seem more relevant or forward-looking today than, say, the gigantic circular Apple headquarters in Cupertino, California, designed by Norman Foster at the same time. The old quarries in Jinyun, China, with their traces of centuries of hard labour and recently transformed into a library designed by Xu Tiantian, are far more inspiring to students than, say, the colossal Harbin Opera House designed by MAD.

Yasmeen Lari, Women's Centre, Darya Khan, Pakistan, 2011.
Raised on bamboo stilts to avoid flooding, the building is part of an ensemble designed for vulnerable people.

The architecture offices featured in this section of the book on 'embodiment' are part of this penchant. The notion of 'biogeology', the mixture of minerals and human-made materials that dominates the surface in urbanised areas that BC architects & studies & materials bring into play, highlights the interaction between architecture and the material quality of the building ground. The 'Light Fever' research by design conducted by BRUTHER (Stéphanie Bru and Alexandre Theriot) treats light as matter in its own right, as an active force and primary material capable of transforming experience. TEN's 'Nautilus' proposal for a temporary structure on the stone embankment of the Vardar river in Skopje, North Macedonia (2015), a building 'without foundations', helps us to see gravity as a key reference for design. And in projects such as the Tâmega House (2022) by Hugo Mendonça Ferreira and Nuno Melo Sousa in Favões, Portugal, the man-made concrete and the natural rocks intertwine as if they were performing a geological metamorphosis. All these practices contribute to architecture's growing – or renewed – focus on concrete, tangible materials, on their specific potential, their transformation, extraction, refinement, arrangement, dismantling and dissolving.

This new architectural attitude differs from the aim to triumph over natural forces, to overcome gravity, the predominance of abstraction, representation and conception that characterised architecture for much of the twentieth century. Becoming rather than being, processing rather than projecting, planting rather than planning, entropy rather than expansion are now the trends. The white, empty page, the tabula rasa from which every design starts anew, is less appealing for the current discussion than the so-called palimpsest, where traces of earlier inscriptions are overlapping, erased and overwritten. The *terrain vague*, to refer to the famous notion coined by the Catalan architect Ignasi de Solà-Morales Rubió thirty years ago, is not empty; rather, it is saturated like a sponge with traces of the past.[5]

5. Ignasi de Solà-Morales Rubió, 'Terrain Vague', in C. Davidson (ed.), *Anyplace*, MIT Press, 1995, pp. 118–23.

The penchant towards the ground and embodiment is not backward-looking at all. The design research of BC architects, TEN, BRUTHER and Nuno Melo Sousa goes hand in hand with the latest research in materials science, construction technology and structural engineering, with the pressing issues of social and climate justice, and with a genuine interest in new forms and a new aesthetic. It is open to new technologies, digitalisation and artificial intelligence. It is a call for architecture to take responsibility for the here and now, to strengthen it as an element of connection between humans and non-humans, and to improve the conditions for people to live together with their environment, whether animated or not.

Grounded utopia?

When did this trend begin? And why does architecture change? Although signs of the trend were already apparent in the late twentieth century, the global economic crisis of 2007 and the Great Recession between 2007 and 2009 were crucial factors because they abruptly shifted the ground architecture stood on. When the real-estate bubble in the United States burst, countless families lost their homes. Architects around the world lost their jobs and formerly booming architecture offices, particularly in Southern Europe, had to close. The recession caused another blow to the postwar order of the welfare

Above, left to right:

Assemble and BC architects & studies & materials, Lot 8, Atelier LUMA, Arles, France, 2021.
Training of architects and contractors in a workshop about local earth: the appropriate composition and humidity are demonstrated to achieve a suitable mixture for compressed earth blocks.

BRUTHER and BAUKUNST, FRAME media house, Brussels, Belgium, 2025.
The multifuncional building is literally a robust physical frame for the immaterial contents of media and audiovisual communication.

TEN and the City Creative Network (CCN), Nautilus, Skopje, North Macedonia, 2015.
An ephemeral, graceful open structure on the banks of the river designed in a participatory process with a local NGO, welcoming gatherings and performances.

Hugo Mendonça Ferreira and Nuno Melo Sousa, Tâmega House, Favões, Portugal, 2022.
Partially emerging out of a former quarry, the concrete structure both frames the terrain and is framed by the land.

state and further accelerated economic disparities.[6] One of the lessons of Tomas Piketty's 2014 bestseller *Capital in the Twenty-First Century* is that 'When the rate of return on capital exceeds the rate of growth of output and income, as it did in the nineteenth century and seems quite likely to do again in the twenty-first, capitalism automatically generates arbitrary and unsustainable inequalities that radically undermine the meritocratic values on which democratic societies are based.'[7]

6. OECD, *Divided We Stand: Why Inequality Keeps Rising*, OECD Publishing, 2011.

7. Thomas Piketty, *Capital in the Twenty-First Century*, trans. Arthur Goldhammer, The Belknap Press of Harvard University Press, 2014, p. 1.

In this phase of ongoing crisis, and in the wake of the growing pressure from authoritarian regimes and political parties, architecture is changing. 'Starchitecture' lost much of its lustre, particularly in the West where it took shape during the 1990s. Designed mainly with the purpose to attract attention and capital, it is no longer a symbol of identification but one of segregation. On the other hand, new offices such as BC architects, BRUTHER, TEN and Nuno Melo Sousa began to emerge, concerned with repair and reuse – small-scale interventions with moderate budgets. Their focus on public institutions, housing and public infrastructure redirected the attention of architecture towards the grounded and the specific. It also shifted the aesthetics from being primarily a visual impression – think of the notion of 'iconic architecture' – towards an architecture that is experienced with all the senses.

The pandemic in the early 2020s accelerated the trend. On the one hand, economic inequality rose even further. Banks, insurance companies and universities were the first to protect their employees in home offices, while people working in care, maintenance and construction remained exposed to the disease. Architectural values changed. A balcony, a stairwell, a door to the garden, a window that can be opened or a small park to walk the dog became more important than, say, a panoramic window or an air-conditioned penthouse. What counted most in this period of social distancing and isolation was the ability to access help and to interact with other people, with neighbours, friends and family. This was a new kind of connectivity, a feeling of togetherness and mutual care. As Ece Temelkuran recalls in her book *Together*: 'It was as if a worldwide network of neighbours were telling each other "We'll get through this".'[8]

8. Ece Temelkuran, *Together: A Manifesto Against a Heartless World*, Canongate, 2025, p. 58. First published in 2021.

The perception of air also changed during the pandemic. Once the very emblem of hygiene, purity and freedom, it became, literally, contaminated, a carrier of invisible danger, a medium that transported the virus with potentially deadly consequences. This strengthened the earlier impression that air space had fallen into the wrong hands. While medical staff struggled to find desperately needed respirators for patients, Elon Musk planned to send rockets to Mars: 'To many of us, his rocket looked like an escape plan for the super rich.'[9] Rather than a space of freedom and limitless possibilities, it turned into a domain of surveillance and control. Our data, stored in a 'cloud', means that it is mostly out of our control.

9. Ibid., p. 134.

Architectural utopia, that mysterious force that sets the imagination in motion and indicates the direction in which architecture could unfold its potential, seems today to be not boundless air space, but the tangible objects, the ground, the landscape. The understanding of space is less that of a neutral or empty medium, within which people and objects move, and more that of a substance that can condense, dilute, transform and change. The very notion of space that inspired the architectural realm in the twentieth century – from Ludwig Mies van der Rohe's proposal for the Friedrichstrasse Skyscraper (1921) to Ivan Leonidov's series on Tommaso Campanella's *City of the Sun City* (1940s–1950s) and Yona Friedman's Spatial City (1958) – is giving way to something else. Rather than speaking of space, we now talk about minerals, bricks, sand, cables, electric currents, light sources, air flows and sound. The very insistence on 'becoming' indicates that the discipline is moving, experimenting, developing and playing. It is not yet clear where this road will lead us. In architectural discourse, the notion of utopia is hardly used these days. It is time to reactivate it.

BRUTHER (Stéphanie Bru and Alexandre Theriot), with Studio Theriot ETHZ

LIGHT FEVER

Snell-Descartes : $n_1 \sin\theta_i = n_2 \sin\theta_t$
Réflexion (amplitudes)

$$R_s = \left|\frac{n_1\cos\theta_i - n_2\cos\theta_t}{n_1\cos\theta_i + n_2\cos\theta_t}\right|^2, \quad R_p = \left|\frac{n_1\cos\theta_t - n_2\cos\theta_i}{n_1\cos\theta_t + n_2\cos\theta_i}\right|^2$$

Brewster : $\theta_B = \arctan(n_2/n_1)$ (réflexion p annulée)
Seuil critique : $\theta_c = \arcsin(n_2/n_1)$ pour $n_1 > n_2 \rightarrow$ réflexion totale & champ évanescent.

A change in angle is enough to alter an entire volume. Luminous material therefore imposes a logic of phenomena rather than a logic of objects. Unlike traditional materials, which offer themselves to the hand, light cannot be grasped – only oriented. It exists only in relation: to a surface, a body, dust, humidity, a moment. Its power comes precisely from this instability. At every instant it oscillates between revelation and disappearance. It produces visibility as much as it threatens it. Wherever it spreads, it creates zones of exposure; wherever it withdraws, it opens chambers of shadow – perceptual refuges. It is never neutral: it establishes sensory hierarchies, redistributes intensities, and organises gestures and proximities. Luminous architecture is therefore not illuminated architecture: it is an architecture that treats light as an active force, a primary material capable of transforming experience.

Studio Theriot ETHZ, Luminous specimen 01, Flickering.
Battery-powered motor, LED lights, steel frame and cables, repurposed Fresnel lenses from overhead projectors. In collaboration with Benjamin Frei, Jonathan Troger, Valentin Wegenstein, Leslie Majer, Lui Jung and Toby Büchel.

Light does not only unfold in space; it fabricates its own space. It thickens or hollows it, stretches or compresses it. Grazing light transforms a flat surface into a topography. Diffuse light generates a directionless, almost liquid atmosphere. Orbital light, slow and repetitive, produces a structured experience of space-time, a perceptual cycle. This luminous material thus acts as a motor: it sets architecture in motion, not by moving masses but by shifting perceptions. Where solid materials fix, light activates. Where construction stabilises, light drifts.

This drift is essential. Light introduces time into matter. It reveals architecture not as a uniform presence but as a succession of states. The same wall may appear dry, porous, sharp or velvety depending on the hour, angle or climate. Light is the operator of these metamorphoses: it makes visible the latent temporalities of matter – its variations of texture, warmth and granularity. It reveals that nothing is fixed, even in what seems most stable. Treating light as a material therefore embraces architecture as a phenomenon: an articulation of forces, rhythms and appearances.

Light also directly affects bodies. It modifies our behaviour before we are even aware of it. A dark zone slows movement;

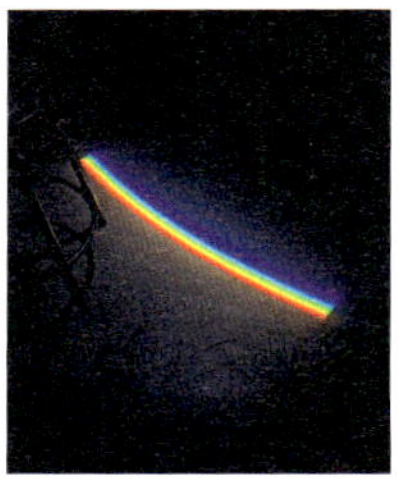
1

a halo attracts and exposes;

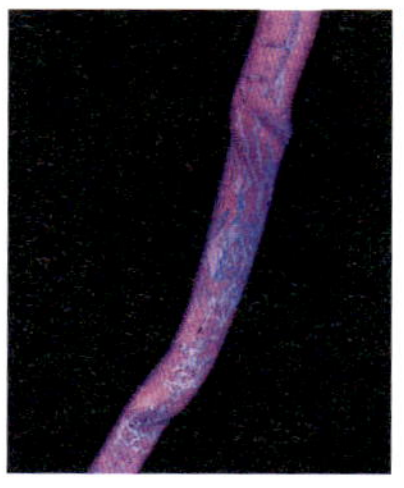
2

an oblique beam creates an involuntary alignment of gestures;

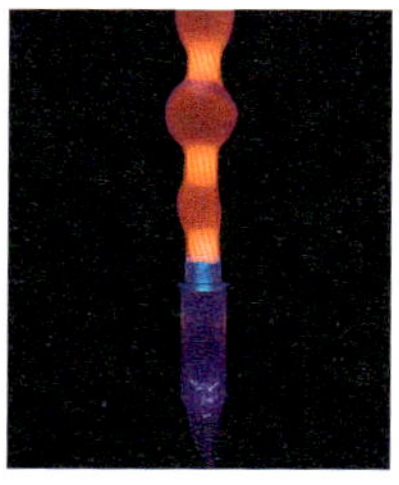
3

a vibrating glow introduces unease or expectation.

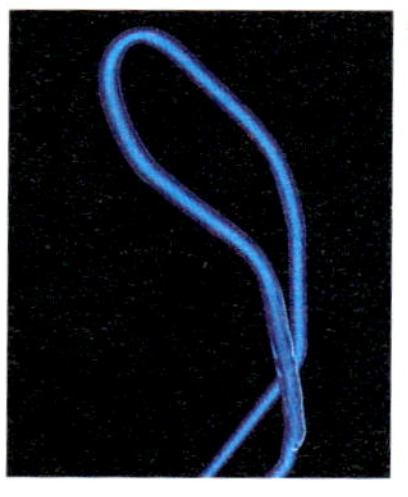
4

Light therefore acts as a silent dramaturgy, composing intensities, distances, relationships. It shapes temporary communities, gathered by a shared luminous climate. In this sense it exceeds perception: it becomes political, social, relational.

1. Studio Theriot ETHZ, Luminous specimen 03, Refract. Prism, lens, daylight. 'LIGHT' Seminar Week, Autumn 2025.
2, 3, 4. Studio Theriot ETHZ, Luminous specimen 03, Glow.
Glass tubes, noble gases, fluorescent powder, electrodes, transformers. In collaboration with Roland Amman, Blanka Major, Leslie Majer and Arnaud Bostelmann.

Studio Theriot ETHZ, Process model 1:20 scale of the Three Chimneys site. In collaboration with Benjamin Frei and Jonathan Troger.

Considering light as a material also means accepting its elusive nature. One does not build with it; one composes with its conditions of existence – an angle, a gap, a surface, a transparency, a mist, a movement. This composition is always open, exposed to uncertainty, dependent on the real. Light resists closure; it calls for experience rather than control. It demands a form of radical, almost microscopic attention to phenomena that cannot be stabilised – only accompanied.

Studio Theriot ETHZ, Process model 1:20 scale of the Three Chimneys site. In collaboration with Benjamin Frei and Jonathan Troger.

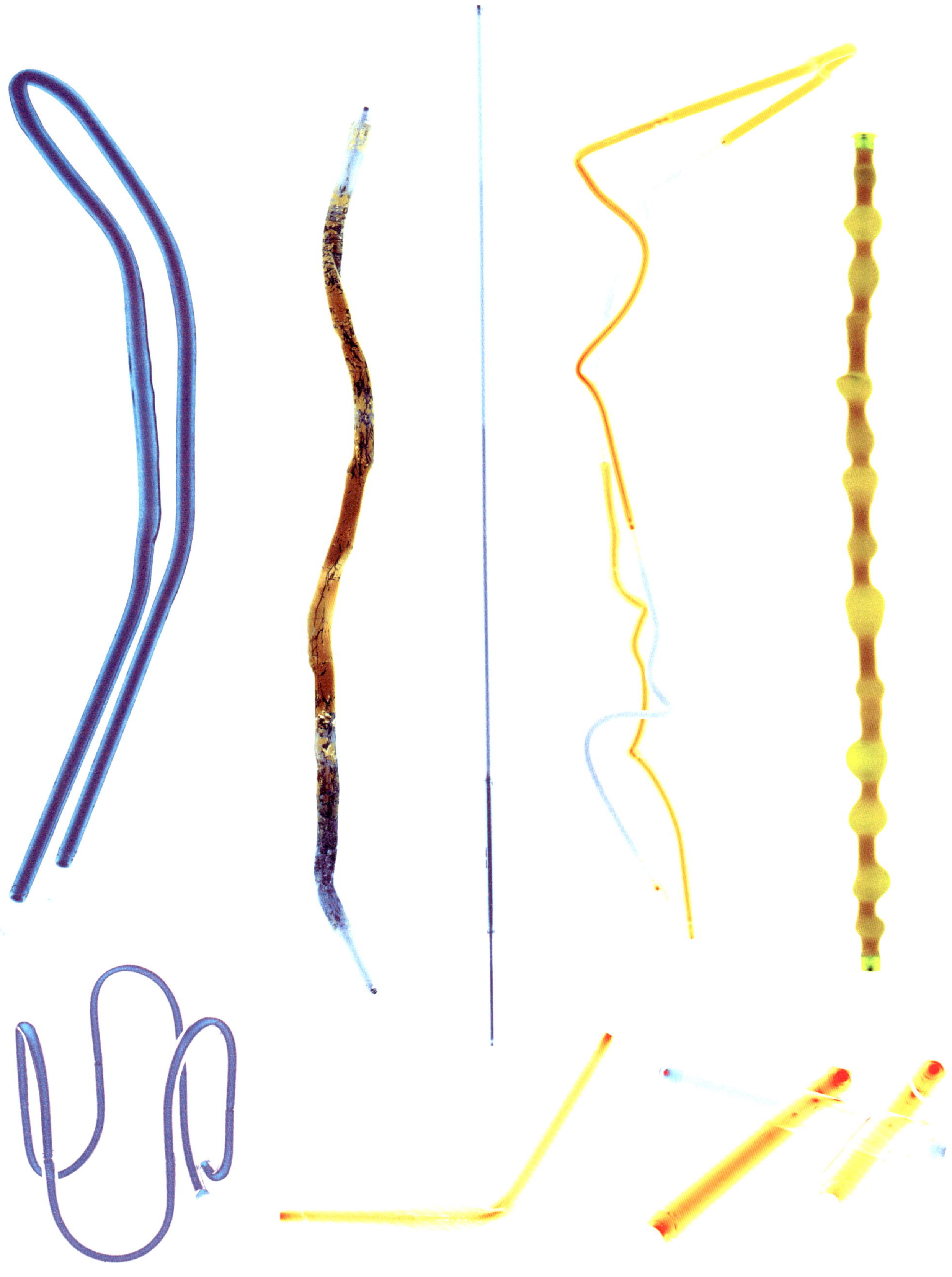

Studio Theriot ETHZ, Luminous specimen 03, Glow.
Glass tubes, noble gases, fluorescent powder, electrodes, transformers. In collaboration with Roland Amman, Blanka Major, Leslie Majer and Arnaud Bostelmann.

It is in this spirit that the in-situ experimentation in the Turbine Hall at UIA 2026 Barcelona takes on its full meaning. The aim is not to produce a spectacular device, but to confront this unstable material directly with the immensity of the space: to observe how it is lost, amplified, diffracted within it. A few gestures are enough – a tilting mirror, a translucent surface, a barely perceptibly oriented beam – for light to invent its own trajectories. The building becomes an atmospheric laboratory where the goal is not to control light but to let it act, to let it reveal the tensions, latent volumes and sensitive potentialities already contained in the space. The intervention is nothing more than the trigger that allows light to manifest fully as a material, and the place to become a medium for directly experiencing its power.

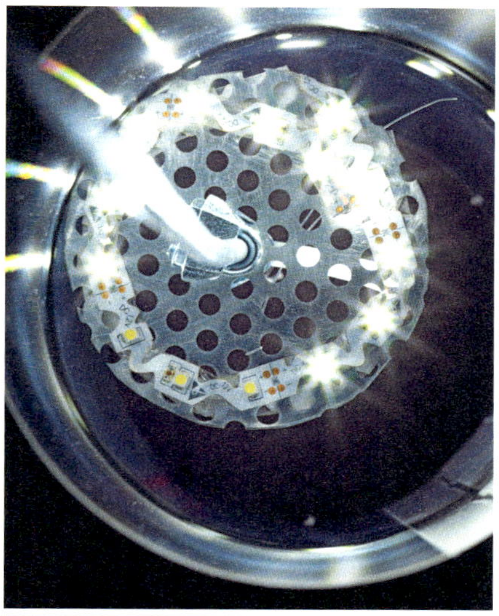

Studio Theriot ETHZ, Luminous specimen 01, Flickering.
Battery-powered motor, LED lights, steel frame and cables, repurposed Fresnel lenses from overhead projectors. In collaboration with Benjamin Frei, Jonathan Troger, Valentin Wegenstein, Leslie Majer, Lui Jung and Toby Büchel.

Studio Theriot ETHZ, Luminous specimen 02, Diffuse.
Fresnel lenses, white LEDs, aluminium profiles, stainless-steel sheet, welding curtain. In collaboration with Leander Areni, Adriana Balagué Reventos, Santiago Madueno, Leslie Majer, Lui Jung and Toby Büchel.

At every interface, Fresnel's laws operate silently. A change in refractive index, an infinitesimal variation in angle, and luminous energy redistributes itself between reflection and transmission. A translucent surface thickens a volume through internal reflections; an oblique mirror cancels a glare; an edge becomes vibrant under the effect of the evanescent wave. The most delicate phenomenology – glare, veil, halo, blur meets the most precise science. Light is a lived phenomenon, but also a measurable one, and our gaze navigates between these two regimes without distinguishing them.

For several years, the prototypes developed by BRUTHER have formed a territory of experimentation where solid matter meets unstable phenomena: airflows, heat, sound, mechanical oscillations, structural vibrations. Each one is a way of testing architecture at full scale, not through form but through behaviour. These artefacts – motors, mobile panels, sensitive membranes, resonant surfaces – have always sought to reduce matter to its minimum in order to liberate action, flow, phenomenon.

The luminous devices designed for the UIA 2026 Barcelona extend this lineage precisely: the same economy, the same rigour, the same attention to the invisible forces that shape space. They do not seek to produce a form but a behaviour. They activate light as a living, unstable, relational material. They explore its physical limits – diffusion, polarisation, total reflection, dispersion – as one would explore those of a raw material. They articulate mechanical gestures and optical phenomena, Fresnel's laws and perceptual shifts, technical rigour and sensory drift.

These prototypes are not answers. They are instruments of observation – luminous organisms, always in imbalance, always in the process of becoming.

Studio Theriot ETHZ, Luminous specimen 01, Flickering.
Battery-powered motor, LED lights, steel frame and cables, repurposed Fresnel lenses from overhead projectors. In collaboration with Benjamin Frei, Jonathan Troger, Valentin Wegenstein, Leslie Majer, Lui Jung and Toby Büchel.

Studio Theriot ETHZ, Process model 1:20 scale.
In collaboration with Benjamin Frei and Jonathan Troger.

TEN

TRY AGAIN. FAIL AGAIN. FAIL BETTER

'What works good is better than what looks good, because what works good lasts.'
Ray Eames

Capable structures are not merely buildings, they are sustainable, societal and representative civic tools. In this sense, design is a continuous discovery of form, material and spatial offerings, but also a creation of value that addresses the community and environmental challenges our planet faces. A capable structure is therefore a programme that can host any use either public or private. It is a platform, playground or prototype that is ready for the unknown while leveraging the programmatic, material and spatial characteristics at hand.

Our research focuses on such architecture beyond life expectancy, in pursuit of a desirable building model that can be appropriated, adapted, repurposed, public and continuously changing. Working between design prototyping, and digital and physical model-making, we explore how experimentation becomes creation, how limitation becomes choice, and how design learns, transforms and, ultimately, shares its discoveries with others while shifting the idea of what is possible. We address resources and durability, beauty and ownership, comfort and public impact to create desirable models for the way we build and design architecture to address current sustainability issues.

Capable structures can be found, repurposed or imagined as a new reality in every context. Our design mission is a social and architectural prototype, a good building model everyone wants to keep. The ongoing investigation of this architectural model is a journey of experimentation, reflection and transformation. Each attempt marks a step that turns process into insight, and decision into a desirable form that welcomes everyone and can be appropriated by designers.

TEN, Cooperative housing, Bern, Switzerland, 2020.
High-rise development model leveraging different material properties while bringing together various building principles within a singular system as a future-proof adaptable and capable building.

TEN with Maria Karaivanova and Mattia Bäggli, Capable structures, Institute of Design and Architecture, ETH Zürich, Spring 2025.
Material and dry construction research focused on the possibilities of stacking principles, structural balance and as-found objects.

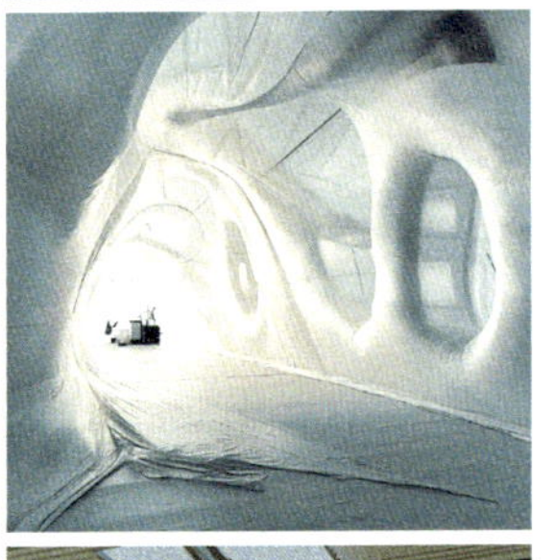

TEN with Leonardo Dietz and Nick Baumann, Capable structures, Institute of Design and Architecture, ETH Zürich, Spring 2025.
Research design project investigating the adaptation of under-utilised infrastructure into buildings for temporary dwelling, focusing on sufficiency, material scarcity and climatic evaluations of living conditions.

TEN and Babini Geysen Architects, Recycling centre, Brussels, 2026–.
Ongoing construction project for a recycling centre where existing site debris is repurposed and reused as part of the new infrastructure.

Nuno Melo Sousa

ONE, TWO, THREE, MORE, MANY TABLES

A roof can be a table.
With legs, arms, feet, supporting bodies light or heavy, opaque or diaphanous, smooth or rough.
A plane with four legs. Or just three. Or two attached to the ground with a flat surface on top.
They create spaces above, where we perch to see beyond.
They shelter spaces below, where we lie in the shade or in fear of rain and wind.
Tables for sitting and making, for conversation and joy, for reflection or sleep.
Spatial structures of steel, iron, plastic, concrete and even fabric.
Inside or outside: a building, the park, the beach, the hill or mountain.
For action or leisure.

Working inside and outside the Tres Xemeneies (Three Chimneys) site, workshop participants start from a list of 'desires' from which to reflect on purpose and place in close relationship with both its indoor and outdoor spaces. Fifteen words to lean on and wander: the void(s), the monumental, the forgotten, the sand, the meadows, the water, the wall(s).

The workshop evokes the permanence and experimentation on-site as fundamental tools for learning – consistency might come from bending time to question, following deviations and iterations within the same line of thought, or making time to acknowledge where and how to place the 'stone'.

The design process thus emerges as a synthesis of the archaic, the possible, the capable, or even the technological, while focusing on the strength of a gesture: that of ingenuity and virtue.

The methodology follows both a pragmatic and active stance* made of steps and jumps.

#1 action
a desired action. choreography. feeling
#2 frame
search a spot. photograph
#3 gesture
approach within the framed subject. finger drawings on images
#4 preview
select one image. collage a gesture
#5 scale / proportion
one size fits most but ain't true here. find a relation between the parts
#6 mockup 1/5 **
build a model of your gesture. materials to be adjusted
#7 words
one sentence to make one wander.

* Scale of the model to be adjusted. Material too. By the moment I am writing this, I am still thinking about it.

** Yes, still far from it, many questions and relations arise. Some will be answered soon, some might just be solved while doing. Trial and error is the way. To avoid certainties and comfortable truths.

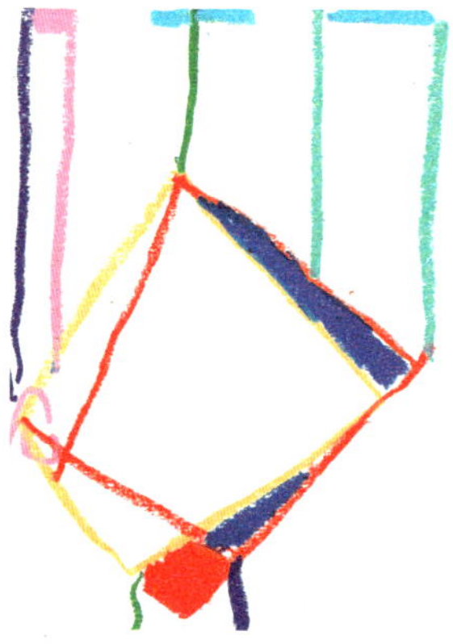

Nuno Melo Sousa, Study for a bungalow, 2022.
Sousa's drawings are both therapeutic and research – into ongoing structures, spaces, desires. Some are already built, some are thought to be built now. Others are yet to have a place, client, budget, will. But all serve as safe spaces of thought, without limits or boundaries.

Nuno Melo Sousa, Studies for car parking and a concrete cabanon, Harambee house, Florianópolis, Brazil, 2022.
The drawings are not intended to mean something. They are just there as rudiments, exercises – as a musician practises scales to warm-up their fingers and sharpen their mind for a concert.

Emerging Workshop

Nuno Melo Sousa, Finger drawing, 2022.
The finger drawing on the photograph is an instant exercise in imagining something on top of a real subject that stands just in front of us – what might, a couple of years ago, have been called augmented reality. It is a way of augmenting this reality, by crossing the finger drawing in strong colours and opposing the will of the real space. The tiny drawing has scale and needs proportions which then are adjusted on the drafting table, CAD drawings and scaled models.

The Grounded Futures investigation is part of the 'Mineral: Architectures of Urban Mining' urban innovation challenge developed during 2025 and 2026 in collaboration with the World Capital of Architecture and the Barcelona City Council through the Manager's Office for the Chief Architect, the BIT Habitat foundation and BIMSA (Barcelona d'Infraestructures Municipals), together with DIBA (Diputació de Barcelona), the Mies van der Rohe Foundation, and the UIA World Congress of Architects 2026 Barcelona. Based on the curatorial framework of the Congress, 'Becoming. Architectures for a planet in transition', the challenge explored urban mining as a design and production strategy, focusing on the potential reuse of the thousands of tons of mineral waste (asphalt, concrete, granite, paving and earthwork) generated every year in the renovation of public works in Barcelona's streets. From the international open call, Brussels-based BC architects & studies & materials was selected to develop a research-driven process exploring different decarbonised material systems – testing and producing a mock-up for the Congress, followed by a pilot intervention in public space, as well as presenting a series of long-term visions that expand the potential of the project in the future.

BC architects & studies & materials

GROUNDED FUTURES

Barcelona's geology offers a unique ground for new biomineralised building materials. Combining algae and calcium-rich construction waste, Grounded Futures proposes a low-carbon return to soft, regenerative mineral matter, placing each material exactly where it belongs and connecting its architecture within Barcelona's bioregion.

A new biogeology …

Geology describes the structure of the Earth; its surface, its subsurface, and the geogenic processes that shape them. Today, however, human-made mass has begun to alter these definitions. In urbanised regions, the upper layers of soil in human settlements are now dominated by technosols: soils formed or heavily modified by human activity.[1] These layers contain complex mixtures of mineral matter with elements of concrete and brick, and they increasingly form the substrate on which new structures are built, from concrete, bricks, glass and steel. This accumulation of technosols and built layers on top can be understood as a new biogeological stratum of human-made mass, which today globally outweighs all living biomass.[2]

1. Stephan Mantel, Stefaan Dondeyne and Seppe Deckers, 'World Reference Base for Soil Resources (WRB)', *Encyclopedia of Soils in the Environment*, 4, 2023, pp. 206–17.
2. Emily Elhacham et al., 'Global Human-made Mass Exceeds All Living Biomass', *Nature*, 588 (7838), 2020, pp. 442–44.

Humanity is creating this stratum at unprecedented scales, mirroring biomineralisation[3] by marine organisms, plants and bacteria, which continuously form shells and limestone. However, unlike marine biomineralisation, which absorbs calcium and carbon dioxide from seawater over medium- to long-term cycles, human activity contrasts with these processes by operating on radically shortened timescales and generating excessive carbon emissions.

3. H. A. Lowenstam, and S. Weiner, *On Biomineralization*, Oxford University Press, 1989.

BC architects & studies & materials, Grounded Futures, Porriño, Spain, 2026.
Brown macroalgae collected by Compañía Española de Algas Marinas, ready to be processed into alginate.

BC architects & studies & materials, Grounded Futures, Barcelona, 2026.
Excavated earth sourced from the Torre Diagonal 00 skyscraper construction site in Esplugues de Llobregat.

Construction and demolition waste sourced from public construction sites across the city.

… from Barcelona's calcium-rich construction waste

Barcelona's geology is inseparable from its location between the Mediterranean Sea and the ancient Atlantic Ocean that once approached from the west deep into present-day Catalonia. Millions of years of marine biomineralisation, such as calcium sediments from seashells or formed by algae, created the vast calcareous deposits of the Catalan Central Depression and Garraf Massif to the west and the south of Barcelona.[4] These deposits define the specific nature of today's construction and demolition waste in the city in two principal ways.

4. Institut Cartogràfic i Geològic de Catalunya (n.d.), Geologia [Geology]. Retrieved from www.icgc.cat/en/Sustainable-territory/Subsoil/Geology and others.

Firstly, the Llobregat river has eroded and transported calcium-rich matter from the Catalan Central Depression at the extreme east end of the Ebro Basin, and laid this down beneath present-day Barcelona; today, this calcium-rich matter is excavated in urban construction sites.

Secondly, calcium-rich materials extracted from the Garraf Massif have been the main source for cement production and concrete used throughout Barcelona. When today's buildings reach the end of their life cycle, their construction and demolition waste will again be calcium-rich, echoing its geological origins of millions of years of biomineralisation.

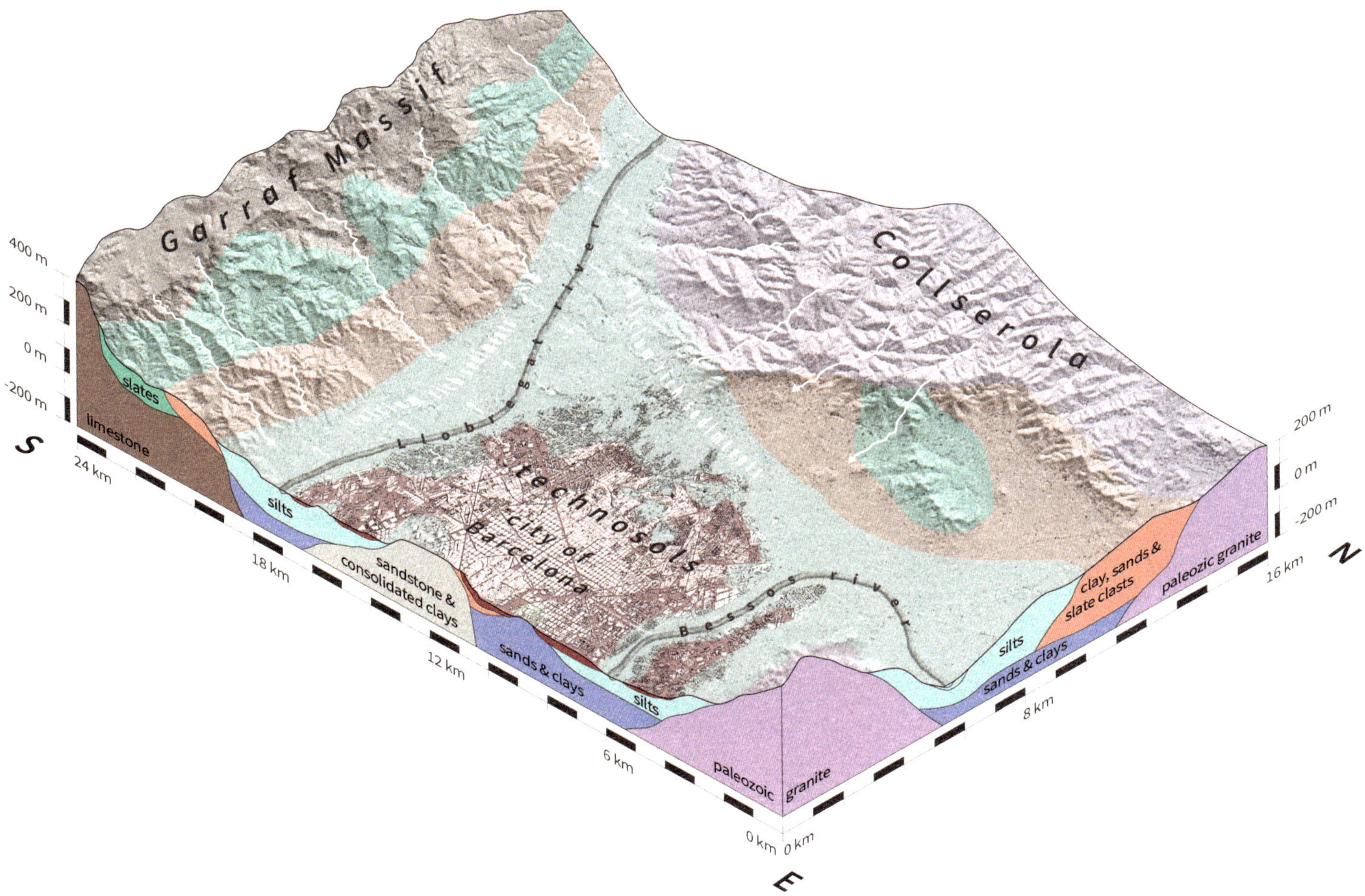

A cross-section of Barcelona's Biogeological Stratum: natural geological layers point to a marine past while anthropogenic layers are new but omnipresent.

The innovative yet ancient chemistry of algae …

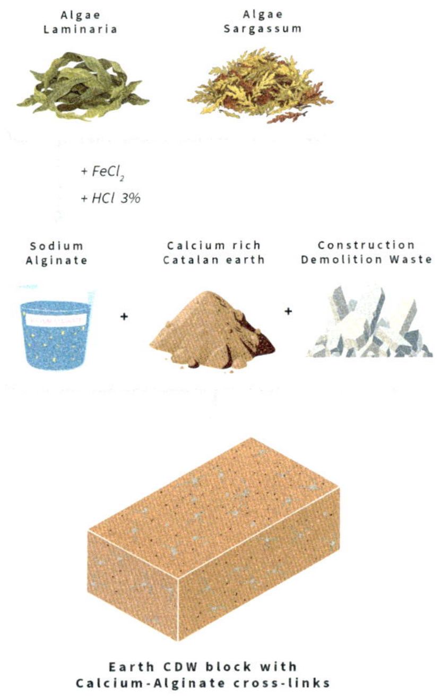

The soft chemistry of macroalgae: cross-linking alginate by replacing sodium atoms with calcium atoms inside a building material for added strength and water resistance.

Algae capture CO_2 for photosynthesis and combine with calcium for biomineralisation. Today, as rising CO_2 concentrations accelerate algal growth, Europe's beaches increasingly receive large quantities of 'stranded' algae, which are often treated as waste despite the continent's immense (yet underused) potential for micro- and macroalgae cultivation.[5] But this biomass need not be discarded. When it is mixed with Barcelona's construction and demolition waste, which is rich in calcium, the mixture begins to bind and biomineralise. This reaction creates new mineral structures that can be shaped into blocks, mortars and plasters capable of resisting loads, rain, wind and sun.

The CO_2-capturing machinery of microalgae: not only through photosynthesis but also biomineralisation by combining carbon dioxide and calcium into newly formed limestone.

5. In Europe, up to 1.17 million tonnes of stranded algae every year is treated as waste. See European Climate, Infrastructure and Environment Executive Agency (CINEA), *Study to Support an EU Sustainable Algae Industry: Final Report*, Publications Office of the European Union, 2025: https://cinea.ec.europa.eu/publications/digital-publications/study-support-eu-sustainable-algae-industry_en

These processes of binding operate at ambient temperatures, avoiding the enormous energy inputs and corresponding CO_2 emissions of conventional materials (for example, 1,600°C for cement clinker, or 1,200°C for fired bricks). In contrast, algae blocks, algae plasters and algae mortars can be produced with minimal emissions and even significant net carbon uptake through its use of CO_2 for photosynthesis and biomineralisation, while being biocompatible, and biodegradable at the end of its life cycle.

… to create soft materials: the right material in the right place

In early industrialised countries and newly urbanised areas, hard materials such as concrete, glass and steel have been overly ubiquitous, driven by their unparalleled structural and mechanical qualities. Today we know that this leads to excessively high carbon emissions as well as unhealthy indoor climates and unadapted outdoor climates. The Grounded Futures project hence advocates for the reintroduction of soft materials such as biomineralised matter next to wood, fibres and earth, as the main building materials to create healthy and well-adapted spaces. By deploying hard and soft materials precisely where their performance is required, we can mimic nature's subtle cycles and transitions between hard and soft layers; we can bring the built environment in balance with the ecosystem of which it is a continuation.

BC architects & studies & materials, Grounded Futures, Lleida, Spain, 2026. Fetdeterra and BC materials' vibro-compaction process uses alginate with excavated earth and construction and demolition waste from sites across Barcelona.

Material prototyping of mortars for plaster or masonry using microalgae as a binder with calcium-rich aggregates.

BC architects & studies & materials, Grounded Futures, Pierra, Spain, 2026. The Piera Ecoceramica and BC materials extrusion process.

BC architects & studies & materials, Grounded Futures, Brussels, 2026. Material lab testing of blocks according to European standard EN 1015.

BC architects & studies & materials, Grounded Futures, Brussels, 2026. Material prototyping of blocks with alginate as a co-binder and biopolymer stabiliser, rendering the blocks water-resistant while remaining biocompatible.

BC architects & studies & materials, Grounded Futures, Brussels, 2026. Material lab testing of plasters at BC materials according to German standard DIN 18947.

BC architects & studies & materials, Grounded Futures, Barcelona, 2026.
Speculative image of Nau 8 de Can Batlló, demonstrating the diverse potential applications of extruded alginate-earth and compressed lime-earth blocks utilised according to their specific material characteristics.

Speculative detail of Nau 8 de Can Batlló, featuring weather-resistant pavement and plinths, while soft material compositions are strategically implemented for vertical façade repairs and integrated wall infill.

Speculative image of CDIAP Ciutat Vella, illustrating the deployment of soft materials based on performance metrics, purposefully differentiating various structural and aesthetic functional uses throughout.

Speculative detail of CDIAP Ciutat Vella, where the material synthesis achieves a unique visual identity, intentionally evoking the textures and atmospheres of the local Mediterranean coast.

Continuous matter, connected matter …

Reintroducing soft materials in the right place restores an architectural logic that is differentiated in functionalities and situated within its context. A plinth reads as a dense, moisture-resistant base; corners articulate rigidity and protection; infill surfaces remain light and soft. Each part appears according to its task, its limits and its materiality, giving buildings stratification instead of homogenised envelopes or concealed assemblies.

But the shift is more than constructive; it changes how buildings are perceived, lived and understood. The material colours, textures and transformations reveal where they come from and how they might evolve in time. A building appears not as a collection of neutral materials but as a continuity of the context: a timely mineral and biological passage between environment, built form and human activity.

This relational understanding transforms the role of architecture. No building is an island made of controlled, stable materials; it is a temporary constellation of agents such as materials, people, organisms, climates and infrastructures, each influencing the others. The building itself becomes an actor within networks, shaping architectural practice, knowledge, material flows, production chains and people's imagination. Recognising this immanent connectedness of architectural undertakings establishes both a framework and a responsibility: to design with awareness of the networks we join, the practice we instil, the ecologies we transform, and the environments we help bring into being.

… becoming Grounded Futures

The Grounded Futures project unfolds through four distinct actions, each expressed in its own medium and format. Together, they construct a layered and multifaceted narrative.

Maps, diagrams and collages visually reinterpret the emerging production chain, from microscopic views of biomineralised material to the broader bioregion of Barcelona and the city's metabolic flows.

Raw materials and small-scale prototypes anchor the installation to its bioregion. Their tactile presence links the origin of each component to its transformed state, revealing inherent qualities, textures and behaviours that are often invisible in conventional material supply chains.

A film by Alexandre Humbert introduces the people, infrastructures and networks involved in this 'becoming' process. It reveals both the practical machinery and the immanent interdependence between place, people, material and production.

A final mock-up demonstrates the architectural possibilities, properties and vulnerabilities of these biomineralised materials.

The Grounded Futures project demonstrates a process of implementing Barcelonian, Catalan and Spanish actors within new production chains for building materials made from algae and construction and demolition waste, with the ambition that these collaborations continue beyond its installation at UIA 2026 Barcelona. Piera Ecoceramica and Fetdeterra serve as primary production partners, supported by resource partners Microalgae Lab, Ceamsa, Hercal, Puigfel, Benjumea, and GRC, alongside the academic expertise of RWTH and UPC as knowledge partners.

Alexandre Humbert, Film still from *Grounded Futures*, 2026.
The film documents the newly established material cultures in Barcelona, Catalonia and Spain.

Critical Antagonist 6/12

A conversation between Marina Tabassum and the Congress curators on Becoming Embodied and material's grounding in place, practice and collective knowledge

PRACTICE ROOTED IN WHAT EXISTS

Becoming

Embodied

CURATORS The UIA Congress departs from an awareness of 'becoming' – from the idea of activating time as a design tool in order to carefully transform pre-existing realities. How do you interpret this notion, both conceptually and in relation to practice?

MARINA TABASSUM 'Becoming' is a process. It starts with realisation and acknowledgement of our questionable living practices that have led to the decline of a balanced environment, which poses a threat not only to human existence but also to all living beings. The next step is to seek ways to mend, to heal, to rectify and transform. It is an awakening that is calling for change on a global scale.

We cannot reverse time, but age-old values of living symbiotically with nature can inform our responses through appropriation in the context of time.

Architecture conditions the way we live socially and individually. It impacts our physical, emotional and psychological health and growth. As such, every aspect of our design thinking influences the built environment and how we shape our lives in and around it.

Becoming needs to begin with the belief that we are part of the ecosystem, and that we need to restore the balance by transforming our living patterns.

C We are particularly interested in your position as a practitioner regarding the capacity of material technologies to embody social and ecological values. Drawing from your own experience, to what extent do you believe such values can become embedded in built work, rather than remaining at the level of intention or discourse?

MT In our practice we try to source locally, focusing on local materials for construction. These can be natural, recycled, artisanal, industrial or waste. This practice reduces long supply chains and imports, vitalises the local economy and building industry, and substantially reduces the construction budget. In addition, employing local builders, the community and craftspeople, and the appropriation of local building techniques, helps to create a social and cultural cohesion with a language of architecture that is rooted in place. My learning is embedded in studying vernacular architecture from around the world. Architecture responds to the uniqueness of geography and climate. Our cultural diversity is our becoming, and in a global sense needs to be celebrated and integrated within our contemporary lifestyles.

C We often refer to your Khudi Bari (Small House) project as operating on multiple levels: it empowers local communities through a low-tech, contemporary vernacular construction system; it responds to transforming wetland landscapes and enables appropriation over time; and it develops a precise material and lightweight architectural expression. Could you elaborate on how these interrelations – between material resources, construction technology, material expression, community engagement and temporal adaptability – come together in this project?

MT Khudi Bari was designed in response to the displacement of marginalised people living in the sand-beds of the Padma, Jamuna, Meghna and Teesta rivers. The Ganges-Brahmaputra hydrological system creates these sand-beds in the middle of the rivers. These '*chars*', as we call them, are constantly being reshaped by the water current, forcing the families who live here to move their houses from one location to another. Some families have moved more than twenty times in their lifetime. In addition, when the rivers flood, the families disperse to higher grounds on the mainland for safety. Young children, mostly adolescent girls, are especially vulnerable during these times of flooding.

A Khudi Bari in a rural *char* area in Bangladesh, 2023.

Our self-initiated research looked into a structural system for elevated homes to protect these families from flooding; a knock-down system they could assemble and disassemble themselves, enabling movement from one place to another. The structure also needed to be low cost and employ locally sourced materials.

We designed a steel joint that connects bamboo arms to form a rigid, two-level structure. It is sturdy enough to withstand the lateral pressure of flood water and high wind velocity during thunderstorms. We shared construction knowledge with the *char* communities through a series of community engagements, and together built the structures in various locations in Bangladesh. We then monitored how the communities appropriate Khudi Bari. In many instances, families moved their houses and also benefitted during the floods. There is demand from the *char* communities for more houses. Our foundation [Foundation for Architecture and Community Equity] is working with them to provide assistance to build them.

C Following Khudi Bari, your work has been widely discussed in relation to community involvement and self-construction. Could you reflect on how knowledge is transferred in these processes – through which techniques, tools or forms of collaboration – and how you negotiate the balance between architectural expertise and local agency? Where does the project stand today in terms of replication or scalability?

MARINA TABASSUM Our community engagements focus on men, women and children. We have a scale model of Khudi Bari that the community members learn to assemble. It's an easy system that even the children can put together as a game. Our community engagement focuses on various topics such as physical mapping of the settlements, wealth ranking of the community, forming savings groups and discussing livelihood opportunities. These activities are important to growing a trustworthy relationship with people. Once the relationship is established, we ask the communities to prepare a list of families who they

A women-led community centre in a refugee camp in Cox's Bazar, Bangladesh, 2022.

think deserve the first twenty houses. Together, the community decides and helps to build the houses.

The houses are built in partnership with the homeowners. They make the first investment by making the plinth. Our foundation provides the bamboo and steel joints for the structure, and corrugated tin for the roofing. The homeowners build the floors and façades according to their affordability. After the first twenty houses, the community is equipped with the knowledge to build. In the later phases we only send them the steel joints and structural bamboo. They can build the houses themselves. We are now looking at how the steel joints can be made locally, to reduce cost and make them more accessible for people.

Bangladesh has hosted more than a million forcefully displaced Myanmar nationals in Ukhiya, Cox's Bazar, since 2017. We built community centres for the refugee women in the camps by scaling up the Khudi Bari structure, adding series of modules to create larger spaces for gathering. We organised co-design workshops with women to finalise the spatial layouts and design. This was a very fruitful process through which we were able to accommodate their aspiration for a garden in the dense refugee camps that impacts their mental health in a positive way.

Khudi Bari, Char Hijla, Chandpur, Lower Meghna River, Bangladesh.

C Dhaka is often described through the lens of crisis – density, informality, climate vulnerability – but in your work it also appears as a place of intelligence, adaptation and spatial knowledge. From your perspective, what can rapidly transforming cities of the Global South like Dhaka teach architecture today about density, resilience and social coexistence under conditions of political, ecological and environmental pressure?

MT Dhaka is one of the fastest growing cities in the world. Due to lack of decentralisation, people are compelled to be Dhaka-bound for better work opportunities and quality of health, education and living. The city of twenty million people cannot provide decent housing to low-income families, who pay the highest rent per square metre. It was not designed for the growing population and suffers from a lack of infrastructure. In addition to the physical challenges, it also lacks the public functions that are essential to a healthy city.

The informal settlements of Dhaka, such as the Korail slum, are self-organised. Despite the lack of formal infrastructure and road networks, the community has established its own systems and governance that help to operate a superblock of 300,000 residents spread over 90 acres of land.

Overview of the Korail slum, Dhaka, Bangladesh, 2024.

I believe that innovation comes from challenges. As such, fast-growing Asian cities like Dhaka also offer many opportunities and room for innovation and healthy growth. It requires collaborative approaches where architects, urban designers, social activists and landscape architects invest their skills and knowledge into community-driven problem-solving to find intelligent, cost-effective solutions for a better living environment.

C Several of your projects in Dhaka, such as the Comfort Reverie apartment building, engage directly with climatic conditions through spatial and material strategies – cross-ventilation, deep façades, filtered light – rather than relying primarily on mechanical systems. How do you approach the question of environmental comfort in dense urban contexts where resources are limited and climate stress is increasing? And how transferable do you think these architectural logics are beyond their local context?

MARINA TABASSUM In our subtropical climate, we experience six distinct seasons that are a variation of hot and humid summers, monsoon rains and dry, cool winters. We grew up without air-conditioning. My memories of growing up are of cross-ventilation with a deep shaded verandah, a courtyard with trees for cool air and shade, thick walls of mud

Marina Tabassum Architects, Comfort Reverie apartment building, Banani, Dhaka, 2011.

or brick with lime mortar, and semi-open pavilion-like spaces. The advent of artificial means of climate control meant architecture underwent massive change. A verandah, a semi-open space encircling a house, was not only important for airflow but was also a lived space for the family. Now, verandahs have become tiny balconies for potted plants and drying clothes.

The history of air-conditioning is not even a hundred years old. Yet 3 per cent of global carbon emissions is due to air-conditioning, and it consumes more than 7 per cent of global demand for electricity. If we look not too far back in history, at pre-Second World War dwellings, we find ingenious systems of climate control that responded to local needs. The global standard of 18–22 °C in an artificially cooled or heated environment is unhealthy and weakens our immune system and our tolerance to anything above or below this temperature range.

In most places in the world there are days in the year when we can open our windows to let nature flow into the spaces we occupy. I do believe that both artificial and passive systems can work side by side in our buildings. It is imperative that we revisit and re-examine the climate-responsive and adaptive architecture of pre-air-conditioning eras to seek solutions that can be reappropriated in our contemporary context as passive means of climate control.

Limitation of resources is never a challenge; it is a path to innovation. In subtropical climates and dense urban contexts, the focus needs to be on planning neighbourhoods that ensure reduction of heat gain and uninterrupted airflow. Climatic responses vary based on location, but the fundamental architectural and planning logic of addressing climate – from individual buildings to neighbourhood and city scales – is universally valid.

C The conversations and sessions within 'Becoming Embodied' span a wide range of topics, from material gestures to the role of technology and the vernacular. What do you think can be learned from these debates? Is there a particular theme, tension or practice that you find especially relevant or revealing?

MT We are transitioning to becoming embedded in environment-friendly building and construction industries. The UIA Congress is seeking alternative approaches to architectural thinking/practice as a new norm in a post-depletion, post-capitalist paradigm. As its curators, in Becoming Embodied you have gathered practitioners, academics and researchers who are already actively contributing to this transition, introducing new material research that investigates local resources, and construction techniques informed by local knowledge and climatic responses. Related topics and concerns are addressed in pedagogy and in policy dialogues.

This platform offers opportunities for conversations, discourses and learning, and encourages us to do better. It is also a great moment to build new connections and collaborations. As such it is important to see, listen to and learn about the research and approaches being undertaken, and at the same time explore ways to develop 'situated responses' through process-driven methods. Only through dialogue and combining our knowledge, experience and intelligence can we find our way back to a symbiotic world of coexistence.

C Beyond invited talks, the Congress seeks to contribute to architectural knowledge through a series of year-long Research by Design investigations. One of them, Grounded Futures by BC architects & studies & materials, explores the reuse of demolition waste from Barcelona's public space – largely calcium-rich concrete – in combination with alginate to generate new biomineralised materials for construction. What is your impression of this research?

MARINA TABASSUM I admire BC architects' practice. They have pioneered many groundbreaking building materials by combining available resources such as urban waste with natural materials. For the Congress, they have created a recipe using Barcelona's urban debris and microalgae. The mixture binds together to form a new material that can be shaped into building blocks. I'm excited by this and by the outcome. Turning waste into a resource is an idea every city can learn from.

C The investigation Light Fever, developed by BRUTHER, approaches artificial light as a fragile and relational material, focusing on its capacity to subtly drift, modulate and transform spatial and social experience. Does their approach challenge or expand your own understanding of human-made light as an architectural material?

MT BRUTHER is working with light. Stéphanie Bru and Alexandre Theriot position light as a phenomenon instead of an object. In their text they explain it quite poetically, that light 'exists only in relation: to a surface, a body, dust, humidity, a moment.' Personally, I am always intrigued by the immense possibilities light offers as a material in architecture. It is integral to atmosphere and emotion as we experience architecture.

BRUTHER investigates the phenomenon of light, the immensity of the site and human perception through in-situ experiments with devices such as a tilting mirror and a translucent surface, where light invents its own trajectories in Barcelona's Turbine Hall. In their sensory orchestration of light and space, 'the building becomes an atmospheric laboratory where the goal is not to control light but to let it act, to let it reveal the tensions, latent volumes and sensitive potentialities already contained in the space.'

C Both workshops within Becoming Embodied, led respectively by TEN and Nuno Melo Sousa, focus on the design of primary structures. One investigates large-scale civic supports adaptable over time, the other explores essential structural variations through the seemingly simple figure of a table. What is your view of these approaches?

MT I think Nuno Melo Sousa's process liberates the simple structure of the table of its preconception and allows exploration of its potentials through material, situation and scale, while TEN challenges the visual realm by focusing on the embedded potential of an existing situated establishment, leveraging programmatic, material and special characteristics to renew the values of making or creating a new reality. Both processes are very much aligned to current thinking in architecture. Our overbuilt cities with abandoned infrastructures or buildings falling into decay as they have lost their original purpose are the new sites of the immense possibilities of becoming.

C To conclude, we would like to ask you about the Congress itself. What do you believe should be the role and purpose of an architecture congress today?

MT There is no 'one solution fit all' in architecture. Our challenges are situation specific and our solutions need to address the contexts and communities they serve. But the processes can be replicated/adapted or used as inspiration for appropriation on the ground. I believe in collaborative approaches through dialogues and learning. At times I am also surprised to find out how related our problems are and also our solutions. International congresses play an important role in providing a space where architects and allied professionals meet and share, and learn about different research and different ways of thinking and working. As we transition to new design thinking, they are becoming more important platforms of dialogue, showcasing the possibilities and ideas being generated and tested.

Curators

AGENCY AND TECHNOLOGIES OF MATERIALS

Technological vernacular

Materials of belonging

Fabrication research

Material gestures

Primary structures

Temporal stratification

Architectural materials are not neutral. Nor are they passive, apolitical substances distributed in space by the certainty of disciplinary abstraction and geometry. The constellation of architectures contributing to 'Becoming Embodied' provides a wide range of stimulating examples in which material assemblies are activated as agents, carrying ecological, political and poetic resonances. Performing as 'actants' in space, these materials produce effects on their surroundings, influencing carbon footprint, thermal conductivity, distributions of power, social disputes, technological shifts, sensorial experience, and even perceptions of time and meaning.[1] This understanding of the material world does not seek to replace the pleasures of beauty and aesthetics. On the contrary, it expands them, calling for the exploration of broader imaginative poetics of construction capable of embodying richer interrelations.

1. Bruno Latour, *Reassembling the Social: An Introduction to Actor-Network-Theory*, Oxford University Press, 2005.

Grounded in cultural and environmental specificities, several practices draw from vernacular traditions to activate construction toolkits rooted in collective knowledge, climatic intelligence and resource awareness. These approaches reinterpret the vernacular as an operative system capable of responding to contemporary conditions of scarcity and transformation. (1, 2) Timber construction, in this context, emerges as a low-emission relational practice linking forest ecologies, technological research and refined spatial expression. (3, 4, 5) Similarly, the renewed interest in earthen construction unfolds through processes of technical

(1) Marina Tabassum, Khudi Bari, Bangladesh, 2023.

(2) DnA_Design and Architecture, Jinyun Quarries, Zhejiang province, China, 2022.

(3) Tomoaki Uno Architects, Terabe Guest House, Nishio, Japan, 2023.

(4) Aulets Architects, Arimunari school, Mallorca, Spain, 2021. Wood construction by EGOIN.

(5) Enric Vadell, Construction of a biomass warehouse at the Conca nursery, Tremp, Lleida, Spain, 2016.

innovation embedded in ancient material knowledge, reinterpreting industrialised variants of traditional rammed earth while enhancing their reduced-carbon, hygroscopic and structural capacities. (6, 7)

Other investigations operate through experimental material research, testing new forms of construction grounded in reuse, transformation and performance. Mineral demolition waste is reconstituted into stone-like blocks, produced directly on-site and stored in open-air conditions to enable processes of carbon absorption before being reintroduced into construction cycles. (8a&b) Other processes combine calcium-rich construction debris with biological agents such as algae to generate biomineralised materials, ranging from softer plasters to more resistant blocks and tiles (see the Research by Design by BC architects & studies & materials). These approaches move beyond recycling as an engineered solution, proposing instead new material ecologies where tectonic character, process and

(8a&b) Roger Boltshauser, *Respira*, Barcelona, Spain, 2026.

(7) David Adjaye, Dot Ateliers, Accra, Ghana, 2022. Rammed-earth construction by Hive Earth.

(6) Lehm Ton Erde, Lehm Ton Erde factory building, Schlins, Vorarlberg, Austria, 2020.

(9) BC architects & studies & materials, Assemble and Atelier LUMA, The Hanok, Gwangju, South Korea, 2024.

decarbonisation become integral to architectural production. (9)

In some practices, attention shifts to material expressions, where construction unfolds through the direct manipulation of matter. Materials are not simply selected as finished products, but acted upon – cut, cast, eroded, assembled or even hacked – to produce forms, gestures and performances that emerge from their internal logic rather than preconceived imposition. (10, 11) This material blooming emerges as a direct, somehow raw and uncontrolled form of expression, recalling practices where spatial transformation is produced through acts of cutting, removal, and exposure.[2] (12) And not only of solids – light is embraced as an active, unstable material that, through its relational and temporal behaviour, shapes space, perception and social interaction not by forming objects but by continuously transforming architectural experience (see the Research by Design by BRUTHER).

(11) AAU Anastas, *All Purpose*, Venice Architecture Biennale, Italy, 2021.

(10) Studio Anne Holtrop, Green Corner Building, Muharraq, Bahrain, 2019. Structural engineer Mario Monotti.

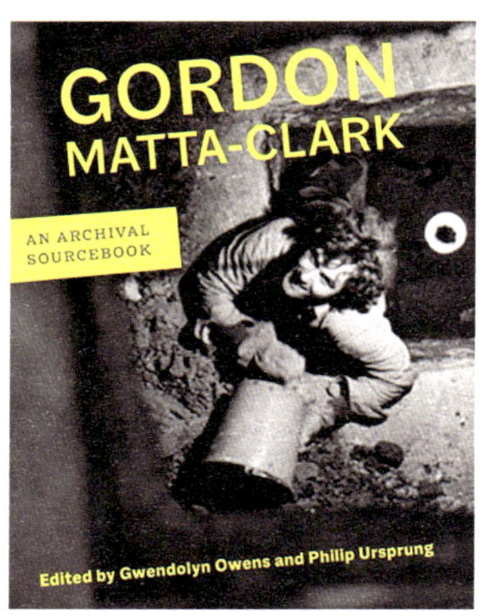

(12) Gwendolyn Owens and Philip Ursprung, *Gordon Matta-Clark: An Archival Sourcebook*, 2022.

Embedded within constructional technologies, all of these gestures transcend ornament and texture by generating specific structural configurations and particular types of space, such as vaulted roofs, interconnected chambers, lightweight skeletons and tensile enclosures. (13, 14, 15, 16, 17) As they scale up and hybridise with their environment, they have the capacity to extend into larger material patterns, shaping not only surfaces but buildings, cities, landscapes and territories.

2. Gwendolyn Owens and Philip Ursprung (eds), *Gordon Matta-Clark: An Archival Sourcebook*, University of California Press, 2022.

Other work approaches technology as an expanded and accessible spectrum embedded in everyday practice. Drawing from catalogues, standard components and shared construction systems, these architectures operate through open frameworks that enable adaptation, modification and collective appropriation over time. Their technical logic resonates with vernacular practices – not as nostalgic references but as operational knowledge rooted

(13) Max Núñez Arquitectos, Casa Doble Bóveda, Santiago de Chile, Chile, 2025.

(14) Palinda Kannangara, Frame Holiday Structure, Imaduwa, Galle, Sri Lanka, 2018.

(15) Josep Ferrando Architecture, Fire Station, Moià, Barcelona, Spain, 2020.

(16) Manthey Kula, Forvik Ferry Port, Vevelstad, Norway, 2015.

(17) Go Hasegawa, Yoshino Cedar House, Nara, Japan, 2016.

in use, repetition and resourcefulness. From this condition, construction becomes a precise yet open system capable of accommodating variation across sites and uses. Standard elements are recomposed into specific structural and spatial configurations, engaging topography, material availability and patterns of habitation. Against the dull standardisation and spatial homogeneity of global production – and despite sourcing from ready-mades and catalogues – these architectures articulate grounded differences through precise, situated and sometimes playful material assemblies. (18, 19, 20, 21, 22)

Architecture is approached here as a stratified assemblage of layers unfolding over time, avoiding the notion of a unified, static object. Primary structures operate as enduring supports – base frameworks that stabilise infrastructural space while enabling great freedom of appropriation. (23, 24, 25) Upon them, lighter and more adaptable layers accumulate, detach, slide and evolve, shaped by changing uses, habitation patterns and everyday belongings.

(18) BRUTHER, New Generation Research Center, Caen, France, 2016.

(19) Adamo Faiden, Edificio Bonpland, Palermo, Argentina, 2018.

(20) gru.a, Let's Fly Biofactory, Papucaia, Rio de Janeiro, Brazil, 2024.

(21) Arrhov Frick, Adelsö house, Adelsö, Sweden, 2025.

(22) Jun Sato Lab, Base Camp on the Moon / Mars, University of Tokyo, Japan, 2021–26.

(26, 27, 28) Material properties condition these temporal behaviours: mineral and heavy systems tend towards permanence and collective management, while lightweight assemblies invite individual alteration, transformation and incremental growth. (29) Rather than opposing permanence and change, these works articulate a readable coexistence of multiple temporalities, where construction becomes an open field of negotiation between long-term support and short-term change. In this layered condition, architecture may never be 'completed' but continuously reconfigured, accommodating diverse forms of agency across time. (30)

Taken together, these practices suggest a shift in how architecture understands matter itself; no longer inert and fully subordinate to form. Instead, materials appear as political agents and active participants in the production of space, interrelated in processes that exceed human intention. Echoing broader philosophical reflections on the vitality of matter, the works reveal construction as a field of

(23) Arquitectura G, Costa House, Barcelona, 2021.

(24) Nuno Melo Sousa, Corcet Headquarters, Penafiel, Portugal, 2025.

(25) BeL, Cooperative housing, Neunburg vorm Wald, Germany, 2024.

(26) Shigeru Ban Architects Europe, IE Madrid Paper Pavilion, Spain, 2019.

(27) Shigeru Ban, Naked House, Kawagoe, Japan, 2000.

(28) Langarita Navarro Arquitectos, Red Bull Music Academy, Madrid, Spain, 2011.

(29) TEN, 500-Year Tower, Bern, Switzerland, 2021.

distributed agency, where minerals, fibres, organisms and environmental forces co-produce architectural outcomes.[3] The act of designing, in this sense, must refuse disciplinary autonomy and imposition, opening towards the uncertainty and ambiguity of transdisciplinary interrelation. Sometimes, this way of approaching the practice of space may feel closer to a curatorial task than to a conventional architectural one. This pathway rejects the simplicity of a fixed aesthetic and technological paradigm, advocating for a plural and evolving material awareness. Architecture, in this manner, operates as an attentive, responsive and embedded mediator within fluctuating values and meanings.

3. Jane Bennett, *Vibrant Matter: A Political Ecology of Things*, Duke University Press, 2010.

(30) ZAV architects, Type-less Building Center for Handy, Iran, 2021.

Becoming Interdependent

'We are undone by each other.
And if we're not, we're missing something.'

Judith Butler, *Precarious Life: The Powers of Mourning and Violence*, 2004

How can we design politics of space that activate interpersonal relationships?

Far from being neutral, space can be either a tool of institutionalised violence or a catalyst for social empowerment. Architecture has historically played a pivotal role in constructing spatial regimes that reinforce regulatory bodies, perpetuating social asymmetries and exclusion. 'Becoming Interdependent' re-evaluates traditional notions of space and labour, recognising the increasingly blurred boundaries between productive and reproductive spheres.

Alternative common economies, non-hierarchical forms of governance, cooperative ways of living, and urban places grounded in coexistence are tested while integrating gendered and postcolonial perspectives. These recognise interconnected dependencies and advocate for collective rights to appropriate spaces and shape environments over time.

Within these processes, conflict, conversation and negotiation entwined with empathy, solidarity and care appear as necessary daily situations of interaction at multiple scales. In the context of the climate emergency, unrestrained capitalistic patterns of exploitation, and rising politics of oppression these attitudes intend to design more feminist, decolonial, non-normative, non-anthropocentric and careful worlds of commons.

Juan Herreros

INTERDEPENDENCE: DUALITIES, FRAGILITIES AND FUTURES

The slogan 'Architectures for a planet in transition', proposed by the Congress curatorial team, strongly echoes the evident reality that we are living through turbulent times. On the one hand are those obsessed with independence, autonomy and security. From policies of self-sufficiency to the ideology of 'not in my backyard', self-protection and defence against what is different have become normalised, underpinning resounding violations of the logic of coexistence. On the other hand, a global outcry calls for maintaining and stimulating bonds, interrelations and symbiotic metabolisms at all scales, attempting to foreground the fact that interdependence is the fundamental equation of living together, and here 'together' involves everything human and non-human. This essay seeks to visualise this struggle in the context of architecture, proposing it as a major ally, in joint action with other disciplines, in discerning this dichotomy.

Dualities

Western thought has developed since Plato through a systematic search for duality. No element of reality is understood without the existence of its complementary opposite. The outlines of paired elements remain clearly defined, and duality insists on their difference. This rational framework manifests in architecture through the confrontation of pairs related to the physicality of the built environment, such as building versus urban context, centre versus periphery, city versus countryside, as well as through deeper visions of reality that dissociate the artificial from the natural, technique from craft, or the human from the non-human.

However, since the late nineteenth century, philosophy, with Nietzsche at the forefront, has been forging a slow revision of dualism, its dehumanisation and obsession with objectivity, which forgets the vital origin of knowledge and its relationship with what surrounds human beings, whether other people or their inhabited environment. Coinciding with the emergence of the architectural avant-gardes of the 1930s, Edmund Husserl developed his work on 'transcendental phenomenology', confronting lived experience with technical rationalisation, and thus subjectivity with prevailing objectivity.[1] By extrapolating Husserl's phenomenology and its opposition to positivism for being considered reductionist, we can discern an implicit critique of Modern Movement manifestos led by Le Corbusier. Husserl's influence would crystallise in Maurice Merleau-Ponty and, through him, in the philosophy of the crisis of modernity led by Jacques Derrida. Grounded in this context, the world described through clearly delimited dualities exploded at the end of the twentieth century with key moments such as the publication of *The Limits to Growth* (1972) by the Club of Rome,[2] the emergence of awareness regarding the artificiality of gender boundaries that would give rise to feminist and queer developments, and the establishment in the 1980s of the concept of the 'non-human' by Bruno Latour,[3] to end the rupture between society and what had been referred to as 'nature'.

1. Edmund Husserl, 'Ideen zu einer reinen Phänomenologie und phänomenologischen Philosophie', *Jahrbuchs für Philosophie und phänomenologische Forschung*, Vol. 1, Max Niemeyer, 1913.

2. The Club of Rome is an international organisation of scientists, economists, business leaders and former politicians founded in 1968 at the Accademia dei Lincei, Rome, to tackle 'world problematique' and the future of humanity. See Donella H. Meadows, Dennis L. Meadows, Jørgen Randers and William Behrens III, *The Limits to Growth*, MIT Press, 1972.

3. In the early 1990s, Bruno Latour fully established the concept of the 'non-human' as a central contribution to his Actor-Network Theory (ANT) within the context of the Centre de Sociologie de l'Innovation (CSI) at the École des Mines de Paris. His principal collaborators in developing these concepts were the sociologists Michel Callon and Steve Woolgar.

Although the persistence of the postulates of the Modern Movement remains a recurring foothold to avoid the slippery terrain of losing clearly drawn definitions, the truth is that since the 1980s we have been relearning to describe reality as a set of intertwined and overlapping systems that do not admit reductions to the magical rationality of the twentieth century and its reassuring inventions such as the autonomy of architecture, functionality, modular logics or other forms of order that over time have slipped through our fingers. The consequence is evident: we can no longer speak of the building as an individualised entity, as a design exercise, without dialogue with the ecosystem in which it is inserted and which it affects. We cannot conceive the city centre without the crucial role of its peripheries mutually feeding back into one another and, with this, recognise the mistake of building suburbs in imitation, and envy, of the centre, forgetting that their implantation processes could have been other, more exciting ones in tune with the space between cities; that the city is not only the great laboratory of architectural experimentation but also lives from and can give life to the natural void of the territory, more or less artificialised, and so on. If to these already indescribable pairs as such we add the dissolution of the boundaries between the natural and the artificial, and the desperate evidence that human dependence on how we use the planet is the most important crisis we face, the emergence of interdependence as the great opportunity becomes an unavoidable reality.

To consolidate this conclusion, we can rely on the environmental and colonial content (another exhausting form of duality) of many of the social crises, migrations and conflicts whose true roots lie in power over water, minerals or forests, and on the powerful eloquence of the Earth Overshoot Day or Day of the Earth's Overexploitation.[4]

4. This index, developed in 2006 by the Global Footprint Network, seeks to visualise the moment of the year when humans have consumed all the natural resources that the planet can regenerate in twelve months. In 2025 that date was 24 July at the planetary level, while in some countries, such as Spain, it was at the end of May. Its retrospective application sets 1971 as the last year in which annual expenditure and production of consumable natural resources were equal.

Conscious work on interdependence and its assumption as the basis of architecture and urbanism of the present and the future is not only an inescapable necessity for the installation of humans in the universe, it is perhaps the only opportunity for survival with an acceptable quality of life.

Fragilities

The strength and energy invested for centuries in the establishment of cities, the overwhelming mechanisms of subjugating nature and the multiple colonialisms that have only very recently begun to be revised, have revealed the harshness and impunity of human actions in their struggle against the world. Since the Venustas-Firmitas-Utilitas of the classical Vitruvian hut and its orders, architecture has been conceived as a defence against the external, as protection from climate and non-humans, and as an exercise of rationality. Emerging at a time when human fragility in relation to nature was evident, its persistence across too many industrial revolutions eventually led it into crisis and enabled the recognition of fragility's conceptual weight as an indicator of the most subtle balance among species. Since then, when catastrophic imbalances are reported – when animals and plants disappear, human groups are subjected to difficult vulnerabilities and unwanted displacements, and territories are devastated by extractivism – it becomes clear that the fragility of environments, human groups and living or inert natural beings is a value to be cared for, encouraged and incorporated into architecture as a matter of design.

The message associated with this observation would be that expanding the field of architecture to everything and everyone, broadening the right to architecture to the whole of humanity and other species, above all entails working with the most subtle fragilities and considering them of architectural interest. The much-mentioned 'architecture of care' finds, in this context, a field of development that assumes that contemporary design actions must embrace the valorisation of those fragilities and even the design and construction of new, highly subtle relationships. New fragilities, after all, are among the ingredients that construct the world. Architecture therefore has a fundamental role in developing a new sensibility that makes interdependence essential working material for contemporary practice.

An example is the overwhelming capacity into which once-innocent tourism has evolved, which only forty years ago we described as a valuable mechanism of exchange. The reality is that, fuelled by social media, it has become an extreme expression of FOMO (fear of missing out), subjecting territories and communities to a colonising action that only displays what can be mercantilised and hides everything that cannot be incorporated into a paradisiacal yet secure scene transited by the fascinated traveller. The exoticised touristification of enclaves stimulates inequalities, generates enormous quantities of waste, and turns water and other resources into merchandise. In its democratic appearance, there is a form of tourism for almost everyone, with diverse manifestations from extreme sports to music festivals in deserts. Our aim here is not to denounce mass tourism, but to demonstrate how it is evidence that there are phenomena that have entered a phase of inadaptation, overexploitation and lack of harmony with their own essence that must be corrected.

Futures

The question of interdependence may seem to call for a return to a 'zero moment' in which apparently more exchanges, integrations and symbioses among all relational systems accompanied the unfolding of events. However, such nostalgia does not seem very productive, first because there is no objective critique of that supposed value of past times, and second because we already inhabit a completely different planet, not only from centuries ago but from that just fifty years ago.

For this reason, it is crucial to consider the course of events of recent decades and ask ourselves: How did we get here? What have we done all this time besides repeatedly citing the Club of Rome report while navigating the 'Great Acceleration'[5] between punctual reference and impotence? Returning to the mid-1980s and the famous slogan 'time to stop' by the artist César Manrique when he saw his bond with the rugged and desert territory of the island of Lanzarote threatened by real-estate development that today pales in comparison to what was built four decades later,[6] now more than ever we must ask not only what should be done, but also for whom do we do it?

5. W. Steffen, W. Broadgate, W., L. Deutsch, O. Gaffney and C. Ludwig, 'The Trajectory of the Anthropocene: The Great Acceleration', *The Anthropocene Review*, 2(1), 2015, pp. 81–98.

6. César Manrique, 'Time to Stop', *c.* 1985. Available at: https://fcmanrique.org/recursos/actividad/54c64a23time%20to%20stop.pdf

Architecture has an obligation in the face of these questions, as it is considered responsible for 40 per cent of global CO_2 emissions related to energy, encompassing both operational carbon (use of energy) and embodied carbon from greenhouse gas emissions. How can our discipline convince society that many of these problems have architectural solutions? From our point of view, that path can only be pursued through research, multidisciplinarity[7] and innovation nourished by a wise mixture of ambition and humility.

7. Perhaps one of the most elaborated defences of multidisciplinarity as a tool to alter the course of the 'Great Acceleration' is T. McPhearson et al., 'Radical Changes are Needed for Transformations to a Good Anthropocene', *npj Urban Sustainability*, 1(5), 2021.

Even while rooting architectural practice in its many centuries of history, new formulations cannot be based solely on what is already known. Establishing new ways of working, incorporating knowledge and experts from other disciplines and inventing new typologies offer a glimpse of a future in which architecture will not only chronicle its time but act as a critical, activist and committed force in the face of present contradictions. To achieve this, it is not enough for academia or professional practice to propose experimental approaches with generous conviction; political and economic institutions capable of administering trust in architecture and its related disciplines as never before in history will also need to be willing to change.

MAIO and Care., ETHZ
(Ethel Baraona Pohl, Pol Esteve Castelló and Anna Puigjaner)

PUBLIC PLEASURES: THE ARCHITECTURES OF CARE AND DESIRE

Public Pleasures explores how architecture can foster expanded forms of care through accessible spaces for dancing and collective celebration, framing pleasure as both a right and a cure. By centring ageing and non-normative bodies, it positions design as an agent of desire, understood as a fundamental force within the caring infrastructures of contemporary life.

MAIO, Care. & Pol Esteve Castelló, Building Pleasures, Barcelona, 2026.
Finding the way.

Pleasure as a practice of care

Care exceeds the management of needs, and is equally constituted through desire. Understood in this way, care is not opposed to pleasure but produced through it. As a growing number of studies and initiatives demonstrate, embodied enjoyment can support and relieve, from everyday duties to medical needs. Audre Lorde's theorisation of the erotic offers a critical counterpoint: the erotic as a generative, sustaining force, 'a measure between the beginnings of our sense of self and the chaos of our strongest feelings. It is an internal sense of satisfaction to which, once we have experienced it, we know we can aspire.'[1]

1. Audre Lorde, 'Uses of the Erotic', *The Master's Tools Will Never Dismantle The Master's House*, Penguin Books, 2018, p. 7.

Discourses of pleasure have long been shaped by normative assumptions that privilege youth and able-bodiedness. Yet for marginalised communities, pleasure has historically functioned as a mode of survival, relation and resistance, as Prishita Maheshwari-Aplin notes.[2] Approaching pleasure through the lens of care for non-normative and ageing bodies exposes the exclusions embedded in dominant imaginaries of enjoyment and opens the possibility of rearticulating pleasure as a right rather than a conditional reward. Such a shift reframes joy as a political, spatial and embodied question, inseparable from access recognition and equity.

2. Prishita Maheshwari-Aplin, *Roses for Hedone: On Queer Hedonism and World-Making Through Pleasure*, 404 Ink, 2025, p. 4.

What water brings.

The architecture through which accessible practices of dancing and socialising are enabled – from the scale of the body to that of the building – remains a contested terrain. Handrails, grab bars, ramps, platforms, elevators, bar counters, tabletops, water fountains, tabs, signage, lighting, speakers and many other objects, spatial artefacts and atmospheric instruments conjunctly shape the environments of the collective, becoming, regardless of their scale, barriers or facilitators for bodies to meet and thrive in their togetherness. As Léopold Lambert observes, 'a cane does not constitute an object designed to cope with age but, rather, one designed to cope with ableist spaces'.[3]

3. Léopold Lambert, 'Introduction: Abstract Normative Bodies vs. Anti-ableist Architectures', *The Funambulist*, 19, September-October 2018. https://thefunambulist.net/magazine/space-of-ableism/introduction-abstract-normative-bodies-vs-anti-ableist-architectures

Accessibility, understood as a wide spectrum of architectural decisions that enable non-normative bodies to be present in, move through, and enjoy a space should be intrinsic to architectural design. This means designing to allow all bodies with diverse abilities to physically access, navigate and inhabit a space, to create conditions in which bodies are represented and acknowledged, because as disability justice activist Mia Mingus writes, 'access for the sake of access is not necessarily

Blowing over bodies.

liberatory'.4 In other words, accessibility means allowing the whole of society to participate in the networks of support embedded in current spaces of congregation and celebration. Therefore, to provide accessibility means designing so that the libidinal pleasures of dancing are open to everyone, making music, body movement and sensuality a public resource.

4. Mia Mingus, 'Access Intimacy, Interdependence, and Disability Justice', Leaving Evidence, 12 April 2017. https://leavingevidence.wordpress.com/2017/04/12/access-intimacy-interdependence-and-disability-justice/

Holding.

At a moment in which new building codes of accessibility are being implemented, architecture is key in imagining the potentiality of accessibility as a quality of design beyond the strict application of legal parameters. The debate should not be reduced to the morphopragmatic functionality of given elements – such as their capacity to support an unstable body or to nuance the sensory experience of a neurodivergent person – but to their affordances: the ability of spaces and objects to mobilise affect as an open call to transversal forms of participation. In this sense, architecture makes desire a means towards accessibility.

We must see 'disability as something generative, a site of value-making, an integral part of life'.5 What does a go-go dancer podium for a wheelchair user tell us? What happens when materiality brings together the neurodivergent experience and the cool? What is the outcome of taking the morphological diversity of bodies as an aesthetic vector of spatial design? Thus, bodily difference emerges as an aesthetic and political force rather than a limitation. The question is no longer how space accommodates difference, but how morphological diversity actively reshapes spatial imaginaries. Desirability, accessibility and care thus converge in a single, interdependent field.

Encountering materials.

5. Sunaura Taylor, 'Care and Solidarity in the Age of Disability', *Green European Journal*, 19, September 2024. https://www.greeneuropeanjournal.eu/care-and-solidarity-in-the-age-of-disability/

Public joy

Public and institutional provisions of care overwhelmingly render non-normative bodies – disabled, ageing or chronically ill, among others – through medicalised, corrective or paternalistic frameworks, while their capacity for joy remains largely unacknowledged. Focusing on pleasure as a political agent rather than as a conditional reward for normative bodies allows architecture to be understood as a medium for diverse embodiments of desire and as a facilitator of intergenerational encounter. Care must operate through the formal and informal infrastructures of kinship and support that permeate contemporary life, including the rituals of gathering, dancing and clubbing, and the accessibility of which determines who

Becoming

Sustaining.

Pause.

Diversities meeting on the dance floor.

Sustaining.

may participate in the joy of collective interdependence.

Dance and clubbing spaces have often been overlooked by public policies of care, yet these environments constitute social infrastructures in which the pleasures of collective dancing become forms of caring practice. Despite the heterogeneity of their forms and practices, these spaces – often associated with the nocturnal, though not confined to it – converge around a common premise: the shared experience of dancing sustains collective life. Through music, movement and presence, such environments cultivate forms of sociality that exceed service-based productivity and normative temporalities. By questioning these spaces, and their use, it becomes possible to challenge the architectural role of pleasure as a right and a form of care.

Leaning on.

Emerging Workshop 7/12

Plan Común (Kim Courréges, Felipe De Ferrari, Nissim Haguenauer and Marcelo Cox)

A HOME FOR US

Plan Común, Santiago markets' area, Santiago, Chile, 2015.
Transformation of one of Santiago's most active and transited areas through the strategic implementation of a series of specific interventions in between.

The workshop focuses on designing and producing a series of spatial devices of diverse scale to reproduce the collective daily and annual rituals of Barcelona's inhabitants.

> 'I think the institutionalisation of space in special building types divides our life in fragments. On the contrary, our lives always happen in between them. Therefore, spaces in-between institutionalised facilities are quite important, and our attempt is to imagine them based on people's demands and behaviour.'[1]

Becoming

Interdependent

1. Yoshiharu Tsukamoto of Atelier Bow-Wow in conversation with Felipe De Ferrari and Diego Grass of OnArchitecture, 2014. www.onarchitecture.com/interviews/yoshiharu-tsukamoto-iv

Our cities and built environments are informed and affected by ideologies. Today, an all-encompassing capital-based market logic is the dominant ideology worldwide, producing increasing economisation, privatisation and commodification of all resources and social needs. Based on private property and perpetual debt, the current world order privileges a few at the expense of the many, globally eradicating existing forms of commons, no matter if the ruling system appears under the guise of liberalism or a burgeoning authoritarian capitalism.

In this context, spatial practices function as a primary battlefield for defining the future of collectivity. To strengthen commons through the organisation of matter and space is not only desirable but necessary.

If a wise (critical and optimistic) reading of the existing conditions allows an understanding of the behaviour of the people, nature, buildings and objects around us, a clear weaving of priorities can identify specific spatial devices capable of introducing qualitative environmental conditions for diverse social rituals.

Precise observations allow learning from concrete realities while revealing their (hidden and specific) potentials. The city therefore becomes a field of opportunities and also a laboratory for strategic interventions to maximise what is already there: more with less.

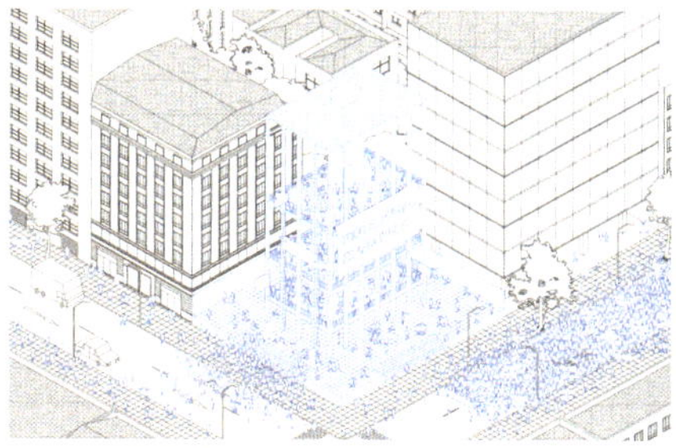

Plan Común, Public Buildings, 2012.
Public Buildings is part of the 'Common Places' collaborative research led by Plan Común between 2012 and 2018.

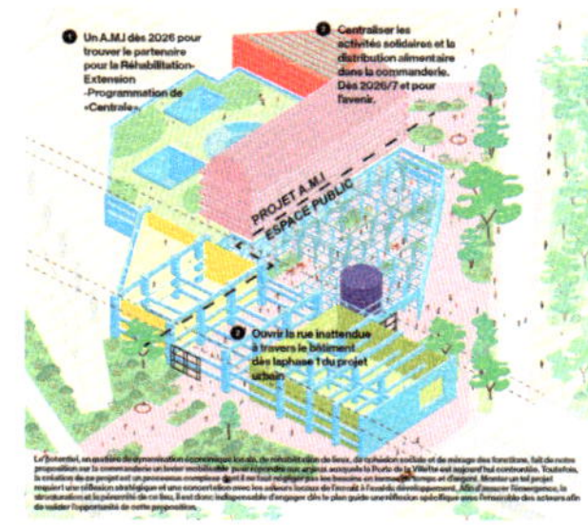

A self-commission in which we designed the brief from the very beginning, leading the administrative, financial and architectural studies and processes.

51n4e and Plan Común, Porte de la Villette, Paris, 2025.
Proposal for the adaptive reuse of the 'Commanderie' in the context of Porte de la Villette's transformation.

Plan Común, Maison Commune, Pantin, Paris, 2023.
Still from a short film about everyday life in Maison Commune.

Kuehn Malvezzi, Plan Común and Nicolas Dorval-Bory, Petit Social Housing, Paris, 2019–26.
Vertical in-between spaces (*palier partagés*). Four neighbourhood units are organised around these spaces which, partially doubled in height, are designed as living spaces that residents can appropriate.

A home for us

The workshop proposes learning from Barcelona and, in particular, from a series of case studies on public space and collective housing. Findings and lessons are collected and potentially transferred to the projects by the participants. The reproduction of shared spaces *in-between*: neither inside nor outside, simple yet effective devices always in relation to climate and environmental conditions – sun exposure, shadow, noise, fresh air, rain, landscape, etc.

Everything can become an architecture project, but it needs to be properly evaluated, studied, framed and designed. As detectives, the participants look to 'build a case' and design their own briefs: collective oases, places for a good life together, a home for us. No matter the scale or complexity, projects are initiated through synthetic discourse and a limited set of representational tools.

A Home for Us[2] understands the design process as a common field of knowledge that requires fluid collaboration and teamwork. The workshop projects are designed in dialogue – discussed, adjusted and reinforced collectively – to create a constellation of interventions within the city fabric, bringing maximum communication and dignity through humble means.

2. A Home for Us continues the design research on collective spaces initiated by Common Places in 2012 and extended through a series of local and international workshops: micro-architectures at Santiago's General Cemetery in Chile (2015), urban playgrounds for Amadora, Portugal (2016), the Andreas-Hofer-Platz in Graz, Austria (2016), a system of devices for gathering in Basel, Switzerland (2017), the transformation of a hypermarket in Ghent, Belgium (2018) and shared spaces in collective housing (2022–23).

Emerging Workshop 8/12

Assemble (James Binning) and Common Treasures (Camille Sineau)

MERCHANTS & WARRIORS

Assemble, Common Treasures and Films M/T, Merchants & Warriors, 2025.
Chickens grazing in the orchard at Cider Apple Trees nursery, an Ecological Land Cooperative site at Wyvern Fields, Somerset, UK.

Green Fingers Organic Farm, Zhuhai, China, 2025.
Salad-harvesting at the community-supported farm.

The early twenty-first century marked a major shift as the global population became predominantly urban for the first time. Driven by aspirations for employment, prosperity and improved living standards, this urban migration is expected to continue. Cities are increasingly framed as the critical sites for managing resources efficiently, mitigating the impacts of human activity and responding effectively to climate breakdown. Barcelona and its metropolitan area exemplify this dense urban model, yet also reveal its vulnerabilities and limitations. Cities are increasingly reliant on fragile global networks of food production, processing and distribution, and while investment in green infrastructures can reduce the impact we have on our daily lives, life in the contemporary city remains predicated on access to and use of energy-intensive systems and global supply chains.

Merchants & Warriors is an ongoing research project that challenges the assumption of urban primacy, proposing instead a vision of interdependence in which rural and urban realms are conceived as mutually constitutive, sustaining and reciprocal. Through a bottom-up perspective of local agricultural work, using interviews, audio recordings, photography and videography, it highlights small-scale farming practices, cooperative systems, and rural households' strategies that underpin ecological resilience, economic stability and social vitality. This survey and documentation work is a means of critiquing prevailing narratives of urban superiority, but more importantly of positioning rural communities not as passive peripheries but as active, interdependent partners in shaping sustainable, resilient futures for their regions.

To date, we have surveyed small farm sites in the UK and Southern China, and are now focusing on Barcelona's evolving peri-urban and rural territory, where demographic shifts and agricultural restructuring intersect with the urgent need to nourish a growing, urbanised population. The contrast between Catalonia's attempts to sustain rural vitality and other European trajectories is fertile ground for comparison. The UK's century-long turn towards industrialised agriculture has triggered renewed interest in agroecological, small-scale systems; in Catalonia, too, small farms and food cooperatives are emerging as vital nodes of urban-rural reciprocity and interdependence. These practices become not just desirable alternatives, but essential transitions: they allow the city to draw on healthier local systems while reinforcing the capacities of rural communities. Together, they form a mesh of economic, ecological and social interdependences that offers a more resilient, regenerative urban-rural continuum.

Assemble and Films M/T, AgroVallbona, Barcelona, Spain, 2023.
Small allotments and occupied farming lands on the periphery of Barcelona in Nou Barris, now part of the AgroVallbona urban agriculture plan to drive agro-ecological activity, the preservation of heritage, connectivity with the surroundings, and the creation of housing and facilities.

Colectivo C733 (Eric Valdez, Israel Espín, Carlos Facio, Gabriela Carrillo and José Amozurrutia)

JAGÜEY: WATER COMMONS

In the face of environmental crisis and urban fragmentation, Jagüey stands as a radical act of interdependence: a public space that reclaims water infrastructure as a shared civic resource, reconnecting communities to ecological cycles, collective responsibility, and a dignified vision for the future of Mexico City. For Mesoamerican cultures, the *jagüey* was a hydraulic engineering system designed for the collection, open-air storage and management of rainwater. This resource was vital for survival in regions with prolonged dry seasons, serving both domestic needs and agriculture.

Interdependence, rather than water as a technical object, is the core of the Jagüey project. This idea guides Colectivo C733's research by design proposal, where water becomes a material lens for understanding how people, ecological systems, and infrastructure shape one another. In Mexico City, discussions around water tend to be highly specialised. Methods and scales differ, but most agree that any meaningful response must embrace regeneration. Within that context, Jagüey presents itself not as a technical fix but as a way to reinforce social and ecological interdependence through vernacular, community-based design.

A collective response to Mexico City's water crisis

The project responds to the city's water crisis, which is particularly acute in areas like Iztapalapa, a densely populated borough in the eastern part of the city afflicted by the lack of water, green space and soil seismic fractures, by proposing local infrastructure that functions as a social, ecological and spatial system. Instead of seeing infrastructure only as pipes or supply lines, the project treats water flows as everyday socio-ecological processes shaped by collective care and shared governance. This shifts attention away from large-scale grey systems towards flexible, place-specific strategies that can ease scarcity and flooding while strengthening community cohesion, reflecting Mexican architect Mario Schjetnan's long-standing argument that water management in Mexico must reconnect ecological processes with lived public space.[1]

1. Mario Schjetnan, 'Reconciling City and Nature', National Autonomous University of Mexico (UNAM Press), 2017.

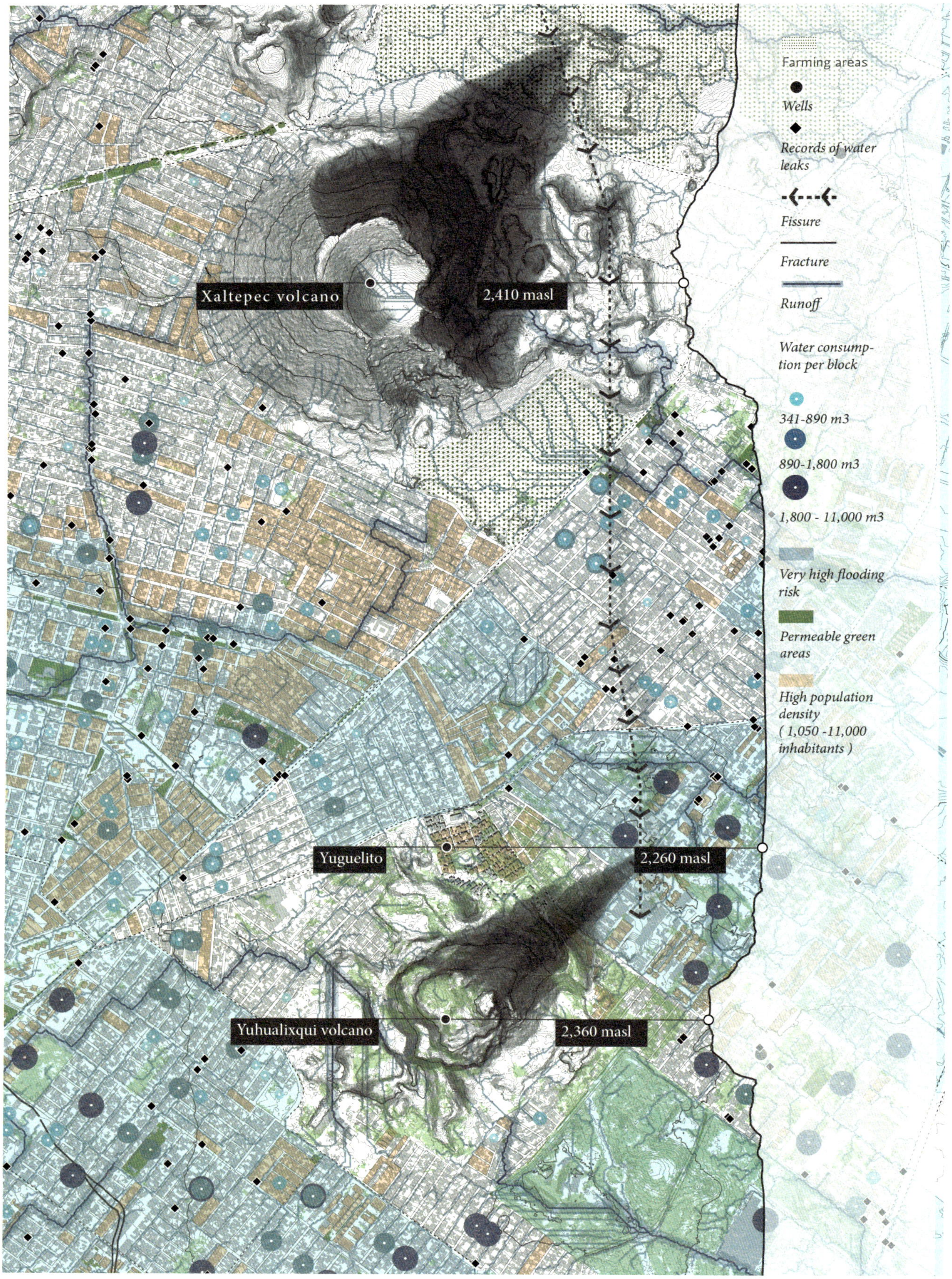

Interdependent

Colectivo C733 and Monserrat Loyola, Site analysis, Mexico City, 2025.
Site analysis of Yuguelito that includes soil cracks, seismic fractures, runoffs, scarcity of water supply, lack of green permeable areas and flooding risk.

Mexico City's disregard for its lacustrine origin has produced a recurring contradiction: seasonal abundance paired with chronic scarcity. For many neighbourhoods formed through informal construction, insufficient services increase vulnerability.[2] These areas illustrate the need to rethink governance through the lens of socio-environmental justice. The Jagüey system does not attempt to offer a universal solution; instead, it provides a framework for rebuilding autonomy and collective responsibility that can be adapted to different terrains and social conditions.

2. Miriam Alfie-Cohen et al., 'Socio-hydrological Vulnerability and Adaptive Capacity in Cuajimalpa Municipality, Mexico City', *Economía Sociedad y Territorio*, 22 (70), 2022, p. 865.

Colectivo C733, From Lake City to Hidden Infrastructure, Mexico City, 2025.
Mexico City's transformation: from lake and canal networks to buried rivers and pipe-based infrastructure, and finally the Jagüey as a visible rearticulation of the urban water cycle.

Structural challenges in the city, from uneven distribution to aquifer depletion, subsidence and recurrent flooding, are rooted in governance models that overlook territorial specificity. Addressing them requires understanding how water, space and power shape access and risk. Interdependence refers to the relationship among communities, ecological systems and infrastructure. The disconnect between urban expansion and environmental processes has deepened vulnerability, showing the limits of technocratic approaches. More integrated models that combine local knowledge, shared governance and incremental technical components are therefore essential.

Santiago Arau, Aerial view of the Yuhualixqui volcano, Mexico City, 2023.
The dense urban fabric built on a former lake-bed meets the exposed slopes of the Yuhualixqui volcano – flat urbanisation abruptly stopping at uncompromising geology.

Colectivo C733, Interim water infrastructure in Yugüelito, Mexico City, 2023.
With no municipal water connection, residents rely on irregular deliveries, storing water in barrels, an interim system slated for formal connection to Mexico City's network in 2026.

The site

These dynamics became visible in Yuguelito, a self-managed community in the haeart of Iztapalapa that, after nearly 20 years, still lacks municipal services but maintains a powerful social organisation. People from neighbouring areas recall arriving in 2008 at a site used to dump waste, rubble and even bodies after the 1985 earthquake. They levelled the land with sand, divided plots, and built with whatever they could reuse: wood, tin, cardboard. Over the years, these first structures slowly became houses of block, reinforced slabs and waterproofed roofs. A landscape first defined by lakes and later by debris turned into a concrete crust through sustained collective labour.

This long history showed how material scarcity, self-construction and territorial care are intertwined, and a workshop on building with debris made this explicit. It began with an assembly, followed by interviews with fifteen families to understand their needs. The process ended with a hands-on session led by a master builder who demonstrated that nearly all materials from a house slated for demolition could be recovered and reused, grounding the project's vernacular approach and its commitment to incremental, cooperative transformation.

Jagüey emerged from years of research and community engagement. We opened our process to architects, ecologists, hydrologists, artists, officials and neighbours. Expertise was shared horizontally, turning interdependence into both a method and an outcome.

Colectivo C733, Community consultation in Yugüelito, Mexico City, 2025.
The presentation of the Jagüey project included open discussions with residents, and incorporation of local knowledge through direct dialogue and collaborative decision-making.

The immaterial gives meaning to the material. Society collectively defines what individuals cannot grasp: beauty, belonging and survival.

Interdependence means sharing infrastructure materially and symbolically, rooted in collective ecology, culture and social responsibility.

To go far, we must act together: whales and chinampas prove that collective care fosters vital interdependence.

Collective awareness begins with deep listening; it transforms relationships and activates interdependence.

State absence in peripheries is unquestionable. The question is whether it fosters collective care among residents.

Communal labor functions like microbial symbiosis. This collective logic extends to nutrition: grasshoppers are the sustainable future of urban food.

Art and architecture break boundaries, creating poetry, new questions and awkward silences that reshape meaning.

Mortality makes interdependence urgent. Art, accepting its own impermanence, demands our constant attention.

Reciprocity offsets extractivism's destruction. It is the key for future generations to learn how to live together.

Colectivo C733, Sketches of Interdependency, Mexico City, 2025.
Nine explorations of interdependency, presented through collages, based on three dinners held with interdisciplinary experts.

A riparian device

The proposal combines low-tech co-design with targeted technical components. These elements operate together across the neighbourhood, particularly around the viaducts and adjacent commons. Although the project does not execute infiltration wells directly, these spaces are conceived to host or connect to future infiltration points. Their integration helps define a territorial system where each component – *jagüey*, *apantle* (a traditional communal irrigation channel used to distribute water across agricultural and settlement landscapes), greywater channels and community spaces – reinforces the others.

Colectivo C733, Isometric view of the Jagüey at Yugüelito, Mexico City, 2025.
Isometric, aerial view of the *apantle* water conduit.

Technically, treated greywater moves through an open, gravity-fed sequence of basins, planted wetlands and mineral filters. Purification is visible at every step, echoing urban design studio Taller Capital founder Loreta Castro Reguera's argument that making water flows legible helps shift public culture.[3] The *jagüey* itself stores and regulates water through layers of compacted soil, clay, permeable aggregates and vegetation. This combines vernacular knowledge with ecological engineering to ensure durability.

3. Loreta Castro Reguera, *La imágen del agua en la ciudad*, Arquine, 2022.

Water is captured from the drainage system and channelled back into a biodigester tank, where solid waste is separated. The water then flows through an elevated ceramic pipe that reduces salinity, supports hydroponic plants, and irrigates the soil below via drip irrigation. From there it is directed to a nursery of *Araucaria* (conifer) seedlings arranged in two lateral rows, where water enters at the base and rises by capillary action. After passing through the nursery, excess water is discharged into an artificial wetland, the Jagüey, where it infiltrates the soil. The project's social value lies in making the water's journey visible and revaluing it, helping neighbours understand its potential to generate life and mitigate waste in an area with irregular water supply.

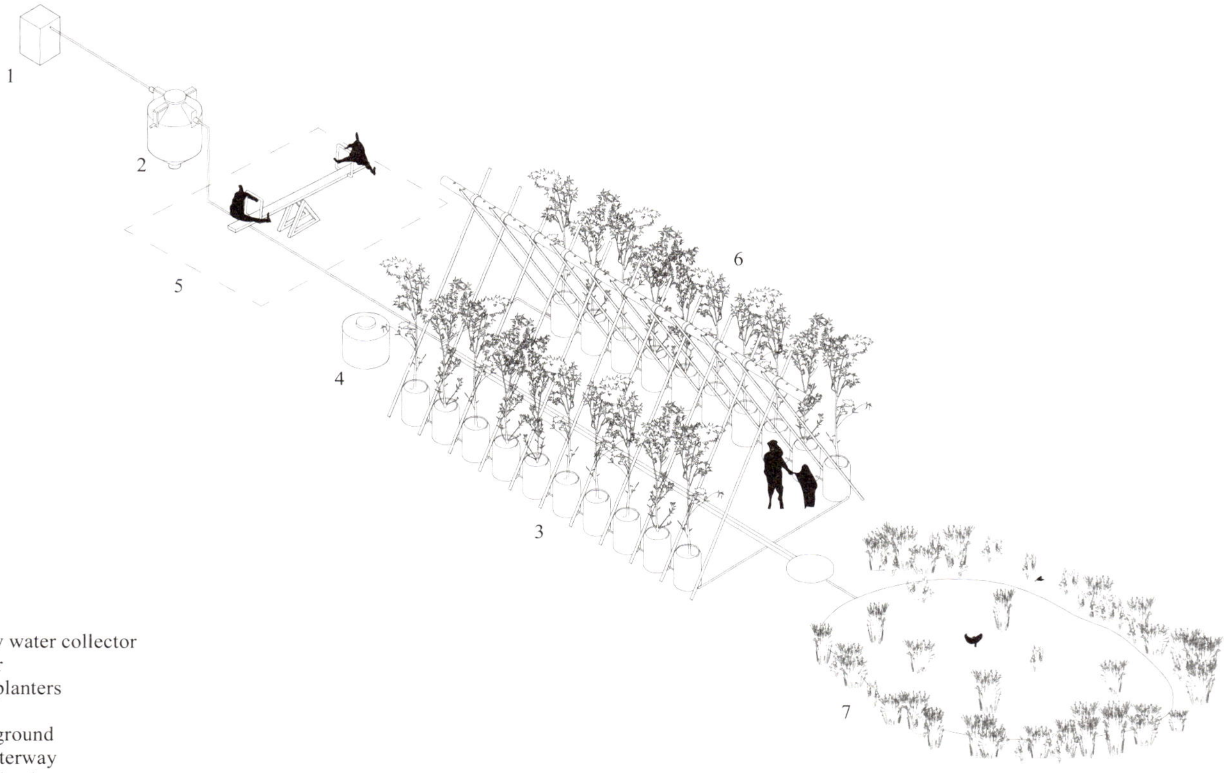

1. Community water collector
2. Biodigestor
3. Treatment planters
4 Deposit
5. Pump playground
6. Apantle waterway
7. Jagüey Wetland

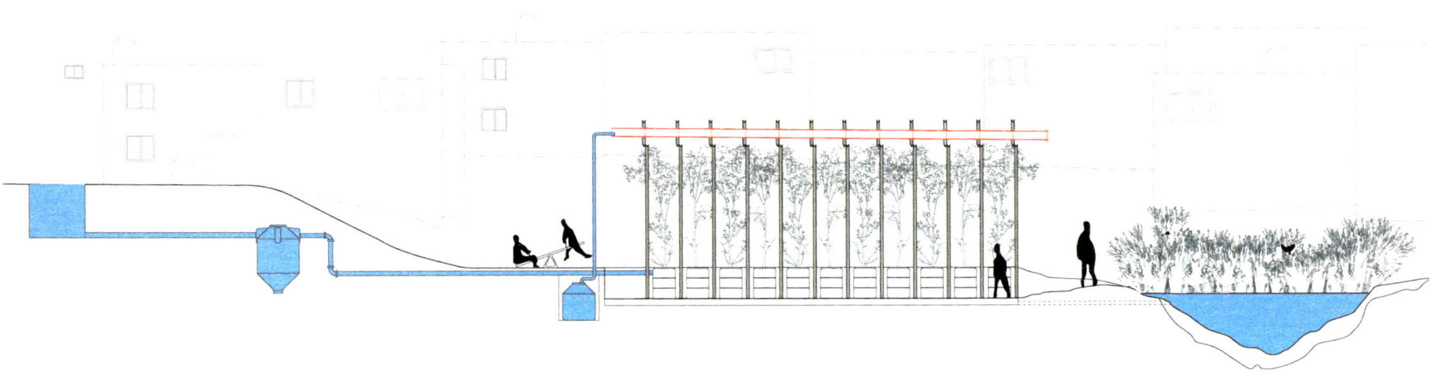

Colectivo C733, Diagram of the Apantle and Jagüey system, 2025, Mexico City.
Diagram of the *apantle–jagüey* system illustrating water capture, filtration, storage, reuse, and social integration, linking landscape, infrastructure, and daily life in Yugüelito.

Jagüey as a scalable strategy

Recycled concrete, salvaged brick and stones from local demolitions shape the architecture. Porous boundaries, shaded areas, native gardens and stepped ground create spaces for gathering and adaptation. The resulting place is open-ended: not quite a park or a plaza but a commons built through collective use. This commons depends on shared protocols that distribute responsibility among families and institutions. Families connecting to the system contribute greywater, participate in maintenance cycles, and take part in assemblies that define agreements for use and care.

Because the system uses low-energy and accessible materials, it can be transferred to other contexts with similar environmental and social challenges. The aim is to work with Mexico City authorities to create pathways for replication at different scales.

Jagüey therefore proposes an integrated view of water where infrastructure is inseparable from territory and community. In a city historically disconnected from its hydrological reality, the project imagines public space as a place of mutual support, where ecological restoration and social cohesion reinforce one another. It offers not only a device but a way of inhabiting water together.

Colectivo C733, Infiltration portrait: Yuguelito, Mexico City, 2025. Conceptual work illustrating the water-infiltration capacity of volcanic terrains such as Yuguelito.

Colectivo C733, Transversal section of the Jagüey, Mexico City, 2025. Transversal section of the *apantle-jagüey* system.

A conversation between Giovanna Borasi and the Congress curators on Becoming Interdependent and architecture's expanded responsibility

ARCHITECTURE SHOULD NOT CURE BUT CARE

CURATORS You have long approached architecture as a discipline embedded in social, ecological and political relations, engaging themes such as housing, health, migration and the everyday. At a moment when architectural autonomy appears increasingly untenable, what does the idea of 'interdependence' make newly visible for architecture today? How might it reshape the way architects understand responsibility, scale and the relationship between domestic life and planetary conditions?

GIOVANNA BORASI Architecture has always, or should always have been concerned with many things at once. That necessity is what differentiates it from art, which has the freedom to choose its concerns or whether it has any. An architectural response to a social issue must take into account many bodies, many factors, many scales simultaneously.

Today we know much more about the Earth, about our bodies, about what generates environmental crisis. Interdependency is not simply necessary; it is the only way to approach a project. It compels us to understand long-term consequences. A housing project is not only housing. It intersects with environmental impact, political structures, economic systems and real-estate development.

The difficulty is that these entanglements are now fully visible. When a house lacks a balcony, the consequences are not only spatial but social and psychological. Covid revealed that proximity, access to outside space, and mental health are deeply connected. We are more aware of how even the smallest intervention participates in much larger systems.

Interdependence requires that architects do not minimise their role. A project may be small, but it belongs to planetary conditions. This awareness expands responsibility beyond architects to mayors, developers and institutions. The architectural act is never isolated.

C Much architectural thinking still privileges completion, efficiency and permanence, even though the conditions in which architecture operates demand openness, adaptation and long-term engagement. How might time be understood not simply as the background of architectural production but as an active design tool that allows buildings, systems and institutions to evolve, adapt and remain open to negotiation and change?

GB The equilibrium between specificity and long-term adaptability remains difficult. Older architecture can often be transformed precisely because it was not overly specialised. By contrast, highly specific buildings can become obsolete. Shopping malls are a global example. At the same time, in Montreal, for instance, churches have been converted into housing, which shows the value of openness to transformation.

Time is also an urban question. What we appreciate in historical cities is stratification, layers of meaning accumulated over time. Contemporary masterplanning often fixes a project at a single moment and leaves no space for verification or adjustment. If time is integrated into the design process, projects can respond to residents, evolve with use, and adapt to shifting conditions.

Yet architecture frequently serves real-estate development, where immediacy and short return periods dominate. In that context, time becomes a constraint rather than a design tool.

This tension between immediate impact and long-term thinking leads to a fundamental question: what does architecture make possible? Once the core question is understood, the appropriate response may not necessarily be a building at all. In 'The Other Architect', a 2015 exhibition and a related publication by the CCA,[1] this idea was central: architecture does not only resolve a given set of problems; it *establishes what requires attention today*.

1. *The Other Architect: Another Way of Building*, Canadian Centre for Architecture (CCA)/Spector Books, 2015.

Cedric Price's 1973 proposal for spreading architecture education formats, called AA/AD/Polyark, illustrated this clearly. Rather than proposing a monumental university building, he imagined a bus system connecting institutions: a network, a route, a recording device. In this case, time, movement and adaptability became the architectural response.

Cedric Price and Peter Murray, Poster for the AA/AD/Polyark Bus Tour, 1973. Printed by Basement Graphics.

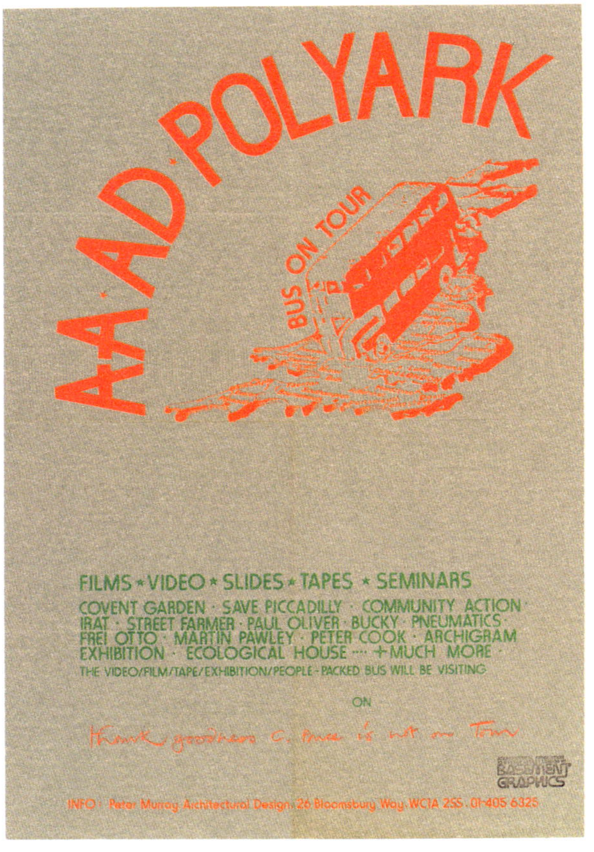

To design with time, then, is to accept uncertainty and broaden our understanding of what architecture can be. It suggests that architecture can operate through systems, relationships and evolving structures, not only fixed construction. This approach aligns architectural practice with inquiry, with responsiveness and with an expanded set of tools, rather than only conventional building.

C Care is often framed in architecture as maintenance, something secondary, reactive or subsequent to design. Yet many contemporary practices suggest that care can be generative, shaping how spaces support encounter, belonging and collective responsibility. How might rethinking care as a design practice transform architecture's political agency and its capacity to engage with everyday life?

GIOVANNA BORASI Care has often been associated with maintaining architecture itself. The question now is how architecture can care for its inhabitants and the city.

When architecture attempts to cure, it risks becoming instrumental. In the CCA's 2011 exhibition 'Imperfect Health',[2] we examined how architecture was mistakenly taken as 'correctional', for the obesity crisis, for example, as absurdly as to hide elevators to encourage stair use. This presumes a norm and excludes certain bodies. Architecture should not cure; it should care.

2. Giovanna Borasi and Mirko Zardini (eds), *Imperfect Health: The Medicalization of Architecture*, CCA/Lars Müller, 2011.

Giovanna Borasi and Mirko Zardini / CCA, 'Imperfect Health: The Medicalization of Architecture', installation view, Canadian Centre for Architecture, Montreal, 2011–12.

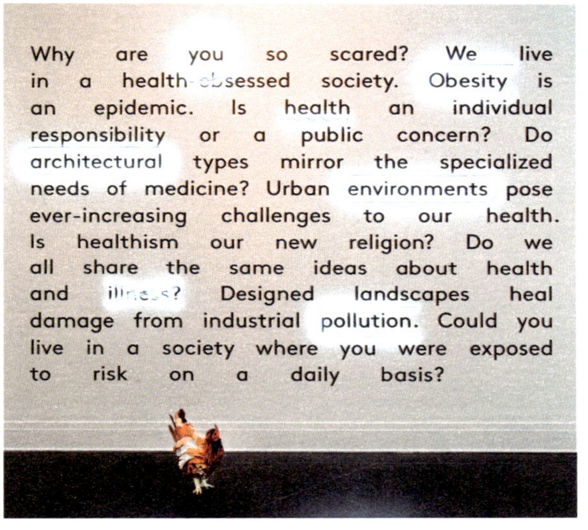

Care is relational. It concerns what you see outside your window, how you transition from the sidewalk to your home, whether you encounter others. Architecture has progressively eliminated opportunities for small encounters in the name of efficiency or real-estate pressures. Lobbies and mailrooms once facilitated everyday interaction.

A generative understanding of care means creating opportunities rather than prescribing behaviour. Architects cannot determine how spaces will be used, but they can establish conditions for shared responsibility and belonging. Care becomes political when it moves from individual assistance to collective implication.

C The Research by Design led by MAIO, Pol Esteve Castelló and Care. challenges the idea that care is primarily a response to need, instead foregrounding pleasure, desire and embodied joy through everyday rituals such as cooking, eating, dancing or celebrating. What happens when these activities are treated not as informal or peripheral, but as spatial practices capable of sustaining collective life and interdependence?

GIOVANNA BORASI If the architect is understood as a community builder rather than merely a builder of bricks, facilitating collective life becomes fundamental. Community cannot be imposed; conditions must be created for it to emerge.

Practices such as cooking, dancing or celebrating generate exchange and knowledge. Historically, they have been considered informal or secondary, yet they form networks of mutual support.

Reconsidering the kitchen illustrates this shift. While the Frankfurt Kitchen prioritised efficiency of movement, reimagining it as a place of connection and conversation, it acquires an entirely different spatial meaning.

As the investigation by the Chair of Architecture and Care at ETH Zürich claims, care should not be structured as a one-directional relationship between caregiver and recipient. Collective caring implies shared starting points where pleasure and joy are integral. Ageing populations are frequently treated as passive recipients of care, yet autonomy and participation extend well-being.

Pilot projects demonstrate that when elderly residents maintain autonomy while engaging in collective activities, longevity increases. Architecture contributes to this by enabling rituals that sustain interdependence.

C Recent architectural approaches have begun to reconsider infrastructures such as water, land and energy systems not simply as technical services but as shared civic resources. What possibilities does this shift from infrastructure as service to infrastructure as commons open for architectural practice? How do you think a proposal such as Colectivo 733's Research by Design might reshape ideas of responsibility, governance and care in contexts of ecological vulnerability and social inequality?

GB Infrastructures such as water or land form the basis of collective life. The work of Colectivo 733 approaches these as shared civic resources rather than purely technical systems. At their Ecoparque Bacalar in Mexico, for example, a modest wooden structure defines public access to a lagoon increasingly threatened by privatisation. It allows ecological regeneration while affirming collective use. The intervention appears fragile yet becomes powerful through the relationships it establishes, between inhabitants, species and the territory.

The scale is significant. The project seems small but addresses systemic issues. It seems temporary, but at the same time it becomes very difficult to dismantle because it reshapes territorial meaning. Fragility and power coexist.

Infrastructure as commons rearticulates responsibility. It connects ecological processes, governance and everyday life. Architecture operates not only as a physical answer but through precise interventions that activate interdependence.

C Several contemporary practices are shifting attention away from architecture as a self-contained object and towards the everyday systems and rituals that sustain collective life, through food production and distribution, shared spaces of gathering or the negotiation of common resources across urban and non-urban contexts. In these approaches, such as the ones Plan Común and Assemble are proposing, interdependence is not an abstract principle but something enacted through daily practices, cooperation and shared responsibility. What can architecture learn from these forms of situated interdependence, where cooperation, reciprocity and collective responsibility are enacted through daily practices rather than through abstract principles?

GB Food and common space are essential to collective life. However, such practices require engaged communities.

In Montreal, back lanes have been transformed into shared gardens and play areas. The municipality provides materials, while residents commit to maintenance. Children play, elderly neighbours participate and collective life takes shape.

These models reveal reciprocity between administration and citizens. Architecture alone cannot create community; it must collaborate with policy and social will.

For practices like those proposed by Plan Común and Assemble, the question is how projects situate themselves within communities while also helping to generate them. Interdependence operates as a reciprocal process.

C In a global context architectural imaginaries are shaped not only by what becomes visible, but also by deeper structures of knowledge production: by who defines the problems, whose expertise is recognised, and which histories, material practices and ways of inhabiting space are legitimised. Within a field still largely organised around Western-centred epistemologies, many spatial practices remain marginal not because they are peripheral, but because they operate according to different logics, temporalities and forms of authorship.

Architectural institutions, congresses and exhibitions play a powerful role in shaping how knowledge circulates, whose expertise is recognised and which histories become visible. How can institutions such as the CCA engage with postcolonial perspectives while avoiding the risk of turning these debates into fixed categories or institutional rhetoric?

GB The CCA's archives reflect a past reality of dominant histories: Western, male, often Anglophone. Recognising this, we developed the 'c/o' programme, collaborating with curators in Tokyo, Buenos Aires, Lisbon and Dakar, for a few years in each city. Rather than exporting our perspective, we seek to learn from local conditions.

CCA c/o Dakar, 'How the École d'Architecture et d'Urbanisme de Dakar Imagined Senegalese Modernities' symposium, Dakar, Senegal, 2024.

In Buenos Aires, inflation reaching 120 per cent reshapes architectural temporality. Long-term planning becomes uncertain. Architects adapt their practice accordingly. Sharing this experience challenges assumptions held in North America.

Engaging postcolonial perspectives requires allowing institutions to be inhabited by other ways of thinking. The risk lies in homogenising diverse practices into Western presentation formats. True plurality demands coherence with different logics and temporalities.

C Housing and domestic space are often treated as neutral or universal, yet they are deeply shaped by assumptions about gender, sexuality, family and care. In light of changing forms of kinship, work and care, how can architecture rethink domestic space so that it supports more diverse ways of living together, beyond the normative model of the nuclear family?

GIOVANNA BORASI

Housing models often assume a nuclear family structure. Yet lifecycles and kinship models have transformed. Architecture has not kept pace. This falling-out-of-step was the core observation behind the 2021 CCA exhibition and book 'A Section of Now: Social Norms and Rituals as Sites for Architectural Intervention'.[3] The project examined works not only in architecture but also in art, real estate, industrial design, communications, etc., that highlighted where architectural thought and practice were lagging behind societal changes and offered solutions, often quite experimental ones, or critiques.

3. Giovanna Borasi (ed.), *A Section of Now: Social Norms and Rituals as Sites for Architectural Intervention*, CCA/Spector Books, 2011.

Giovanna Borasi / CCA, 'A Section of Now: Social Norms and Rituals as Sites for Architectural Intervention', installation view, Canadian Centre for Architecture, Montreal, 2021–22.

We continue to construct apartments for a heteronormative couple with two children, despite changing employment patterns, longevity, fertility treatments and ownership structures.

Interdependence requires acknowledging diverse bodies and trajectories. Domestic space should support shared care and collective responsibility rather than reinforcing rigid norms.

C Editorial practices, through acts of selection, framing and omission, are among the most powerful ways in which institutions shape how architectural knowledge circulates and whom it addresses. Museums, schools and cultural organisations shape architectural discourse through acts of selection, framing and omission. How can institutions take responsibility for this editorial power while still creating space for disagreement, plurality and conflicting perspectives within architectural culture?

GB Editorial practice is inherently selective. Institutions operate within dependencies. Responsibility begins with recognising this and allowing space for disagreement.

Congresses and biennials are powerful devices. They do not merely reflect discourse; they shape it. They generate agitation and collective attention.

Plurality is essential, but it involves risk. Not all actors share commitments to interdependence. Some remain driven by spectacle or profit. The challenge is to extend discourse beyond those already aligned.

To curate is to remain in the complexity of relation, and to invite others into it.

C Across many regions, the consolidation of right-wing and authoritarian political forces has increasingly shaped how societies imagine identity, territory and belonging, often through narratives that simplify complexity, instrumentalise fear, and frame dependence as weakness. These shifts have tangible spatial consequences, influencing housing policies, borders, infrastructures and the everyday organisation of life.

In this context, what risks do authoritarian simplifications pose to ideas of interdependence, care and collective responsibility within architectural culture? And how can architectural practices and institutions remain attentive to these pressures while sustaining dialogue and complexity in increasingly polarised societies?

GB Unfortunately, what we are experiencing today is not new. But maybe this time it is on a bigger global scale.

This is why an institution like the CCA collects ideas, practices and projects from the past. You might not find your answers there, but you might understand the answers others have given to similar questions. 'Architecture in Uniform', Jean-Louis Cohen's research project, 2011 CCA exhibition and publication,[4] looked exactly at this: what architects did or did not do in an era dominated by Nazism and Fascism, and how their ideas or oppositions not only shaped practice in those years but also defined the outcomes we are still operating with. Architects, or responsible architects, should have an ethical stand and the confidence that architecture at large – built and non-built – could help to allow better conditions to prevail. Right now, we observe an increasing number of practitioners turning to design policies and laws as a way to have an impact at a systemic level, as we see, for example, in B+'s work with HouseEurope! to campaign for the reform of European legislation to promote renovation and disincentivise demolition and rebuilding, a change which aside from having great environmental benefits could mean a paradigm shift in the discipline of architecture in Europe.[5] That is the beauty of architecture: it is an art that through dialogue with society could take the form that society needs.

4. Jean-Louis Cohen, *Architecture in Uniform: Designing and Building for the Second World War*, CCA/Hazan, 2011.

5. B+'s work on the HouseEurope! campaign was explored in *To Build Law*, the second chapter of the CCA documentary film/exhibition trilogy 'Groundwork' (2024–25).

Jean-Louis Cohen, 'Architecture in Uniform: Designing and Building for the Second World War', installation view, Canadian Centre for Architecture, Montreal, 2011.

Curators

SPATIAL POLITICS FOR THE COMMONS

Co-design

Decolonising practices

Gender policies

Mutual care

Housing as commons

Politics of space

Becoming

Architecture should not be elitist, and the persistence of this idea must be dismantled. The practice of space has always belonged to the ordinary, to the ways we dwell, share rooms, organise care and sustain life. To reclaim architecture is to return it to this common ground, to recognise it not as an abstract discipline or a means of control, but as a communal condition, socially produced and continuously changed through use, time, negotiation and everyday life. This is a deep political condition grounded in the collective right to appropriate and transform the environments we inhabit after our hearts' desire.[1] The idea that architecture could be neutral, purely technical or autonomous has been fundamentally challenged for a long time, proving that hidden regimes of control always act behind the mask of impartiality.[2] The planetary crises of our time – environmental, social and political – make clear that every built form is an act of positioning. Each project expresses values and organises relationships: between people, between species, between bodies and institutions. Architecture is political not only because it embodies ideologies, but because it structures the material conditions through which life unfolds.

1. David Harvey, *Rebel Cities: From the Right to the City to the Urban Revolution*, Verso, 2012.
2. Henri Lefebvre, *The Production of Space* [1974], trans. Donald Nicholson-Smith, Blackwell, 1991.

To practice today is to work within fragile and precarious systems. These systems – ecological, economic and social – are not failures to be corrected but assemblages and entanglements to be engaged.[3] Fragility reveals the networks that sustain us, making visible the interdependent relations through which human (and more-than-human) life persists under conditions of capitalist precarity.[4] Yet precarity is not equally distributed: it is structured across geographies shaped by extraction, dispossession, gender and colonial legacies, where spatial control organises differential exposure to harm and survival. It produces what can be understood as necropolitical conditions in which some lives are systematically exposed to death.[5] Designing within this condition means shifting from stability to coexistence, from spectacle to solidarity, and from isolated objects to 'interconnected systems'.[6] Practices such as cooperative housing, urban commons and shared infrastructures show that alternatives can be built in the present, fostering collective governance, economies of care and cooperative ways of living. Yet they operate within the systems they seek to transform, negotiating market pressures, institutional frameworks and regulatory constraints. Their relevance lies in this tension, in their capacity to act both within and against existing conditions.

3. Anna Lowenhaupt Tsing, *The Mushroom at the End of the World: On the Possibility of Life in Capitalist Ruins*, Princeton University Press, 2015.

4. Judith Butler, *Precarious Life: The Powers of Mourning and Violence*, Verso, 2004.

5. Achille Mbembe, *Necropolitics*, Duke University Press, 2019.

6. Keller Easterling, *Medium Design: Knowing How to Work on the World*, Verso, 2021.

Across different geographies and scales, a set of practices exposes how space has long been used as an instrument of control, extraction and environmental violence. These works reveal territories marked by invisible toxicities, infrastructures

(1) Samia Henni, 'Performing Colonial Toxicity' exhibition, Framer Framed, Amsterdam, The Netherlands, 2023.

(2) Malkit Shoshan, *BLUE: Architecture of UN Peacekeeping Missions*, Venice Architecture Biennale, Italy, 2016.

(3) Estudio Teddy Cruz + Fonna Forman, Santuario Frontera, San Diego-Tijuana border, 2023.

(4) Rural Urban Framework, Rethinking the Collective, Shizhong County, Fujian, China, 2019.

(5) RMA Architects, Visitor Centre, Chhatrapati Shivaji Maharaj Vastu Sangrahalaya (CSMVS) museum, Mumbai, India, 2011.

that operate under the guise of neutrality while reorganising power, and border conditions where spatial systems enforce exclusion. To work against these legacies is not only to denounce them, but to reconfigure the ways in which knowledge is produced, situated and shared. (1, 2, 3)

Other approaches shift attention towards the infrastructures that sustain life. They operate through distributed forms of support where care is not centralised but embedded in everyday environments, from therapeutic landscapes and spaces of recovery to civic frameworks that prioritise mental and social well-being. (4, 5) These practices understand that architecture participates in broader economic and ecological systems, and that transforming them requires collective forms of responsibility capable of reorganising how resources, attention and value circulate. (6, 7, 8, 9, 10, 11, 12, 13, 14)

This shift is particularly evident in new forms of inhabitation that challenge the isolation of the

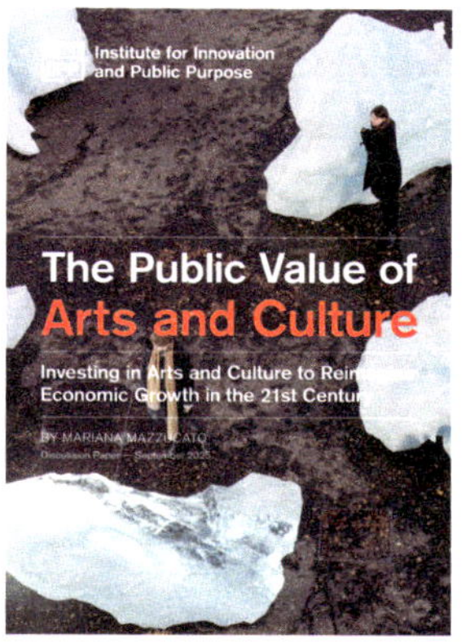

(6) Mariana Mazzucato, *The Public Value of Arts and Culture: Investing in Arts and Culture to Reimagine Economic Growth in the 21st Century*, 2025.

(7) MAIO, Nursery: 1306 Plants for Timisoara, Romania, 2023.

(8) Giovanna Borasi / CCA, 'Imperfect Health: The Medicalization of Architecture', installation view, Canadian Centre for Architecture (CCA), Montreal, 2011.

(9) Colectivo C733, Tapachula Station, Tapachula de Córdova y Ordoñez, Mexico, 2022.

(10) Estudio Herreros, Trosten Sauna, Oslo, Norway, 2024.

(11) Colectivo C733, Ecoparque Bacalar, Bacalar, Mexico, 2023.

(12) Román Meyer Falcón, Balneario Las Ventanas, El Colomo, Colima, Mexico, 2023.

domestic unit. Housing is reimagined as a shared condition, where intermediate spaces, collective thresholds and adaptable frameworks allow for multiple forms of living together. Rather than fixed typologies, these projects propose open systems that can be appropriated over time, enabling communities to construct their own modes of coexistence while resisting the reduction of housing to a financial asset. In this context, public institutions, policy frameworks and design practices play a crucial role in fostering forms of living that move beyond market-driven models, enabling more equitable and sustainable ways of inhabiting the city. (15, 16, 17, 18, 19)

Within these transformations, it becomes necessary to confront how spatial organisation has historically reinforced unequal distributions of labour, visibility and agency. Since the Industrial Revolution, the separation between productive and reproductive spaces – the division of work

(13) Raquel Rolnik, *Urban Warfare: Housing Under the Empire of Finance*, 2019.

(14) Elizabeth Añaños, Mayuriaga School, Plan Selva Project, Mayuriaga, Morona District, Peru, 2019.

(15) Peris + Toral Arquitectes, Social Atrium, Barcelona, Spain, 2022.

(16) EMI Architekt*innen, The Well-Tempered House, Regensdorf, Switzerland, 2025.

(17) Josep M. Borrell / IMPSOL AMB, 136 social housing units by H arquitectes, Gavà, Spain, 2022.

(18) Andreas Hofer / IBA '27, Neckarspinnerei neighbourhood by Rustler Schriever Architekten, Wendlingen am Neckar, Internationale Bauausstellung Stuttgart, Germany, 2027.

(19) Silvia Hofer / Wohnfonds Wien, Wald, wir kommen! (Forest, Here We Come!), Währing, Vienna, Austria, 2024.

and family life – has marginalised housewives' unpaid labour as domestic slavery, raising and sustaining the male workforce through the perverse virtue of love and care.[7] To design otherwise is to dilute production and reproduction, to redistribute proximity, to make visible what has been hidden, and to acknowledge that bodies, identities and forms of life are not neutral but situated within structures that must be actively resignified. (20, 21, 22)

(20) Yasmeen Lari, Zero Carbon Cultural Centre, Makli, Pakistan, 2016.

7. Silvia Federici, *Caliban and the Witch: Women, the Body and Primitive Accumulation*, Autonomedia, 2004.

Some practices redefine how architecture is produced, or co-produced. Design is not treated as a singular act of authorship, but as a negotiated process where multiple agents participate in shaping space over time. Through collective decision-making, open-ended construction and iterative development, architecture becomes a platform for engagement and participation rather than a finished object. What is built is less a form than a frame-

(21) MAIO, 40 social housing units, Sant Feliu de Llobregat, Spain, 2022–23.

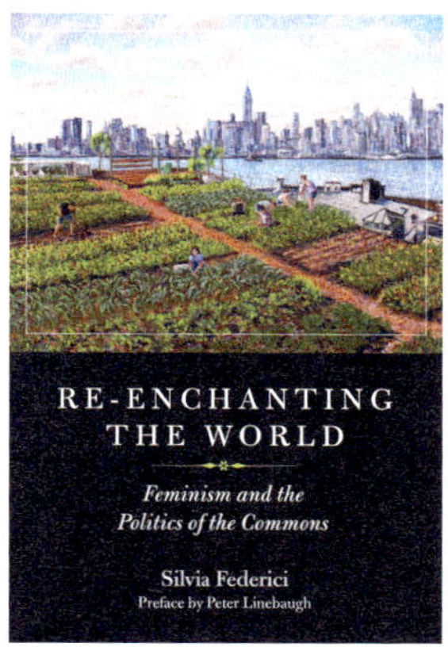

(22) Silvia Federici, *Re-enchanting the World. Feminism and the Politics of the Commons*, 2018.

(23) Assemble and Granby Four Streets CLT, Granby Winter Garden, Liverpool, UK, 2019.

(25) Lacol, La Borda cooperative housing, Barcelona, Spain, 2018.

(24) Plan Común, Maison Commune, Montevideo, Uruguay, 2026.

work, capable of evolving through use, conflict and adaptation. (23, 24, 25, 26)

'Becoming Interdependent' is not a universal model nor a call for an abstract ideology. It suggests an operative, situated framework for engaging with complexity, acknowledging mutual dependencies amongst diverse forms of agency. The tension between individual desires and freedoms and the collective rights and aspirations of communities is at the heart of its interplay (27, 28, 29). Conflict, negotiation, empathy, care, reciprocity, solidarity, play and pleasure emerge as forms through which interdependence is enacted. If architecture embraces these conditions, creating spaces where people can rely on one another, it can contribute to repairing the fragile systems that sustain life. In doing so, it can reclaim its fundamental role, not as an elite discipline, but as a shared practice rooted in the common.

(26) Clauss Kahl Merz Atelier, Lyse-Lotte, Lysbüchel Süd, Basel, Switzerland, 2023.

(27) Gehl Architects, Times Square transformation, New York, 2009.

(28) Raumlabor, Plastische demokratie / third space, Düsseldorf, Germany, 2021.

(29) Teco Studio, Kasugadai Center Center, Kanagawa, Japan, 2022.

Waterborne absorption fluids
Pr_20_31_01_96
Waterborne absorption fluids
Pr_20_31_01_96
Cavity
ORCHAMP
WEATHER STATION
Kodak

Waterless toilets
Pr_40_20_93_85
Kodak

Becoming Hyper-conscious

'A hyperobject is a thing so vast in both temporal and spatial terms that we can only see slices of it at a time; hyperobjects come in and out of phase with human time; they end up "contaminating" everything, if we find ourselves inside them.'

Timothy Morton, *Being Ecological*, 2018

What actions can arise from a deeper awareness of global and local interplays?

In our daily lives we consciously or unconsciously traverse a vast array of networks of interrelations. They are so big and implacable that we can barely see them. These phenomena operate at a higher level of awareness, escaping usual perception yet crucially conditioning human and more-than-human life. Baconian scientific reasoning, based on objectified facts and linear certainty, limits our capacity to understand them.

A new planetary contract depends on our capacity to orient ourselves towards – even if we cannot fully grasp them – planetary matters of concern: the climate crisis, loss of biodiversity, capitalistic abuse, the accumulation of legislation, and worldwide phenomena like the internet and algorithmic rule in the form of AI, among other huge entities. These concerns present challenges at a global scale with direct local, everyday impacts.

'Becoming Hyper-conscious' calls for a deeper, immanent awareness – beyond data accumulation and critical description – as an ongoing, collective effort to inhabit and compose with entanglement, one that remains incomplete and sensitive to uncertainty, enabling us to carefully and projectively transform our worlds.

Marina Otero Verzier

HYPER-CONSCIOUSNESS: RE-ORIENTATION IN THE AGE OF OVERLOAD

We live in an environment of uninterrupted updates. Of bleeps coming from screens animated by satellite signals and algorithmic feeds. As we scroll up and down sleek surfaces, we struggle to make sense of an overwhelming abundance of information. Conflicting facts are simultaneously confirmed and denied, compelling audiences (now users) to continuously scrutinise information, distinguish signal from noise, and test their capacity to filter and trust. This overload is not accidental; it is structural; it is designed, with consequences manifesting across social, political and environmental realms. It also shapes how we imagine, inhabit and practise architecture.

The UIA World Congress of Architects 2026 Barcelona does not attempt to ease this condition; rather, it intensifies it. Through six interconnected research lines – More-than-human, Circular, Embodied, Interdependent, Hyper-conscious, Attuned – and a range of formats including plenaries, keynotes, panels, duos, trios and open forums, it generates deliberate density. It orchestrates an encounter with the excess that defines contemporary life. To start with, it is impossible to absorb the entire programme when sessions run concurrently. However, this impossibility constitutes the terrain in which we operate and make sense of the world. The Congress thus serves as a rehearsal for navigation and action.

Let us focus on the research line 'Becoming Hyper-conscious'. The field of philosophy has long sought to clarify what it means to think, to perceive and to exist. As certainty about the nature of consciousness remains elusive, the very effort to think, to be conscious, attentive and ethically awake, I would argue, should already be understood as an achievement. That's why the prefix 'hyper' initially appears to me as a disturbance, suggesting the risk of another instance in which architecture amplifies its own rhetoric. One might suspect a trace of disciplinary ego in the aspiration to become hyper-anything.

However, rather than dismissing it as mere inflation, can this intensification be productive? If 'hyper' signifies heightened relational awareness (an ability to perceive the distributed systems, technological mediations and planetary entanglements within which architecture operates), then it may indicate not arrogance, but urgency.

Orientation

The conceptual framework of Becoming Hyper-conscious emerges from the work of Timothy Morton, and particularly his notion of the 'hyperobject',[1] which refers to entities so massively distributed in time and space that they exceed direct human perception: climate change, global capitalism, nuclear waste, the internet. Hyperobjects are viscous, nonlocal and temporally extended. They are everywhere and nowhere. We cannot step outside them; we are surrounded and penetrated by them. We encounter them through fragments: a drought, a broken supply chain, the residual heat coming from a server farm.

1. See Timothy Morton, *Hyperobjects: Philosophy and Ecology After the End of the World*, University of Minnesota Press, 2013.

Architecture is within hyperobjects. They are the medium within which design occurs. Therefore, if we take Morton's hyperobjects as a loose and generative framework, a hyper-conscious architectural practice might be understood as an attempt to operate within systems that exceed comprehension, to act from within something we cannot see in its entirety. Hyperobjects are not only large, they destabilise habitual scales of thought and blur temporal limits, both human and non-human, biological and computational.

Take, for instance, climate change. It unfolds over centuries and milliseconds, melting glaciers and triggering sensors that simultaneously adjust thermostats. Whereas architecture is implicated as a mediator of scale, architects confront the impossibility of engaging these dynamics as a whole. What remains possible is the task of orienting among the fragments we can grasp and, at the same time, among the exposure to a deluge of data that does not necessarily translate into more well-informed decisions or more precise knowledge.

Hyper-consciousness, we could argue, becomes a practice of calibration: Where to look? What to look for? Which signals matter? Which patterns are structural and which are episodic? Which fragments reveal systemic relations? The aim is not to know everything but to be able to orient within this complexity.

Today, many turn to artificial intelligence systems to filter this complexity. As hyperobjects transcend human perception, machines promise to help make sense of them. We trust synthetic intelligences with this task even if, by training, they are not neutral. Machine-learning models detect patterns inside cascading datasets on a scale no human could process. They find correlations in climate models, urban mobility flows and military intelligence, and feed them to predictive algorithms. Sensors detect movement and air quality; surveillance networks monitor public space; algorithms allocate mortgages, assess insurance risk and potential romantic matches, control autonomous vehicles, curate social media streams and generate architectural proposals. Together, they contribute to a decision-making infrastructure that is not exclusively human.

Once the idea of the centred human observer has been destabilised, architecture has no option but to recognise that design decisions are entangled with planetary processes and scales that exceed human cognition. Architecture, after all, has always mediated between the scales of body and territory, interior and exterior, individual and collective. Yet, when we zoom out of the scale of a building, a work of architecture operates as a distributed system that includes energy grids, data infrastructures, carbon cycles, material economies, and the human and non-human lives bound up within them. From this perspective, to be hyper-conscious as an architect is to nurture the capacity to think of these scales, cycles and economies, and, crucially, to attend to them, without being paralysed.

This requires resisting two temptations: the fantasy of total control, that is, the belief that humans can master these systems through technical sophistication; and the surrender to fatalism, or the conviction that action is meaningless. Between these extremes lies a third position that involves relational awareness, attunment and situated intervention that does not attempt to dissolve complexity.

To be hyper-conscious is to identify directions and leverage points within systems too vast to fully comprehend, too powerful to confront alone, too intricate when viewed from a distance, and to act within them without presuming mastery. It also entails recognising the necessity of collective practice and of forging unlikely alliances amid uncertainty. And, of course, to take responsibility for the distributed consequences (or externalities) of design and the forms of violence it carries. Architecture has always been an instrument of power, operating through systems of governance that regulate the distribution of rights and belonging: organise space, allocate resources, and produce regimes of inclusion and exclusion.

Hyper-conscious design requires confronting these forms of violence. It asks us to acknowledge our complicity within systems of power while still proposing alternatives, particularly in fields where design contributes to inequality even as it claims ethical commitments.

Situated nonlocality

Eyal Weizman's works make these tensions explicit. Through Forensic Architecture, Weizman mobilises architectural expertise to expose state and corporate violence. The agency has developed spatial methodologies through counter-mapping, modelling and open-source investigation. Their work in Gaza, for example, traces patterns of annihilation, turning diverse sources of data into a spatial argument that can be mobilised as evidence in court, NGO and UN contexts. Architecture is, in this context, both a vehicle of violence and a means of its exposure. This dual role complicates the discipline's ethical position, as its tools may either reinforce or contest power structures.

Yet, Forensic Architecture's work is grounded less in design solutions than in increasing resolution, that is, intelligibility. Their investigations unfold in environments where information is often controlled and concealed, requiring the laborious identification and aggregation of distinct sources, datasets and testimonies into spatio-temporal assemblages. Buildings, cities and landscapes are treated as political sensors, as witnesses and archives in which events are inscribed. Using multimedia techniques, these fragile constructs are modelled with precision yet in an accessible manner to facilitate their inclusion in forums that demand accountability.

Each case requires the development of new investigative techniques, evidence-gathering methods, representation and dissemination, and this often involves using technologies that are not neutral. Consequently, Forensic Architecture's models do not merely represent reality; they actively produce it – a reality grounded in ruins, in fragments painstakingly gathered in an unequal struggle against hegemonies that control access to resolution and the monopoly of truth.

One might ask: Does becoming hyper-conscious necessarily involve machine mediation, even those used by the powers whose actions are under investigation? Forensic Architecture's work makes the answer explicit: while technology helps gather and put together a piece of evidence, it is the collaboration with communities exposed to violence, negligence or state persecution, and the organisation of public forums – whether courts, media platforms, public events or museums – that ultimately help to generate solidarity, shift public opinion and create change.

Not by chance, Forensic Architecture's work in Gaza is one of the two commissioned Research by Design investigations for the Becoming Hyper-conscious section of the Congress. The other is Brandlhuber+, b+ and HouseEurope!. Together, these two projects materialise the Congress's ambitions through practice. They provide structural poles: one working through evidence as spatial counter-power, the other through law as design medium. Their juxtaposition foregrounds the multiple realms of architectural agency, and social and environmental justice, that extend beyond the human.

HouseEurope! understands law as the architecture that shapes everyday life. This proposition reframes legislation, zoning and regulation not as external constraints to design, but as design media in their own right. Earlier projects in the 'legislating architecture' trajectory operated tactically, exploiting loopholes and reinterpretations to produce alternative architectures from within the system. HouseEurope! marks a shift: from working within legal frameworks to intervening in their production.

By relocating architectural agency into policy-writing, advocacy and the European Citizens' Initiative mechanism, HouseEurope! challenges the assumption that architecture's primary field of action is the building itself. Architects operate in a context where financialisation determines housing long before a wall is drawn. Today the built environment is structured primarily through legal and financial instruments (often hyperobjects that resist scrutiny) rather than architectural drawings. What is at stake is not simply legal literacy, as architects have long been involved in planning processes, regulatory frameworks and compliance regimes. In fact, legal instruction remains part of professional qualification in many countries.

Rather, HouseEurope! reframes architectural work. From this perspective, a hyper-conscious architectural practice means identifying where power is operationalised and intervening precisely there. It involves acting at targeted points even when broader control is lacking, assuming financial and legal mechanisms are often structurally engineered to evade scrutiny. Architects, therefore, should not be positioned only as interpreters or enforcers of legal frameworks, but as the community's mediators and political actors, capable of redefining these frameworks through specific, coordinated actions.

Both Forensic Architecture and HouseEurope! deal with systems that extend across distributed networks while grounding themselves in specific territories. When these systems touch the ground, however, they encounter that which exceeds them. Attending to this excess[2] requires making space for what cannot be fully translated into infrastructural or computational terms.

2. The notion of 'excess' draws on the work of the anthropologist Marisol de la Cadena, who uses the term to describe entities, relations and worlds that cannot be fully translated into modern epistemic frameworks. See Marisol de la Cadena, *Earth Beings: Ecologies of Practice Across Andean Worlds*, Duke University Press, 2015.

Collective celebration

In addition to the investigations conducted by Forensic Architecture and HouseEurope!, the Congress features two workshops that facilitate situated actions within Barcelona, the host city. While the Research by Design projects engage with legal and evidentiary systems, the workshops focus on remapping and restaging the urban environment.

Ibiye Camp's workshop, Revised Cartographies, investigates the persistent presence of colonial systems in urban space. Through expanded forms of architectural representation, Camp proposes a rereading of spaces such as the Columbus Monument, Plaça Idrissa Diallo, Port Vell and Kumasi Market to expose and reinterpret the flows connecting Barcelona to West and Central Africa, past and present. Camp has long reflected on the power of representation. To represent is to select, to emphasise certain aspects of reality while omitting others; to render distant phenomena plausible and measurable; to determine who or what is represented or included. Every line, every point, carries implications for how bodies, spaces and phenomena are categorised. This power can be devastating when it enables the construction of realities that serve violence and social injustice.

These questions are central to the workshop. During site visits, participants digitally scan fragments of the city, which are later translated into calico textiles using the Kalabari practice of *pelete-bite* ('cutting thread'). For Camp, the acts of cutting and pulling threads serve as both literal and symbolic methods of reclamation. Although representation and digital technologies are embedded within structures of power and colonial legacies, Camp demonstrates how these tools can be repurposed for counter-hegemonic practices and become vehicles for restitution. Against this background, hyper-consciousness becomes a material process through which the city's colonial and geopolitical entanglements are sampled, cut and re-threaded. The resulting cartographies encode strategies for dismantling colonial spells and for reimagining and reclaiming space. They are far from the polished digital cityscapes that circulate across every screen. The incompleteness and intentional disruptions introduced during translation (first into digital images and later into textiles) create openings across the boundaries imposed on imagination.

As these investigations and practices show, to become hyper-conscious is to accept that architecture is always already implicated in planetary systems – legal, financial, climatic, colonial, technological. It is to recognise that design operates within and upon those systems. It is to act, collectively, to transform them, and this collectivity necessarily exceeds the human.

Common Accounts' PARADE! approaches this collectivity performatively, highlighting the undeniable power of bodies in space. Their work mobilises bodies, media and ritual in an urban parade. In doing so, they connect to the long history of festivals as forms of collective intelligence. Whereas their festive character makes us lose sight of their capacity to challenge conventional norms and generate new ones through a seemingly ephemeral occupation of space, they are, as pointed out by Henri Lefebvre and the Situationists, able to transgress the control and order of everyday life. Or, in Lefebvre's words, 'the bureaucratic society of controlled consumption'.[3]

3. Henri Lefebvre, 'The Bureaucratic Society of Controlled Consumption', *Everyday Life in the Modern World* [1968], Continuum, 2002, p. 68.

Despite their appropriation and domestication by brands and corporations, parades remain a tactical device frequently used by activists to catalyse change. They reorganise urban hierarchies, challenge the status quo, and bring to the centre what is often pushed to the margins. In doing so, they construct spatial configurations through which worlds can be imagined, rehearsed and enacted. If becoming hyper-conscious carries the risk of paralysis, resulting in overwhelm rather than action, embodied collective action restores desire for transformation.

The parade mobilises bodies, affects, alliances and forms of visibility, merging the symbolic and the infrastructural. In motion together, bodies reclaim the capacity to dissent, to occupy spaces otherwise governed by circulatory regimes and consumption, and to act within structures that might otherwise appear totallising. In this sense, the parade counters the disembodying effects of abstraction and reintroduces friction through celebration.

All these propositions exemplify what 'Becoming. Architectures for a planet in transition' ambitiously sets out to do: to embrace architecture as a collective practice of orientation. And, as becoming indicates a direction rather than a destination – the curators remind us – it is always an incomplete task through which we attune to and make sense of the world through its fragments. It is to acknowledge that actions will produce consequences, though without certainty about how, when or for whom. It is an act of care that sustains the imaginative capacities necessary for transformation, even in the absence of hope. It is a celebration that moves beyond the anthropocentric, for becoming hyper-conscious can only emerge through intersubjective and more-than-human relations.

Almost nothing. And yet, it is far from heroic. It is simply necessary.

Forensic Architecture
(Eyal Weizman, Elizabeth Breiner and Júlia Nueno Guitart)

EARTHWORKS: FROM *A CIVILIAN OCCUPATION* TO 'A CARTOGRAPHY OF GENOCIDE'

In July 2002, the Israel Association of United Architects announced its last-minute cancellation of the exhibition it had commissioned to represent Israel at the UIA World Congress of Architects in Berlin later that month. Of particular concern was the accompanying catalogue, edited by architects Eyal Weizman and Rafi Segal and titled *A Civilian Occupation: The Politics of Israeli Architecture*,[1] most copies of which the association subsequently destroyed, calling it a form of 'one-sided propaganda'. Laid out across a series of essays examining the history and common infrastructure of Israeli settlements in Gaza and the West Bank, the publication makes a case for the Israeli state's co-opting of architecture and urban planning as strategic tools of occupation, and its reshaping of the natural landscape as an expression of its national and geopolitical objectives. *The New York Times* account of the episode was titled 'Are Politics Built into Architecture?'[2] In indirect answer, the controversy would become the first in a series that Weizman's and later Forensic Architecture's work would generate, arising most notably from the application of architectural tools and thinking to expose historical and contemporary Israeli crimes throughout Palestine.

1. *A Civilian Occupation: The Politics of Israeli Architecture* was first published by the Israeli Association of United Architects (IAUA) for the Union Internationale des Architectes (UIA) Congress in Berlin, July 2002, before being banned. A very limited number of original copies are still circulating. A revised edition of the catalogue was published the following year by Babel (for the Hebrew language edition) and Verso (for the English language edition).

2. Alan Riding, 'Are Politics Built into Architecture', *The New York Times*, 10 August 2002. https://www.nytimes.com/2002/08/10/arts/are-politics-built-into-architecture.html

Ma'on
Area: Hebron
Population: 250
Established: 1981
Location on map: E14
Latitute: 770
Type: Community Settlement

Ateret
Area: Ramallah
Population: 300
Established: 1981
Location on map: E7
Latitue: 720
Type: Community Settlement
Planner: S. Melman, A. Kaplan

Hermesh
Area: Jenin
Population: 1981
Location on map: E2
Latitute: 270
Type: Community Settlement
Planner: Shahar Yehoshua

El'azar
Area: Bethlehem
Population: 200
Established: 1975
Location on map: E11
Latitude: 910
Type: Community Settlement
Planner: Settlement Planning Department

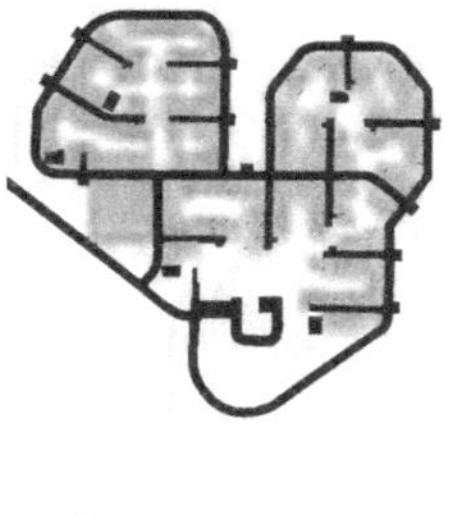

Gitit
Area: Jordan valley
Population: 100
Established: 1971
Location on map: G6
Latitude: 305
Type: Moshav

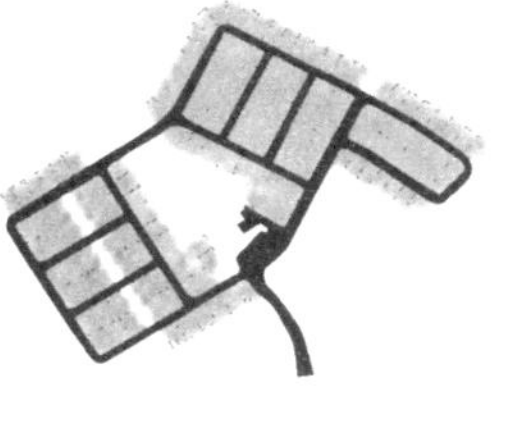

Mechora
Area: Jordan valley
Population: 150
Established: 1973
Location on map: H5
Latitude: 225
Type: Moshav

Rafi Segal and Eyal Weizman, Plans of settlements in the West Bank, *A Civilian Occupation: The Politics of Israeli Architecture*, 2002.
In Segal and Weizman's analysis of Israeli settlements and accompanying infrastructure, they highlight the spatial typologies that emerge across them as a means of understanding the landscape as a 'battlefield' whose terrain 'dictates the nature, intensity, and focal points of confrontation'. The conflict itself, they suggest, may be read most clearly 'in the process of transformation, adaption, construction, and obliteration of the landscape and the built environment' – a new kind of more durational warfare.

Weizman went on to found the human rights research agency Forensic Architecture in 2010 as a critical practice dedicated to challenging settler-colonial violence in Palestine, with locally situated 'counter-investigations' incorporating new forms of spatial analysis, immersive interviewing and open-source investigation. Its work has since expanded to encompass over a hundred investigations into state and corporate violence worldwide, findings from which have been submitted to and presented in the International Court of Justice, International Criminal Court, European Court of Human Rights and United Nations General Assembly.

Since Israel launched its military campaign in Gaza in October 2023, the investigative practice of Forensic Architecture has in some ways come full circle, with the work it has undertaken in support of South Africa's historic genocide case against Israel at The Hague prompting the most dramatic refocusing and reconceptualising of the agency's practices and priorities since its founding.

As a way of reading the present moment, this proposed project begins by revisiting Weizman and Segal's 2002 exhibition and publication, displaying elements of the original censored show for the first time, supported by the same institution under whose auspices the controversy first unfolded. From there, it disassembles the methods developed by Forensic Architecture in response to the genocide in Gaza, and the translation and reworking of subsequent findings across forums. It seeks to bring together two key moments within a long continuum of critical reinvention as a means of intervention – in both instances, the normalisation of acute violence necessitating new approaches to deconstructing the impenetrable architecture of Israeli occupation into its physical and psychological dimensions, and through different scales of pattern analysis translating the hieroglyphs of Zionist control and oppression into an intelligible language.

This legibility has relied on establishing the historicity of each observed Israeli tactic, the strategic aims contained in every allegedly isolated incident. The 2002 project offers an expansive array of examples from different scholars illustrating the common characteristics not only of settlement architecture but of settler logic, observed over three-quarters of a century. Weizman and Segal, for instance, produced a map locating all of the settlements in the occupied West Bank, and across them identified three common types of 'civilian occupation' that represented distinct military, economic and ideological aims. *A Civilian Occupation* was radical in its formulation of the relationship between spatial organisation and population control as foundational to Israeli statehood, addressing in particular the dual mechanisms of 'fortification and observation',[3] contributor Sharon Rotbard wrote, built into the architecture of its settlements starting in the 1930s during the pre-state period of the Great Revolt. These 'spatial technologies', as Segal and Weizman call them, would form the basis for all future Israeli urban planning[4] – necessitating, in turn, the invention of a different set of 'spatial technologies', also subverting conventional architectural practice, in order to expose the political power dynamics enmeshed in the Israeli built environment.

3. Rafi Segal and Eyal Weizman (eds), *A Civilian Occupation: The Politics of Israeli Architecture*, Verso, 2003, p. 52.

4. Ibid, p. 21.

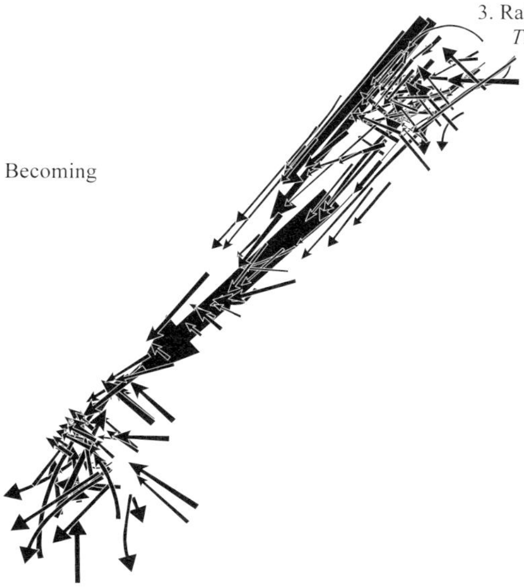

Forensic Architecture, Map of arrows showing Israeli evacuation orders in Gaza between October 2023 and October 2025, *Gaza Atlas*, 2025.
Between October 2023 and October 2025, Israel issued over a hundred and fifty evacuation orders directing Palestinians from one part of Gaza to another. With every evacuation order, a new arrow or set of arrows was superimposed over a map of Gaza, crude indicators of the supposed direction of 'safe' areas to which Palestinians were being continuously instructed to relocate. Seen together, these directional devices form a network of disorder, instructions reduced to empty symbols that were never designed to be understood or serve their purported humanitarian function.

Today, nearly two-and-a-half decades later, a sophisticated technical and analytical framework for spatialising and interrogating state violence has evolved out of these early conceptual foundations, informed by dozens of investigations undertaken both in Palestine and elsewhere around the globe. *A Civilian Occupation* moves deftly between bird's-eye-view sketches, aerial images and ground-level photographs of Israeli settlements; from an interview with an Israeli architect known for his influential design of mountaintop settlements in the West Bank, to accounts of the Palestinian experience of such settlements from below. The interest in representing these multiple axes of vision as parts of a common whole can be seen translated into Forensic Architecture's pioneering invention of the 'image complex', through which discrete visual data can be precisely situated within a modelled environment, offering a unique form of multiperspectivalism that erodes the primacy of any one vantage point. And it is only by synchronising and situating a combination of satellite and ground imagery that the guiding principles of 'fortification' and 'observation' addressed in Rotbard's essay may be understood as common characteristics of contemporary Israeli military strategy. Her analysis of the dynamic nature of settlements as 'permanent construction site[s]' transforming every aspect of the landscape offers a key insight into Israel's strategic weaponisation of earthworks or earth berms in Gaza. As part of a wider strategy of spatial control, the Israeli military has deployed bulldozers to shape these large mounds of earth and rubble into fortified compounds, military outposts, detention facilities and checkpoints facilitating the involuntary surveillance of Palestinians. The temporary nature of this new occupation architecture, which has turned Gaza into an ever-evolving construction site, makes it no less of a precursor to permanent military presence; rather, it serves as a blueprint for a future in which this military infrastructure is fully actualised, a means to 'transform the temporary into the quotidian, the quotidian into the permanent and the permanent into the eternal'.[5]

5. Ibid, p. 53.

Forensic Architecture and Studio Folder, Satellite images showing earth berms created by the Israeli military to serve a range of architectural functions, 2024–25. As the built environment of Gaza has been progressively decimated, the military has used bulldozers to execute a new masterplan of spatial control, piling mounds of earth and rubble in various configurations, also known as earth berms, to enclose fortified compounds, military outposts, checkpoints and detention facilities. Forensic Architecture has traced some of the common features and functions of these berms over the course of the genocide, cross-referencing photographs and footage from Palestinians on the ground with satellite imagery to locate and analyse the development of this temporary architecture of occupation. Satellite imagery: Esri World Imagery.

As the Forensic Architecture team progressively gathered, categorised, geolocated and verified thousands of incidents being reported from the ground in Gaza, simultaneously constructing a new digital platform to host and visualise these data points, the destruction (through which the aforementioned construction became possible) began to take a clear shape, with emergent subtypes and observable strategic objectives: the foremost objective, a culmination of the rest, being the comprehensive and calculated annihilation of the fundamental conditions of life for Palestinians in Gaza. This ongoing project documenting Israel's military campaign in Gaza is referred to as 'A Cartography of Genocide'.

Such an expansive form of mapping allowed for the visualisation of the overlapping and intersecting strata of Israeli violence, from the targeting of medical and agricultural infrastructure to the gouging out of raid routes and military corridors directly through the built environment of Gaza – eliminating essential infrastructure for survival while establishing the groundwork for a permanent military presence. Both *A Civilian Occupation* and 'A Cartography of Genocide' demand that each contemporary example be read through the historical continuum of Israeli settler colonialism extending back to the Nakba, and extending, too, the charge of intentionality as something compounding and durational rather than confined to a particular moment. But where the former builds a steady chronology of Israeli mechanisms of architectural control, the latter flattens time and space into a series of stratified layers of categorical violence that mirror the layers of rubble to which Gaza has been reduced, a means of digitally sifting and preserving these inaccessible evidentiary repositories.

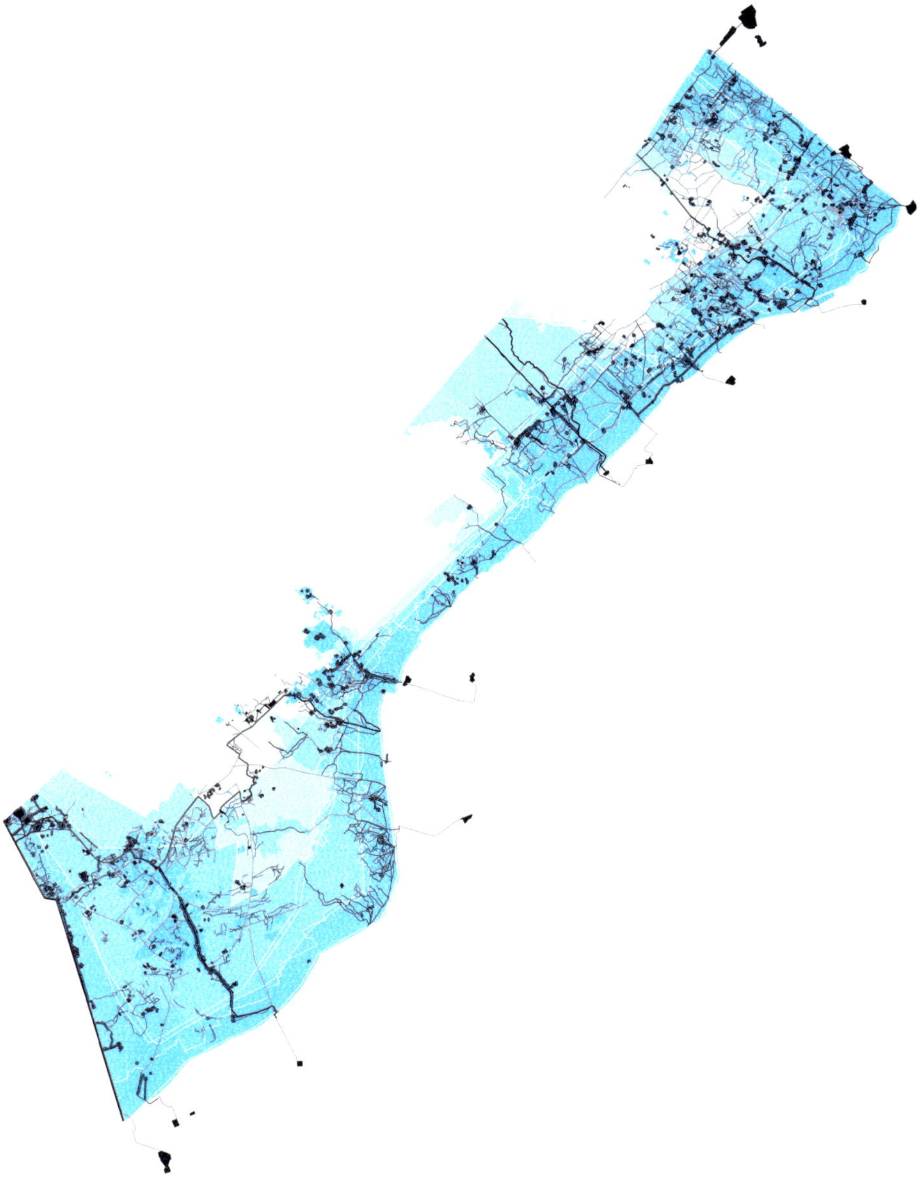

To attempt to disprove each piece of state propaganda and investigate each incident in Gaza as a singular event would have been to fall into the Israeli trap of normalisation through physical and mental bombardment, to be chasing the ever-shifting, ever more distant threshold for challenging its impunity. As a result, it became necessary to limit the application of the long-term investigative approach for which Forensic Architecture is best known – driven by individual testimony and a combination of collaborative and open-source reconstruction – to select representative events with wide reverberations: the bombing of al-Ahli Hospital or the targeting of the Palestinian Red Crescent Society medics and attempted cover-up. Certain sites subject to repeated attacks like

Forensic Architecture and Studio Folder, Map showing Israeli systems of spatial control in Gaza between October 2023 and October 2025, *Gaza Atlas*, 2025.
Israel's military campaign has involved the reshaping of Gaza's cultivated and built environment through parallel acts of destruction and construction. Forensic Architecture has documented the clearing and likely contamination of agricultural land and destruction of homes and other features of the built environment to facilitate the construction of military raid routes leading from the perimeter to the interior of Gaza, part of a wider system of spatial control.

al-Shifa Hospital have been modelled based on witness documentation, so that new incidents and testimonies can be easily situated in place and time – Forensic Architecture's model of the medical complex paradoxically acquiring greater resolution with each new assault that has, in turn, contributed to its progressive destruction. Further close investigations into the 1948 ethnic cleansing of a series of different Palestinian villages, undertaken with living survivors, have run alongside these contemporary projects, offering critical insights into the continuities between past and present Zionist mechanisms of expulsion, displacement and false historicisation.

Looking from *A Civilian Occupation* to 'A Cartography of Genocide', we seek to illuminate the relationship between established spatial techniques and experimentation – procedure and invention – in attempting to make legible the Israeli modus operandi. By deconstructing these two formative bodies of work into the raw materials that shaped them, we aim to draw

Forensic Architecture, Map showing the cumulative destruction of Gaza's built environment by Israeli forces between October 2023 and October 2025, *Gaza Atlas*, 2025.
By the end of October 2023, the Israeli army had already dropped over 25,000 tons of munitions on Gaza's cities and camps, the majority targeting Gaza City. Forensic Architecture has since analysed and cross-referenced hundreds of satellite images to map the progressive destruction of Gaza's built environment, finding that public infrastructure was repeatedly targeted even after it had been previously damaged and was unlikely to be occupied.

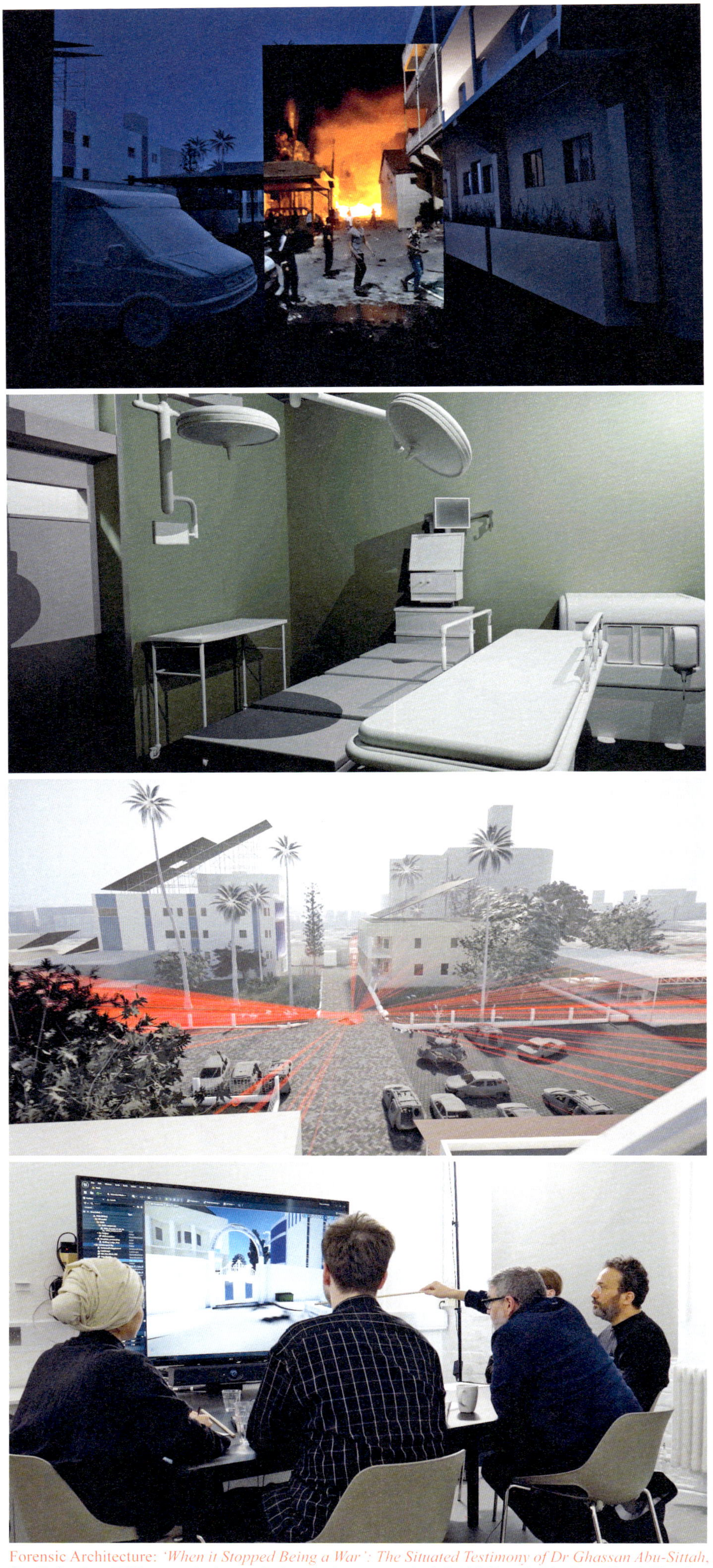

Forensic Architecture: *'When it Stopped Being a War': The Situated Testimony of Dr Ghassan Abu-Sittah*, 2024–25.
On 17 October 2023, an explosion took place in the courtyard of al-Ahli Hospital in Gaza City, killing hundreds. British-Palestinian surgeon Dr Ghassan Abu-Sittah was working in the hospital at the time of the blast and recounted his efforts to try to treat the mounting numbers of injured people, many of whom had been sheltering in the hospital grounds. The Forensic Architecture team was in close contact with Dr Abu-Sittah, and after his return to London after five weeks of treating patients in Gaza decided to collaboratively reconstruct the events of the night as he experienced them using Forensic Architecture's 'situated testimony' interviewing practice.

a line between the combination of theoretical and technical methods that evolved over time to allow for assemblages of visual data to be transformed into multidimensional models. Our new body of work presented at the 2026 UIA World Congress foregrounds the process of typologising as a form of pattern analysis, showing the way in which different organising principles expose different findings and continuities within the available data, and bringing viewers into this complex process of aesthetic attunement. Gradually, these disparate elements assemble and coalesce into a composition through which the distinct architecture of Israeli occupation and genocidal violence may be understood transparently as the sum of its many parts.

6

Forensic Architecture and Palestine Land Society, Return to al-Ma'in, 2025.
Al-Ma'in was a village located in the Beer al-Saba District of Palestine that was ethnically cleansed in 1948 and subsequently destroyed. The territory is occupied today by four Israeli-Jewish kibbutzim and is just a few short kilometres from what is now known as the Gaza Strip. Forensic Architecture worked with Palestinian scholar Dr Salman Abu-Sitta to reconstruct his home of al-Ma'in as it stood in the early 1940s.

Ibiye Camp

REVISED CARTOGRAPHIES

Ibiye Camp, *Barcelona Containers*, 2025.
Screen capture of mapped point clouds of containers at Port Vell using the 3D-modelling software Agisoft Metashape.

Ibiye Camp, *Kumasi Market Barcelona and Columbus Statue*, 2025.
Collage of an OBJ 3D model of the Columbus monument and point clouds of the Kumasi Market, scanning techniques explored during the site visits.

Ibiye Camp, Prototypes of laser-cut fabrics from point-cloud studies, 2025.

Revised Cartographies investigates how colonial and geopolitical systems continue to circulate in a contemporary city. While Barcelona's prosperity was historically tied to colonial exchange, it was also one of the first places in Spain where publishers, artists and activists resisted Francoist censorship and openly critiqued colonial culture.

Workshop participants interrogate colonial inscriptions and the geopolitical flows emanating from Barcelona by deconstructing scans of its architectural legacies to develop new forms of cartography that expose and rework the flows connecting the city to West and Central Africa, past and present. Using historic textiles and natural dyes, we reclaim and reveal these material exchanges to explore how these flows and systems can be represented in non-Western cartographic form.

Site visits

The workshop begins at Port Vell, where participants are introduced to photogrammetry and point-cloud capture technologies. As a historic port shaped by trade, extraction and movement, Port Vell offers a starting point to consider how technologies of mapping and visualisation can reveal hidden infrastructures and layered histories embedded in the landscape.

The second site visit examines spaces of colonial contention and reassessment, including the Columbus Monument and Plaça Idrissa Diallo. These sites foreground how public memory is actively contested and rewritten. The removal of a monument to a man who profited from slavery, and the renaming of the square in honour of Idrissa Diallo, a young Guinean man who died in a migrant detention centre, open discussions around power, erasure and resistance within urban space.

The third visit focuses on contemporary West African presence through sourcing materials at Kumasi Market. Participants trace the movement of ingredients such as cocoa, kola and hibiscus from Nigeria, Côte d'Ivoire and

Ghana, revealing diasporic networks, cultural continuity, and the living afterlives of colonial trade routes in Barcelona.

Cutting thread

The mapped routes from the port, contested colonial monuments and contemporary diaspora sites are examined by generating point-cloud information from the scans. Participants work with film and laser-cutting techniques to convert the point-cloud information into a calico textile. In eighteenth-century Spain, calico (a fine cotton cloth from India) was highly prized for its brilliant, colourfast prints and designs. The importance of this fabric led to the development of a major domestic cotton industry, particularly in Catalonia.

The process of cutting into fabric is inspired by *pelete-bite* ('cutting thread'), practised by the Kalabari people of the Niger Delta. In this process, the cutting and pulling of thread acts as both a literal and symbolic method of reclamation. Participants use this logic of removal and exposure to reinterpret their site research on the calico fabric. These revised textiles become new cartographies, material proposals for how the city might be re-read, dismantled and reimagined.

Emerging Workshop 10/12

Common Accounts (Igor Bragado and Miles Gertler)

PARADE!

Common Accounts, Clima Fitness: Rituales de Adaptabilidad, Matadero Madrid, 2023. With artwork by Faysal Altunbozar, and curated by Maite Borjabad, Clima Fitness was an exhibition, a gym, and a year-long programme that considered planetarity and the human body's capacity to negotiate, mutate and adapt in the context of climate change.

Within the context of 'Becoming Hyper-conscious', which calls for a heightened awareness of planetary interdependencies and the material consequences of our spatial decisions, the PARADE! workshop reflects on the potential of urban parades, processions and rituals – as well as their attendant structures – as pragmatic tools for city-building. How can ephemeral architectures produce lasting changes to enhance the civic realm? How might architectural form materialise tactically to improve daily life? How can we adapt the spatial strategies

Common Accounts, Parade of Verifiable Truths, 2021.

Common Accounts, Parade of Remote Rituals, 2021.

Common Accounts, Parade of Cancelled Personalities, 2021.

'Verifiable Truths', 'Remote Rituals' and 'Cancelled Personalities' are part of FOMO-STOCK, a speculative project commissioned for the Yale Architectural Journal *Perspecta 54: Atopia*. These parades imagine the traditional urban procession/parade as a way to address contemporary societal preoccupations, niche cultural concerns and internet-driven anxieties.

of historical parade traditions to address urgencies in the contemporary city?

Historically, parades and festivals organise civic space, transmit messages to publics, and often model prospective worlds or realities yet to come. Parade itineraries have produced urban form in cities like Athens and Rome. These ephemeral events often produce lasting vestiges in the lived environment. Across time, parades have been organised to articulate urban and trans-urban relationships to power and value, for example between frontier and capital, or labour and market. Perhaps unsurprisingly, architecture has a disciplinary history in their design. Architect Charles Robert Cockerell designed the environment to host the lying-in-state of the general and politician Arthur Wellesley, 1st Duke of Wellington, in London in 1852, and architects Richard Redgrave and Gottfried Semper designed his funeral carriage. From Victorian-era London to the queue of mourners waiting to visit Queen Elizabeth II in state in 2022, processions have gathered publics and materialised the urban with crowds, media and monuments.

Barcelona is a locus for processions, festivals and the ephemeral architectures that shape them, and thus presents an ideal testing ground with a discernibly receptive public. The workshop additionally draws on the history of maintenance and service-oriented artistic practices like that developed by Mierle Laderman Ukeles, to account for ways in which ephemeral and processional architectures can institute lasting material transformations of public space.

PARADE! learns from existing parade and festival cultures along Spain's Mediterranean coastal region and adapts their space-making strategies to an ephemeral architectural intervention enacted in Barcelona's streets and plazas. The project expands disciplinary awareness of parades and processions as a valuable architectural genre, develops an arsenal of material, formal and logistical design strategies for ephemeral architectures, and identifies useful, democratic tools for city-building tailored to UIA 2026 Barcelona's curatorial priorities and the civic urgencies of this moment.

Brandlhuber+, b+ and HouseEurope!

FROM BUILDING TO POLICY – THE RIGHT TO HOUSING

'From Building to Policy – The Right to Housing' understands law as an architectural medium that ultimately determines who gets to live where, how and under what conditions. Rooted in the practice of building, it presents a way of thinking that translates real-life knowledge and experience into policy and narrative. The goal is to design and build arguments for the socioecological transformation of the built environment.

The project unfolds across buildings, research, films, publications and campaigns, reflecting a continuous development of practice. It traces a process in which architectural work expands from designing buildings to designing practice itself, questioning whom architecture serves, under which conditions it operates, and how it can act beyond the scale of a single building.

Designing with the system: Legislating Architecture (Brandlhuber+)

It all started with a building – or was it a ruin? And who decides what can be used and what cannot; what counts as the norm? 'Legislating Architecture' is a mindset. Instead of treating legislation – from building codes to zoning rules and legal constraints – as obstacles, it is read as a material: something to be interpreted, designed and built with.

Canadian Centre for Architecture (CCA), 'To Build Law' exhibition, CCA, Montreal, Canada, 2024–25. Graphics by HIT.

This approach focuses on what is possible within the existing: rules and ruins alike. The Brandlhuber+ buildings in Berlin, such as the gallery and studios at Brunnenstrasse 9 (2010), the Antivilla or the St Agnes church conversion (both 2015), emerged from the as-found. They treat legislation and market logic as generative forces, exploiting gaps, bending norms, and reframing risks and potentials. In doing so, they show how different readings of the same law produce different architectures. Legislating Architecture, in this sense, is a practice of designing with the system. It works with legislation and the market while foregrounding the speculative potential of architecture.

Crisis of architectural agency: Between fact and fiction (b+)
How can we not only design a building, but also the desire for it? And how can we build a self-sustaining practice without costing people and the planet? These questions mark a shift in perspective. For a younger generation of architects, the central challenge is the awareness of being part of the problem.

Canadian Centre for Architecture (CCA), 'To Build Law' exhibition, 2024–25.

Architecture is deeply embedded in the value chain of the construction industry and building sector. In Europe, they produce more than a third of Europe's CO_2 and more than a third of its waste. Real estate is the largest store of household wealth in Europe, more than all other financial assets combined. Housing is the single largest expense, and for a growing number of Europeans, it is becoming unaffordable. Construction is one of Europe's biggest employers and engine of growth. No other sector touches as many lives, budgets and emissions at once, leaving little room for neutrality.

Architects are part of this chain. Agency therefore becomes the central question. How can practical knowledge of buildings, materials and spatial organisation enter the processes that actually govern the sector: laws, incentives and regulations?

Addressing this question requires a change in what is built and for whom. It means no longer following market demand alone or reducing architecture to a planning service, but questioning the very reasons for building in the first place. Projects such as the ongoing San Gimignano Lichtenberg and Mäusebunker CC challenge not only what is built, but also how architecture communicates and to whom. Here, the public becomes the client, one that needs to be addressed, involved and made aware of what architecture could be.

Joshua Frank and the Canadian Centre for Architecture (CCA), Film stills from *To Build Law*, 2024.

From working with(in) to working on the system: Power to the people (HouseEurope!)

When is working with and within the system no longer enough? What happens when designing buildings through loopholes, narratives and interpretation no longer affects the system they depend on? This moment marks a shift. Architectural agency moves from working with and within the system to working on it. Rather than addressing individual projects alone, the focus turns to the systemic structures that shape the built environment. The task of design expands towards writing laws (policy) and shaping public understanding (advocacy).

As a community-driven platform, HouseEurope! brings together people operating in and around the construction and building sector. Rooted in practical experience, it understands itself as part of the value chain – from material to finance and law. This position makes it possible to identify not only the most relevant issues, but also the most effective levers for systemic change. Practical knowledge and lived experience are translated into policy proposals and narratives, connecting citizens, organisations and institutions across Europe to share knowledge, build arguments and act across different scales.

Canadian Centre for Architecture (CCA), 'To Build Law' exhibition, 2024–25.

A central instrument in this work is the European Citizens' Initiative (ECI), an EU tool of participatory democracy that allows citizens to place legislative proposals on the agenda of European policymakers. In this sense, ECIs are not only legal mechanisms, but also design projects: bringing together research, spatial analysis, design studies, campaigning and public narrative around a concrete legal goal.

The first initiative, Power to Renovation (2025–26), focused on shifting legal and economic frameworks so that renovation and transformation of existing buildings become the norm, rather than their demolition.

Joshua Frank and the Canadian Centre for Architecture (CCA), Film stills from *To Build Law*, 2024.

Canadian Centre for Architecture (CCA), 'To Build Law' exhibition, 2024–25.

The Right to Housing: The next European Citizens' Initiative

While the European Union defines overarching legal and economic frameworks, housing is regulated and realised across multiple levels: European, national and local. These layers interact, overlap, and at times contradict one another. Their effects, however, are always concrete. They materialise in buildings, neighbourhoods and cities. It is within this multi-level system that the Right to Housing becomes a design question – one that must be addressed across scales.

The Right to Housing is understood here in a broad and differentiated sense. Housing crises across Europe are driven by different conditions in different places. Each city, region and country faces specific pressures: vacancy, overtourism and short-term rentals, real-estate speculation, rising energy costs or overcrowding. Accordingly, each local group and initiative participating in the Right to Housing ECI contributes its own perspective and proposal to a collectively developed legal framework. The resulting proposal does not seek a single solution, but brings together diverse legal positions and their distinct spatial consequences.

Canadian Centre for Architecture (CCA), 'To Build Law' exhibition, 2024–25.

Within this collective process, HouseEurope! contributes the concept of the Right to Remain based on three key pillars:

(I) Incentives for renovation that protect tenants, preventing displacement.
(II) Financial incentives for the reuse and transformation of vacant offices into housing.
(III) Public funding for affordable housing developed by non-speculative private actors.[1]

1. www.righttohousing.eu

(I) European Level –
Legal & Economic Framework

Defines the legal and economic conditions that structure housing across Europe. Through energy, climate, competition and state-aid law – as well as funding programmes – the EU indirectly determines what can be built, renovated, financed or reused, and under which conditions.

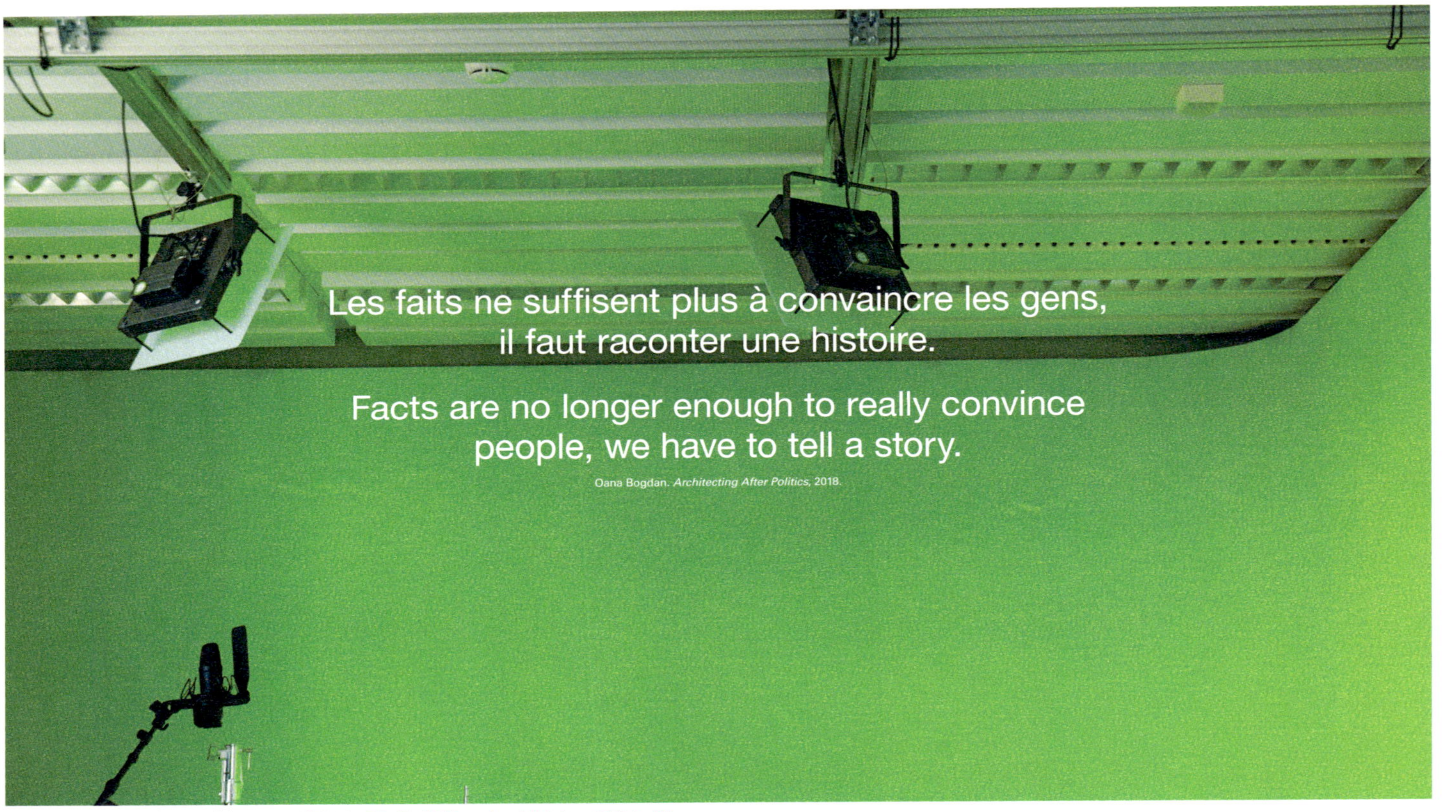

Canadian Centre for Architecture (CCA), 'To Build Law' exhibition, 2024–25.

(II) National Level –
Housing Law & Rights

Translates European frameworks into national law. Constitutions, housing acts, tenancy law, energy standards and social policies define rights, obligations and protections – shaping who is entitled to housing, under what terms and with which safeguards.

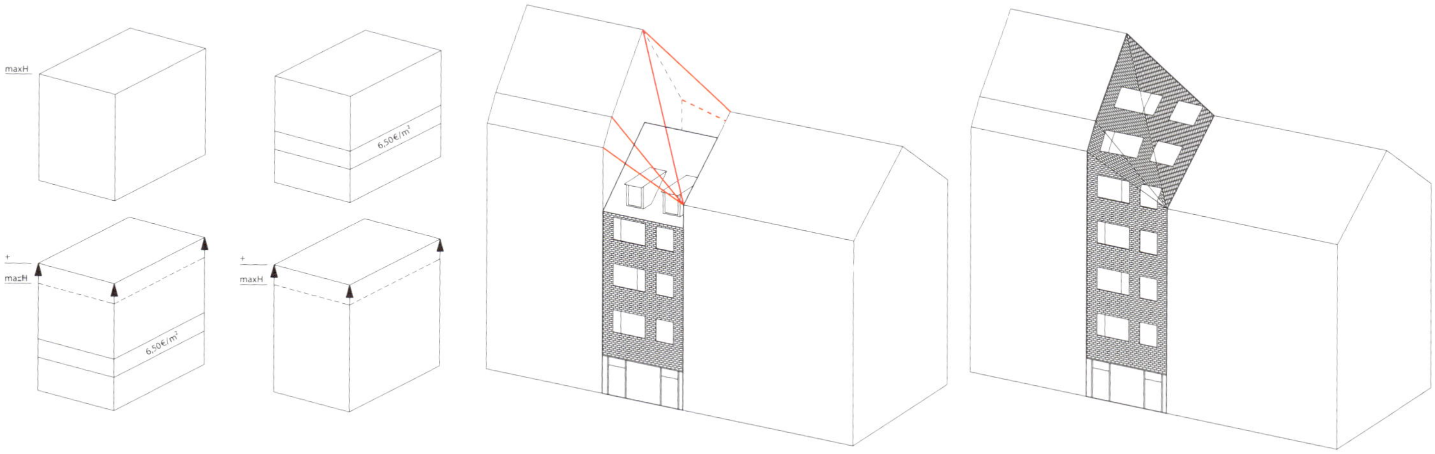

(Left): Brandlhuber+, '+1', from *The Dialogic City*, Cologne, 2017.
(Right): b&k+ Markus Emde, Martin Kraushaar + Marc Frohn, Over the Top, Cologne, 2006.
Planning regulations often limit building height and floor area, restricting the housing potential of existing buildings. At the same time, high-demand areas face a shortage of affordable housing, while rooftop extensions are economically attractive for property owners. This Dialogic City proposal links both interests by allowing additional building height beyond current regulations, on the condition that an equivalent amount of floor space within the same building is permanently secured for socially affordable housing, with optional allocation rights for the municipality. By coupling market-driven extensions with binding social obligations, new housing is created while affordability is secured locally – countering neighbourhood homogenisation and strengthening social and cultural diversity.

(III) Local Level – Planning & Implementation

Implements and interprets national law through planning regulations, zoning, permits, subsidies and municipal housing strategies. Here, abstract legal frameworks become concrete decisions affecting neighbourhoods, buildings and everyday life.

Cornelia Müller for Brandlhuber+, Bikini Tempelhof, Berlin, 2015.
In 2014, Berlin held a referendum about the future of Tempelhofer Feld, the former airport in the centre of the city. The city wanted to build thousands of apartments on the open field. The citizens voted to keep it 100 per cent empty. Bikini Tempelhof is a proposal developed during this debate. Instead of building on the empty field and sealing new ground, it suggests building on top of the existing, unused airport structure. The project was meant to overcome the either-or logic of both sides and to show that social goals (housing) and ecological goals (park) are not a contradiction, and that both are possible.

(IV) Architecture

Absorbs and materialises the consequences of these layered regulations. Buildings, renovations, vacancies, evictions and spatial inequalities materialise where laws, markets and policies meet – making architecture the physical outcome of legal and political decisions.

Building on the first ECI and its objective of establishing renovation and transformation as the new norm, the Right to Remain seeks to ensure that tenants are able to stay in – or return to – their homes after renovation or upgrading. In this sense, the Right to Housing today cannot be separated from the question of existing buildings. It includes the continued use, adaptation and transformation of the built environment so that housing remains liveable and affordable under conditions of rising energy costs and increasing temperatures.

Methodologically, the project combines comparative legal research with typological analysis and situated knowledge from local initiatives. By tracing how different legal definitions translate into different spatial realities, it aims to formulate concrete policy proposals that can operate across jurisdictions while remaining grounded in everyday life. An accompanying film and exhibition, *To Build a Law*,[2] conceived by Francesco Garutti and Irene Chin together with film director Joshua Frank, produced by the Canadian Centre for Architecture (CCA) and launched in Montreal in 2024, introduce these questions through a combination of documentary material and narrative, connecting legal structures, architectural expertise and lived experience. The project follows the development of HouseEurope!'s first initiative, 'Power to Renovation', and is the second chapter of *Groundwork*, a three-part series that traces the conceptual development and field research of contemporary architects cultivating alternative modes of practice in response to the urgency of the climate crisis and its impacts on multiple communities.

2. The film and further information are available at: cca.qc.ca/tobuildlaw

Critical Antagonist 10/12

A conversation between Timothy Morton and the Congress curators on Becoming Hyper-conscious and architecture as a practice of attunement and opacity

BECOMING HYPO-CONSCIOUS

CURATORS — At a moment of geopolitical and ecological transition, how do you perceive an endeavour like the UIA Congress? What does it mean to gather transnationally under these conditions?

TIMOTHY MORTON — Well, first of all, thank you for inviting me. It's a great honour to be part of this. What is really happening in the world is a transition to planet-scale politics. It's happening somewhat by accident, somewhat deliberately – but it's a big shift. The idea of the nation-state – which is really a scaled-up version of the classical concept of the person – is now in serious jeopardy. *Persona* in Latin means mask. It implies a transparency behind the mask; a sovereign interior will. The nation-state is a collective persona that imagines it can abstractly impose its will on the world.

But philosophically, that imposition never truly worked. Colonialism and imperialism were attempts to enact sovereignty at scale, yet what they ultimately relied on was violence. At its core, the nation-state depends on violence – it has a monopoly on violence. All those flags and symbols are just public relations secondary to the basic illogical violence. Hitting someone is hitting someone; it's not teaching them a lesson. Teaching involves words and symbols. Violence is the breakdown of symbolisation – the end of speech.

The nation-state assumes a toxic holism: that a whole subsumes all its parts. All the trees, all the water, all the people belong to that whole. That is a fascist holism. Ecological politics demands a completely different holism. Belonging to a planet cannot mean belonging to a super-nation scaled up to planetary size. That would simply repeat the same mistake. So, if architecture – or a congress of architecture – is going to speak to this moment, it needs to be thinking in terms of holistic action and thought, although this has nothing to do with default holism. When we think of scaling politics up, we need to be thinking differently.

C How do you think this should happen? Perhaps this can connect to the notion of 'becoming' approached by the Congress: as an awareness of planetary transformations rooted in spatial practice. This approach follows specific architectural legacies, but also philosophical ones – Bergson, Derrida, Lefebvre, etc. How do you understand this term today?

TM The word 'becoming' can be imagined in a number of different ways. I think the way human beings are living the experience of becoming right now is in a state of crisis, disruption and agony. Ideology is telling us that we're feeling this agony because it's the end of the world. But this is part of the problem: that's advertising language. That's why I wrote *Hyperobjects: Philosophy and Ecology After the End of the World*.[1] 'After the end of the world' doesn't mean after everything stops. It means after the concept of the end of the world has been shown to be untrue. Very basically, very simply, the 'end of the world' is really just the end of the nation-state and the end of the person defined as a willing subject imposing its will on objects. That is what is ending. Empires might crumble, but regular people might not end up having too bad of a life.

1. Timothy Morton, *Hyperobjects: Philosophy and Ecology After the End of the World*, University of Minnesota Press, 2013.

When we say 'becoming', it refers to a time when something is approaching, something is emerging, but we have to think carefully about what that means. On the one hand, if we think of it as a sort of smooth transition or as some kind of fluid that just keeps flowing and then magically transmogrifies itself, that's not convincing. On the other, planet-scale political change imagined in terms of violent apocalypse – revolution as revelation, ripping the appearance off to get to reality – that's also part of the same problem.

C We often debate the tension between slow and abrupt change, which might connect to your argument about the nation-state. Historically, colonialism was imposed spatially through violent tabula rasa transformations. Many modernist architects approached change in a similar revolutionary yet careless way. This recalls Walter Benjamin's Angel of History:[2] facing backwards to the past while being propelled forward by the storm of progress, unable to see the path ahead and the destruction it leaves behind.

What is your position in this debate?

2. An allegorical figure from his 'Theses On the Philosophy of History' (1940). Available at: https://www.sfu.ca/~andrewf/CONCEPT2.html

Paul Klee, *Angelus Novus*, 1920.

TIMOTHY MORTON Of course, that image has a problematic resonance. Many thinkers act like the Angel of History: they like to tell you that if you look wide enough, everything is a catastrophe and, therefore, their vision is more correct than yours. There is a deep cynicism in this view, which, however, I believe Benjamin did not intend. I think that what he was really doing was criticising the Communist Party for not working closely enough with the Social Democrats to stop Hitler – and wrote the Angel as a satirical image. It's not an image of what we should be doing, but an image of what is not good, which is to see the big picture in such a way that it's all bad.

C If the whole can't be seen, what does it mean to stay attentive to it? We've been using 'Becoming Hyper-conscious' as a directional term – a collective effort to orient ourselves towards political and ecological entanglements across scales.

TM Actually, if I had been in charge of this title, I would have called it 'Becoming Hypo-conscious'. The hyperobject demands the hypo-subject. 'Hypo' as in 'hypodermic' (under the skin) or 'hypotension' (low blood pressure); as lower down. A hyperobject is any entity that is so large in space and time terms that it drastically constrains the ability of human beings to understand, compute and comprehend it … and deal with it politically and aesthetically. It is literally impossible to grow 'big' enough, 'hyper' enough, to do any of that regarding a hyperobject. Instead, the task is to become 'small'. Hypo, not hyper. Hyperobjects are not necessarily evil. The biosphere is a hyperobject. The solar system is a hyperobject.

Consciousness has been 'hyper' all the time: we think of the subject as hyper. The nation-state is hyper, bigger and better because it transcends everything. But planet-scale awareness actually involves becoming hypo-conscious. Hyperobject awareness is hypo, because you can only ever see a little bit of it at any time. Hyper-consciousness is impossible, that's the beauty of hyperobject reality: now that human beings know about massively distributed objects, such as global warming, the galaxy, the dark energy, capitalism and so forth, it is no longer possible to imagine that consciousness is hyper.

One task of philosophy – and I think of architecture – is to allow human beings, especially people who look like me, to step off the precipice of being the hyper-subject and to enable us to become the hypo-subject. To become smaller. More humble. More personable. The concept of 'person' is richer than the idea of a command-control will-imposing being. If one is the subject and zero is the object, a person is fractally just a little bit less than one and quite a lot more than zero. Not a manipulable object, not a command-control subject, but something infinitesimally less than one. Architectural design allows human beings to live that truth rather than to keep on – as you very rightly say, like in modernism – reproducing the physical structure of a violent untruth.

C This is a valuable critique – any attempt at collective consciousness must remain below the hyper-subject: sensitive, vulnerable, incomplete, uncertain. Hypo-consciousness is fascinating because it seems less a knowledge and more like a feeling: a process of attunement. This connects to another of the Congress lines, 'Becoming Attuned', deliberately positioned in the schedule after 'Becoming Hyper-conscious', and closing the Congress. How do you understand attunement in this context?

TM Attuning is an interesting concept, because attunement is more than passive and less than active, in the same way that a person is less than a subject and more than an object. If you've ever been in a band – especially in a free improvisation band – you know that playing is the same as listening. When you're playing music, you're listening to the other person, to your instrument, to your musical inheritance, your knowledge, your skills. You're listening out for what the audience might like. If you're a DJ, you're really listening to the crowd and channelling it. In a very strict sense, attunement has to do with the future. You are attuned to the possibility of the future. Listening is primordial. When I speak, I'm listening for what you might be interested in and what words might persuade you. You're doing the same. This implies a kind of uncanny precognition of the future.

Even the Angel of History implies this. They say they aren't looking behind their head, but they know there is a catastrophe arriving. They know there is a future that might be destroyed. The image is a lie, because intuitively they know there is a future. Even the most cynical person is actually hoping that if people listen correctly to their paralysing argument, they might want to change things. Even this feeling of paralysis implies awareness that there is a future that could be different.

I do believe that the way in which a planetary politics will succeed is through a decolonisation of thought. In particular, white European and American thought based in the idea that all that is available is the past. And if attunement means anything more than blurring active and passive, it means being aware of the future in some way; anticipating a future response. There is something about the DJ putting a record on a deck in a club that is futural: it is oriented towards the future. Derrida, who you mentioned, has the wonderful idea of the *arrivant*,[3] that is to say, a radically unpredictable future. A future that intrinsically cannot be predicted in the sense of build-out from present assumptions, but of which, nevertheless, somehow sentience can be aware. When we strengthen this idea a bit more, we understand that the *arrivant* is actually something that can be sensed, felt, noticed. From an architectural point of view, the question is: how can we design the way people live so that they are enticed into orienting towards that future, rather than simply accepting fate?

3. Jacques Derrida, *Aporias*, trans. Thomas Dutoit, Stanford University Press, 1993.

C The ambiguity of this idea is especially suggestive. On the one hand, the future retains a degree of open-endedness; on the other, it implies that this future was already somehow oriented. In the past you have said that 'free will is overrated'. If we are willing to move towards an unplanned future, perhaps we should accept that we are engaging with a context that is already partly oriented. At the same time, as architects, if we want to transform environments that may endure over time and affect many beings – yet avoid doing so through violence, tabula rasa and imposition – how can we design spatial transformations that catalyse future processes of engagement?

TIMOTHY MORTON This is a deep question. In the past, I have had a tremendous anxiety about the idea that free will is either overrated or non-existent. One of the greatest things about object-oriented ontology (OOO) is the insistence that free will is overrated. I loved it when I first read it, and I love it even more now.[4] If it's true that there never was such a thing as free will, then we can relax. We've been doing things, being creative, conducting our business – without this 'free will' ambition. The absence of free will doesn't mean the presence of complete mechanism. That's the difficulty. Thinking about this difficulty must be part of decolonising thought.

4. See Graham Harman, *Object-Oriented Ontology: A New Theory of Everything*, Penguin, 2018.

Neurologically, when you intend to do something, you've already started doing it. A few hundred milliseconds before you think, 'I'm going to pick up this pencil,' you've already begun. Free will is a kind of timestamp: an aesthetic experience that's always secondary to what's actually happening. The body, including the brain, is literally in the future relative to awareness. The environment is already there before I am aware of it. And my sense of self is even later, responding as a kind of silhouette inversion of my environmental awareness. So, when I'm willing to lift up the pencil, several hundred milliseconds ago, the body has already started doing so, including the brain.

The brain as part of the environment isn't just some kind of puppet – it is imagining something. This brain is 'preconising' picking up the pencil, and then my sense of willing to do that is always late. That doesn't mean there's no freedom. Just because there's no free will, doesn't mean there's no freedom. It means freedom was imprisoned in a one-dimensional idea of conscious control. That distinction – between freely imposing will and acting mechanically – feeds person versus machine, human versus animal, master versus slave, human versus inhuman, and all the ways in which racism, transphobia and misogyny play out in our world. Politics, culture and architecture must take into account an awareness that isn't just of the future; it is the future.

C If we try to translate these concepts into spatial terms, we may think of places that have a sense of open-endedness and yet a certain orientation. We inhabit, take care, adjust and distort them. We're embedded in these contexts, so there is a degree of freedom without free will. What are the architectural qualities of such places?

TM

I'm looking at your room right now. What I like about your space is its play of light and shadow. There are parts I can't quite see – a plant behind your shoulder, I can't quite see their leaves, it's quite dark, and there are shadows between the books and the bookcase. My eye is invited not to fill it in, but to explore the opacity, to explore the shadow. The psychological equivalent of a black hole is not darkness, but total illumination. The narcissistic, command-control position – like Foucault's Panopticon[5] – is a space where everything is lit the same. All the lights are on. Everything is illuminated. And it's bleak.

5. Michel Foucault, *Discipline and Punish: The Birth of the Prison* [1975], trans. Alan Sheridan, Vintage Books, 1995, pp. 195–228.

By contrast, think of Giorgio de Chirico's oil *Mystery and Melancholy of a Street* (1914). There's a girl playing with a hoop, she's rolling it. You can see the giant buildings with their shadows – it's the late afternoon. You want to see around the corner. You can feel there's something because you see the shadow there. It's this very suggestive sense that there is something that you cannot see, but you know it's there. This is your hyperobject awareness. You can't see all of it, but you can feel it, you can sense it, you can feel the future. Because that space around the corner is the future. If you want to translate it into spatial terms, the suggestive corner of your room is the future.

Giorgio de Chirico, *Mystery and Melancholy of a Street*, 1914.

In the same way, one of the things I love about Cézanne is how he paints a container and the way he paints the whole – the vase, the jug, the cup, the bowl – as if the gap, the void is kind of inviting you in. It's not a strict point perspective, so there is a feeling of movement. You're not still looking at the picture, you feel like the jug is pouring itself towards you a little bit, just kind of inviting you. This sense of being invited – a space that invites you in – is the architectural analogue of welcoming the stranger.

The stranger is the neighbour. Love your neighbour as yourself – the guy in the Bible says. It's not saying: love your neighbour in the same way that you love yourself. It's much more than that: you can only love yourself when you love the neighbour. If we're talking about becoming here, the most radical form of it would be love your neighbour as yourself. The neighbour is the future, in a very radical sense – a sort of unpredictable, actually existing person, whom I find myself near to, not in tape-measure terms, but proximate to me phenomenologically speaking. We're talking about a kind of architecture that would allow for me to love the neighbour as myself.

C Thinking about the current state of architecture, we are interested in how you approach very serious concerns – colonialism, racism, global warming – without relying on ideological knowledge, but through a fragile sensitivity that seems rooted in art. It appears both subjective and collective – a form of intersubjective awareness. How do these feelings operate?

TIMOTHY MORTON There is a term by a somewhat Marxist thinker I like a lot, Raymond Williams. He calls it 'structure of feeling'.[6] He never quite develops it enough, but you could think of it as ideology from the future that hasn't happened yet. It hasn't crystallised out into a determinate set of beliefs and practices. It is still in a process of becoming. Not waiting for one thing to turn into another thing, but emphasising the process itself.

6. Raymond Williams, *The Long Revolution*, Chatto & Windus, 1961.

Structures of feeling are new ways of being. They necessarily appear as evanescent, fleeting, wavering. There's an analogy in the *Tibetan Book of the Dead*. When you die, you see different possible gateways into different realms. You're freaked out, you don't have a body anymore, you want to know where you're going. You see a nice doorway with a soft, smoky atmosphere, and you think, that looks reassuring – but that's the door to hell. Before that, you saw the Buddha mind directly, but most people delete it. They think it's just a glitch, some flickering illusion. The glitch is the thing. But because it looks like nothing, you ignore it.

Art is this glitching of appearance. Ethically speaking, true progress always looks like regress. It looks childish. Think of Nietzsche crying and hugging the horse being whipped. At the time, that looked stupid, regressive. Now we would all feel the same way if we saw an animal being beaten like that. Not just sympathy – almost becoming the animal and feeling that level of agony. True political progress looks like regress. The ultimate power of art is to negate the world. But if you truly negate it, it won't look like an obvious gesture within current symbolism. It will look hazy, wispy, stupid – like something a child could do.

Art creates structures of feeling to invite future ways of living. They are structures because they are intersubjective, as you say. They are collective. That's the whole trick behind political progress. So, I can't tell people exactly what to build and design, but I can tell them what it might look like and feel like when it's going right, and it might look like something incredibly playful, childish, stupid, ridiculous.

C As an alternative to analytic research in architecture, a series of Research by Design initiatives have taken place in the past months with the excuse of the UIA World Congress. How do you see these attempts at engaging with massive political situations and trying to change things?

TM What I like about HouseEurope! is the idea of approaching architecture through engaging with the law, as opposed to simply designing something within an existing legal framework. That is a sort of crossing of the streams: an imagining of what an architect could be that is not constrained by the concept of being an architect, but collaborating with other people, such as lawyers or politicians. It's a visionary approach. But I think also that something as grounded as Ibiye Camp's work, which is looking at changing the way in which we map and do cartography, it's an equivalent kind of way of doing architecture differently. There are all kinds of aesthetic and geographical rules in cartography and, it looks to me that, to map the world differently speaks already about how to transform it. It reminds of the famous *dérive* by Guy Debord, where you're mapping the city by walking around it, almost by dancing about it – as a deeply embodied movement whose significance might always be in the future.

The work of Forensic Architecture is a process of accounting for trauma. Part of it is a kind of truth and reconciliation, where people begin to fess up to the trauma that they've caused and allow for people to speak the trauma that is being caused to them. Without it, violence would be, to some extent, senseless. We go back to the beginning here – violence always represents the breakdown of communication and symbolisation. So, by definition, to restore symbolisation and meaning to something violent that has happened is a way to lubricate the past so that the future can be different. It's a kind of grief work. Grief is where everything that happened to you becomes a kind of body worker and starts to massage you so that your future can be different. It happens without your conscious will. Grief is something that always happens to you, it's never something you can do.

And looking at the urban parades, processions and rituals proposed by Common Accounts, I like the idea of acting collectively, without necessarily an agenda. I like the necessarily aesthetic – that is to say non-teleological – quality of this notion of parade. In other words, there is not necessarily a direction, conceptually speaking. I think that this emphasis on ritual is more radical than the amoral or licentious carnivalesque structure. The parade is a way of inviting a future that could be different – an invitation to create a different world. I think it's a kind of reimagining of what pleasure can be in the context of transmogrifying the power.

Curators

COLLECTIVE AWARENESS OF PLANETARY ENTANGLEMENTS

Data ecology

Geopolitics of space

Synthetic intelligence

Design by law

Cultural depth

We practise architecture immersed in colossal oceans of information – overloaded by layers of legislation, global warming indicators, accelerated geopolitical threats, developments of synthetic intelligence and much more. These planetary phenomena are experienced at an exponential rate of complexity that seems impossible to digest, exceeding the limits of individual perception and cognition.[1] However global, these systems translate within every localised situation, provoking a significant impact on everyday habitational and design actions. As humans we can barely grasp minor fragments of these hyper-dense entanglements. They are so overwhelming and incremental that we can easily feel paralysed or alienated by them.[2] (1) The work of those gathered under the 'Becoming Hyper-conscious' pillar engages with these fragmented encounters, from evidence of violence embedded in tropical rainforests to algorithmic environments shaping contemporary life. Rather than attempting to represent totalities, they construct situated readings of complex systems, where architecture becomes a medium for collectively sensing, orienting and acting within phenomena that remain structurally incomplete to human awareness.

(1) Timothy Morton, *Hyperobjects: Philosophy and Ecology After the End of the World*, University of Minnesota Press, 2013.

1. Benjamin H. Bratton, *The Stack: On Software and Sovereignty*, MIT Press, 2016.
2. Timothy Morton, *Hyperobjects: Philosophy and Ecology After the End of the World*, University of Minnesota Press, 2013.

Across several investigations, data is not approached as an abstract layer of information, but as a material, political and spatial condition. Cloud infrastructures, sensing systems and image-based platforms show how information is anchored in territories, resources and physical environments.[3] (2) Data centres reshape landscapes through energy

3. Marina Otero Verzier, 'Data Architectures and the Ontologies of Depth', *Log*, 60, 2024, pp. 177–86.

(2) Marina Otero Verzier, *Computational Compost*, Tabakalera International Centre of Contemporary Culture, Donostia/San Sebastián, Spain, 2023.

(3) Lev Manovich / Cultural Analytics Lab, TimeLine, 2009.

consumption and thermal impact, while digital images reorganise public perception through algorithmic circulation in social media. Images operate beyond analogy and representation, as platform-based tools designed and programmed to classify and reshape how architecture is accessed, valued, desired and produced. (3, 4, 5) Several practices explore alternative forms of cartography and digital mapping to unveil network patterns and phenomena otherwise invisible to everyday sight. In parallel, critical spatial practices mobilise data as a political and ecological tool, tracing connections between extraction, biodiversity loss and colonial legacies, revealing how information infrastructures are entangled with systems of power and environmental transformation. (6, 7, 8, 9, 10)

Computation reconfigures design through algorithmic processes, artificial intelligence and emerging forms of digital reasoning that

(4) Javier Fernández Contreras, *The Interiors of Social Media: Architecture, Space, and Technology in the 21st Century*, 2026.

(5) John May, *Signal Image Architecture*, 2019.

(6) Paulo Tavares, Trees, Vines, Palms and Other Architectural Monuments, Brazil, 2017–21.

(7) Ibiye Camp, Data, the New Black Gold, Freetown, Sierra Leone, 2019.

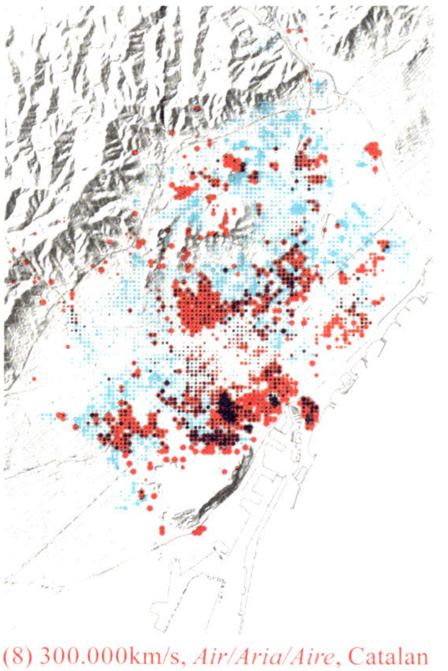

(8) 300.000km/s, *Air/Aria/Aire*, Catalan Pavilion, Venice Architecture Biennale, Italy, 2021.

(9) Limbo Accra, The Liminal Archive, Accra, Ghana, 2022.

redistribute authorship and decision-making. The historical shift towards variation and automation has intensified with contemporary AI systems, where architecture is equipped with tools capable of generating, analysing and simulating complex conditions. These systems open new possibilities for design, enabling alternative forms of iteration and participation. (11, 12) At the same time they raise critical questions regarding bias, extractive data practices and the carbon footprint of computational infrastructures, revealing how artificial intelligence operates through material supply chains, labour conditions and energy-intensive systems at a planetary scale.[4] Rather than neutral instruments, these systems are portrayed as contested environments; they enable new and collective forms of agency while at the same time structurally reproducing existing asymmetries and distributions of power. It falls to architects to investigate and negotiate their

(11) Mario Carpo, *Beyond Digital: Design and Automation at the End of Modernity*, 2023.

(12) Lluís Ortega / JL-Office, *Recycling Intelligences*, Venice Architecture Biennale, Italy, 2025.

4. Kate Crawford, *Atlas of AI: Power, Politics, and the Planetary Costs of Artificial Intelligence*, Yale University Press, 2021.

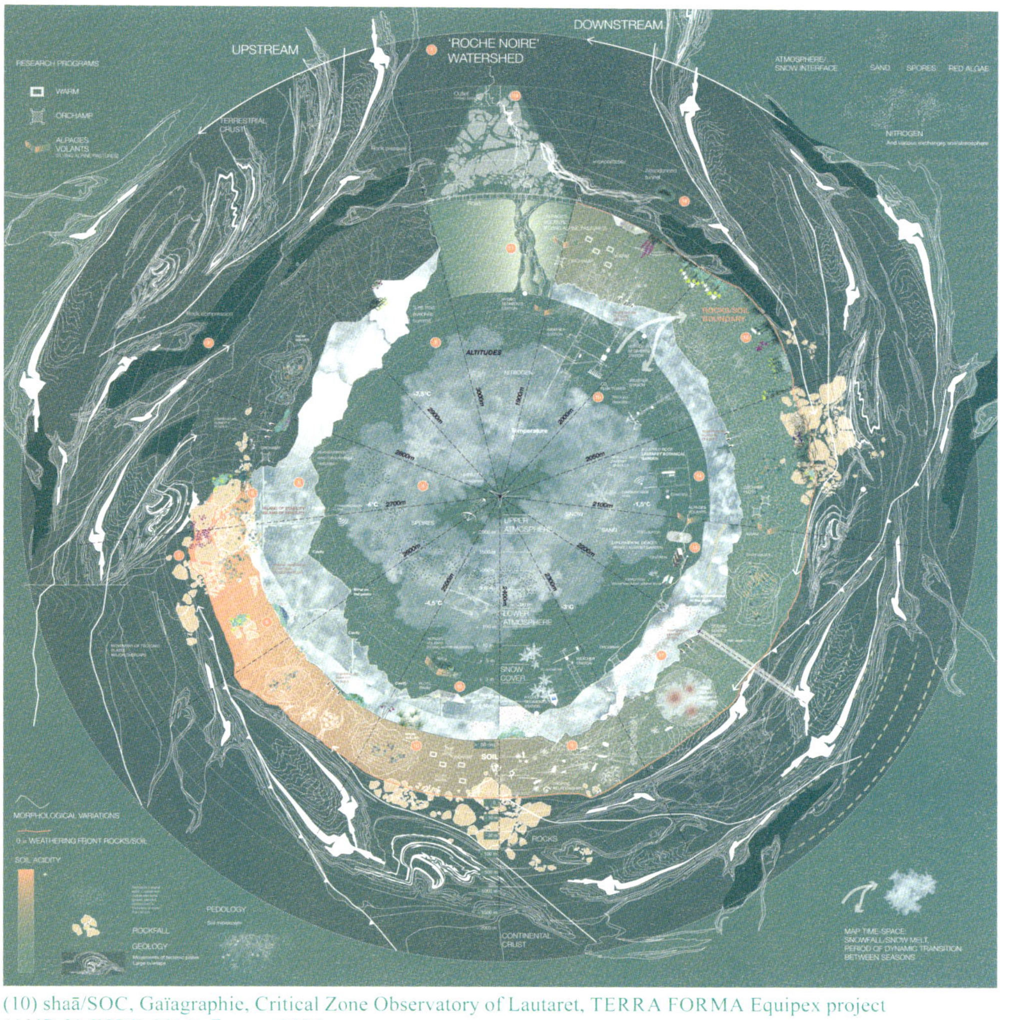

(10) shaā/SOC, Gaïagraphie, Critical Zone Observatory of Lautaret, TERRA FORMA Equipex project (ANR-21-ESRE-0014), France, 2024.

(13) Lydia Kallipoliti, Areti Markopoulou and Post-Spectacular Office, *Metabolic Home: New Forms of Cohabitation and Decarbonization in the Dense City*, Venice Architecture Biennale, Italy, 2025.

political, ecological and cultural potential in the realm of spatial practice. (13)

At the territorial scale, these dynamics become interrelated with geopolitical interests that shape environments through extraction, violence and resource control. Hydrological systems are redirected and weaponised, mineral landscapes reorganised through global supply chains, and infrastructures of energy and communication produce inequitable spatial distributions. Within these extreme conditions, architecture operates as a tool for investigation. Tools such as virtual reconstruction and geolocation allow the emergence of spatial witnesses of human rights abuse. Examined as repositories of evidence, they are assembled into juridical and political claims. In short, these practices construct situated readings of structural violence, revealing how conflict is inscribed in space and how spatial knowledge can contribute to processes of

(14) Center for Spatial Technologies, Russian Attack on Kyiv TV Tower, Kyiv, Ukraine, 2022.

(15) Forensic Architecture, *'When it Stopped Being a War': The Situated Testimony of Dr Ghassan Abu-Sittah*, 2024–25.

accountability, a sense of truth and a path to reconciliation. (14, 15)

Legal and regulatory frameworks appear as operative layers within architectural production. They are acknowledged as materials to be read, interpreted and designed with, functioning as forms of infrastructural governance that shape spatial outcomes.[5] Planning systems, building codes, legislation and contractual structures define the parameters within which architecture takes shape. However, their application is neither fixed nor singular; through selective readings, loopholes and reinterpretations, these frameworks can act as generative constraints, catalysing unexpected and joyful spatial outcomes. (16, 17, 18a&b) In parallel, architectural agency extends beyond individual building projects towards the design of legislation itself. Through instruments such as the European Citizens' Initiative, legal frameworks are approached as collective design projects where

(18a&b) Hiroyuki Ito, Tenjincho Place, Tokyo, Japan, 2023.

(16) Brandlhuber+, Antivilla, Krampnitz, Berlin, Germany, 2015.

(17) XDGA, Melopee School, Ghent, Belgium, 2022.

spatial knowledge is translated into policy proposals advocating desired horizons such as the right to housing. In addition, labour conditions, fee structures and institutional frameworks reveal how legal and economic systems organise not only the built environment, but the discipline itself. (19)

5. Keller Easterling, *Extrastatecraft: The Power of Infrastructure Apace*, Verso, 2014.

(19) The Architecture Lobby, *Organizing in the Lobby*, Venice Architecture Biennale, Italy, 2025.

Curatorial and editorial practices further articulate how architecture operates within networks of discourse. Small magazines and digital platforms act as lubricants for the collective formation of today's architectural sensitivities, in addition to framing debates and positioning architectural work within broader cultural and political contexts. Through selection, narrative construction and visual language, these carefully curated platforms influence how architecture is interpreted and valued. (20, 21, 22, 23) At the same time, curatorial practices rooted in ecological interactions, food systems, body interface and popular culture

(20) Quaderns d'Arquitectura i Urbanisme, *les imatges es queden curtes*, issue 278, Barcelona, Spain, 2026.

(21) Accattone / Arc en rêve, *MBL: Impasse des Lilas*, 2024.

(22) *Real Review: What it Means to Live Today*, Summer 2016.

(23) *PLOT Especial 21: Suelos, Ecologías, Territorios, Comunidades*, Buenos Aires, Argentina, 2024.

reposition architecture within metabolic processes, where cultivation, consumption, pleasure and fun become operative frameworks to imagine and prototype alternative futures. (24, 25, 26, 27) Finally, a range of pedagogical environments engages diverse teaching and research practices. Learning unfolds across different cultural, geographic and institutional contexts, redefining how architectural knowledge is transmitted, transformed and produced. (28, 29, 30, 31)

The juxtaposition of these works suggests a shift in how architecture engages with large-scale complexity. A multiplicity of partial views and grounded interventions are prioritised over comprehensive models based on universal solutions. The orientation suggested by Becoming Hyperconscious does not seek to reveal a final condition of total knowledge, but a path towards intensified awareness of situated entanglement – an ability to recognise how multiple systems overlap,

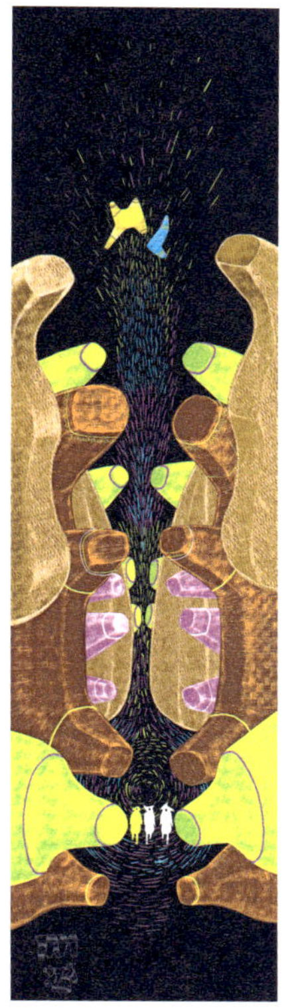

(24) Afreetekture, *Architecture South Africa Issue 101*, Johannesburg, South Africa, 2024.

(25) Lluís Alexandre Casanovas, Invernáculo new cultural billboard system for Madrid, Spain, 2025.

(26) Cooking Sections, *Becoming Xerophile*, Sharjah Architecture Triennial, United Arab Emirates, 2019.

(27) Common Accounts, Clima Fitness: Rituales de Adaptabilidad, Matadero Madrid, Spain, 2023.

(28) Rural Studio, Newbern Town Hall, Newbern, Alabama, 2011.

interfere and co-produce spatial realities. In this expanded field, architectural practice becomes a form of mediation, navigating between data and territory, computation and representation, regulation and agency, culture and environment.

(29) Tongji University, Robotic natural log fabrication, Co-Poiesis project, Shanghai, China, 2025.

(30) MASS Design Group and theAfrican Design Centre, Ruhehe Primary School, Ruhengeri, Rwanda, 2018.

(31) EPFL Domestic City Lab (DC-Lab), Final reviews, Lausanne, Switzerland, Fall 2025.

Becoming Attuned

‘I wouldn’t be surprised if poetry…
is how the world works.’

David Byrne, *Bicycle Diaries*, 2009

What kinds of meanings and poetics can we address with our everyday practice?

The traditional aesthetic paradigm, grounded in Western-centred perspectives and entrenched notions of beauty, seems increasingly limited in dealing with the complex challenges posed by today's rapidly changing world. The poetics of becoming recognise the fluidity and contingency of architecture: no longer fixed, it is subject to negotiation and exchange.

This position advocates for alternative paradigms, calling for a shift from passive observation to active engagement in specific, diverse contexts that interrelate a multiplicity of beings. It fosters a process of attunement that guides us to listen, not just to physical landscapes but also to the stories they tell, the needs they express and the cultures they embody.

The perception of our manifold pre-existing realities may be attuned in order to curate the meaning of our actions in spatial practice. 'Becoming Attuned' claims an approach guided by empathy and desire, to acknowledge usually dismissed values: sensitivities that embrace uncertainty, the ordinary, mundane accidentality, physical and digital phenomena, and unexpected pleasures and delights.

Matilde Cassani

A TRIP TO THE JUNGLE

Pimpa is a famous little white dog with red polka dots and long ears, created by Italian cartoonist Francesco Tullio Altan in 1975. The star of comic strips, cartoons and a monthly magazine embarks on fantastical and poetic adventures with her owner Armando, talking to both objects and animals in a child-friendly, yet completely realistic, world. In one episode, while walking through the Amazonian jungle, she hears a chameleon, but she cannot see him.

When asked why he is invisible, he replies that every time he moves from one place to another he becomes the same colour as his background. Next to yellow he becomes yellow, next to Pimpa he becomes like Pimpa. When she asks why, he replies: 'I'm afraid they'll eat me.' A few seconds later, a carnivorous animal emerges from the nearby foliage. Terrified, Pimpa becomes the same colour as the jungle – she becomes attuned.

Scenes from 'Una gita nella giungla' (A trip to the Jungle), Season 1, episode 17 of the Italian animated children's series *La Pimpa*. © ALTAN/QUIPOS

Being attuned can thus be considered as being aware of the unique, deep-seated identity and distinctive historical, cultural, natural and sensory characteristics that define a specific place. The concept transcends physical space to entrench something both hyperlocal and global, micro and macro, and transcalar.[1] In this context, as Christian Norberg-Schulz suggests, architecture should not merely provide functional shelter;[2] rather, its purpose is to help people inhabit their surroundings in an existential sense, allowing them to find their bearings and identify with their environment.

1. Andrés Jaque, *Superpowers of Scale*, Columbia Books on Architecture and the City, 2020.
2. Christian Norberg-Schulz, *Genius loci: Paesaggio ambiente architettura*, Mondadori Electa, 1997.

In their book *Echo of Space / Space of Echo* (2009),[3] which explores the relationship between physical space ('echo of space') and human behaviour ('space of echo'), Atelier Bow-Wow describe another experience of becoming attuned when staying in a lodge in the Costa Rican jungle. The book advocates for an architectural ethnography, analysing how users adapt, inhabit and shape their urban environments. What guided the designer of the lodge if not the tone of the place? What did they experience there? By immersing themselves in the humidity and sounds of their context, the book's authors experienced the overwhelming presence of the jungle rather than just observing it, and the overwhelming spirit of the lodge – how it related to and operated within the forest as a form of being and a form of doing.

3. Atelier Bow-Wow, *Echo of Space / Space of Echo*, INAX-Shuppan, 2009.

Yoshiharu Tsukamoto of Atelier Bow-Wow entering the lodge immersed in the jungle.

Architectural drawings and photography have traditionally represented a finished form as a natural outcome of the design process, but perhaps they should be seen as provisional, depending on what is encountered on site, capturing both human and non-human behaviour, as Atelier Bow-Wow's Nocturnal Tokyo research by design project for the UIA World Congress proposes.

Thinking of architecture as a series of bodies in space reflects Maurice Merleau-Ponty's phenomenology of embodiment, in which the world is not a collection of external objects but a sensitive fabric to which we belong, where the flesh of the body and the flesh of the world are interchangeable and in constant relation.[4] Here, our bodies are attuned; human beings, time and space are made of the same magma, constituting not chaos but a sort of circular growth where each is determining and determined.

4. Maurice Merleau-Ponty, *The Possibility of Philosophy: Course Notes from the College de France, 1959–1961*, Northwestern University Press, 2022.

Attuned is also an individual in a crowd. The crowd has a common goal and, as such, its protagonists experience a sense of equality in this moment of excitement, a temporary sense of relief from the rigid social hierarchies and personal burdens of distance.[5] The crowd is thus the messenger of a collective memory which is renovated, with time, in the spaces we interact with. Public gatherings and rituals serve to refresh citizens' participation and strengthen social ties. Today's large public gatherings reveal the complex and diverse territory, under constant re-actualisation, of the necessities and visions of the community. They constantly attune and generate spatial implications.

5. Elias Canetti, *Masse und Macht*, Claassen, 1960 and *Crowds and Power*, Viking Press, 1962.

Becoming

The quest to become attuned generated by public gatherings was clear in *Tutto* (2018), my mixed-media installation for the Manifesta 12 international art event in Palermo, which drew on Sicilian Baroque traditions and updated them by revealing the complexity of the new and different cultural inputs the city experiences today. The project took its inspiration from the specifically Palermitan case in which the Christian and Hindu Tamil communities have developed a profound syncretic devotion to, and participate in the traditional Palermitan rituals of Santa Rosalia, the city's patron saint. The work focuses on the idea that a celebration is a tool to describe a wider system of societal changes which are, or will be, reverberated into the city fabric.

Matilde Cassani, *Tutto*, Manifesta 12, Palermo, Sicily, 2018.
Performance and installation at the Piazza dei Quattro Canti.

Based on Maurice Halbwachs' theory that collective memory is not a static repository but a dynamic, socially constructed process that constantly updates the past to align with the present, as in Baroque times celebrations are agents of urban change where performative acts anticipate how the city will look in the future. Their ephemeral architectures are thus more attuned than permanent structures, in anticipating what is not yet visible in the urban fabric. They act as a sudden interlude, an 'intermezzo', during which the climate consequences, political choices and social battles that inform future, more stable architectures are displayed.

Intermezzo

A musical interlude, an intermezzo, is a piece of music, usually instrumental, performed between two acts of an opera, or between movements of a composition, which serves as a pause, a break in the action, or a dramatic link. In the eighteenth century, it was even a comic pause, performed between the acts of a serious opera. In the Romantic and Modern eras, the term referred to a piece that connected two parts of a longer work, also known as a 'bridge'. An intermezzo is also an independent orchestral composition, not linked to the opera.

Thanks to their strong emotional charge, many intermezzos have become iconic. As an example, Pietro Mascagni's intermezzo from *Cavalleria Rusticana* (1890) accompanies the opening credits of Martin Scorsese's *Raging Bull* (1980) and the final scene of *The Godfather Part III* (1990). Here, a marginal part of the play becomes the protagonist of some of the most renowned movie scenes of the twentieth century.

Intermezzo can even be just a short break, an interval. Its function is typically to fulfil the technical needs of the spectacle: manage the timing, allow for scene changes, or offer the audience a break to reflect, a more logistical purpose.

A spatial connection, an emotionally charged moment, a functional connection between two sides, a pause – all these short definitions of the musical term can be easily translated into architecture and to what being attuned could mean.

Known as Chapex, the Palais des Expositions in Charleroi, Belgium developed by AM AjdvivgwA - architecten Jan De Vylder Inge Vinck (A JDVIV) + AgwA and completed in 2025, is a profound embodiment of the idea of intermezzo as something marginal that becomes identitarian in its own right. This transformation of a city centre industrial exhibition space into a modern, multifunctional exhibition, congress and concert venue, perhaps also touches upon all of the previous definitions. The project embraces the scarcity of means and takes de-industrialisation as a fact. One side uses only a third of the budget, while the other opens the central part of the former factory to become a terraced park. It reconnects the two sides of the city and above and below it, energy-free and using only the architecture of what is available.[6]

6. https://divisare.com/projects/507008-a-jdviv-agwa-architects-filip-dujardin-chapex

De Vylder Vinck defines the operation as an 'ENTR'ACTE' – an intermezzo or pause, then. Selective in its goal, contained in the intervention, and poetic in its architectural choices, it 'works in times of scarcity, changing needs to better practice, but never without beauty'.[7] The project looks at the urban fabric and transforms the building into an action by re-establishing movement around the inside, outside and within the city. De Vylder Vinck does not change the building, nor try to tame an architecture of such scale; he retains the architecture and works with its matter to design walls, columns and even seating. The architecture is thus attuned to its context.

7. Excerpt from Jan De Vylder, speech at the 'Award Ceremony of the European Prize for Urban Public Space 2024', Barcelona.

Until recently, before climate change and rising global temperatures, for most cultures night was an intermezzo, a blank moment of the day, the opposite of the day, when the city ceased being a crossroads of activities. Traditionally seen as a moment of pause, time without content, in some regions of the world it is now often considered the most productive moment of the day, or even a substitute for it. In Michelangelo Antonioni's film *La Notte* (1961), set in Milan, the transition from day to night signifies a shift from restless alienation in the city to a desperate, hedonistic attempt to escape it. While the day involves sterile professional obligations and individual wandering, the night, and more specifically the long party attended by the film's protagonists at the infamous Villa Gherardini, enables behaviours, interactions and emotional exposures that do not occur during the day.

Atelier Bow-Wow's speculative Nocturnal Tokyo adds to these examples in proposing a transition towards nocturnal urbanism as a form of adaptation to climate change in a city that is not yet fully prepared or organised for the shift. They imagine a workday starting in the late afternoon instead of early morning, and the logistical barriers that would need to be overcome in this new urban planning scenario: scarce means of night-time transportation, the absence of urban furniture and resting infrastructures, and low public activity. Their research focuses on people's behaviour and rituals after dark, and on 'day-fying' the night, highlighting the need for a new attunement that moves away from traditional urban planning and instead embraces nocturnal rhythms and behaviours, where the intermezzo becomes a moment for a new form of collective city life.

In their UIA Barcelona proposal, Bangkok Tokyo Architecture explore an architecture of plurality of design and inhabitation, where the process is kept open and negotiable at all scales and moments of design. Indeed, in their Collective Completions workshop, the existing architectural form continues to update as the participant groups exchange ideas and work, embodying the very notion of the contemporary city and creating a feeling of being attuned. Given that construction is considered one of the most polluting industries, it is increasingly necessary to imagine cities that maintain a stable physical form while rapidly adapting their uses. Observing societal changes and engaging with them will produce ever-changing architectural results. Today, more than ever, there is a need for a multi-authorial approach to interpreting the complexity of architectural practice.

Elements of Dissidence, the workshop led by BeAr, articulates the idea that a souvenir is the minimal exported unit of identity of a place: 'a portable object that condenses simplified urban narratives and disseminates a codified image of the city outward'. A souvenir is a scale replica of the identity of a place, a substitute for a map of geographical extensions, of an atlas for data, of a travel guide for places to visit. It is a condenser of a collective identity that is constantly negotiated and reimagined. Collective memory reconstructs and selects from the past in function of the present. The shared memory of a nation, tradition or city originates in an individual memory and gives continuity and cohesion to collective life.[8] New souvenirs continue to be designed through time and sold in markets next to great classics – replicas of the famous monuments. An architecture focused on what heritage to preserve and what image to export is a form of being attuned to the collective past and a collective present of a city like Barcelona, where identity has historically been at stake.

8. Maurice Halbwachs, *On Collective Memory*, ed. and trans. Lewis A. Coser, University of Chicago Press, 1992.

The UIA World Congress in Barcelona is also an intermezzo, a space of encounter and friction between different perspectives, a form of collective celebration. Becoming attuned means looking at the distinctive historical, cultural, natural and sensory moments that define a specific place in a specific moment. The Congress brings together a multiplicity of contexts, practices and voices, not only to discuss architecture but to experience it collectively.

Research by Design 11/12

Architecten Jan de Vylder Inge Vinck, with ETHZ D ARCH IEA. CHAIR/SHARE OF JDV ON ARCHITECTURE AN(D) ATTITUDE; and KADUS KUNSTAKADEMIE, DÜSSELDORF. BAUKUNSTKLASSE INGE VINCK

’ ’ ’

%%%

’’’

ENTR’ACTE ATTI’TUDE ATTU’NE

The triple ENTR’ACTE ATTI’TUDE ATTU’NE is no more no less a way of rewording the idea that the BECOMING and the ATTUNE are looking for. Architecture as a matter of the behaviour of availability – ATTI’TUDE. Architecture as matter of moment amongst other perspectives – ENTR’ACTE. Architecture as a matter of precision though without parallax – ATT’UNE. The truncation mark – borrowed from the word entr’acte and propelled into the other words – stands as a sign for that precision, that momentariness and that availability.

3.33% 33.3% 333%

This triple ENTR’ACTE ATTI’TUDE ATTU’NE mirrors in another triple 3.33% / 33.3% / 333% and vice versa.

This triple numbering – this time accompanied by a comma – orients the ENTR' ATTI' ATTU' triple towards the discussion on ECONOMY, ECOLOGY and ERGONOMICS – the order of these words here presented is not per se linked to the order in which the percentages appear.

ECONOMY ECOLOGY ERGONOMICS

The word ECONOMY goes back to the Greek word *OIKONOMIA* being the combination of the words *OIKOS* and *NEMEIN* or *NOMES*. *OIKOS* is related to the idea of HOUSE, and *NEMEIN* or *NOMOS* to the idea of managing. In short: the however nowadays modern definition frames ECONOMY as a large-scale systematic; in origin it framed the idea of keeping a household.

The word ECOLOGY goes equally back to the same Greek origin. Also, the word *OIKOS* – ECO- is here visible and the word *LOGOS* speaks for itself; but together they stand for – as one could say – the understanding of the logics of a household. In later interpretations rather to the logics of the environmental conditions – the German zoologist Ernst Haeckel did widen the origin to the nowadays interpretation by introducing the word ECOLOGY into biologic perspective studying microorganisms and their environments.

The word ERGONOMICS, in turn, finds origin in the Greek words *ERGON* and *NOMOS*. *ERGON* stands for work and *NOMOS* stands for – in a wider understanding starting from law – standards; together they can be understood as the organisation of the environment in favour of the human.

INTERFERING, INTERVENTION and INTRODUCING

To link ECO' NOMY & 'LOGY & ERGO' – the play with the truncations is not just a game – with triple %'s again three other words are to be added: INTERFERING, INTERVENTION and INTRODUCING.

The attitude of not aiming or ambitioning – nor maybe as first not expecting or demanding – a total conceptual control – and by that total economy of means – is linked to these words INTERFERING, INTERVENTION and INTRODUCING and are as they sound to be understood as minor acts and at the same time acts with a certain precision.

These acts do not need all means – MATTER OF ECONOMY –; and these ACT'S – it is not a spelling mistake but once again the play of the truncation mark – are as well the outcome of thinking and acting as the conscious start of thinking and acting.

Is 3.33% the most DARING REFRAINING, being the almost nothing, the 33.3% act – 33.3% of what one mostly sees as the 100% architecture acting generally is about – the most FEASIBLE REFRAINED and aims to become – BECOME! – a 333% UN-REFRAINED CHANGES since this PRECISE REFRAINED act – both the 3.33% and 33.3% – comes to leave space for past and future, however the acting accordingly to today's questions or needs, even longings.

333% points to the past, the today and the future: how to act understanding the given – the past – the needs – the today and the not known – the future. Or how to act the past still to be, the today without loss of the needs at all and the future to be free at all.

REFRAINED, ATTU'NE isn't it? REFRAIN to UN-REFRAINED, better than that it doesn't get when it is about seeking for a reality in the political shout of STOP this – like demolishing –

and STOP that – like building. STOP as the lack of imagination or fantasy or dare or capacity. REFRAIN or ATTU'NE as mastering the chances above HALTING the fears.

ADD ON TAKE AWAY into ADD AWAY TAKE ON

And maybe this idea on REFRAIN UN-REFRAIN and ATTU'NE can be even more inspirationally reworded by twisting the idea of ADD ON TAKE AWAY into the idea of ADD AWAY TAKE ON.

To clear the idea of STOP this – like building – and STOP that – like demolishing – meanwhile seemingly an uncritical premise – who is not with us is against us – can be transcended by the belief that it is RATHER A MATTER OF TWIST – FREEING – than SHIFT – HALTING.

A twist that believes that it is about daring but refraining – that is daring!

FORM LIFE URGE

The TWIST of ADD ON TAKE AWAY in ADD AWAY TAKE ON is not only just a WORD TWIST giving other perspectives on meaning, but by it FORM TWIST, finding that other perspective. A TWIST by FORM. A TWIST by the ACT of FORM.

In the order ADD ON TAKE AWAY the words are the FORM of the idea or CONTENT. Twisting the words around delivers first just a FORM but seemingly a FORM that equals a TWISTED thinking of content. The formal twisting seems to be recognisable by the on-the-move thinking and even more by giving that thinking a further understanding; an understanding it was looking for. ADD AWAY TAKE ON is first just a FORM, but by that FORM the CONTENT finds base.

But there is more – next to the daring though refraining and the form making content; the PLAY of WORDS also lifts the discussion if it is about demolishing or building. As the words left their original place in QUADRUPLE it points also to the free act surpassing the idea of demolishing and building: it is in the act of making – read: FORMING – that which is eventually taken away – demolished – and what is eventually added – build – become by FORM one act and one outcome.

Understanding this, the triple word-set FORM LIFE URGE explains itself: the essence is LIFE, no one discusses that. The URGE should be not less discussed. But the idea of FORM comes possibly rather unexpected. But not if ADD AWAY TAKE ON comes into place.

UNIVERSUM CAROUSEL JOURNEY

The word LIFE. If the triple word-sets ATTI'TUDE ENTR'ACTE ATTU'NE and ECO' NOMY & 'LOGY & ERGO' and the %%% sets of words are setting out a way of thinking or an approach of method, then is UCJ the reason why and at the same time the outcome of. Not the political discussion of STOP & STOP is matter of change – STOP does just STOP – but only FORM is the matter: TWIST is the change and it is about a MATERIAL as much as about a MATTER OF change.

Daring to FORM, however REFRAINING the ACT makes that an UN-REFRAINED REALITY that can be given SPACE. And that SPACE will not just be for the NOW but WITH the EVER and this BEFORE and AFTER. UNIVERSUM as SPACE and CAROUSEL as TIME and JOURNEY as LIFE.

PALAIS DES EXPOSITIONS – A PRISM

AM AjdvivgwA - architecten Jan De Vylder Inge Vinck (A JDVIV) + AgwA, Palais des Expositions (CHAPEX), Charleroi, Belgium, 2025.

PALAIS DES EXPOSITIONS – CHARLEROI – is a transformation of a city centre-situated industrial exhibitions space – 66.000 m² being 500,000m³; dividing above and below city – into a nowadays open programmed exhibition, congress and concert venue. The special challenge however was that only ⅓ of the needed means were available: 33 M€ instead of the usual normal expected 100 M€.

This led to a review of all thinking – conceiving – and doing – forming – needed to conduct the project. Key was the competition proposal. As the brief stated to give advantage of action to the middle-situated large lobby space – 12.000 m² – and upgrading it to a state of the art of what is today expected of architecture expression and nonetheless a zero-energy building; the proposal stripped the centre part from unnecessary additional buildings and from its façades to turn it into a revised multilevel terraced open space and by that even not needing the 33 M€ budget but only – irony – only ⅓ of the 33.3% not less checking in on the idea of zero-energy – there being no building anymore – and what architecture is about today: connecting. In space and in commune. From the 1950s onwards the building did disconnect above and below city, the terraces today reconnect. And ⅔ of the budget was now available for other actions; actions not foreseen in the original budget. As said: this challenge did challenge everything – not only regarding the transformation of the venue as such; but even more the transformation of the architecture practice as such: utmost all usual operational habits needed to be reviewed.

Looking backwards; the PALAIS DES EXPOSITIONS PROJECT became a new PRISM on looking and understanding. All sets of words above – like from ⅓ to 33.3% situating ATTI'TUDE – came in the whilst and by repeated reflection on the meaning of the project and process. Not only on the project but on how to understand the nowadays language of urges – ST0P & STOP – in a more adequate and precise but also at the same time more to a realistic understanding and not pamphleteer shouting, and this never without what it only is about: life, the poetry of life.

architecten Jan De Vylder Inge Vinck (A JDVIV), Lieve Bloemen Lus, Lievegem, Belgium, 2025.

architecten Jan de Vylder Inge Vinck (AJDVIV), Rot-Ellen-Berg, Oudenaarde, Belgium, 2011.

At the same time and moment this project balances with a 66m² house LIEVE BLOEMEN LUS realised for 100 k€ where 300 k€ is the average expected. 2026. But also, yet in 2010 HOUSE ROT-ELLEN-BERG the same economy. And in 1996 HOUSE OVO II even half the economy: 50.000 k€.

As the PALAIS DES EXPOSITIONS became the MOMENT being a PRISM of thinking and talking about the matter; actually, the way of ACT'ING and REFL'ACT' ING yet so long. And in a matter that makes architecture not a matter of one or another political novelty but a matter of architecture.

ARCHITECTURE IS (NOT) A MATTER OF ARCHITECTURE

However, a paradox is to be situated. Here above stated ARCHITECTURE IS A MATTER OF ARCHITECTURE; however once before saying ARCHITECTURE IS NOT A MATTER OF ARCHITECTURE. How to understand this now?

DREAM / D-RE-AM
(D)-REA-L-(M) / (D)-REA-L-M

IR-RE-SPONSIBILITY

Therefore, the next came along. For long – and still going on – the RE-word is today overarching the architecture thinking at all. Endless streams of RE-words. From RE-USE to RE-COMMON to even more specialist ADAPTIVE RE-USE and RE-SOURCE and RE-CLAIM and RE- and RE- and RE – and with an ironical note: however re-lated to the STOP & STOP, the fog of RE- never stops …

The IS (NOT) points – Oh irony – towards two dear words that are clearly key – personal and to the matter of the ATTI' ENTR' ATTU' and %%%: 'dream' and 'irresponsible'. To rewrite these words: D-RE-AM and IR-RE-SPONSIBLE. The PRISM is about that: not a SHIFT IN POLITICS but a TWIST IN FORM; and a certain degree of IR-RE-SPONSIBLE ACTING often energised by D-RE-AM_ING away is what made possible from ROT-ELLEN-BERG HOUSE to PALAIS DES EXPOSITIONS.

D-RE-AM till it becomes not only RE-AL but a new RE-ALM: UNIVERSUM CAROUSEL JOURNEY.

DO WE TEACH WHAT WE PRACTISE?
DO WE PRACTISE WHAT WE TEACH?*

Attuned

AM AjdvivgwA - architecten Jan De Vylder Inge Vinck (A JDVIV) + AgwA, Palais des Expositions (CHAPEX), Charleroi, Belgium, 2025.

Holding CHAIR ON ARCHITECTURE AND DESIGN at the ETH ZÜRICH DEPARTMENT OF ARCHITECTURE – chair of Jan De Vylder renamed as SHARE OF ARCHITECTURE AN(D) ARCHITECTURE – a year before (Fall 2024) delivery of PALAIS DES EXPOSITIONS (2025) a graduation design studio studied PALAIS DES EXPOSITIONS into a next future. A future in which housing and work and many other ideas were freely tested on the just about to be delivered project. Now a year after (Spring 2026) the chair of Inge Vinck at the Baukunstklasse and Kunstakademie Düsseldorf (KADUS) explored further on speculating possible futures for PALAIS DES EXPOSITIONS.

Today at the ETHZ D-ARCH a special research project has begun on the future of the campus building. The project aims to collectively re-design the actual building – ADAPTIVE RE-USE to state it in academical vowing. The SHARE OF deviated away from just the expected all over transformation by first studying a doubling of the actual volume of 66.666 x 66.666 m2 by new construction – NOT STOP – and in the outcome of that IR-RE-SPONSIBLE D-RE-AM-ING what the available existing might all ever mean: BECOMING! DO WE TEACH WHAT WE PRACTISE? DO WE PRACTISE WHAT WE TEACH?

BRAVIOUR SCARCITY BEAUTY
UNLESS EVER PEOPLE
AVAILABLE ACCEPTANCE ADORANCE

ENTR'ACTE ATTI'TUDE ATTU'NE inscribes itself in the series of triple word-sets above situated and by that is part of an ever ongoing thinking caused by different acting but also causing action differently, but all bring words to the front that do PLAY so long yet always KEY roles in whatever whenever however: IR-RE-SPONSIBILITY and BEAUTY and PEOPLE and FORM and …

ABOUT THIS
AND ABOUT THAT
ALSO THIS
AND SO ON
THAT MAYBE
IF NOT
ALWAYS

Yes. Let's move on. ADD AWAY TAKE ON.

Bangkok Tokyo Architecture
(Wtanya Chanvitan and Takahiro Kume)

COLLECTIVE COMPLETIONS

Bangkok Tokyo Architecture, House C, Chiang Mai, Thailand, 2023. Construction of House C, showing the assemblage of commonly found materials.

Architecture is not a finished form fixed in time, nor always the product of a single author, but something that is continually modified, adapted and reinterpreted. Our involvement as architects is temporary and partial; we are only the initiators of the transformations to come. Rather than seeking singular or exceptional outcomes, we look to the ordinary and familiar, assembling typical things in ways that can generate multiple possibilities of use, meaning and authorship.

The Collective Completions workshop explores an architecture of plurality, questioning conventional ideas of authorship and completion, and considering how building new and renovating might coexist. By finding potential in generic forms and working with common materials, simple rules and shared frameworks, the project proposes an architecture that can be adapted and transformed over time.

It begins with the simplest architectural form: a platform, a horizontal plane supported by vertical elements, made from common leftover materials through breaking, cutting, stacking and assembling. These initial platforms establish rules of material and structure. The work is then exchanged between groups to be arranged into spatial compositions, reveal-

Bangkok Tokyo Architecture, House K, Bangkok, 2023.
Working model of House K, an open-ended medium that allows modifications and add-ons as the project develops.

ing relationships, connections and emerging possibilities. Next, architectural elements such as walls, roofs, openings and circulation are added, along with a consideration of scale and accessibility. Finally, inhabitation brings purpose to the structures, furniture, programmes and use scenarios that suggest how life can unfold within these spaces. The finished works are exhibited together to show how each model evolved through multiple authors and decisions.

Across each phase, workshop participants must work with what already exists, responding to discoveries made by others. Through collaboration and the unpredictability of the process, open-ended architectures are created that emerge from the ordinary and belong to no one and everyone. Here, making becomes a conversation; each decision leaves traces, enabling new possibilities, and reveals the potential of the intentions of previous authors. The project is never fully controlled nor completely known, but continuously negotiated. It is, in a way, seeing architecture as an act of discovering new in the familiar, one that involves continuous interrogation, reconfiguration and letting go.

Bangkok Tokyo Architecture, Various structural models, 2018–25.
Structural models from various projects, read as modifications of a simple system. Open-ended, each structural completion is one among many.

Emerging Workshop 12/12

BeAr (Iñigo Berasategui and Ane Arce)

ELEMENTS OF DISSIDENCE: NEW POETICS OF RESISTANCE

Elements of Dissidence is articulated around the souvenir as the minimal exported unit of identity: a portable object that condenses simplified urban narratives and disseminates a codified image of the city outward. These artefacts – serially and industrially produced – act as distorted mirrors through which cities observe themselves in reduced form. Their global circulation transforms local fictions into universalised iconographies stripped of nuance. The Elements of Dissidence workshop aims to intervene in these objects to reveal what standardisation usually conceals: tensions, historical discontinuities, latent layers of meaning and marginal aesthetic components that lie beneath the commercial surface of the souvenir.

In a context where urban identity becomes a marketable resource, and cities seek differentiation while reproducing globalised patterns, ornament emerges as a domain of singularity capable of resisting cultural homogenisation. In dialogue with the congress theme of 'Becoming Attuned', which calls for a heightened sensitivity to cultural and environmental contexts, the workshop sharpens attention towards elements

Enbor Beretik/BeAr, Proposal for the 100th anniversary of Villa Noailles, 'Fragments d'architecture la Villa Noailles 1923–2023' exhibition, Villa Noailles, Hyères, France, 2023.
An object-fragment where narrative becomes ornament.

often taken for granted – minor ornamentations, vernacular patterns, commercialised or displaced iconographies – that constitute the cultural epidermis of Barcelona. Their apparently minor condition renders them carriers of micro-narratives, vernacular gestures and collective memories. Analysing and manipulating these fragments activates a critical reading of the micro-aesthetic structures underpinning everyday experience. At this minimal scale, ornament operates as a condensed visual language that can articulate micro-worlds and symbolic tensions which, once reinterpreted, can extend towards broader urban scenarios, granting beauty a cohesive role within a socially fragmented environment.

The workshop adopts Sir John Soane's Museum as a methodological reference, the logic of accumulation and fragmentation of which constructs a model of knowledge grounded in the articulation of heterogeneous pieces. This framework enables the workshop to function as a contemporary Wunderkammer, a cabinet of curiosities in which transformed objects generate new narrative constellations about Barcelona and foster a curatorial and design practice that understands objects as relational elements capable of producing collective meaning.

Rather than proposing long-term futurist speculations, the project is situated within the domain of present-fiction: a space where the real and the potential coexist, and make possible critical examination of transformations already underway. From this standpoint, the workshop develops three speculative scenarios – utopian, dystopian and ambiguous – conceived as analytical tools through which to explore contemporary tensions within the city.

The resulting ornaments or souvenirs function as speculative micro-monuments that can condense current issues – tourism, identity, climate, memory, desire – while suggesting possible reconfigurations of Barcelona's urban narrative.

BeAr, Mundo Cebra: Reappropriations of the Uniformising, 2024.
Standardised urban imagery reinterpreted as a device of aesthetic resistance.

BeAr, Fake and Popular, Ailarak Museoa, Artea, Spain, 2024.
Renovation and exhibition design for the new Museum of Basque Landscape and Traditional Music.

Enbor Beretik/BeAr, Proposal for the 100th anniversary of Villa Noailles, 'Fragments d'architecture la villa Noailles 1923–2023' exhibition, Villa Noailles, Hyères, France, 2023.
Narrative fragments assembled as a contemporary micro-monument.

Atelier Bow-Wow (Momoyo Kaijima and Yoshiharu Tsukamoto)
and Tsukamoto Lab, Institute of Science Tokyo

NOCTURNAL BEHAVIOUROLOGY: TRANSITIONING TOWARDS A NOCTURNAL URBANISM AS CLIMATE CHANGE ADAPTATION

Tokyo has been experiencing record-breaking temperatures in recent years. While this intensifying heat has significantly altered environmental conditions, the city's social structures have remained largely unchanged. As a result, behavioural patterns have struggled to adapt and are 'locked' into patterns shaped by a time when summers were much cooler.

It is important to understand that these social structures – strict schedules, shared rituals, and a transit-oriented lifestyle – were not planned, but largely established through years of accumulated contingent events, repeated practices, decisions, infrastructural systems and spatial constraints. This process of 'path dependency' stands in contrast to 'planning', the premise of which tends to simplify complex conditions into a set of problems to be solved to achieve a predefined goal, treating unexpected encounters along the way as noise.

What would it mean for Tokyo to shift towards nocturnal urbanism as a form of climate adaptation? How could activity migrate into cooler hours in a city whose daily rhythms have not yet adjusted to its changing summers?

Our research consists of three parts, the first of which looks at nocturnal urbanism not as a programme to be introduced but as a condition that some cities have already learned, over time, to sustain. Through fieldwork in warm-climate cities – Bangkok, Rio de Janeiro and Cairo – it asks how nocturnal life becomes possible, and what kinds of paths allow it to persist. These cities are not models to be copied. They are situations in which night has taken shape differently.

Our Tokyo case study introduces the hypothesis of nocturnal urbanism into existing practices, revealing frictions with prevailing social structures. It examines the barriers that hinder a nocturnal Tokyo: train schedules, long commuting distances, zoning regulations and social routines.

Finally, we propose a methodology for understanding social structures through path dependency, challenging the barriers to a nocturnal Tokyo through speculative interventions imagining summer night behaviours adapted to contemporary climatic conditions.

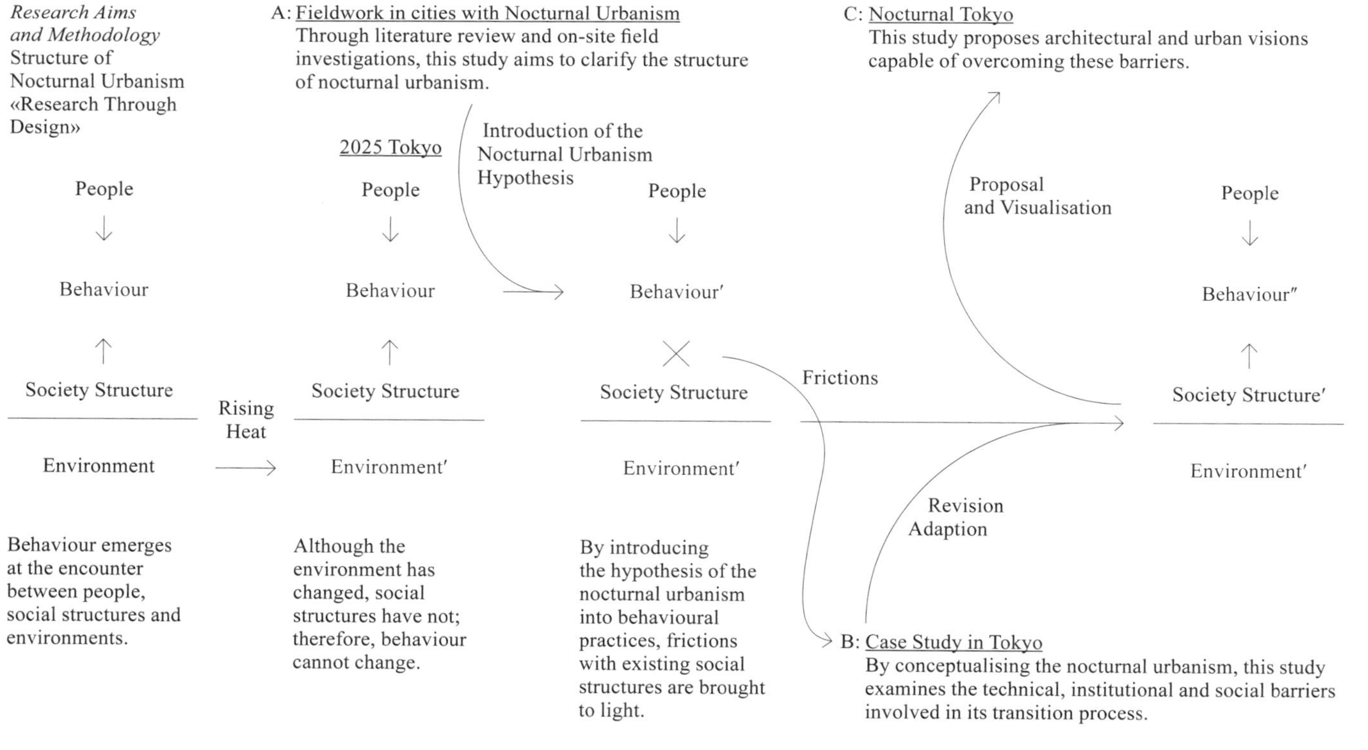

Atelier Bow-Wow and Tsukamoto Lab/Institute of Science Tokyo, Nocturnal Tokyo research aim and methodology, Tokyo, 2025–26.

Bangkok, Thailand

In Bangkok, nocturnal life is assembled every evening through a chain of small urban operations. As the heat subsides, vendors pull carts from hidden alleys, draw electricity from shops, and the edge of the road is temporarily redrawn by barricades, stools, tables and food smoke. Alleys are reclaimed where domestic life spills outside turning narrow passages into communal rooms for cooking, washing, eating and sleeping, dissolving the boundary between public and private. Some streets pedestrianise after sunset as night-market tents go up. At dawn, everything is washed and returned to traffic. Nothing is permanent, yet everything is prepared to happen again.

Reclaiming the streets: barriers repositionned to claim street space for tuk-tuk parking in Khao San, Bangkok, 2025.

This repetition did not happen by planning. It has been built path-dependently. In Yaowarat, the vibrant heart of the city's Chinatown, a dense commercial fabric, shophouse morphology, tolerated informal occupation, shared electricity, tourism, and later transit investments have all layered onto one another, reinforcing a nocturnal economy already embedded in the street. Rather than erasing it, authorities evolved a system of negotiated tolerance. In Patpong, the clustering of bars during the Vietnam War era, private ownership, later market activity, and accumulated reputation produced a nightlife identity that still resists major transformation. In newer cases, such as EmSphere, a fashionable, modern, ten-storey mall in the Sukhumvit area, a gap in the city's late-night commercial landscape generated a different kind of lock-in, pulling future development towards a 24-hour mixed-use node.

Night street-vendors redefining the street edge in Yaowarat, Chinatown, Bangkok, 2025.

Domestic life spilling outside: a resident doing laundry in the alley at night, Batthathong, Bangkok, 2025.

Bangkok shows that nocturnal urbanism can grow from overlap of formal and informal systems rather than separation. Taxis, tuk-tuks and low-cost motorcycle-taxis play a central role in sustaining these nocturnal practices, filling the gap of public transit. Night survives because the city does not close all at once.

After-work dining in the side streets, the van's trunk serving as a table, Chinatown, Bangkok, 2025.

Atelier Bow-Wow and Tsukamoto Lab/Institute of Science Tokyo, *Nocturnal Bangkok* collective drawing, 2026. Pencil on paper, 2,376 mm x 840 mm.

ok 2028 Atelier BOW-WOW & Tsukamoto Lab

Drawn by Abir Ezzedine, Anri Koyama, Hibiki Saji, Hinako Kobayashi, JaeJin Kim, Jin, Keita Yoshihira, Kenshin Hosaka, Kota Kashiwagi, Liza Grishchenko, Mai Sakauchi, Noe Naganuma, Ochi Masato, Sota Ominato, Ryo Oyama, Seishin Azuma, Seo Kawakami, Sogo Kurihara, Takeru Mizuno, Tento Nishiumi, Yoshitaka Suto, Chenye Yu, Yukako Masui

In Bangkok, nocturnal life is assembled every evening through a chain of small urban operations. ... At dawn, everything is washed and returned to traffic. Nothing is permanent, yet everything is prepared to happen again.

Atelier Bow-Wow

Rio de Janeiro, Brazil

Stadium-scale floodlights and unauthorised vendors at Copacabana, Rio de Janeiro, 2026.

Night-time activity in Rio de Janeiro is concentrated within urban clusters: the beaches, the *botecos* (informal neighbourhood bars), samba circles, sports warehouses, the lit sidewalk, the suburban cluster. A patch of light, a few chairs, a bar counter, 24-hour service (or anchors), human presence: these are often enough to create a collective sense of safety, functioning as 'nocturnal acupoints'. When people eat, talk, watch, circulate and linger, they generate their own informal surveillance. The 'eyes on the street'[1] are not a metaphor here. They are the nightlife itself.

1. A concept from Jane Jacobs emphasising that urban safety depends on human presence and 'attentive eyes' rather than lighting alone. See Jane Jacobs, *The Death and Life of Great American Cities*, Random House, 1961.

Locals Playing Altinha, a popular local beach sport where players stand in a circle and keep a football in the air without using their hands, Copacabana Beach, Rio de Janeiro, 2026.

Rio also shows that nocturnal life can emerge through loopholes and resistance. Footvolley (*Futevôlei*) – a sport born on the city's beaches in 1965, combining football techniques with volleyball rules, and played without goals and using a volleyball net – emerged to work around a municipal ban on daytime beach soccer. Following the 'Rio Orla' municipal interventions to reorganise the beachfront, including the installation of powerful floodlight corridors, beach practices shifted into cooler hours. The ban intended to control public space, but instead it catalysed a new way of occupying it that endures to this day; public space that resists top-down control and is reshaped from the bottom up by its users, visible in the unauthorised street vendors occupying Roberto Burle Marx's iconic mosaic sidewalks (*calçadão*) and where the street bands and parades of the *Blocos de carnaval* invade the streets, synchronising bodies, traffic, vendors and music into a temporary condition in which social behaviour seems to unlock all at once.

Blocos de carnaval: the street temporarily reclaimed, a live band playing atop a slowly moving truck, the crowd following behind. The entire city becomes a shared public space, driven by collective occupation and held together by the 24-hour metro, Lapa, Rio de Janeiro, 2026.

Yet these nocturnal intensities remain fragile. Light dictates Rio's night; where it is absent, safety fractures, mobility narrows, and the street empties into taxi dependency. Rio's night is not a stable condition. It is sustained by repeated social persistence under pressure.

Surveillance by *botecos*, acting as nocturnal urban acupoints, creating a collective sense of safety through constant social presence and light, Rio de Janeiro, 2026.

Cairo, Egypt

During Ramadan, Cairo introduces another path entirely. Fasting from sunrise to sunset shifts eating, gathering and movement into the evening and night, not as a special event but as an ordinary social reorganisation around *iftar* (the meal taken at sunset) and *suhour* (the meal taken before dawn). By late afternoon the city is already turning, and what follows *iftar* is not rest but acceleration. Streets fill, cafés overflow, and the city remains in motion well past midnight.

An alley transformed into an open kitchen, the street itself becoming infrastructure for a collective *iftar*, Ezbat Hamada, El-Matariya, Cairo, 2026.

What matters here is not only the shift in time, but the way an annual rhythm gathers force through repetition. In the historic, densely populated district of El-Matariya, what began (around 2012) as a single family breaking their fast with friends on the sidewalk due to a cramped, hot apartment, evolved as participation increased annually. Kids paint murals, youth manage crowds, *mahshi* (stuffed vegetables) are stuffed on sidewalks, food comes down from balconies in baskets, and what nobody planned became large enough for the government to support. It is path dependency in plain view: a contingent gesture, repeated and amplified until it acquires its own urban structure.

Kids playing billiards at night in the alleys of Old Cairo, set up by a shop owner, his premises demolished for a hotel, Cairo, 2026.

Workshops open at night: a metal workshop opening after *iftar* until late at night – light and noise mixing with the neighbourhood's lively soundscape, Imbaba, Cairo, 2026.

In older districts and informal neighbourhoods, where the urban fabric is dense, walkable and socially thick, night extends into the street. Residents take over the sidewalks to play *tawla* (a popular board game), watch television, share shisha, pray or keep workshops open. This rhythm peaks after the Tarawih prayers, fuelled by extended metro hours and 24-hour affordable tuk-tuks, motorcycle-taxis and taxis. In New Cairo, with its wide streets and car-dependent layout, the same night retreats indoors, into malls and restaurants. Here, path dependency is morphological as much as temporal. Night follows the form of the city that receives it.

Residents reclaiming the street in Old Cairo after Tarawih prayers, watching Ramadan dramas, sharing shisha and coffee, Imbaba, Cairo, 2026.

The fieldwork here suggests that nocturnal urbanism is not a ready-made urban type. It is the visible effect of paths that have formed over time. In Bangkok, the path is sustained by tolerated logistics, negotiated overlap and continuous mobility; in Rio de Janeiro by nocturnal anchors, light, collective occupation and a culture practised in surfing its own regulations; and in Cairo by temporal inversion and a fabric capable of holding the street as a social room. In each case, contingent acts accumulate, align with infrastructures and gradually become durable urban behaviour.

Tokyo case study

Tokyo reveals a more rigid path. Its rhythm is oriented towards daytime productivity and synchronised precision. But this very precision also shapes the limits of its night. The last train is not only a transport deadline. It is the moment the city decides to end. People rush home before it happens. Activities contract in advance. The city empties in coordination. When the tracks go silent between night and morning, Tokyo enters a spatio-temporal void: a state of suspension.

Empty stations and platforms after the last train, Tokyo, 2026.

Once the train network stops, a space that was accessible no longer supports staying. School grounds, station platforms, commercial streets, parks and sidewalks remain physically present, yet they cease to function as a nocturnal public realm. They are corridors of circulation with scarce urban furniture, designed to move bodies during the day rather than to host them at night. The city's existing structure locks behaviour into a narrow temporal window.

Empty commercial streets after midnight: vending machines and street lights, Tokyo, 2026.

Yet this void is utilised for the maintenance and recovery of its stressed infrastructure. Therefore, it is never entirely empty: convenience stores remain open, vending machines and street signs hold their light, the city is stocked and cleaned. But it is serviced, not inhabited.

Street and infrastructure maintenance after the last train, Tokyo, 2026.

And while Hanabi summer fireworks festivals occasionally reclaim the night only in brief and highly regulated windows, the *nomikai* culture of gathering for drinks – a social ritual rooted in Tokyo's era of rapid economic growth – pushes social life into after-work hours yet anchors it to the major transit hubs. The rigid functional zoning introduced by Japan's 1968 City Planning Act severed the central workspace from the residential suburb, resulting in long commuting distances and holding the city's nocturnal life hostage to the last train. In the absence of affordable taxis or alternative transit, 'salary-men' (office workers) who miss the last train get 'trapped' on the sidewalk, in manga cafés, karaoke booths or capsule hotels, waiting for the first morning train.

Nomikai culture in *izakayas* (Japanese gastropubs), clustering around major transit hubs before the last train, Tokyo, 2026.

These are not yet forms of nocturnal urbanism. They are signs of a city whose behaviour has been locked into daytime rhythms, even as environmental conditions begin to ask for something else.

The question, then, is how to read the path dependencies that currently organise its behaviour.

Tokyo's rhythms were not always rigid. The flexible temporal cycles of the pre-industrial Edo period (1603–1868) in which time itself was measured differently across seasons, suggest that another relationship with time is latent within the city and worth rethinking. If hotter summers increasingly strain the daytime regime, what would it mean for Tokyo to develop nocturnal life as another path? What happens to the spatio-temporal void when it is no longer read as dead time but as latent capacity? What would it take for public spaces, school grounds, parks and waterfronts to remain active once the daytime path ends? What would it mean to seed secondary nodes of nightlife closer to the suburbs? Which minor supports – mobility, access, tolerance, comfort, light, a place to sit, a reason to linger – would allow another rhythm to appear?

Nocturnal Tokyo begins by locating how night becomes possible elsewhere, how paths are formed through contingency, and how behaviour comes to be locked within them. Could Tokyo, only then, be read again as a place where another nocturnal path is waiting to emerge?

A conversation between Enrique Walker and the Congress curators on Becoming Attuned and the pursuit of what spatial practice cannot fully anticipate

DESIGNING FOR THE UNEXPECTED

CURATORS The central thread of the Congress is the idea of 'Becoming' and the temporal dimension of architecture. Do you see this as a central issue in architecture today?

ENRIQUE WALKER It's a strong proposition, but I would make one distinction from the the outset. The question may be less whether time is explicitly a theme in architecture today, and more whether time becomes visible as a consequence of a particular way of practising.

In that sense, time tends to appear when architecture no longer imagines itself as the production of a closed object, but as an intervention within an ongoing process.

When Umberto Eco wrote *Opera aperta* in 1962,[1] he observed that many artists – especially writers and composers – had begun to recognise that a work is, by definition, open in meaning, and could therefore be produced differently from the classical model of the finished, self-contained work: one in which content is fully inscribed by an author and simply transmitted to a reader, viewer or user. As a result, works could be left unfinished or opened to participation, completed through interpretation or through continued involvement in their becoming – a sensibility very close to what you are calling 'Becoming' here.

1. Umberto Eco, *Opera aperta* (*The Open Work*), Bompiani, 1962.

In architecture, the parallel shift was to think of buildings not only as objects, but as frameworks with an ongoing life – structures capable of sustaining changing uses, readings and later transformations – moving the discipline away from monumentality towards an understanding of architecture as a system that continues evolving after construction.

So perhaps the relevant question today is not simply whether architecture is open, but what kind of openness is at stake under current conditions, and what the discipline does with that awareness when architecture still tends to be debated primarily as a product.

C In your Open Work academic studios, you revisited the legacy of metabolism as a way of thinking about impermanence, flexibility, uncertainty, and the ongoing life of buildings after construction. Did those exercises helped you test what openness means today in operative architectural terms?

EW What interested me was whether the historical idea of the open work could still be productive today once translated into project decisions.

In that sense, Lacaton & Vassal are exemplary. Their premise is that a building that answers the brief exactly, one-to-one, tends to limit appropriation, informal use and transformation. So their key move is to give the double – to increase the programme by a hundred per cent – pairing spaces that are strictly organised according to the brief with additional open-ended space that can absorb overflow, change and unforeseen forms of life over time.

What makes this so powerful is precisely that it is not rhetorical. It is a conceptual project built through radical pragmatism. The use of greenhouses, inexpensive systems or off-the-shelf components is not a stylistic statement, but the practical consequence of a very clear ambition: to provide more capacity, more freedom and more possible uses within the same economic constraints.

C Lacaton & Vassal's work is also compelling for the way it links spatial generosity to environmental responsibility. In that sense, the Congress suggests a shift in perspective. If thirty years ago the UIA World Congress in Barcelona – 'Present and Futures: Architecture in Cities' – framed the city as architecture's laboratory, 'Becoming. Architectures for a planet in transition' reframes that lens towards planetary interdependencies shaped by socioecological crises and global infrastructures. How do you interpret this shift?

EW I find it stimulating, but I think it is crucial to distinguish between the scale of awareness and the scale of intervention. There is clearly a growing awareness of large-scale problems – ecological, territorial, social – yet architecture still operates through very concrete, often very small projects.

What matters is the discipline's ability to connect those two registers without confusing them: allowing a planetary horizon to shape the questions we ask while accepting that architectural work takes place through limited, situated actions.

Architecture is most effective precisely in that intermediate zone – between the abstraction of large issues and the immediacy of real constraints – because it translates broad questions into specific decisions while allowing specific situations to reframe those broader questions in return.

The decisive point is not to equate the magnitude of the problem with the physical scale of architectural action, but to maintain a productive oscillation between them.

C How do you see this planetary awareness operating in architectural discourse today?

ENRIQUE WALKER

I would say that a planetary awareness has existed for quite some time. I remember attending the UIA congress in Chicago in 1993, which was devoted to sustainable architecture. At the time, even the terminology felt relatively new. Since then, the debate has continued almost uninterrupted for more than three decades.

What is striking is not the lack of awareness, but the difficulty of translating that sustained awareness into decisive disciplinary transformations. We have technical frameworks, metrics and regulatory systems, of course, but the question remains what impact this has had on architecture beyond compliance and technical response. From that perspective, it can feel like a question that is perpetually present in the discipline, perpetually addressed, and yet somehow perpetually suspended.

And precisely because it has circulated for so long, the term itself also risks losing precision. 'Sustainability' can begin to function almost as a cliché – repeatedly invoked and at times instrumentalised – rather than as an operative framework.

So the open question, for me, is whether architecture still needs to explicitly thematise that awareness, or whether it should assume that awareness and respond through practice – through buildings, through project decisions, through the way specific conditions are related to other questions. The issue is not to abandon ecological responsibility, but to avoid reducing it to rhetoric. If we assume that the awareness exists, then perhaps the next question is what architecture does with it.

C The Congress uses the notion of 'attunement' to describe this kind of situated awareness, not only at the planetary scale, but also in relation to the immediate environments in which practice operates. Do you see a connection with what you have often described as architecture's attention to the 'ordinary'?

EW

Yes, I think there is a clear connection. What I've called the 'ordinary' emerges when architects learn to look beyond what the discipline has traditionally recognised as architecture – infrastructures, anonymous buildings, commercial landscapes, everyday environments that shape how people actually live.

Denise Scott Brown described this as a 'non-judgmental gaze':[2] the capacity to observe what surrounds us without immediately classifying it as good or bad architecture, but simply acknowledging that it exists, produces spatial and cultural effects, and can therefore become material for architectural thought.

2. Denise Scott Brown, 'On Pop Art, Permissiveness, and Planning', *Journal of the American Institute of Planners*, 35(3), 1969, pp. 184–86.

What matters is not only what is being looked at, but the operation itself: learning to look, and being willing to bring into the discipline something that had previously remained outside it. Attention to the ordinary is fundamentally a question of awareness – of attunement, if you like – to things architecture had left outside its own disciplinary territory.

C When that attention turns towards what already exists, it also raises questions of place and identity. How do you see that operating today?

EW There is always a delicate balance between engaging what already exists and simply reproducing it. What interests me in the ordinary is its role within a vanguard tradition – looking outward in order to push the discipline forward.

What has always made me uneasy is when that outward-looking posture hardens into a doctrine of correctness: a form of extreme contextualism in which architecture is expected to emulate what is already there, as if preservation were the ultimate goal.

At the same time, ignoring context produces another problem: an autonomous architecture detached from lived conditions.

The work that tends to matter operates between those poles – of a place, but in productive tension with it.

C Earlier you suggested that a term can become a cliché when it keeps circulating after the question that gave it force has weakened. Do you think something similar can happen with the ordinary?

EW Often, yes. The ordinary matters when it produces insight – when it forces you to notice something that had not yet been conceptualised. But there is a paradox: once architecture identifies something as ordinary and brings it into the discipline, it ceases to be neutral. It becomes charged, reframed, almost extraordinary.

At that point imitation becomes easier. What circulates is no longer the act of looking but its surface effects. The ordinary shifts from being a method to becoming a repertoire of recognisable gestures.

Because those gestures are legible, they travel quickly. So the problem is not the ordinary itself; it is what happens when it stabilises into a formula.

C So perhaps the crucial point is how architects operate once those materials have entered the discipline. Do you think architecture is shifting from design towards something closer to curatorship – selecting, assembling and reorganising what already exists?

EW Two issues intersect there. One is the shift from design towards curatorship; the other is the distinction between using references to advance a project and simply repeating them as a formula.

Yes, a significant amount of contemporary work operates through selection and recombination – systems, typologies, images, off-the-shelf elements. But I still defend design, not as form-making but as the act of formulating the problem and assuming responsibility for the decisions a project requires.

Architecture is always a negotiation among constraints that rarely resolve into a single clean solution. In that sense, design is not the production of a pure answer; it is the organisation of a complex question.

Curatorship can be powerful when it produces friction and generates new questions. The risk appears when it simply assembles culturally approved elements because they circulate well. Then what spreads is not the underlying inquiry, but the recognisable outcome. Repetition without the original question becomes a cliché.

C That also raises the question of authorship. If architecture increasingly works with what already exists – references, fragments, systems – does authorship become diffuse?

ENRIQUE WALKER I would distinguish between authorship and its representation.

There can be strong authorship in the intellectual operation – deciding what matters, what to bring in, how to frame it – even if the work shows little stylistic signature.

The paradox today is that we have more authorial branding than ever, but often less authorial responsibility. Authorship is not only the visible hand; it is also the willingness to assume responsibility for an operation. Even interventions based on found elements can be highly authorial. The decisive act is intellectual.

Roland Barthes's 'Death of the Author'[3] is often misundestood. He was not eliminating authorship but questioning the author as a sole source of meaning. Meaning emerges through interpretation, use, time and transformation. In architecture, occupation and temporal change are integral to the work. Authorship is redistributed rather than erased.

3. Roland Barthes, 'The Death of the Author', *Image, Music, Text*, trans. Stephen Heath, Hill & Wang, 1977, pp. 142–48.

C When so much production is driven by repetition and recognisable positions, where do you still see architecture generating genuinely new operations?

EW For me, the key notion here is error – what philosophy calls 'clinamen'. It comes from Epicurean thought and is developed by Lucretius in *De rerum natura*.[4] The basic idea is that the universe is organised as a system of atoms, but at some point one atom inexplicably swerves from its trajectory. That small deviation – the swerve – is precisely what allows the system itself to exist. So the error is not simply failure; it is the condition for encounter, change and form. It has often been read as a figure of free will within a predetermined system, and therefore also as an operation proper to art.

4. See Lucretius, *On the Nature of Things*, trans. W. H. D. Rouse, rev. Martin F. Smith, Loeb Classical Library/Harvard University Press, 1924.

That is why I find Jan de Vylder and Inge Vinck's proposal so interesting. Instead of taking the theme directly, they begin to work through words that sound alike – 'attuned', 'attune', 'attitude', 'entr'acte' – playing with signifiers more than with meanings. The apostrophes, shifts and near-homophonies open the words up and allow associations to emerge, to see what the signifiers themselves can produce. Meaning becomes a later consequence of having first manipulated the signifying material.

It is very close to an Oulipian operation – and, in a way, to the writer Raymond Roussel:[5] first a formal operation with language, and then the need to discover what implications and meanings can be drawn from it. The point is not incapacity to follow a rule, but the deliberate induction of a deviation within a system. One sets up an open procedure to produce an accident, trigger a finding or open something unexpected.

5. Raymond Roussel, *Comment j'ai écrit certains de mes livres (How I Wrote Certain of My Books)* [1932], Alphonse Lemerre, 1935.

The counterpoint is Atelier Bow-Wow, which I think is an excellent pairing with Jan de Vylder and Inge Vinck, because they are looking for something similar by almost opposite means. Atelier Bow-Wow's project on nocturnal urbanism proceeds through close, patient scrutiny of a condition we do not usually look at. And I like very much their premise of 'path dependency': the idea that many accidents accumulate over time and become a tradition, rather than the result of prior planning. So there too, what is being studied is a mixture of planning and accumulated accident – a way in which to form through repetition and contingency.

In both cases, the question is how to produce a finding: by inducing an accident through a procedure of language, or by methodically examining a condition until it reveals what had remained unseen. The issue is what discovery is triggered, what kind of awareness or attunement emerges.

This is also where humour becomes important. Not as a decorative trait, but as a deliberate intellectual operation for detonating error. What I find remarkable in Jan de Vylder and Inge Vinck, for example, is that the approach is as serious as it is irreverent: they take the subject completely seriously, but work through play, word shifts and a Dada-like attitude that introduces a fissure in what is taken for granted. That matters because the ordinary is difficult to see precisely when it is too familiar. Humour and irreverence can create that fissure, prevent the procedure from becoming ceremonious, and make room for discovery.

C These two commissioned projects are conceived as Research by Design: forms of projective research that can reach a level of speculation that ordinary practice rarely allows. What do you think this kind of work adds to the discipline?

EW What seems important to me, again, is a question of balance. We are in a moment in which professional practice is increasingly dissociated from argument, while research is increasingly dissociated from practice; academia and profession may never have been more distant.

That is why I think these Research by Design commissions are so valuable – and why the pairing of De Vylder Vinck and Atelier Bow-Wow's is so strong. They are very different from one another, but they pursue comparable ambitions through very different mechanisms.

In both cases, they are strong practitioners who use the academy not only to situate their work within a disciplinary tradition, but also to expand the spectrum of what that work can do.

C The Congress leans on dialogues rather than one-way presentations. Do you think that kind of exchange is now necessary?

ENRIQUE WALKER Yes. I think what you are trying to do is useful: to establish a provisional common ground on which people can debate for a few days. We are in a moment of enormous production but very little shared debate; there is a great deal of work and discourse, but few common frameworks that allow us to situate that work in relation to larger questions. In that context, dialogue matters not only as a format for presenting positions, but as a way of producing friction and testing them.

The challenge, of course, is duration: how to extend that conversation beyond the event itself. Part of the difficulty is temporal, because debate now moves quickly through events and media while buildings take years to materialise, so architecture often arrives late to debates that accelerate without it. That mismatch is significant, and it is one of the central conditions the discipline has to work with.

C Perhaps that returns us to the initial question of time?

EW Exactly. Architecture is always negotiating different temporalities: the slow time of construction, the accelerated time of discourse, the long duration of environmental processes, and the immediate pressures of culture and media. Understanding those layered temporalities – rather than collapsing them into a single narrative – may be one of architecture's most important tasks today.

Curators

POETICS AND ETHICS OF ATTENTIVENESS

Uncertain beauty

Ordinariness

Specific indeterminacy

Displacement

Poetics of belonging

Architectural meaning today can no longer be secured by formal order alone. Form and space are inherently related with worlds already dense in material, social, ecological and symbolic conditions. Beauty, in this sense, exceeds predetermined forms of coherence, harmony or completion, emerging instead through ambiguity, displacement, ritual continuity, attention to the ordinary, and fragile forms of indeterminacy. Attunement is the feeling of listening to these entangled contexts while gently beginning to act upon them, transfiguring them towards the future.[1] Rather than accepting linear historicity, attunement opens a passage for change, a door towards unpredictable, new prospects. 'Becoming Attuned' implies cultivating architectural attention to such situations: the ordinary and the overlooked, inherited spatial arrangements, sensed atmospheres, sporadic activities, cultural sedimentations and subtle forms of coexistence that precede the project yet continue to shape it while playfully introducing new elements that generate unexpected charms and delight. This paradigm calls for a shift from passive aesthetical observation to active poetic and technical engagement, where meaning takes shape as art or architecture, and is experienced, interpreted and made public.[2]

1. Timothy Morton, *Being Ecological*, Pelican Books, 2018.
2. Boris Groys, *Going Public*, Sternberg Press, 2010.

In some cases, architecture remains close to what is vulnerable, temporary or unresolved without converting it into a flaw. Uncertainty,

(1) Smiljan Radić, *Guatero*, Bienal de Arquitectura y Urbanismo de Chile, Santiago, Chile, 2023.

(2) Alexander Brodsky, 95 Degrees, Pirogovo, Russia, 2002.

in this sense, becomes one of the conditions through which architecture acquires depth, ambiguity and appearance. Certain works remain deliberately close to fragile constructions, reinterpreting accidental beauty embedded in refined material ensembles and structural skeletons. (1) Radical spatial built and unbuilt experimentation is crossed with temporariness, the sublime and fragile architectures of memory and ruin. (2) Attentive and playful attitudes remain open to accidentality, juxtaposition and mistake, revealing spatial and material interplays culturally embedded in architectural praxis. (3) Speculative images – synthetically produced – operate through slightly altered familiar environments where minimal estrangement unsettles slight recognition. (4) What emerges from these sensitivities is a kind of uncertain beauty that relies on the capacity to remain open, vulnerable and indeterminate, leaving room for delight and irony, and that at once feels

(4) Jean Jacques Balzac, *Budget limité*, Paris, France, 2025.

(3) architecten de vylder vinck taillieu, PC Caritas, Melle, Belgium, 2017.

familiar and strange. This uncanny beauty attunes dimensions of architecture whose significance surpasses utility and depends precisely on what lies beyond instrumental return.[3]

3. Nuccio Ordine, *The Usefulness of the Useless*, Paul Dry Books, 2013.

Attending more closely to the ordinary and the peripheral is another way of approaching attunement. Dense urban contexts, suburban landscapes, domestic encounters and everyday environments matter when habits, proximities and subtle differences come into view. This form of awareness makes the city legible through images that remain at once close and distant. (5, 6) Daily life unfolds through gestures, routines and occupations that reveal how space is continuously produced and inhabited. (7) It brings into focus conditions that the discipline has often placed outside its proper field, redefining its own limits and procedures.[4] (8) Everyday urban conditions are observed through an ethnographic lens where spatial behaviour

(5) Takashi Homma, *Tokyo Olympia*, Tokyo, Japan, 2023.

(6) Maxime Delvaux, *Untitled*, Dilmun Burial Mounds, Bahrain, 2023.

(7) Bêka & Lemoine, *Homo Urbanus*, various locations, 2017–25.

(8) Enrique Walker, *Lo ordinario*, 2010.

(9) Atelier Bow-Wow, *Made in Tokyo*, 2001.

reveals how architecture is shaped by use, proximity and informal practices. (9) Mundane architectural elements may likewise be assembled, superposed and left open enough to accommodate adaptation and completion over time. (10) The ordinary, in this sense, is not simply what architecture looks at; it is one of the grounds from which architectural thought begins again.

4. Enrique Walker (ed.), *Lo ordinario*, Gustavo Gili, 2010.

For one group of architects, a specific primacy of form, type, order and structure prevails – even if remaining open to indeterminate use. Typological rules, interconnected chambers and rigorous geometries do not necessarily produce static usage. These calibrated sequences of rooms and figures, sometimes juxtaposed, construct precise spatial orders that remain open to interpretation and occupation. (11, 12, 13) Clear and almost generic frameworks, in turn, avoid prescribing use too tightly, leaving space for appropriation. (14, 15)

(10) Bangkok Tokyo Architecture, House C, Chiang Mai, Thailand, 2023.

(11) OFFICE Kersten Geers David Van Severen, Solo House, Matarraña, Spain, 2017.

(12) Pezo von Ellrichshausen, REST restaurant, Les Jardins de Médongaule, Gyeonggi-do, South Korea, 2025.

(13) MOS, House No. 10, New York, 2015.

Indeterminacy, here, is not the absence of spatial specificity; on the contrary, it is a latent capacity to absorb open programmes within unprogrammed, well-designed supports.

A further shift concerns architecture as an act of displacement – selecting, reframing, editing and contextualising as-found spatial systems. What matters here is the meaning that emerges when something is moved from its expected place and made to enter into new relations. In this sense, the already formed world appears as a field of latent possibilities open to reinterpretation through proximity, friction and recombination. Whether working with existing conditions and generic elements, or with signs, fragments and references drawn from architectural and cultural repertoires, (16, 17, 18, 19, 20) displacement becomes a way of producing new contingencies without relying on the rhetoric of originality. It is a curatorial kind of work, where authorship becomes diffuse.

(14) Yanfei Architects, Climate Museum, Chengdu, Sichuan, China, ongoing.

(15) Experience, Chris Marker Residence, Paris, France, 2018.

(16) Un Parell d'Arquitectes, Can Sau Emergency Scenery, Olot, Spain, 2019.

(17) KOSMOS Architects, EMA Space, Moscow, Russia, 2016.

(18) Infraestudio, Red Garden, Vedado, Havana, Cuba, ongoing.

(19) Fala Atelier, Fala 143, Porto, Portugal, 2025.

(20) Point Supreme, Ignatiou Apartment, Athens, Greece, 2022.

Questions of place and belonging run through this field as well, understood beyond fixed identity or nostalgic return. Belonging is approached as a relational and negotiated condition, one that emerges through rituals, spatial habits, symbols, climatic intelligence, postcolonial imaginaries and everyday forms of continuity. It is not secured through purity, but through the capacity to sustain attachment while allowing transformation. Vernacular knowledge, shared customs, informal expressions and collective memories are approached as living frameworks that may be translated, edited and recombined through material cultures and situated forms of making, (21, 22, 23) through rituals and spatial forms of collective care and celebration (24, 25) or through questions of visibility, representation and postcolonial narrative, (26, 27) rather than as fixed images to be preserved intact. Belonging, in this sense, is a lived continuity, shaped through reinterpretation,

(21) Ted'A, Casa en Colònia de Sant Pere, Mallorca, Spain, 2025.

(22) Leopold Banchini Architects, Dar El Farina, Al Haouz, Morocco, 2025.

(23) BeAr, Ailarak Museum, Artea, Spain, 2024.

(25) Tatiana Bilbao ESTUDIO and MAIO Architects, *Opera Aperta Pavilion of the Holy See*, Venice Architecture Biennale, Italy, 2025. Curated by Marina Otero Verzier and Giovanna Zabotti.

(24) Matilde Cassani, *Quasi Nessuno*, Principato di Lucedio, Italy, 2023.

coexistence and the careful negotiation of multiple narratives.

The sensitivity emerging from Becoming Attuned is not a style, nor a unified aesthetic language. It is a reorientation of architectural practice. Against detached judgement, it proposes closer forms of involvement. Against fixed beauty, it privileges diffuse meanings that remain negotiated, unstable and shared. Against disciplinary distance, it values practices able to listen, register, recalibrate and reposition. The fragile, the ordinary, the inherited, the ambiguous and the collectively held are not secondary matters surrounding architecture from the outside; they are among the very conditions through which architecture now comes to matter. In that sense, attunement does not name a mood; it names a way of practising architecture within a world that demands more careful forms of attention.

(26) AD-WO, Bole Rwanda apartment building, Addis Ababa, Ethiopia, ongoing.

(27) New South, Muqarnas, Paris, France, ongoing.

Seven Visions of Becoming

This group of seven essays was selected by an international jury composed of Keller Easterling, Lydia Kallipoliti, Marina Otero Verzier, Philip Ursprung, Samia Henni and Raquel Rolnik. The same jury also selected a wider group of 30 essays for oral presentation at the Congress. Both selections were drawn from 63 accepted essays, following a two-stage anonymous peer-review process that received 797 submissions.

Arturo Frediani-Sarfati and Lara Alcaina-Pozo, *Universitat Rovira i Virgili (Unitat Predepartamental d'Arquitectura)*
Larry Barham, *University of Liverpool (Faculty of Humanities and Social Sciences)*
Adriana Hernandez-Aguila, *Universitat de Barcelona (Faculty of Psychology)*

ORIGIN AND EVOLUTION OF ARCHITECTURE: ON HUMAN ARCHITECTURAL ETHOLOGY

THE EVOLUTION OF ARCHITECTURE

Why do we create architecture?

Our last common ancestor with chimpanzees (*Pan troglodytes*) and bonobos (*Pan paniscus*) diverged between six and seven million years ago into species that walked upright and, taking advantage of the fact that they still had arboreal adaptations, probably continued to build platforms or nests for sleeping or resting in trees as all great apes do today (Groves & Sabater Pi, 1985; Sabater Pi et al., 1997; Stewart, 2011).

Architecture is, due to the advantages it provides for survival and reproduction, an adaptive behaviour of numerous species from insects to mammals (Pallasmaa, 2020; Hansell, 2009; Von Frisch, 1974). Its enormous variety of forms, materials and building techniques is only comparable to the great diversity of animal species that take shelter in it. All living species in the hominid family, which apart from chimpanzees, bonobos, gorillas and orangutans includes us humans, build shelters that function to avoid predators, thermoregulate, increase comfort and avoid pathogen vectors (Stewart et al., 2011; Koops et al., 2012a; Fruth et al., 2018; Hernandez-Aguilar & Reitan, 2020; McGrew, 2021).

But is human architecture a biological exception disconnected from our evolutionary history?

This article explores the origin of human architecture prior to the appearance of our own species, argues that the course of human evolution may have been strongly influenced by the need for shelter, and proposes the idea that we enjoy a cross-cultural architectural behaviour that may be governed by a possible set of specific emotions.

The transition to terrestrial shelters

The morphology of animals and their behaviour are connected (Schwab et al., 2023). Thus, evolution not only produces new forms, but also new behaviours. When the environment to which a given species is adapted undergoes major changes, the new scenario can lead to its disappearance or drive evolutionary shifts in its morphology and behaviour.

The gradual aridification of Africa that began six million years ago led to the spread of seasonally dry habitats in once-forested landscapes (Cerling et al., 2011) to which early humans (hominins) adapted. The earliest member of our genus, *Homo habilis* (2.8 million years ago), retained climbing abilities as well as being a terrestrial species (Ruff, 2009). An increasingly open landscape may have made it difficult for them to continue building nests in trees. The reduction of trees also increased the threats from large predators (Vegara-Riquelme et al., 2025). The changes to their habitat must therefore have exposed them to selective pressures that favoured the loss of dependence from trees and, during sleeping hours, demanded alternative protection to that offered by elevated nests (Figures 1 & 2).

Figure 1. A chimpanzee (*Pan troglodytes*) mother with two babies sleeping in a day nest in Gombe Stream National Park, Tanzania.

Figure 2. A chimpanzee nest in Dindefelo Community Nature Reserve, Senegal.

The marked increase in aridity that began two million years ago is related to the disappearance of *H. habilis*, and to the emergence of a new lineage, *H. ergaster/erectus* (DeMenocal, 2004; Hammond et al., 2021). This hominin species had to evolve new ways of responding to this environmental stress.

<u>REM sleep</u>

The REM phase of sleep, associated with the evolution of mammals, produces intervals of muscle paralysis that render them vulnerable to predation during sleep. The increase in REM during human evolution is also related to the altriciality of our species (Kavanau, 2002). This supports the idea that the first *Homo* did not suffer a decline in sleep quality, having found ways to protect themselves and their helpless offspring when they could no longer rely on trees for sleeping (Coolidge & Wynn, 2006; Nunn et al., 2016; Samson, 2021).

<u>Transition to sleeping on the ground</u>

Two behaviours observed in some chimpanzee communities may provide insights into the transition from *H. habilis* to *H. erectus*, particularly in relation to the construction of shelters: terrestrial nesting and fire habituation. Some chimpanzee populations in habitats ranging from rainforest to savannas build nests on the ground rather than in trees, a behaviour that may be explained by low or absent predation pressure, including from humans, or by limited nesting-tree availability (Koops et al., 2012b; Tagg et al., 2013; Romani et al., 2023). Savanna chimpanzees in Fongoli, Senegal, are not afraid of wildfires and their self-control makes them the only animals, apart from humans, capable of conceptualising fire (Pruetz & LaDuke, 2010; Pruetz & Herzog, 2017).

If our hominin ancestors, driven by increasing aridification of their habitats, managed to successfully transition away from arboreal shelters, it was because they must have had a way of defusing the threats of their new environment. The use of fire may have served to keep predators at bay (Wrangham, 2009), but if fire was extinguished, this protection also required an additional physical shield that had to be constructed on the ground.

<u>*Homo erectus*</u>

The 'Turkana Boy', or Nariokotome Boy, fossil is the most complete skeleton of a *Homo ergaster/erectus*. Approximately 1.6 million years old, its height between 1.60 and 1.70 metres and anatomy show adaptations to open spaces and long journeys (Coolidge & Wynn, 2006). The fact that it had lost climbing abilities supports the idea of a life independent of trees (Coolidge & Wynn, 2006). Its thorax narrows from shoulders to waist, with a significant reduction in intestinal volume compared to *H. habilis*, gorillas or chimpanzees, which are distinguished by their funnel-shaped thorax. The dramatic reduction in mandible size and dentition supports the hypothesis that *H. erectus* may have been the first hominin species adapted to a cooked diet, which was easier to chew, digest and assimilate than raw food (Wrangham & Carmody, 2010; Gowlett, 2016; Carmody et al., 2016).

<u>The first dwelling</u>

For decades, there has been debate as to whether certain stone remains adjacent to *H. erectus* sites and dating back more than a million years, were shelters. Specifically, the stone circle found at Olduvai by Mary and Louis Leakey (Leakey, 1971), or the findings of what could be aligned peg holes for wooden supports at Melka Kunturé (Chavaillon et al., 1979; Chavaillon, 2004; Chavaillon & Chavaillon, 2004). These claims for early structures have been strongly contested (e.g. Potts, 1988).

To end the controversy, the discovery of the remains of a waterlogged wooden structure such as the one excavated in 2019 by a team of archaeologists near the Kalambo Falls in Zambia, consisting of two crossed beams with half-lap joints and dating to >476,000 years, has forced us, due to its level of planning, structural complexity and skill with tools (also found in-situ), to grant a descendant of *H. erectus* – *Homo heidelbergensis* (also known as *Homo bodoensis*) – abilities such as felling trees and beam carving that were believed to be exclusive to *H. sapiens* (Barham et al., 2023) (Figures 3 & 4). This discovery marks the earliest evidence of a built environment with human modification of the habitat by creating an elevated structure (platform or trackway) in a seasonally damp setting.

Figure 3. Unearthing wood artefacts from 500,000-year-old deposits at Kalambo Falls, Zambia.

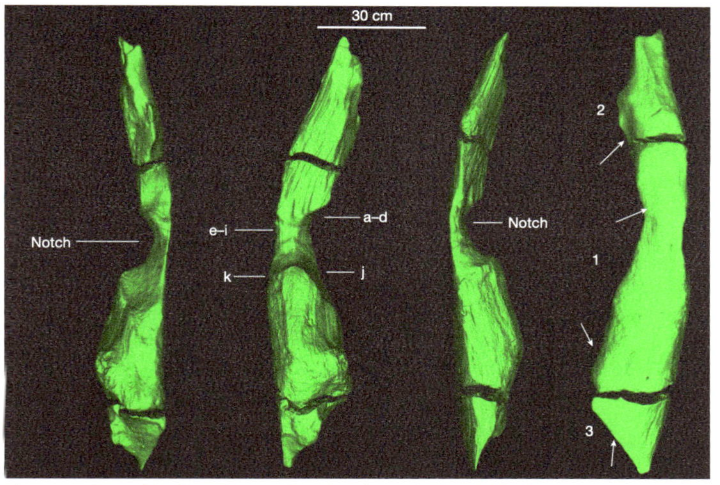

Figure 4. One of the logs/beams found at the Kalambo Falls site, with shaping marks on the margins of the notch (a–k), and pieces separated by cracks and arrows (1–3) signalling shaping facets.

The first architects

The semi-nomadic hunter-gatherer societies of the Great Rift Valley in East Africa, who currently inhabit savannahs where hyenas and lions still roam, use both huts and bonfires to ward off the dangers of the night. The Hadza, a relict fraction of the Khoisan linguistic group, are one of the few remaining hunter-gatherer groups living a nomadic lifestyle in Africa. The shelters they construct have a main structure of branches supporting a plant covering made by stacking leaves with their stems, braiding foliage or overlapping patches of woven plants. Both the raw materials and the construction techniques the Hadza employ to build their shelters are comparable to those great apes use to make nests, with humans delimiting a covered space (Figure 5).

Figure 5. A Hadzabe hunter-gatherer hut in Tanzania.

Sumatran orangutans (*Pongo abelii*) also know how to build complex, completely enclosed nests in which to shelter from the rain and camouflage themselves in trees (Van Casteren et al., 2012). But it is still the tree that gives the nest its impregnability, and to come down from it means to lose that impregnability. To move away from dependence on trees for shelter and colonise Eurasia, *H. erectus*, rather than being a lucky species, was perhaps an accomplished architect.

From evidence to hypothesis

Our hypothesis is that the evolution of human architecture began at least 1.9 million years ago when a climate change first fragmented and then reduced the woodlands in which our ancestors built their nests, forcing them into a more open landscape that required shelters built on the ground. Thus, 'the first dwelling' may well have appeared when a *H. habilis*, instead of sleeping in her nest, covered herself with it, creating a safe enclosure in which to sleep on the ground. Such shelters could hide their occupants and provide a physical barrier against external threats, as well as offer the shade previously provided by trees to rest during the day. The effort involved in their construction would have been somewhat greater than that invested in making nests, but as with chimpanzee nests, they could have been reused, subject to the same pressures that drove our ancestors to transform their tools into objects of recurrent use (Fruth & Hohmann, 1996; Hernandez-Aguilar, 2009, Stewart et al., 2011). If we assume that *H. habilis* was able to survive in a changing environment thanks in part to architecture, we can understand how the selective pressures derived from a greater freedom of movement could have determined its rapid transformation into a very different species. If we consider that *H. erectus* experienced reductions in the jaw, teeth and digestive system (Antón et al., 2014), and probably body hair, it is entirely understandable that this was the first species to use fire, creating a completely new kind of shelter.

The ethology of human architecture

Homo erectus must also have taken advantage of their group bonds to survive in all kinds of contexts (Samson, 2021). Fire, in addition to providing protection from predators and cooked food, enabled a new period of wakefulness after sunset (Gowlett, 2016), during which it was possible to strengthen bonds and share plans for the next day. The hearth could thus become the *axis mundi* of the community and the first hierarchical element of architecture and urbanism. When our ancestors could not depend on trees for shelter, they had to strengthen their bonds or perish. Architecture may have had much to do with the sophistication of cooperation and with greater safeguards for survival.

At least half a million years have passed since hominins made the oldest recorded dwelling, and human architecture has continued to evolve, conditioned by our hyper-social behaviour. It is not surprising, then, that its current form tends to take into account our need to interact with each other, producing spaces that expose us to others and identify us.

Taken together, what we have discussed here allows us to explore a set of emotions that may have played a role in the evolutionary history of architectural aesthetics.

ARCHITECTURAL EMOTIONS

Why are the evolutionary origins of architecture important?

Gathering and articulating evidence on the possible origin of human architecture from the evolution of our ancestors' nesting behaviour is of scientific importance. But, beyond putting forward a hypothesis about such origin, we are interested in what might remain in us of the supposed architectural ethology of those ancestors, and whether, in this transition, our social nature might have favoured the selection of new ties to architecture.

We mentioned above that the morphology of animals and their behaviour are connected, so when we see certain architectural characteristics stubbornly reappearing in different periods and in different human cultures, we must be attentive to possible traits of our architectural ethology that may have been retained by natural selection.

Rather than confirming the existence of inheritable architectural behaviours, we will focus on possible candidates that are worth exploring. Emotions are nothing more than useful adaptations for adequately managing environmental stimuli (both those that come from the physical environment and those that come from other humans). Architecture, on the other hand, is the form we give to that environment in order to survive and thrive in the best possible conditions. Given architecture's enormous impact not only on survival but also on society, it should come as no surprise that certain emotions may have become linked to the way we experience it, and may influence in some way the shape we ultimately give to it.

Some of the emotions on our list of architectural candidates have already been acknowledged in both humans and other species. The rest, studied as ancient virtues of architecture, could be regarded as more than mere cultural expressions (Semper, 1851; Semper, 1860).

Evolutionary aesthetics

Evolutionary aesthetics is the branch of psychology that considers the experience of beauty from a biological perspective. According to this branch, beauty is the attraction we experience towards objects whose biological performance depends precisely on this emotional link (Dutton, 2009). Evolution ends up selecting and highlighting as attractive, exciting or beautiful those objects that contribute to orienting our behaviour towards reducing uncertainty: survival, reproduction and, in a gregarious animal like us, towards the continuance of the community.

Beauty is a constantly changing construct heavily influenced by cultural, historical and environmental contexts.

In certain periods and places it was believed to be a teleological or intrinsic property of objects. In others it was thought to be more of a divine emanation. Throughout Western history, beauty was frequently considered a core value aligned with truth and virtue. Modernity reduced its status to that of a mere conventional reference, nothing more than an agreement between transmitter and receiver. Today we know that beauty is not in objects but in our biased way of seeing them, which depends on an internal model – our brain's 'wiring' – modulated, of course, by learning and cultural context (Appleton, 1975; Orians & Heerwagen, 1992; Cosmides & Tooby, 2001; Falk & Balling, 2010).

Little did Charles Darwin imagine that he would deliver a veritable bombshell to centuries of aesthetic speculation when wondering – admiring the peacock's tail – why natural selection does not always only favour the strongest, but also the most attractive. Darwin was the first to understand that beauty 'is biology's way of acting at a distance' (Darwin, 1871).

Biological basis of human architecture

A list of possible architectural emotions should translate into a set of behaviours that are 'profitable' from an evolutionary point of view. Here we identify seven candidates that, far from discovering new or original architectural phenomena, could offer a biological explanation for common aesthetic categories:

- *Genius loci* or sense of place
- Territoriality
- Cosiness or homeliness (a central emotion of architecture)

- Ornament
- Picturesqueness
- Monumentality
- Grace

The first four categories and their material effects are also observable in the behaviour of other animal species, while the last three are candidates for cultural human behaviours that might have a biological basis. We have ordered them based on their chronological appearance and decreasing frequency in the animal world. Thus, for example, more species establish a territory than those that build shelters in it, while just a few decorate these structures. Similarly, our supposed attraction to the picturesque or the monumental must have emerged later than homeliness, the instinctive force that makes animal architects return to their shelters.

Human manifestations of all the categories discussed have a social or collective dimension that their animal equivalents lack. This collective component may have been retained in our species thanks to the Baldwin effect or self-domestication, a specific form of natural selection described by James Mark Baldwin in the late nineteenth century that has been added to those previously proposed by Darwin: selection of the fittest and sexual selection (Baldwin, 1896; Bateson, 2004).

Just as selective breeding led to the domestication of the dog from the wolf, or the pig from the wild boar, the Baldwin effect takes into account the selective pressures that humans exert on themselves, providing a way to transform a behaviour from cultural to biological. We have seen this mechanism at work when discussing the evolution of human intestines and mandibles after the widespread consumption of cooked food. In that case, the transmitted cultural behaviour that conditioned the evolution of these anatomical traits was the control of fire. In our own hypothesis, the Baldwin effect would explain the virtues, in particular, of behaviours that express the pleasure we feel when creating or admiring a picturesque city or a monument, both of which are the result of a significant collective effort; or even grace understood as an affective performance of architectural form.

Moving on to briefly define how these presumed emotions work, homeliness would be what links us to all other architect species, what lies behind our efforts to create a habitable inner universe; a controlled, safe and reliable version of the cosmic universe capable of adequately protecting us from physical elements and threats that come from both the physical environment and from our competitors.

The *genius loci* – or sense of place – situates each species in its place in the world, as the capacity to discriminate among habitats and select suitable ones is a key evolutionary characteristic of all living organisms (Petit & Petit, 1996). Territoriality, for its part, is a combination of affiliative and dissuasive forces that guides the behaviour of species towards the management of resources and control of a given demarcation. In short, it is the force that divides or aggregates the territory into enclosures, communities, neighbourhoods, cities and countries (Hertzberger, 1991).

In general, ornamental behaviours affect some species which, to attract the opposite sex, apply them to objects to facilitate or improve courtship, mating or procreation (Borgia, 1986; Kawase et al., 2013). Among humans, however, ornamentation superimposes a Baldwinian layer of identification and communication, and/or expression, on objects and architecture.

Probably the most relevant of all collective enterprises and the one that has had the greatest impact on the survival of human societies over the last 10,000 years has been the city. Hence, its picturesque and monumental qualities, the main forces driving global tourism today, are the first presumed architectural emotions without an equivalent in other animal species. Our affinity for the formal eurhythmic structures that emerge in architectural conglomerates produced diachronically by a community – namely, the formal relations that link individual buildings to their neighbouring structures – on the one hand, and for the concentration of these shaping forces in a single, challenging object, on the other, has been examined by a number of architectural theorists and, within the framework of environmental aesthetics, analysed by architects, philosophers and psychologists. However, it has received comparatively little attention from anthropologists and biologists (Nasar, 1988; Habibi, 2016; Ábalos, 2005, 2008).

The last emotion on our list of candidates – the most uncertain and perhaps the one most closely related to the functional performance of architecture – concerns architecture's ability to embody a certain will or influence that may operate upon our socio-affective behaviour. This occurs when architectural form conveys care and attention, expresses closeness or affection, or, at the very least, demonstrates a thoughtful and attentive consideration of the inhabitant. Grace differs from ornamentation in that it arises from the architectural form itself rather than from a superimposed expressive device. It also complements architecture's central emotion – cosiness – by adding a gratuitous and altruistic dimension.

CONCLUSION

You have accompanied us on a journey spanning at least half a million years, looking into an even more distant past through the window of our closest primate relative's behaviour. Along the way, we have explored the possible continuity of architectural ethology in the course of human evolution, and also the distinctive traits that natural selection may have retained via the Baldwin effect driven by the selective force of our own hypersociality.

Accordingly, we have proposed a set of possible forces that, although not always welcomed by architects – precisely because their universal appeal sits uneasily with the authorship or the originality architects often seek – continue to exert a significant influence on architecture and therefore warrant further careful, objective and verifiable analysis within the framework of the scientific method.

Acknowledgements

ASF and LAP are grateful to their research group Centre de Recerca Urbana de El Camp (CRUC), from the Universitat Rovira i Vigil. LB wishes to thank the Arts and Humanities Research Council, UK (grant AH/N008804/1, Deep Roots of Humanity Project) for supporting the research at Kalambo Falls, Zambia. RAHA is grateful to the Serra Hunter Programme, Generalitat de Catalunya, for support. The authors would like to thank Ingo Arndt and the Jane Goodall Institute Spain in Senegal for granting permission to reproduce the photographs in Figure 1 and Figure 2.

References

Ábalos, I. (2005). *Atlas pintoresco Vol 1: El observatorio*. Gustavo Gili.
Ábalos, I. (2008). *Atlas pintoresco Vol 2: Los viajes*. Gustavo Gili.
Antón, S. C., Potts, R. & Aiello, L. C. (2014). Evolution of early *Homo*: An integrated biological perspective. *Science*, *345*(6192),1236828.
Appleton, J. (1975). *The Experience of Landscape*. John Wiley.
Baldwin, M. (1896). A new factor in evolution. *The American Naturalist*, *30*, 441–51.
Barham, L., Duller, G. A., Candy, I., Scott, C., Cartwright, C. R., Peterson, J. R., Kabukcu, C., Chapot, M. S., Melia, F., Rots, V., Taipale, N., Gethin, P. & Nkombwe, P. (2023). Evidence for the earliest structural use of wood at least 476,000 years ago. *Nature*, *622*, 107–11.
Bateson, P. (2004). The active role of behaviour in evolution. *Biology & Philosophy*, *19*, 283–98.
Borgia, G. (1986). Sexual selection in bowerbirds. *Scientific American*, *254*, 92–100.
Carmody, R. N., Dannemann, M., Briggs, A. W., Nickel, B., Groopman, E. E., Wrangham, R. W. & Kelso, J. (2016). Genetic evidence of human adaptation to a cooked diet. *Genome Biology and Evolution*, *8*, 1,091–103.
Cerling, T. E., Wynn, J. G., Andanje, S. A., Bird, M. I., Korir, D. K., Levin, N. E., Mace, W., Macharia, A. N., Quade, J. & Remien, C. H. (2011). Woody cover and hominin environments in the past 6 million years. *Nature*, *476*, 51–56.
Chavaillon, J. (2004). Discovery, geological introduction and study of percussion material and tools on pebble. In J. Chavaillon & M. Piperno (Eds.), *Studies on the Early Palaeolithic Site of Melka Konture, Ethiopia* (pp. 253–69). Istituto Italiano di Preistoria e Protostoria.
Chavaillon, J. & Chavaillon, N. (2004). Comments and conclusion on the lithic assemblage. In J. Chavaillon & M. Piperno (Eds.), *Studies on the Early Palaeolithic Site of Melka Konture, Ethiopia* (pp. 437–48). Istituto Italiano di Preistoria e Protostoria.
Chavaillon, J., Chavaillon, N., Hours, F. & Piperno, M. (1979). From the Oldowan to the middle stone age at Melka-Kunture (Ethiopia): Understanding cultural changes. *Quaternaria*, *21*, 87–114.
Coolidge, F. L. & Wynn, T. (2006). The effects of the tree-to-ground sleep transition in the evolution of cognition in early *Homo*. *Before Farming*, *2006*(4), 1–16.
Cosmides, L. & Tooby, J. (2001). Does beauty build adapted minds? Toward an evolutionary theory of aesthetics, fiction and the arts. *SubStance*, *30*(1&2), 6–27.
Darwin, C. (1871). *The Descent of Man, and Selection in Relation to Sex*. John Murray.
DeMenocal, P. B. (2004). African climate change and faunal evolution during the Pliocene–Pleistocene. *Earth and Planetary Science Letters*, *220*(1–2), 3–24.
Dutton, D. (2009). *The Art Instinct: Beauty, Pleasure and Human Evolution*. Oxford University Press.
Falk, J. & Balling, J. (2010). Evolutionary influence of human landscape preference. *Environment and Behavior*, *42*(4), 479–93.
Fruth, B. & Hohmann, G. (1996). Nest building in great apes: The great leap forward? In W. C. McGrew, L. Marchant & T. Nishida (Eds.), *Great Ape Societies* (pp. 225–40). Cambridge University Press.
Fruth, B., Tagg, N. & Stewart, F. (2018). Sleep and nesting behavior in primates: A review. *American Journal of Physical Anthropology*, *166*(3), 499–509.
Gowlett, A.J. (2016). The discovery of fire in humans: A long and convoluted process. *Philosophical Transactions of the Royal Society of London B: Biological Sciences*, *371*(1696), 20150164.
Groves, C. P. & Sabater Pi, J. (1985). From ape's nest to human fix point. *Man*, *20*(1), 22–47.
Habibi, A. (2016). Environmental aesthetics: The share of environmental aesthetics indices the cognition of urban landscape. *Manzar*, *8*(35), 50–55.
Hammond, A. S., Mavuso, S. S., Biernat, M., Braun, D. R., Jinnah, Z., Kuo, S., Melaku, S., Wemanya, S. N., Ndiema, E. K., Patterson, D. B., Uno, K. T. & Palcu, D. V. (2021). New hominin remains and revised context from the earliest *Homo erectus* locality in East Turkana, Kenya. *Nature Communications*, *12*, 1939.
Hansell, M. H. (1984). *Animal Architecture and Building Behaviour*. Longman.
Hansell, M. H. (2009). *Built by Animals: The Natural History of Animal Architecture*. Oxford University Press.
Hernandez-Aguilar, R. A. (2009). Chimpanzee nest distribution and site reuse in a dry habitat: Implications for early hominin ranging. *Journal of Human Evolution*, *57*(4), 350–64.
Hernandez-Aguilar, R. A. & Reitan, T. (2020). Deciding where to sleep: Spatial levels of nesting selection in chimpanzees (*Pan troglodytes*) living in savanna at Issa, Tanzania. *International Journal of Primatology*, *41*(6), 870–900.
Hertzberger, H. (1991). *Lessons for Students in Architecture*. 010 Publishers.
Kavanau, J. L. (2002). REM and NREM sleep as natural accompaniments of the evolution of warm-bloodedness. *Neuroscience & Biobehavioral Reviews*, *26*(8), 889–906.
Kawase, H., Okata, Y. & Ito, K. (2013). Role of huge geometric circular structures in the reproduction of a marine pufferfish. *Scientific Reports*, *3*, 2016.
Koops, K., McGrew, W. C., De Vries, H. & Matsuzawa, T. (2012a). Nest-building by chimpanzees (*Pan troglodytes verus*) at Seringbara, Nimba Mountains: Antipredation, thermoregulation, and antivector hypotheses. *International Journal of Primatology*, *33*(2), 356–80.
Koops, K., McGrew, W. C., Matsuzawa, T. & Knapp, L. A. (2012b). Terrestrial nest building by wild chimpanzees (*Pan troglodytes*): Implications for the tree-to-ground sleep transition in early hominins. *American Journal of Physical Anthropology*, *148*(3), 351–61.
Leakey, M. D. (1971). *Olduvai Gorge: Excavations in Beds I & II 1960–1963*. Cambridge University Press.
McGrew, W. C. (2021). Sheltering chimpanzees. *Primates*, *62*(3), 445–55.
Nasar J. L. (Ed.) (1988). *Environmental Aesthetics: Theory, Research and Application*. Cambridge University Press.
Nunn, C. L., Samson, D. R. & Krystal, A. D. (2016). Shining evolutionary

light on human sleep and sleep disorders. *Evolution, Medicine and Public Health*, *1*, 227–43.
Orians, G. H. & Heerwagen, J. H. (1992). Evolved responses to landscapes. In J. H. Barkow, L. Cosmides & J. Tooby (Eds.), *The Adapted Mind: Evolutionary Psychology and the Generation of Culture* (pp. 551–79). Oxford University Press.
Pallasmaa, J. (2020). *Animales Arquitectos*. Gustavo Gili. Originally published 1995.
Petit, L. J. & Petit, D. R. (1996). Factors governing habitat selection by prothonotary warblers: Field tests of the Fretwell-Lucas Models. *Ecological Monographs*, *66*, 367–87.
Potts, R. (1988). *Early Hominid Activities at Olduvai*. Aldine
Pruetz J. D. & Herzog N. M. (2017). Savanna chimpanzees at Fongoli, Senegal, navigate a fire landscape. *Current Anthropology*, *58*(S16), 337–50.
Pruetz, J. D. & LaDuke, T. C. (2010). Brief communication: reaction to fire by savannah chimpanzees (*Pan troglodytes verus*) at Fongoli, Senegal: Conceptualization of 'fire behavior' and the case for a chimpanzee model, *American Journal of Physical Anthropology*, *141*(4), 646–50.
Romani, T., Tranquilli, S., Roessingh, P., Menken, S. B., Mundry, R., Konarzewski, M. & Hicks, T. C. (2023). Factors affecting nest height and ground nesting behaviour in Eastern chimpanzees (*Pan troglodytes schweinfurthii*) of the northern Democratic Republic of the Congo. *Folia Primatologica*, *94*(4–6), 173–206.
Ruff. C. (2009). Relative limb lengths in *Homo habilis*. *American Journal of Physical Anthropology*, *138*(1), 90–100.
Sabater Pi, J., Veà, J. J. & Serrallonga, J. (1997). Did the first hominids build nests? *Current Anthropology*, *38*(5), 914–16.
Samson, D. R. (2021). The human sleep paradox: The unexpected sleeping habits of *Homo sapiens*. *Annual Review of Anthropology*, *50*, 259–74.
Schwab, J. A., Figueirido, B., Martín-Serra, A., van der Hoek, J., Flink, T., Kort, A., Esteban Núnez, J. M. & Jones, K. E. (2023). Evolutionary ecomorphology for the twenty-first century: Examples from mammalian carnivores. *Proceedings of the Royal Society B*, *290*(2011), 20231400.
Semper, G. (1851). *Die vier Elemente der Baukunst*. Braunschweig.
Semper, G. (1860). *Der Stil in den technischen und tektonischen Künsten, oder Praktische Aesthetik: ein Handbuch für Techniker, Künstler und Kunstfreunde*. Verlag für Kunst und Wissenschaft.
Stewart, F. A. (2011). The Evolution of Shelter: Ecology and Ethology of Chimpanzee Nest Building. PhD dissertation, University of Cambridge.
Stewart, F. A., Piel, A. K. & McGrew, W. C. (2011). Living archaeology: Artifacts of specific nest site fidelity in wild chimpanzees. *Journal of Human Evolution*, *61*(4), 388–95.
Tagg, N., Willie, J., Petre, C. A. & Haggis, O. (2013). Ground night nesting in chimpanzees: New insights from central chimpanzees (*Pan troglodytes troglodytes*) in South-East Cameroon. *Folia Primatologica*, *84*(6), 362–83.
Van Casteren, A., Sellers, W. I., Thorpe, S. K., Coward, S., Crompton, R. H., Myatt, J. P. & Ennos, A. R. (2012). Nest-building orangutans demonstrate engineering know-how to produce safe, comfortable beds. *Proceedings of the National Academy of Sciences*, *109*(18), 6,873–77.
Vegara-Riquelme, M., Baquedano, E. & Domínguez-Rodrigo, M. (2025). Early humans and the balance of power: *Homo habilis* as prey. *Annals of the New York Academy of Sciences*, *1553*(1), 140–57.
Von Frisch, K. (1974). *Animal Architecture*. Harcourt.
Wrangham, R. W. (2009). *Catching Fire: How Cooking Made Us Human*. Basic Books.
Wrangham, R. W. & Carmody, N. R. (2010). Human adaptation to the control of fire. *Evolutionary Anthropology*, *19*, 187–99.

Víctor Cano-Ciborro
School of Architecture, Universidad Europea de Canarias

COUNTER-CARTOGRAPHIES OF MIGRANTS TO THE CANARY ISLANDS

INTRODUCTION

The Atlantic migration route to the Canary Islands has become one of the most lethal borders in the world. In 2024 alone, 46,843 migrants arrived on 692 boats, representing a 17.4 per cent increase compared to 2023, when 39,910 people reached the islands (Ministerio del Interior, 2024). This figure surpasses the historically significant ‘cayuco crisis’ of 2006, during which 31,678 individuals arrived in the Canary Islands. This humanitarian crisis has persisted for 30 years. It began on 28 August 1994 when two Sahrawi individuals in their twenties reached the fishing village of Las Salinas del Carmen on Fuerteventura after an almost 24-hour journey covering 90 kilometres from the African coast. Word of this feat spread quickly throughout the Sahara, and from 1995 to today the numbers have exponentially increased. What began as an exception in that initial journey has become a normalised practice of migratory ‘necropolitics’ (Mbembe, 2018) influenced by geopolitical tensions, mafias and human traffickers, resulting in staggering figures.

According to the annual report from the collective Caminando Fronteras (2024, p.4), ‘the Canary route remains the most “lethal” in the world with 9,757 deaths in 2024’ (421 women and 1,538 children), and more than 100 boats have disappeared with all the people on board – numbers never seen since Frontex (the EU Border and Coast Guard Agency) began its data collection efforts in 2011. In late 2024, the Canary Islands President stated that the islands were ‘overwhelmed’ and NGOs ‘can’t take it anymore’ (Fumero, 2024) (Figure 1).

In the context of historically high migration flows, a critical, detailed, multiscale and spatially attentive research project on this ongoing humanitarian crisis is urgently needed. Unlike traditional cartography – historically aligned with imperial power, surveillance and the erasure of subaltern bodies – counter-cartography aims to foreground the embodied experiences of migrants, making visible the overlooked geographies of displacement, vulnerability and resistance. This approach visually and graphically communicates the spatial dynamics of migrant movements, including the conditions and strategies of (dis)appearance, (in)visibility and (in)audibility along the entire Northwest African migrants route, from Morocco, Mauritania, Senegal, The Gambia and the disputed territories of Western Sahara to the Canary Islands, across three different scales (Figure 2). At the Atlantic scale, we examine both the journeys and the specific departure points along the African coast, undertaken in *cayucos*, *pateras* or inflatable boats. At the insular scale, we focus on actions, movements and architectures from migrant pickup points to reception centres. At the corporeal scale, we explore not just the architecture of these centres but also the spatial, emotional and affective experiences of migrants in urban environments, especially their interactions with local citizens. Particular attention is given to the 6,000 minors living in overcrowded and under-resourced reception centres on the islands.

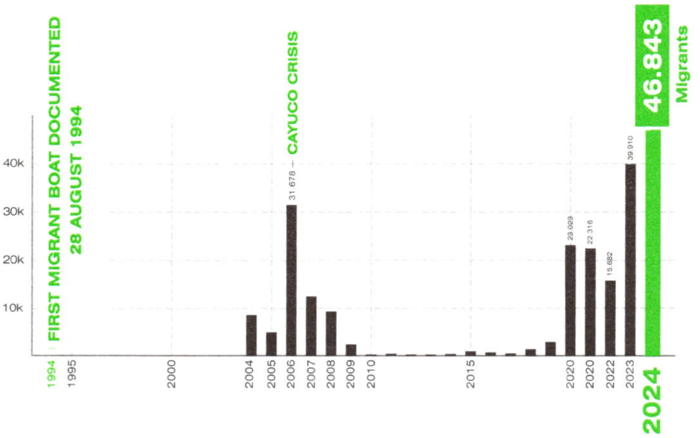

Figure 1. Migrants, Canary Islands route, 1994–2024. *Source*: Author's elaboration based on data from Ministerio del Interior (2024).

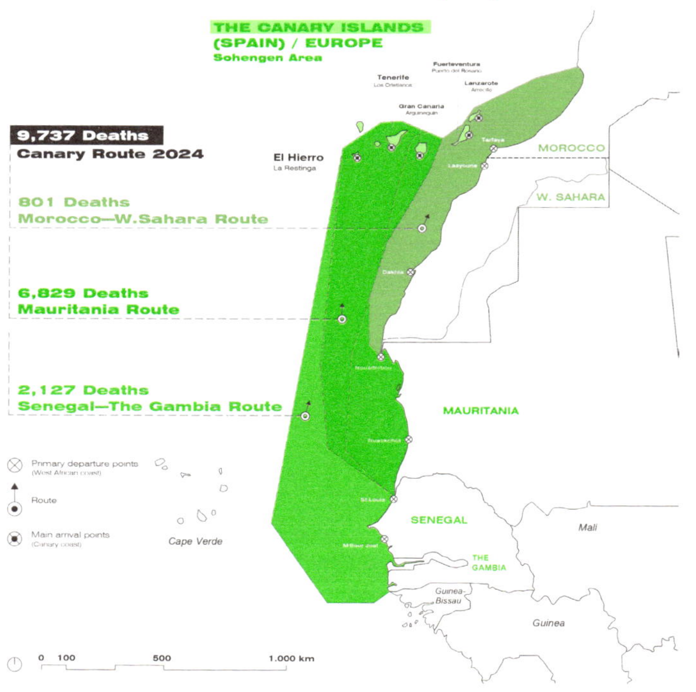

Figure 2. Routes and number of migrant deaths in 2024. *Source*: Author's elaboration based on data from Caminando Fronteras (2024).

SITUATED SPATIAL KNOWLEDGE GROUNDED IN THE CANARY ISLANDS ROUTE

The primary aim of this ongoing research is to make visible the current dynamics of migration along the Northwest African migrant route through critical and technical 'counter-cartographies' from a spatial perspective. This knowledge is developed in direct collaboration with migrants themselves and grassroots associations that work closely with migrants daily. Rather than relying solely on the abstract data of large NGOs, the project is grounded in the lived realities, needs and insights of those directly involved.

At the same time, this locally embedded approach responds to a broader academic gap: while transdisciplinary migration studies have been extensively developed in the Mediterranean context, research on the Canary Islands route remains limited, particularly from the perspectives of architecture, urbanism and territorial studies. This gap has left key spatial dimensions of migration underexplored. Drawing on Donna Haraway's concept of *Situated Knowledge* (Haraway, 1991), this study positions the Canary Islands route as a crucial and urgent case study.

Our hypothesis is that a spatial research approach enables a more effective understanding of the ongoing humanitarian crisis. We contend that this perspective offers a critical advantage over non-spatial methods, which often collect data and narratives without situating events or migrant bodies within specific spatial contexts. The added effectiveness can be measured in two ways: greater accuracy in identifying migratory patterns, and enhanced relevance of humanitarian interventions. Ultimately, the goal is to transform abstract data, raw numbers and spreadsheets into meaningful and contextualised spatial narratives.

COUNTER-CARTOGRAPHIES, FORCES, AFFECTIONS, AND VIOLENCE WITHOUT COORDINATES

The project employs counter-cartographies to highlight the migration experience from the perspective of the oppressed body, making visible the hidden human stories and 'affections' behind the journey, a perspective not previously applied to this specific migratory route. It contributes to scientific knowledge in two main ways: 1) expanding key concepts within migration studies, such as forces, affections, and 'violence without coordinates'; 2) spatialising these concepts through new, countercartographic tools.

Novel and multidisciplinary concepts

This framework incorporates key situations addressed in migration studies – across both liquid and terrestrial territories – that are rarely spatialised through maps or cartographic tools, and include clandestinity, embodied experience, spatial justice, (dis)appearance, (in)audibility, (in)visibility, informal infrastructures of mobility, human testimonies, and tactics of survival, smuggling and resistance. These phenomena converge around three interrelated key novel and multidisciplinary concepts: forces, affections, and violence without coordinates. We begin with the latter to clarify the other two when discussing cartography.

> Can we imagine a crime without a criminal? A violence without coordinates on which transgressions might be plotted? A violence with no 'x' and with no 'y'? A violence with no weapon and no witness, passing invisibly through the human sensorium – leaving no memory, no testimony, and no record? That is to say, can we imagine violence without a violent event? (Lahoud, 2014, p. 496)

The project reflects on these questions by proposing a way to spatialise forms of violence that lack Cartesian coordinates. Our challenge is to make visible, through counter-cartography, events that resist conventional mapping.

Counter-cartography

If cartographic science and maps have historically been tools of empire and power (Harley, 1989), counter-cartography reclaims mapping practices to represent historically subaltern and invisibilised bodies. This shift, latent since the 'spatial turn' (Warf & Arias, 2009) of the 1960s, was formalised in 1995 when sociologist Nancy Peluso coined the term 'counter-mapping' as a radical practice to depict territories and situations that escape hegemonic control and are instead experienced by economically deprived or socially marginalised groups (Lee Peluso, 1995).

Why 'cartographies' and not 'maps'? Deleuze and Guattari understand cartography as an operative tool to think about and inhabit the intensities of reality. Cartography makes visible not just objects, but bodies.

Not just points, but relations. Not just forms, but forces and affections. Not just regulatory lines, but lines of flight that escape control (Deleuze & Guattari, 2012). As Deleuze puts it:

> What accounts for a person's life, whether individual or collective, is a certain ensemble that can be called a cartography. A cartography is made of lines … which vary from individual to individual, from group to group, although there may be common segments (Deleuze, 2005, p. 303).

In contrast, a map is a static codification of reality: it resembles the territory but does not participate in it. Maps are concerned with forms; cartographies engage with relational forces (Cano-Ciborro, 2024). This Deleuzian distinction anchors our methodological approach – counter-cartography – which is oriented towards tracking and intervening in the forces that act upon migrant bodies. While not entirely invisible, these forces often operate with extraordinary subtlety, affecting bodies in unpredictable ways: what the seventeenth-century philosopher Baruch Spinoza termed 'affections' (Deleuze, 2008). These affections are the very forces that move us. They delineate not only what a (migrant) body can do, but also expose what it can endure (Deleuze, 2005).

Research-by-making methodology

This project builds upon the innovative 'research-by-making' approach presented by Laura Kurgan (2013) and Eyal Weizman (2017). Their cartographic investigations, applied to stigmatised territories, humanitarian crises and crimes against humanity, have demonstrated how architectural and cartographic tools can act as both analytical and political devices. Following the geographer Nigel Thrift, this methodology aligns with non-representatioal theory, opening up new possibilities to render visible the 'invisible and excluded' (Thrift, 2008).

Multi-scalar and embodied spatiality

The graphical tool developed in this project operates across multiple spatial scales. It does not limit itself to the migrants' origin territories (e.g., the West African coast) or to the liquid geographies of the Atlantic Ocean. Instead, it zooms in on the embodied spatialities experienced by migrants upon their arrival in Tenerife, which means focusing on their lived spatial experiences: Who takes this route? What specific circumstances prompted their migration? In what kind of vessel did they arrive? What is the spatiality of their place of origin? What is the journey like? And the arrival? What are the reception centres where they stay like? How do they sleep? What and where do they eat? What clothing do they wear? What emotions do they experience? How do they interact with locals? What places do they frequent when they leave the centres?

The goal is to map migration not as a generic flow, but as lived experience inscribed in sensitive bodies and specific spaces.

ATLANTIC, INSULAR AND CORPOREAL COUNTER-CARTOGRAPHIES

The methodology is grounded in the development of multiple counter-cartographies at three analytical scales – Atlantic, insular and corporeal – produced within undergraduate (first- to fifth-year) and Master's courses at the School of Architecture, Universidad Europea de Canarias. Below we describe selected examples, highlighting the results obtained to date.

Atlantic and drifting counter-cartographies

The availability of openly georeferenced datasets – such as those from the International Organization for Migration or the Missing Migrants Project – enable the production of quantitative cartographies using GIS tools (Figure 3). These are complemented by migrant interviews using the forensic-architectural method, aimed at reconstructing spatial events and revealing the lived geographies of migration.

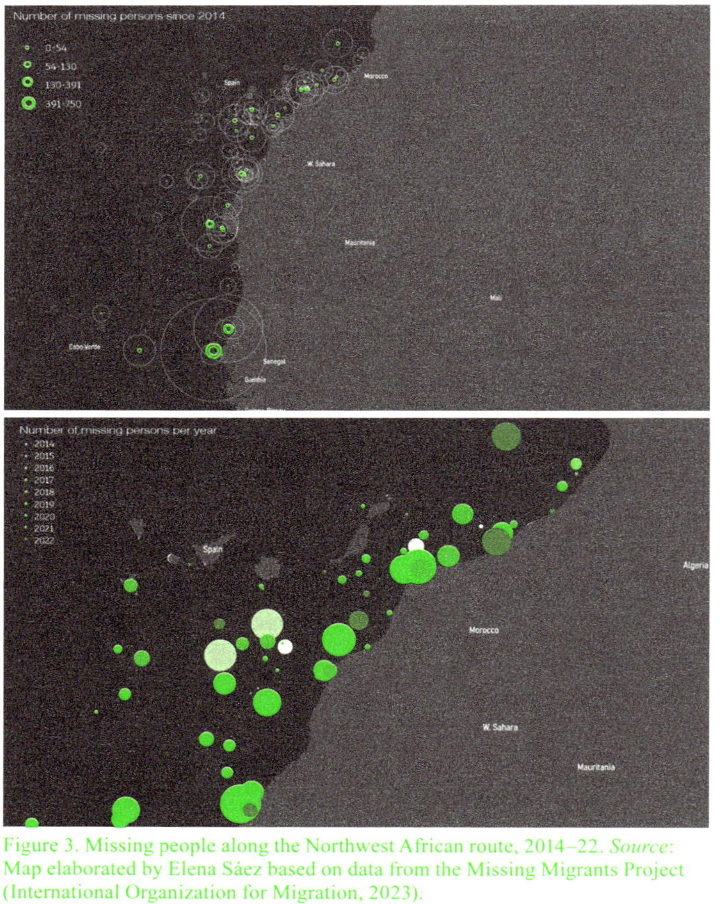

Figure 3. Missing people along the Northwest African route, 2014–22. *Source*: Map elaborated by Elena Sáez based on data from the Missing Migrants Project (International Organization for Migration, 2023).

Understanding the operational dynamics is crucial: Moroccan, Mauritanian and Senegalese authorities patrol sea borders, leading to mostly nocturnal departures for evasion. Migrant boats often carry GPS or compasses but lack satellite phones. Previously, migrants have paid in cash between US$1,500 and $3,700, depending on the route and type of boat, and have waited for days or weeks, packed into cheap hotels or unnoticed private homes near the departure point until the smugglers gather enough ‘clients’, prepare the vessel (boat organisers are other stakeholders), and identify a suitable weather window with minimal risk of interception (sometimes braving coastal guards) (UNODC, 2022). On this basis, the research team is developing counter-cartographies around the three situations outlined below.

1. Internal migrations, violence and refugee camps in Northwest African countries

Using open georeferenced data, quantitative cartographies were produced in QGIS, and complemented by official documents and the narratives of survivors themselves. As shown in Figure 4, internal displacements caused by war, as well as the presence of refugee camps, have been mapped.

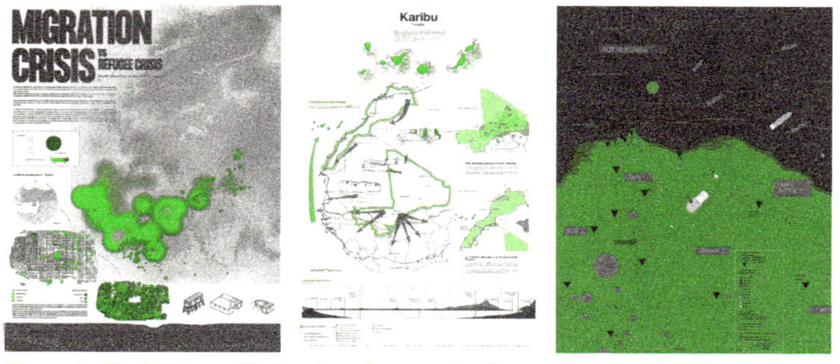

Figure 4. (Left) Internal migratory flows and refugee camps in the West African countries. Map: Ray Pérez, 2025. (Centre) Counter-cartography of conflicts in Northwest Africa, highlighting two cases: the Western Sahara conflict, including the Moroccan Wall, which is heavily mined and serves to protect natural resources such as phosphates and other minerals; and the conflict in Mali, which since 2012 has been affected by jihadist insurgencies that have destabilised the Sahel region. This has caused the displacement of tens of thousands of families, some of whom have crossed into Senegal and onwards to the Canary Islands. The bottom section shows the route from The Gambia to the Canary Islands on a 360-hour journey. Map: Daniel López, Carlota González, Gabriela Pérez and Ana Victoria de Ángel, 2025. (Right) Internal migratory routes, border hazards and physical barriers. Map: Natalia Conrado, Jorge Delgado and Antonio Díaz, 2025.

2. Trajectories and the situation of the boats

Points of departure (African coast) and arrival (Canary Islands) were identified, together with the types of boats (*cayucos*, *pateras*, inflatable boats). The cartographies mapped overcrowding on board as well as ‘common’ trajectories chosen to avoid law-enforcement agents or potentially dangerous tides (Figure 5).

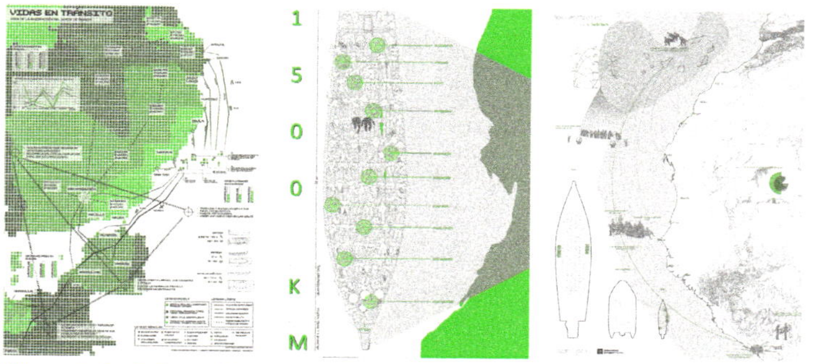

Figure 5. (Left) Quantification and migratory flows rendered in a pixelated aesthetic to emphasise the dehumanisation behind migration data. The map, where Europe is usually shown at the top, is rotated 180 degrees to subvert this cartographic hierarchy. Line types highlight key relationships: flows of interest (projections of European migration pressures and motives), routes from Africa to the Canary Islands, routes from the Canary Islands to Europe, and repatriation or redistribution to countries of origin. Map: Iván Marrero, Diego Marrero and Daniil Sorokin, 2025. (Centre) This counter-cartography does not seek only to quantify the number of bodies aboard a *cayuco*, but to make visible the types of ‘dispositions’ and ‘affects’ embodied by them. To this end it re-creates situations that give rise to states of unease, anxiety, fear, solidarity, frustration, resignation, confusion, concern, exhaustion and uncertainty. These situations are at once corporeal and spatial, unfolding throughout the 1,500-kilometre journey itself. Map: Laura González and Virginia Pérez, 2025. (Right) Types of vessels, number of passengers, and trajectories of the different routes, illustrated with testimonies provided by interviewed migrants describing what was happening at each point along the journey. For example: ‘What felt hardest to me was seeing people falling into the water and drowning, and not being able to do anything.’ Map: Victorina Otero, Laura Sanz and Alejandro Fuhai Tomé, 2025.

3. Shipwrecks

Through the representation of shipwrecks and survivals, the brutal reality of the Canary Islands route – today recognised as the most lethal migration route worldwide – is brought to light (Figure 6).

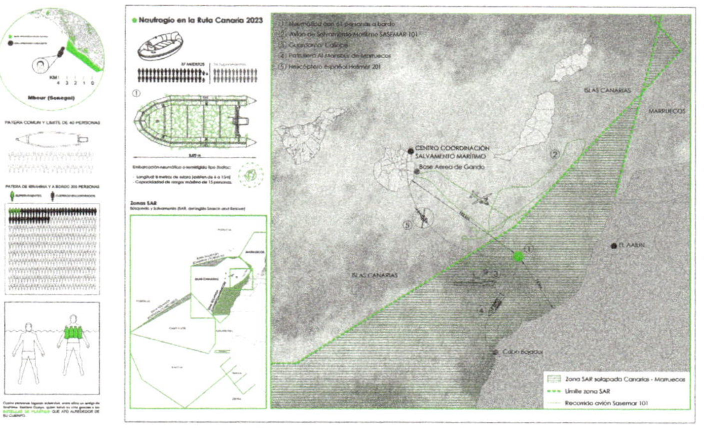

Figure 6 (Left) Sinking of a *patera* off the coast of Senegal, and the flotation and survival tactic of tying empty plastic bottles around the body to stay afloat. Ángel Ripollés, Héctor García and Alejandro Jerez, 2025. (Right) 20 June 2023: an inflatable boat carrying 61 people drifted in a shared search and rescue (SAR) zone between the Canary Islands and Morocco. Despite being located, and despite nearby rescue assets, Spanish authorities transferred responsibility. SAR zones are maritime areas where states are obligated to coordinate and assist vessels in distress and cannot refuse responsibility. Twelve hours later, Moroccan patrols arrived: 24 people were rescued, 36 were missing. Only the body of a child was later recovered. Genaro Capogrosso, Diego Farrais and Sara Reale, 2025.

Insular and landing counter-cartographies

We tracked migrants’ journeys from sea to land, from interception or rescue (by Salvamento Marítimo) to their arrival at the ports of Los Cristianos (in the south of Tenerife) and La Restinga (El Hierro) (Figure 7). We focus on these two islands, as they are the main points of arrival for migrants coming from The Gambia, Senegal and Mauritania. These routes are considered the most dangerous, with crossings that, according to conversations with migrants, can last between 6 and 14 days.

Once the migrants reach land, they undergo interrogation and administrative detention for 72 hours.

According to interviews conducted by the Observatory on Migrant Smuggling, 'facilities dedicated to the administrative detention of newly arrived migrants in the Canary Islands often fall short of meeting minimum standards, such as access to water, hygiene and sanitation facilities, and medical care' (UNODC, 2022, p. 25). Depending on their health, age, nationality and whether they have requested asylum, they are transferred to different emergency facilities – Centres for the Temporary Assistance of Foreigners (CATE) or long-term reception centres across the island. We aim to understand the spatiality of this process, the dynamics, and architectural forms constructed, adapted, rehabilitated or produced on Tenerife.

We conducted field visits to group homes where unaccompanied minor migrants live with caregivers (locations will remain undisclosed for safety reasons) and to the Las Raíces reception centre (La Laguna, Tenerife), which – despite overcrowded and precarious conditions 'housing' around 3,000 people – has become the main destination for migrants (Figure 7).

Figure 7. (Left) Migrant *cayucos* docked at La Restinga port, El Hierro, 1 December 2024. (Centre) Las Raíces centre exterior fence view, 23 September 2024. (Right) Opening of the fence to allow the entry of a bus carrying migrants arriving from the island of El Hierro, 23 September 2024.

Around the area of Las Raíces, located near the city of La Laguna, we mapped the walking routes taken by migrants from the centre to La Laguna along a two-way road without a shoulder, covering more than 4 kilometres and with a 127-metre elevation gain towards the city. Once there, migrants tend to gather at specific supermarkets to ask for food, or at particular establishments where they can recharge prepaid phone-cards and communicate with their families (Figure 8).

Corporeal and affective counter-cartographies

At this scale of the research, cartographies were produced in which the emphasis shifts to the body and the surrounding spatiality. The migrant body is understood not in terms of its form, but as a set of forces, actions, agencies and affects that mobilise it to construct diverse and complex spatialities. The aim is to map relationships that remain invisible in politicised and media narratives: unseen stories, narratives of affect. Drawing on resources from graphic novels, approaches were developed to explore experiences of journeying, waiting and displacement, moving beyond the abstraction of plan-view drawings. Narratives range from apparent successes – a minor arriving on the islands, accessing training in Tenerife, and collaborating with an association to assist other young migrants – to the stark reality of a minor collapsing shortly after reaching the port of La Restinga on Tenerife, who, being undocumented, is reduced to a mere number (Figure 9).

CONCLUSIONS

The analysis of the Canary Islands route – currently the deadliest migratory corridor in the world – underscores the urgent need to rethink conceptual, spatial and political tools in order to co-produce situated knowledge together with migrants and to better address contemporary migration dynamics.

Despite the scale of this crisis, knowledge of the everyday experiences and spatial challenges faced by migrants – particularly minors – remains scarce. To address this gap, the research has introduced a conceptual framework that foregrounds notions such as affects, invisible violence and embodied spatialities, dimensions largely absent from existing studies of the route.

This framework has been tested through the development of counter-cartographies, representing both a methodological and an ethical contribution. Unlike traditional cartography – historically aligned with imperial power and territorial control – counter-cartography seeks to make visible the bodies, trajectories and emotions that

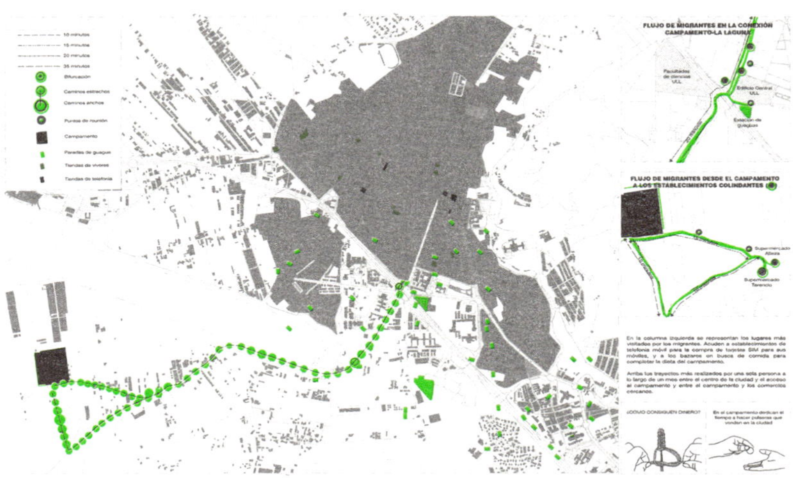

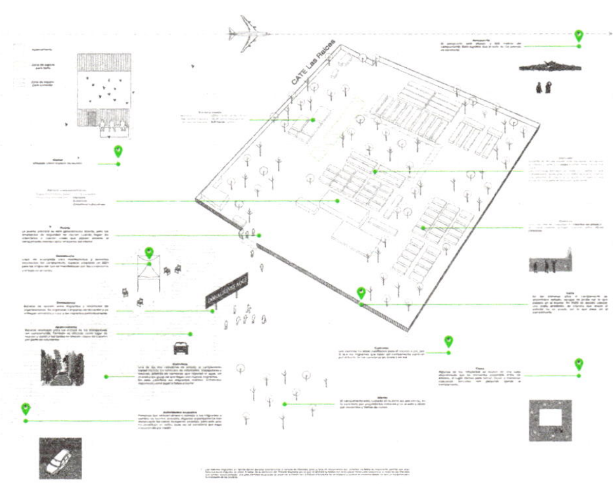

Figure 8 (Left) City map of La Laguna, Tenerife, highlighting the distance between the Las Raíces migrant reception centre (capacity: 3,000 people) and the historic city of La Laguna (a UNESCO World Heritage Site). The route migrants must walk to reach the city is marked by the green dotted line. Green areas indicate zones of restriction and control. The dark-grey square marks the location of the Las Raíces centre.

(Right) Axonometric representation of the Las Raíces centre, emphasising its internal organisation (location of bathrooms, the outdoor queue for showers), the surrounding fence, and the immediate exterior. The drawing also shows the area where donations are received and where sexual encounters between local residents in cars and migrants take place, exposing situations of exploitation linked to migrants' vulnerability. Maria Barroso, 2025.

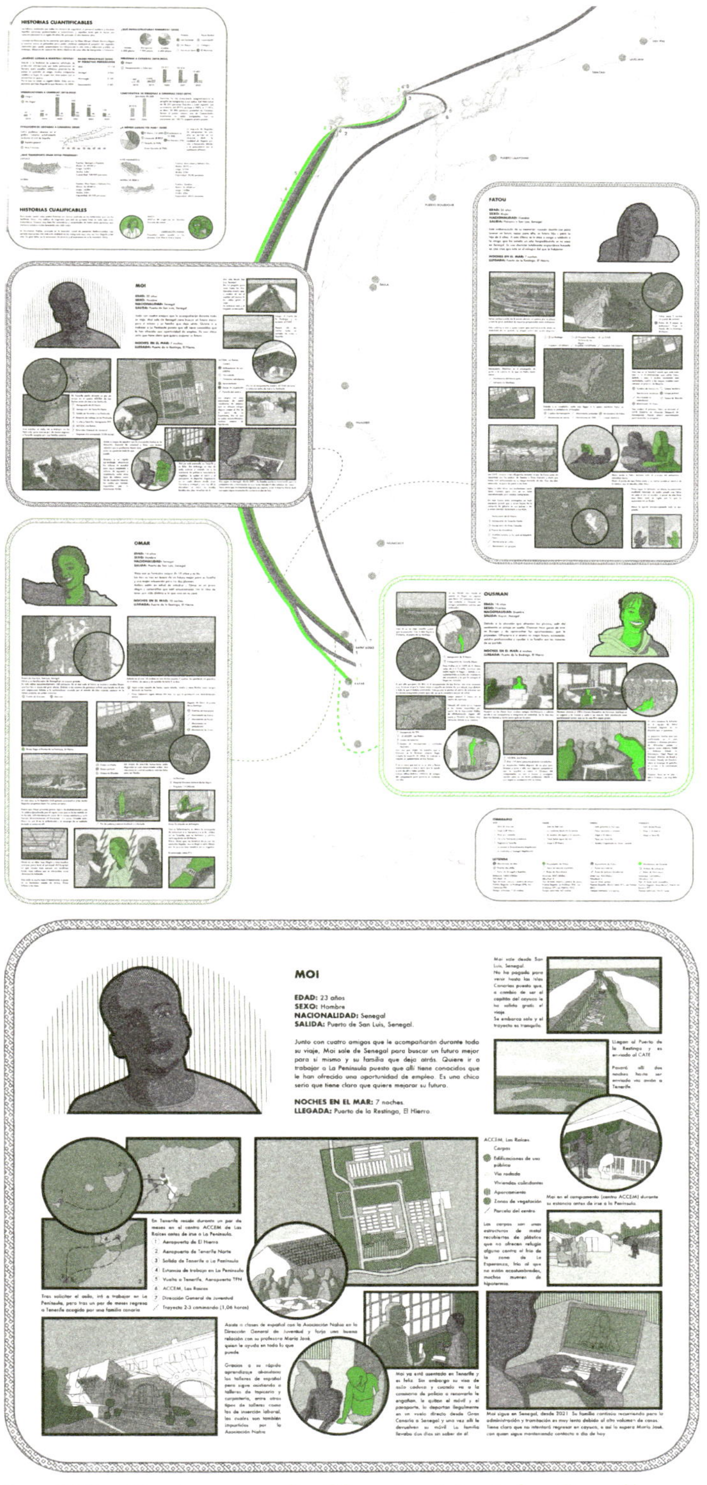

Figure 9. (Top) Counter-cartography of four migrants' route from Senegal/ The Gambia to the Canary Islands. (Bottom) Counter-cartography of a 23-year-old Senegalese survivor whose asylum claim expired after learning Spanish and participating in labour integration programmes, leading to his deportation to Senegal. Sara Cruz and Juan Carlos León, 2025.

official records tend to erase or reduce to abstract figures. By adopting a multi-scalar perspective (Atlantic, insular and corporeal), this initial stage reveals migration not only as geopolitical displacement (mere georeferenced lines and points) but also as lived and affective experience, shaped by violence without coordinates, everyday forms of resistance, situated spatial relations and emotionally charged encounters.

This essay should therefore be understood as part of a broader, ongoing research project. Its purpose at this stage is not to provide definitive conclusions but to establish a foundation for further inquiry into a complex and evolving reality. By articulating counter-cartographies and introducing new conceptual tools, the work aims to advance a more critical understanding of migration, to expose structural deficiencies in reception infrastructures, and to support responses grounded in spatial justice that directly benefit migrants.

Acknowledgements

This project began in 2024 with the participation of undergraduate (First- to Fifth-year) and Master's students from the School of Architecture at Universidad Europea de Canarias, all of whom were involved as members of a research team engaged with this topic.

I am deeply grateful for the commitment and empathy shown by all the students, with special recognition given to those whose counter-cartographies are included in this paper. I would also like to express my sincere gratitude to the associations Nahia and Hay Raíces for their invaluable work with the migrant community, and for helping us to better understand and raise awareness of the realities of this humanitarian crisis.

I acknowledge the use of artificial intelligence to refine and polish the English version of this text.

This research project is currently ongoing with the support of the Social Observatory of the 'la Caixa' Foundation (project code: LCF/PR/SR25/57020016).

References

Cano-Ciborro, V. (2024). Cartografía y resistencia: Líneas y cuerpos en fuga. *Materia Arquitectura, 1*(26), 6–9.

Caminando Fronteras (2024). *Informe del Observatorio de Derechos Humanos de Caminando Fronteras*, December.

Deleuze, G. (2005). *Derrames: Entre el capitalismo y la esquizofrenia*. Cactus.

Deleuze, G. (2008). *En medio de Spinoza*. Cactus

Deleuze, G., & Guattari, F. (2012). *Mil mesetas: Capitalismo y esquizofrenia*. Pre-textos.

Fumero, T. (2024). 'Clavijo: "Seguimos desbordados, con 4.521 menores en centros, y las ONG no pueden más"'. Diario de Avisos, 2 January. https://diariodeavisos.elespanol.com/2024/01/clavijo-seguimos-desbordados-con-4-521-menores-en-centros-y-las-ong-no-pueden-mas/

Haraway, D. (1991). *Simians, Cyborgs, and Women*. Routledge.

Harley, J. B. (1989). Deconstructing the map. *Cartographica: The International Journal for Geographic Information and Geovisualization, 26*(2), 1–20.

International Organization for Migration (2023). Missing Migrants Project data. https://missingmigrants.iom.int/downloads

Kurgan, L. (2013). *Close Up At a Distance: Mapping, Technology, and Politics*. Zone Books.

Lahoud, A. (2014). *Floating Bodies* (E. Weizman & A. Franke, Eds.). Sternberg.

Lee Peluso, N. (1995). Whose woods are these? Counter-mapping forest territories in Kalimantan, Indonesia. *Antipode, 4*(27), 383–406.

Mbembe, A. (2018). *Necropolitics*. Duke University Press.

Ministerio del Interior (2024). Inmigración irregular 2024: Datos acumulados del 1 de enero al 31 de diciembre. https://www.interior.gob.es/opencms/export/sites/default/.galleries/galeria-de-prensa/documentos-y-multimedia/balances-e-informes/2024/24_informe_quincenal_acumulado_01-01_al_31-12-2024.pdf (Informe quincenal)

Thrift, N. (2008). *Non-representational Theory: Space | Politics | Affect*. Routledge.

UNODC Observatory on Smuggling Migrants (2022). *Northwest African (Atlantic) Route: Migrant Smuggling from the Northwest African Coast to the Canary Islands (Spain)*. United Nations Office on Drugs and Crime.

Warf, B. & Arias, S. (Eds.) (2009). *The Spatial Turn: Interdisciplinary Perspectives*. Routledge.

Weizman, E. (2017). *Forensic Architecture: Violence at the Threshold of Detectability*. Zone Books.

Víctor Cano-Ciborro

Valentina Labriola
Politecnico di Torino and Tsinghua University

DESIGNING OTHERWISE: ARCHITECTURE BEYOND THE HUMAN

A CRISIS DIFFICULT TO IMAGINE

In 1965, Susan Sontag, in her essay 'The Imagination of Disaster' (Sontag, 1965), reflected on the role of science fiction in shaping the cultural imagination. Far from dismissing its dramatic visions of catastrophe, she saw in these stories a mirror of our collective anxieties, tools for thinking through crises before they arrive. Today, as the climate emergency unfolds with increasing urgency, this speculative function feels more relevant than ever. In an age defined by planetary instability, how might architects and designers begin to imagine the futures we are already living in?

The climate crisis challenges not only our infrastructures and economies, but also our ability to comprehend and represent it. As Amitav Ghosh argues in *The Great Derangement*, this is 'a crisis of culture, and thus of the imagination' (2016, p. 9). Scientific data is abundant, but data alone rarely moves audiences or practitioners. The difficulty lies in translating abstraction into awareness, and understanding a phenomenon that unfolds over decades, across oceans, and in registers we cannot always see or feel directly. Climate change is everywhere, yet it can often feel strangely distant from our daily lives. We know it is real, but we struggle to picture it, let alone design with it in mind (Figure 1).

Figure 1. Climate crisis on social networks. The constant stream of images saturates perception, often producing paralysis rather than clarity. In this context, the challenge is no longer only to know, but to imagine otherwise.

For architects and spatial thinkers, this crisis of imagination cuts deep. Our work depends on the ability to anticipate, to visualise, to make the future tangible. However, how do we give form to uncertainty? What does it mean to design in relation to forces – like atmospheric shifts, rising seas or slow drought – that resist clear images or fixed boundaries? Architecture, rooted in drawing, modelling and projecting, is inherently a visual practice. Moreover, when the future becomes harder to visualise, the entire framework of design is unsettled.

This essay proposes a method of reframing the climate emergency. Fiction allows us to imagine otherwise. It stretches our thinking, shifts perspectives and opens up spaces where ecological entanglements and more-than-human conditions can be explored and examined. Far from escapist, science fiction offers what Suvin (1979) called 'cognitive estrangement': a way to step outside the familiar in order to see it more clearly. Through invented worlds, speculative timelines and altered viewpoints, fiction cultivates a kind of imaginative literacy that is urgently needed in design disciplines.

Imagination, after all, is not a luxury. As Rendell & Rawes (2007) and others have argued, it is a critical part of the design process, a way of thinking that allows us to move between the known and the possible. Coleman (2018) describes 'imaging' as an interdisciplinary method that helps us question, unpack and reconfigure existing conditions. In architecture, this means more than representing reality; it means generating alternatives, working with abstraction, and drawing futures into being. While imagination enables abstraction and possibility, representation often works to stabilise and communicate those visions. The two are interconnected, but not synonymous: imagination speculates, while representation renders. This difference is essential in design pedagogy, where the goal is not only to draw but to provoke rethinking.

In *Are We Human?* (2016), Beatriz Colomina and Mark Wigley have argued that design is not merely a response to need but a producer of culture and subjectivity. To teach design, then, is not to train for market demands but to cultivate sensitivity: to what is excluded, to what is non-human, to what is yet to be thought. They remind us that design has historically been used to anaesthetise, to smooth-over discomfort, to make environments legible and obedient. However, in a world of rising seas, collapsing certainties and ecological interdependence, pedagogy must do the opposite. It must train for discomfort, for the ability to stay with difficult questions, to listen across difference, and to imagine coexistence where none seems possible.

The following explores how science fiction can help architects engage with the climate emergency, not by offering blueprints, but by nurturing the capacity to imagine. Through stories of submerged cities, hybrid bodies and planetary estrangement, speculative fiction offers new perspectives on space, time and environmental relations. It invites us to ask not just what can be built, but how else we might live and with whom.

FICTION AS METHOD: SCIENCE FICTION AND THE MORE-THAN-HUMAN

Science fiction is often framed as a cultural genre speaking about distant futures, but at its core it is less about the coming than about the present.

In the context of the climate emergency, speculative narratives offer a way of encountering ecological shifts not from above, with distance or detachment, but from within, through altered rhythms, perspectives and environments. These are not stories that predict the future but ones that help readers feel its textures, move slowly into its uncertainties, and reframe what is often taken for granted.

Science fiction works best when it unsettles the reader. It disorients just enough to allow new recognitions to surface. What Suvin (1979) called 'cognitive estrangement' is not about escape, but about thinking differently, estranging us from the habitual in order to return with sharper eyes. In the context of planetary transformation, this becomes a method of 'staying with the trouble', to borrow Donna Haraway's phrase (Haraway, 2016). It lets us imagine environmental conditions that are not theoretical, but lived environments that sweat, flood, breathe and forget.

In Han Song's *Oceano Rosso* (2018), for example, we descend into an oceanic world that is not only physically immersive but spiritually inhabited. Humanity has changed into aquatic hybrids, creatures whose bodies are shaped by water, as well as by a profound sensitivity to its moods and currents. The ocean is not passive. It is aware. It pulses with memory and desire, and the beings who live within it – half-human, half-fish – are attuned to its consciousness in a way surface dwellers never were. Their relationship to water is not extractive or defensive, but reciprocal. In that reciprocity, the ocean emerges not as a threat, but as a companion, a host, perhaps even a forgotten ancestor.

This kind of narrative reframes the environment not as something to be mastered or engineered, but as something to be in relation with. It proposes a mode of existence where survival depends not on controlling natural forces, but on listening to them. Fiction not only makes this idea thinkable; it makes it tangible, giving us sensory entry points into unfamiliar worlds.

In Chi Ta-wei's *The Membranes* (2021), this intimacy with the non-human becomes layered in new ways. Set in an underwater city protected by a synthetic dome, the novel blurs the boundaries between skin, climate and identity. Characters are shaped by biotechnology, but also by longing, memory and uncertainty about what their bodies are made of, who they are and what they are part of. The sea, again, is not a backdrop, but a condition. It presses in on the edges of the world, infiltrates dreams and complicates the distinction between natural and artificial. If the future is wet, then so is memory, and fiction becomes the filter through which we begin to absorb that idea.

These imaginaries do not arrive in isolation. They circulate alongside real concerns – rising seas, disappearing coastlines, shifting habitats – and offer ways to dwell within those anxieties without collapsing into despair. They teach how to think with water, not against it. In J. G Ballard's *The Drowned World* (1962), the world's cities have slowly submerged beneath tropical lagoons, not with dramatic violence but with quiet inevitability. In Ballard's book, time stretches and warps, memories slip away and landscapes turn prehistoric. The protagonist does not fight the change, he drifts with it, increasingly absorbed into the environment's altered rhythms. This surrender is not defeat, but a kind of metamorphosis. What emerges is a different understanding of space, not measured in zones or grids, but in temperature, light, humidity and instinct.

What connects these stories is not only their aquatic settings, but the way they push against the idea of design as control. They suggest that environments are not fixed but mutate, remember and dream. The beings who inhabit them, too, are in flux. In Kim Bo-Young's *On the Origin of Species* (2021), artificial life-forms recount myths of their own creation, questioning evolution, agency and belonging. The world they describe is shaped as much by emotion and intuition as it is by mechanics or genetics. This speculative storytelling challenges the clarity of categories, such as natural/artificial, human/non-human, and self/environment, and encourages us to imagine systems built not for stability, but for resonance.

Across these narratives, fiction does not simplify. It entangles. It lingers in uncertainty, holds competing truths and resists the demand to offer answers. It does not draw blueprints, but opens up space to think, to doubt, to feel. These are not exercises in fantasy; they are exercises in attention. It is a way to focus what usually escapes conventional gaze – currents, pulses, atmospheres – and to recognise them not as background noise, but as part of the shared world we inhabit and co-produce. Fiction becomes a mode of environmental literacy, an attunement to conditions that lie beyond the immediate scale of the human. It offers languages for the unspoken and forms for the unseen. In doing so, it expands the field of what we can imagine, not just technically or formally, but relationally. Not what we might build, but how we might live otherwise.

EXHIBITION AND SPECULATION IN ARCHITECTURE

Architecture is a visual discipline. In fact, before anything is built it is imagined, sketched, drawn, modelled, rendered, represented. It begins not in concrete and steel, but in images. These images are not neutral: they frame, abstract and project. They shape how we understand space, what we consider possible, and with whom or for whom we design. If fiction provides the conceptual ground for thinking otherwise, then visual media – drawings, diagrams, models and exhibitions – translate that thinking into form.

This translation is not straightforward. As Coleman (2018) argues, imaging is an epistemological practice – an act that both produces and questions knowledge. It is through images that we engage with worlds we cannot fully grasp: temporalities beyond the human, systems that exceed perception, environments in flux. Jane Rendell similarly writes of imagination as a 'positive and productive' force in the design process, one that allows us to move between speculation and intervention (Rendell & Rawes, 2007, p. 207). To imagine is not simply to visualise what is not yet there; it is to reconfigure what is already in place.

Speculative exhibitions – especially those addressing climate and more-than-human conditions – take on this function with particular urgency. They are not just platforms for communication, but spaces for rehearsal. Like science fiction, they work through narrative, abstraction and estrangement. They enable us to inhabit unfamiliar perspectives, linger in uncertainty and encounter environments that challenge anthropocentric habits of seeing. In these exhibitions, the more-than-human is not an abstract theme but a palpable presence. Floodwaters rise across large-scale floor maps. Rivers speak through sound installations. Droughts are not displayed as statistics, but as cracked earth, warped wood and silenced crops. Through these curatorial strategies, environmental forces are no longer represented at a distance – they are brought into the room, pressing against the viewer's body and field of vision. The goal is not clarity, but attunement.

In this sense, exhibitions serve as a bridge between speculative fiction and spatial design. They hold space for narratives to take visual form, and for images to exceed representation. The river in a drawing is not only a feature of terrain – it is a character, a force, a memory. The flood is not only a risk – it is a story, a rhythm, a presence. Through such media, the more-than-human becomes not just something we design for, but something we design with.

Recent exhibitions increasingly challenge architectural representation by foregrounding more-than-human perspectives through immersive, narrative-driven strategies. For example, 'Water is Coming' (Danish Architecture Center, Copenhagen, 2025) (Figure 2, top) staged a flooded future through spatialised prototypes, speculative storytelling and environmental soundscapes. Visitors stepped into floating pavilions, listened to fictional narrators from submerged cities, and engaged with water not as a threat but as a relational medium. Similarly, 'Prospecting Ocean' at the Columbia Graduate School of Architecture, Planning and Preservation in New York, 2025 (Figure 2, bottom) presented the ocean as a geopolitical agent, exposing its legal and infrastructural entanglements through forensic cartography and video. In both cases, the exhibition space becomes a narrative environment – a speculative and pedagogical infrastructure that activates more-than-human imaginaries while challenging disciplinary boundaries. These experiments recall the long legacy of architectural speculation, but shift the focus away from anthropocentric futures towards fluid, relational and post-human worlds.

Figure 2. (Top) 'Water is Coming' exhibition, Danish Architecture Center (DAC), Copenhagen, 2025. (Bottom) 'Prospecting Ocean' exhibition, Columbia Graduate School of Architecture, Planning and Preservation (GSAAP), New York, 2025. These curatorial experiments activate more-than-human imaginaries, staging water not as a threat but as a relational medium, and oceanic space as legal, political and narrative terrain.

This shift – from representation to relation – marks a critical transition in this essay. If fiction teaches how to think differently, exhibitions teach how to see differently. They reveal how imagination operates not only in literature, but in lines, colours, scales and textures. They train the eye to hold contradiction, to dwell in abstraction, and to recognise that environments are not backgrounds, but active participants in shaping how we live.

This visual and spatial literacy – this ability to engage with more-than-human conditions through form, story and image – is not a passive skill. It is a pedagogical tool. And it is here, in the tension between fiction, exhibition and design, that the possibility of reimagining architectural education begins to take shape.

This engagement with speculation is not without precedent. Architectural history is rich with visionary projects that imagined future cities and alternative worlds, such as Archigram's mobile infrastructures and the Metabolist megastructures of the 1960s. Many of these imaginaries were first presented through exhibitions, drawings and publications. The difference today lies not in the speculative impulse, but in the subjectivity: where past visions centred the human designer, today's experiments increasingly foreground more-than-human actors – rivers, bacteria, climates – as active agents. Just as historical exhibitions challenged the discipline to think anew, these contemporary examples aim not only to project futures but to question who is authorised to imagine them.

The fact that these exhibitions are staged within architecture institutions such as the DAC and Columbia GSAPP, and, more recently, at the Triennale di Milano which hosted the 'We the Bacteria: Notes Toward Biotic Architecture' exhibition (Columina & Wigley, 2025), signals a growing recognition that architecture itself must be reimagined not just as form, but as a speculative, relational and pedagogical practice.

CONCLUSION: REHEARSING OTHERWISE

The long transition towards post-anthropocentric and post-carbon futures demands not only new materials and policies, but new epistemologies: ways of sensing, thinking and drawing that are attuned to a world where human agency is no longer central. Pedagogy, in this light, becomes a speculative act: a space for training not only professional skills, but perceptual shifts.

In this essay, science fiction has emerged as a tool that cultivates estrangement, dislodging dominant assumptions and creating space for reconfiguring our relationship with the world. Fiction is framed as a form of rehearsal, allowing us to inhabit uncertainty without resolving it, to simulate futures we do not yet know how to navigate. When brought into architectural education, it does not offer ready-made visions of the future, but invites the student into a process of cognitive estrangement. By displacing the human as the default subject and by imagining environments that shift, flood, forget or resist, fiction asks: What does it mean to design with others, other species, other temporalities and other forms of life? Within architectural education it offers students the opportunity to explore new temporalities, agencies and spatial configurations where the environment is not a backdrop but a protagonist.

However, fiction alone is not enough. As argued earlier, architectural imagination is shaped through visual abstraction: the act of drawing as a way of knowing. This visual epistemology is not passive. Imaging is 'a speculative method' (Coleman, 2018, p. 62) that can question and reconfigure existing conditions. When coupled with the destabilising potential of fiction, visual practice becomes a way of not only imagining but also manifesting alternatives. And so, sketches, diagrams and models all become sites for rethinking relations between humans and their environments.

In this way, speculative fiction and speculative design are two sides of the same pedagogical coin. Where fiction narrates the unfamiliar, drawing gives it form. Where story disorients, modelling rearranges. Teaching architecture through this lens means equipping students not only to solve problems, but to frame questions, to live with ambiguity, to embrace contradiction, to move between data and dreams.

What emerges, then, is not a pedagogy of solutions, but one of endurance and attentiveness: a way of learning that accepts discomfort as a condition of thinking, and uncertainty as a shared ground rather than a problem to be eliminated. To imagine otherwise, finally, is to accept unease: to resist the desire for stable ground, and to remain present within the shifting relations that bind humans, environments and futures together.

In his reflections on 'Architecture After Architecture' (2020), Jeremy Till echoed this call for radical reform, arguing that architecture, long complicit in the modern project of growth, order and control, must now reckon with its limitations. The climate crisis, for him, is not a problem to be solved but a predicament to be navigated, a condition that demands not just technical expertise but systemic rethinking. For Till, design pedagogy must shift away from aesthetics and technocratic fixes, and towards forms of 'sense-making' that are collaborative, situated and open-ended. In other words: speculative, relational and more-than-human. This speculative pedagogy is already emerging, not as a curriculum, but as a practice.

In a recent pedagogical experiment I conducted with a team from the Politecnico di Torino and Barnard College, Columbia University, New York, students explored the Bormida Valley – a territory in the Piedmont region of Italy – as a multispecies archive, developing speculative projects through narrative mapping, fieldwork and water-centred storytelling. During an immersive workshop called 'Imagining the Bormida Valley: Interfaces between past and future' (Figure 3), students from both institutions engaged with a diverse set of materials, ranging from technical data on water pollution, flood statistics and GIS layers, to speculative narratives drawn from literature and film about the valley. Their challenge was to confront both the past and the future of the Bormida River not as a problem to be solved, but as an open question to be approached through design. While the studio is still ongoing, it is already demonstrating how site-based pedagogy can foster engagement with more-than-human conditions through fiction, visual abstraction and interdisciplinary collaboration.

Figure 3. A selection of materials from the workshop 'Imagining the Bormida Valley: Interfaces between past and future' (Bormida Valley, Italy, 2025), including a poster, on-site photo and student sketches. Through fieldwork, speculative drawing and narrative design, students from the Politecnico di Torino and Barnard College, Columbia University, New York, engaged the Bormida River as a multispecies archive, rethinking how to design and imagine with water.

This pedagogical reframing is aligned with initiatives such as those developed at the Canadian Centre for Architecture (CCA), which use fiction not to escape architecture, but to expand its field. Its exhibitions and public programmes experiment with form, storytelling and representation. In one such project, speculative environments were imagined not as utopias but as mirrors, reflecting the blind spots of architectural modernism and the extractive logics that continue to underwrite the discipline. These critical framings, often curated as fragmented, layered or incomplete, resist the clarity of a single message; that is, to recognise that architectural thinking must be stretched, disoriented and reconfigured – not to produce certainty, but to build resilience, responsiveness and care. This requires a pedagogy that values attunement over control, speculation over prescription, and relation over separation.

In conclusion, this essay has traced a path from science fiction to pedagogy through the terrains of drawing, exhibition and environmental estrangement. Its argument is not that architecture must become something else, but that it must become more of what it already is at its best: a cultural, imaginative and ethical practice that does not simply represent the world, but participates in shaping how it is perceived, inhabited and shared.

In the face of planetary instability, architecture must stop pretending to be in command. It must begin to listen across species, across mediums, across time. The future does not need more blueprints. It needs stories, rehearsals, drawings and doubts. It needs the slow labour of imagining otherwise, and the courage to stay with that imagination until it starts to reshape practices of teaching, designing and living.

Acknowledgements

This research was developed within the Transnational Architectural Models in a Globalized World programme, a joint PhD curriculum within the framework of the Politecnico di Torino's doctoral programme in Architecture. History and Project, and the doctoral programmes in Architecture at Tsinghua University, Beijing.

The author would like to thank the faculty and collaborators involved in the pedagogical experiments referenced in this essay. In particular, Professor Francesca Frassoldati, Professor Roberto Albano and Professor Albena Yaneva. Thanks also to Paolo Bianco, architects Matteo Novarino and Magdalena Jendras (Novarino Jendras Studio), Anna Gloria Moschetti, Marco Del Fiore, Francesca Moro and Juan José Miranda, as members of the Politecnico di Torino coordination group.

Special thanks are extended also to Professor Kadambari Baxi and Professor Karen Fairbanks at Barnard College, Columbia University, for fostering an interdisciplinary exchange between fiction, exhibition practice and spatial design.

The reflections on pedagogy presented here are deeply indebted to the students from the Politecnico di Torino and Barnard College who participated in the workshop in the Bormida Valley; their openness, curiosity and speculative engagement were fundamental to the development of the ideas discussed.

References

Ballard, J. D. (1962). *The Drowned World.* Gollancz.

Bo-Young, K. (2021). *On the Origin of Species and Other Stories.* Kaya Press.

Chi, T. W. (2021). *The Membranes: A Novel.* Columbia University Press.

Coleman, R., (2018). Imaging. In C. Lury, R. Fensham, A. Heller-Nicholas, S. Lammes, A. Last, M. Michael & E. Uprichard (Eds.), *Routledge Handbook of Interdisciplinary Research Methods* (pp. 61–67). Routledge.

Colomina, B. & Wigley, M. (2016). *Are We Human? Notes on an Archaeology of Design.* Lars Müller Publishers.

Colomina, B. & Wigley, M. (2025). *We the Bacteria: Notes Toward Biotic Architecture.* Lars Müller Publishers.

Ghosh, A. (2016). *The Great Derangement: Climate Change and the Unthinkable.* University of Chicago Press.

Haraway, D. J. (2016). *Staying with the Trouble: Making Kin in the Chthulucene.* Duke University Press.

Rendell, J. & Rawes, P. (2007). Spatial imagination. In T. Inns (Ed.), *Designing for the 21st Century* (pp. 205–19). Gower Ashgate.

Song, H. (2018). *Oceano Rosso.* add editore.

Sontag, S. (1965). *Against Interpretation.* Picador.

Suvin, D. (1979). *Metamorphoses of Science Fiction.* Peter Lang

Till, J. (2020). Architecture after Architecture, lecture, Architecture Foundation 100-Day Studio, 2 April 2020. Transcript available at: www.jeremytill.net/read/130/architecture-after-architecture

Joan Maria Martí Elias
Universitat Politècnica de Catalunya – BarcelonaTech

LEARNING FROM GARCIA FÀRIA: CIRCULAR METABOLISM IN THE LATE NINETEENTH CENTURY

THE CENTURY OF ENGINEERS AND THE RETURN TO THE TERRITORY

The relationship between the city, territorial transformation and the water cycle underwent an exceptional phase during the second half of the nineteenth century. The sudden demographic growth generated by the Industrial Revolution revealed the limits of a linear metabolic pattern which, until then, had ensured a balanced relationship between the city's material flows and the productive capacity of its territory. Within this context, figures such as Pierre Leroux and Élisée Reclus underscored the importance of recovering organic approaches that emphasised a return to the territory within the framework of large-scale works of urban engineering (Kaika & Swyngedouw, 2000).

It was in this epistemological context that Pere Garcia Fària (1858–1927), at the end of the nineteenth century, formulated his proposals for the sanitation of Barcelona and the rectification of the Llobregat River. These projects should not be understood as isolated episodes within a Barcelona still deeply shaped by the shadow of Cerdà's Plan, but rather as part of a European tradition that regarded the management of the water cycle as the final opportunity to re-establish a more organic and balanced relationship between the city and its territory through circular logics of management.

Leroux's *circulus* and the metabolism of the city

When Victor Hugo described the sewers of Paris in the memorable episode 'The Intestine of the Leviathan' in *Les Misérables* (1862), he drew upon and synthesised the principles defended by publisher and philosopher Pierre Leroux (Vandenput, 2019). Leroux applied the principle of the *circulus*, inspired by the theory of natural circulation formulated by the scientist Jean-Baptiste Dumas (Crossley, 2008). Since the second agricultural revolution and the investigations of Justus von Liebig (Finlay, 1991), agronomic science had emphasised the need to continuously fertilise peri-urban lands by accelerating crop rotation, thereby ensuring their productivity and sustaining a growing population (Simmons, 2006). Leroux thus proposed establishing a circular relationship between resources and the environment, a system in which waste was used to re-nourish the productive origin of the resource itself (O'Neil-Henry, 2016).

Within this framework, Hugo defended the use of wastewater for the irrigation of the Parisian hinterland, recognising its value in avoiding more costly and geographically dislocated practices such as the importation of fertilisers, while also mitigating the pollution of the Seine. Faced with the emergence of guano imports to guarantee the productivity of urban hinterlands[1] (within a distinctly colonial and extractive logic), the recognition of the regenerative value of urban waste offered the possibility of reformulating the metabolic model, anchoring it in proximity and reciprocity with the territory. These ideas, rooted in a critical historical moment, found in the transformation of Europe's great cities the ideal context for their implementation (Martí & Crosas, 2023).

Infrastructure, modernity and the imaginary of progress

The Parisian sewer system described by Victor Hugo constitutes one of the most emblematic examples of nineteenth-century urban transformations, designed by engineer Eugène Belgrand under the authority of prefect Georges-Eugène Haussmann.

Between 1852 and 1870, Belgrand designed the city's new sewer network, separating potable water from wastewater within a hierarchical system of collectors discharging into the Seine downstream (Reid, 1991). The project, published in Belgrand's *Les travaux souterrains de Paris* (Belgrand, 1877), depicted the city as a living organism nourished by veins and arteries (Figure 1). This process of reconstruction began with the survey conducted by Pierre Bruneseau between 1805 and 1812, and culminated with the publication of Hugo's novel (1862) and Félix Nadar's photographic campaign (Figure 2) commissioned by Belgrand in 1864. The latter portrayed the sewers as clean, illuminated and sanitary spaces,

1 The question of guano is, indeed, key to understanding the shift of the period. From 1841 onwards, Europe began to massively import these deposits of fossilised seabird droppings from the Pacific coast of South America. This resource became essential for sustaining agricultural productivity and, by extension, the growth of industrial cities.

constructing a social imaginary that associated them with progress and with the strength of the 'City of Light' (Atkinson, 1997; Gandy, 1999).

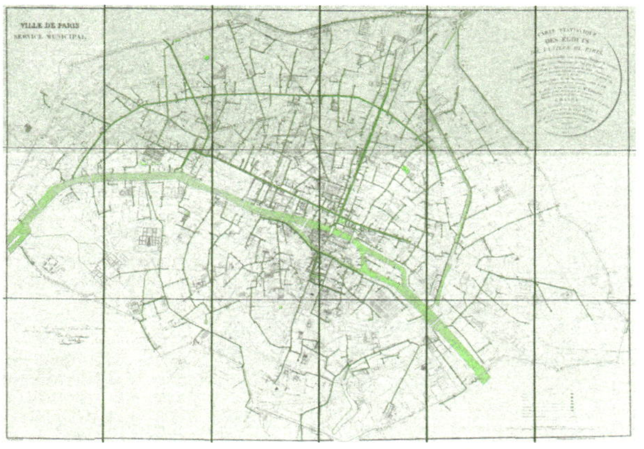

Figure 1. Eugène Belgrand, *Carte statistique des égouts de Paris au 31 Décembre 1885*. Dark green – supply; soft green – sanitation. *Source*: Bibliothèque Nationale de France.

Figure 2. Félix Nadar, *The Sewers*, 1864. *Source*: Gandy (1999).

A crucial aspect was that infrastructure extended beyond the administrative limits of the city: Belgrand proposed connecting Paris with the Dhuis and Vanne catchments, thereby linking the destiny of the metropolis to the hydraulic flows of its surrounding territory. In this sense, the wastewater management project at Gennevilliers (1864–69), directed by engineer Adolphe-Auguste Mille, provided empirical confirmation of Leroux's theories: one-fifth of Parisian effluent transformed barren land into fertile soil (Sturge, 1879).

The roots of this new conception of urbanism, however, lay in a necessity derived from the massive demographic expansion brought about by the Industrial Revolution: the reduction of 'avoidable deaths' (Gorostiza, 2014). This concern was articulated under the umbrella of the so-called hygienist movement, which originated in England.

Hygienism, public health and the politics of water

The Public Health Act (1848), driven by Edwin Chadwick's 1842 report on sanitary conditions in England and regarded as the first explicitly hygienist document, established the regulation of water supply and drainage systems as essential tools for reducing mortality rates (Ringen, 1979; Rosen, 1975). Investigations such as those conducted in neighbourhoods like Bethnal Green in London demonstrated how detailed cartography validated the correlation between overcrowding, insalubrity and premature death, anticipating the celebrated cholera outbreak mapped by John Snow in 1854 (Lewis, 1952).

This body of ideas emerging from England was soon disseminated throughout industrialised Europe, transforming water management into more than a technical question by endowing it with political and social significance. In this regard, the solution to a public health problem was directly tied to the need to fertilise urban hinterlands, as maintaining their productive capacity was indispensable to organic societies (Cuchí, 2011).[2]

For this reason, Chadwick viewed in the design of urban sanitation systems the opportunity to articulate the return of organic matter to the territory through water management. This approach, deeply embedded in the European intellectual tradition, constitutes a paradigmatic example of the transition from organic to industrial society: from a closed metabolic cycle based on the return of matter to the land, to a cycle dependent upon the consumption of fossil materials (Llop, 2017). It reflects a missed opportunity situated between two revolutions (Allen, 2004) and provides the theoretical and ideological framework within which Pere Garcia Fària would later formulate his proposals for the transformation of the city of Barcelona and the Llobregat Delta.

PERE GARCIA FÀRIA AND THE CITY–DELTA PROJECT

In a historical context shaped by the hygienist movement and by the hegemony of engineering as an instrument for the radical transformation of urban life, the proposals of architect and engineer Pere Garcia Fària stand out

2 Specifically, in Europe, until the mid-nineteenth century, the fertility of fields was maintained through the management of organic matter produced in the cities, which allowed nitrogen to be fixed and prevented the desertification of the crops that supplied the urban centres. From that moment on, new sources appeared, such as the importation of guano. The chemical revolution culminated in 1910 with the fixation of atmospheric nitrogen by the Haber–Bosch method, and it is within this temporal framework that numerous claims emerged – such as those indignantly described by Victor Hugo in 1862 – defending urban effluents as far more efficient fertilisers from both a logistical and, above all, a sanitary perspective.

for their singular attention to the territory and for their ambition to integrate city and environment into a unified operation (Sabaté i Casellas, 1994). Whereas in other contexts such undertakings were fragmentary and temporally dispersed, in Barcelona they acquired, through two almost consecutive projects (1889 and 1891), a unitary dimension.

The significance of Garcia Fària's work lies not only in the originality of his contribution within the Spanish panorama, but also in his ability to anticipate a systemic conception of the territory understood as infrastructure. The city could no longer be conceived as an autonomous element defined by administrative boundaries; rather, it had to be understood as a node within an ecosystem encompassing agricultural land, subsoil and water dynamics. In this sense, his projects synthesised the ideological frameworks of the period (the *circulus*, hygienism and the prominence of engineering works) while introducing a decisive shift: defining the Llobregat Delta as both support and receptor of a new urban water cycle (Miranda, 2006). In so doing, he broke with the historical vertical mountain-to-sea relationship in favour of a new city-to-delta vector aimed at recovering circular logics in response to emerging metabolic disruptions. What might have appeared a merely technical reformulation was, in fact, a radical rethinking of the relationship between city and territory, anticipating many of the contemporary discourses on urban metabolism and circularity.

Architect, engineer and hygienist

Garcia Fària was both an architect and a civil engineer. Upon completing his studies he entered the Cuerpo de Ingenieros de Caminos (Corps of Civil Engineers), and his practice (strongly shaped by hygienist concerns) directed his career towards questions of urban sanitation (Esteve & Recaño, 2006). He served as technical secretary of the Municipal Commission for the Sanitation of Barcelona (1884), drafting several reports on the hygienic and sanitary conditions of the city.[3] His intervention at the Sant Boi Sanatorium during the cholera outbreak of 1885 further consolidated his reputation as one of the foremost experts in the hygienist field.

Professionally, Garcia Fària also drafted projects for neighbouring municipalities, such as that for Vila de Gràcia (1888). In 1889 he was appointed Chief Engineer of the Barcelona City Council, tasked with preparing the sanitation plan for the city's subsoil. At the same time, he drafted a project for the rectification of the final stretch of the Llobregat River, producing two parallel projects rooted in a profound understanding of the physical, social and environmental dynamics of the territory in which they were to be implemented.

The sanitation of the Eixample as urban infrastructure

The renowned Eixample project by Ildefons Cerdà also originated in a hygienist document: the 1841 essay *Abajo las murallas!* by Pere Felip Monlau (Monlau, 1841), which argued that the demolition of Barcelona's walls was not only an opportunity for urban expansion but also a means of improving public health, recognising the influence of the physical environment on citizens' well-being (Sabaté i Casellas, 1994).

On the basis of social and scientific criteria, Cerdà elaborated his 'Teoría general de la urbanización y aplicación de sus principios y doctrinas a la reforma y ensanche de Barcelona' (1867).[4] Drawing on epidemiological and demographic studies, and complemented by a detailed survey of the Barcelona plain, he produced a theoretical and practical framework that gave rise to an exemplary project (the Cerdà Plan) that is still widely studied and recognised today (Corominas, 1986).

Garcia Fària adopted this methodological approach, combining it with extensive research into sanitation systems in major European cities.[5] These investigations laid the foundation for his most ambitious project, the Proyecto de Saneamiento del Subsuelo de la Ciudad de Barcelona (1891). This was the most significant operation to equip the grid envisioned by Cerdà with sanitation infrastructure, conceived from the perspective of urban services (mobility and sanitation) as the essential elements of the city (Gómez Ordóñez, 1982). In his 'Teoría general de la urbanización', Cerdà (1867) described sanitation as the 'venous system of a colossal being' (p. 30). Water, sanitation and public transport infrastructures materialised and consolidated the mesh-like structure he had foreseen (Magrinyà Torner, 1995). Garcia Fària's project, therefore, operated within a transforming territory, integrating existing networks while laying the foundations for services in an Eixample still in the process of consolidation.

Beyond guaranteeing the proper sanitation of Barcelona, Garcia Fària's proposal sought to integrate and connect the Eixample with its internal and external peripheries. Cerdà's sanitation system followed a vertical mountain-to-sea pattern: rainwater was discharged directly into the sea, while organic matter was stored in independent cesspits,[6] similar to the systems being

3 Beyond the European context, which Garcia Fària knew quite well, he drew inspiration from the methodology of Ildefons Cerdà who, during the drafting of the Eixample project, published the *Monografía de la clase obrera* (1856), compiling all the hygienic and sanitary parameters on which he would rely to present his proposal.

4 It is not the purpose of this research to examine in depth the work of Cerdà, which already has an extensive bibliography analysing and studying it from various perspectives.

5 He had previously tested this design in his 1888 sewerage Project for Vila de Gràcia.

6 This proposal is reflected in the Anteproyecto de Docks de Barcelona, drafted by Cerdà himself in 1863.

implemented at the time in European cities such as Turin (Figure 3). The Eixample proposal managed its interface with both the plain of Barcelona and the historic centre through peripheral collectors that intercepted waters and diverted them into vertical conduits, effectively severing continuity. By contrast, Garcia Fària's sanitation plan, based on the lateral movement of water across the plain, offered an opportunity to amend Cerdà's design and align it with contemporary European practices.

Figure 3. Comparison between Ildefons Cerdà's Anteproyecto de Docks (1863) and Garcia Fària's Proyecto de Saneamiento (1891).

This new approach, departing from Cerdà's cesspit-based system, introduced several innovations that made Garcia Fària's project exemplary in Spain. It established a networked system that collected not only rainwater but also domestic wastewater, which was conveyed to the Llobregat Delta for irrigation. A network of 29 main collectors was planned, integrating the existing sewers and concentrating flows at three discharge points, from which an outfall carried them onto the plain.

At the architectural scale, the project was equally innovative. The sectional drawings of residential buildings, rooted in the ground through waste evacuation and water supply conduits, also functioned as transversal diagrams to be replicated across the corridor-streets, embodying the urban idea expressed in these projects (Gómez Ordóñez, 1982). These sections represented the outcome of earlier sanitary struggles against insalubrious housing (damp, small, dark and poorly ventilated) which had enshrined the provision of sanitary services as a legal and technical imperative of urban planning (Figure 4).

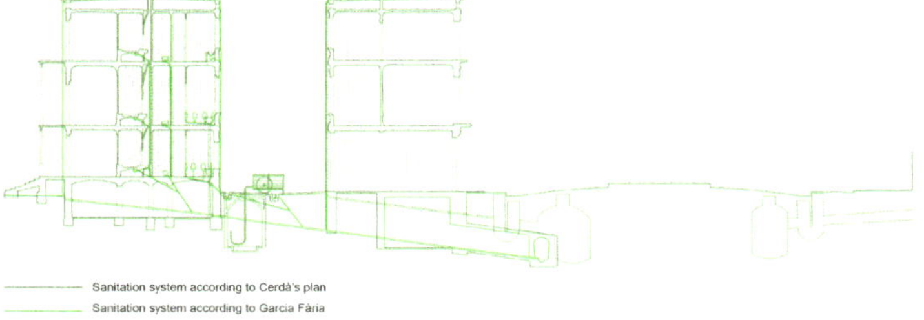

Figure 4. The street section as an integrating element. Comparison between Cerdà's original proposal and Garcia Fària's reformulation.

The rectification of the Llobregat River

Parallel to his Eixample sanitation proposal, in 1890 Garcia Fària published the Proyecto de Saneamiento y Rectificación del Río Llobregat. This ambitious plan sought to address both sudden floods and stagnant waters in the river's final stretch.

The Mediterranean regime of the Llobregat River caused frequent and violent floods in municipalities such as Sant Boi and Sant Joan Despí (Perich, 1996), while stagnant waters in the lowest parts of the delta, below sea level, facilitated the spread of diseases such as malaria (Simo et al., 2005). To address these problems, Garcia Fària proposed a drastic solution: the rectification of the river[7] (Miranda, 2006), beginning at Molins de Rei, passing tangentially to Sant Boi, and debouching near the El Remolar wetland. By minimising meanders, the new channel reduced the risk of flooding. The plan was supported by two principal measures: the definition of the new course and the construction of embankments designed to prevent overflow.

Garcia Fària's design reclaimed the rectilinear section at Molins de Rei while respecting two pre-existing infrastructures: the masonry bridge at Molins and the Canal de la Infanta. From there, the alignment proposed a slight southwesterly curve at Sant Feliu, a straight reach to Sant Boi, another curve before the castle, and a final straight course to El Remolar (Garcia Fària, 1898).[8] Although the project represented a sharp disruption of the territory's hydrological dynamics, it was nonetheless grounded in a contextual reading (both physical and cultural) and respected landmarks such as the Molins bridge, the Canal de la Infanta, the tangential passage by the Sant Boi's hill, and the natural floodplain outlet (Figure 5).

Figure 5. The urbanisation of Barcelona and the reconstruction of the Llobregat Delta: a unitary project.

Joan Maria Martí Elias

7 The design of the river's course is based on a critical analysis of three previous projects, all carried out from the mid-nineteenth century onwards: one by engineers Camon and Ardanúz (1846), another by the architect Josep Maria Bladó (1854) and a third conceived by engineer D. J. de Moulin (1862). It is, therefore, a project framed within a long-standing debate about the territory, seeking to address a problem with deep historical roots.

8 The choice of the outlet point is not accidental, but rather responds to an interpretation of the water dynamics in these flood-prone territories, since it is precisely at El Remolar that a secondary branch of the Llobregat is formed during floods that inundate the delta, giving rise to the largest lagoon in the entire area.

The new course was complemented by works throughout the delta to ensure continuous circulation and prevent stagnation. Garcia Fària analysed and calculated the surfaces of ponds and wetlands, proposing the removal of dunes, the raising of roads, the restructuring of farmland terraces, and the reuse of excavated soil to fill depressions. Once flatness was achieved, he projected a network of equidistant axes, one kilometre apart, radiating from the old trace of Valencia Road.[9] These were conceived as new elevated roads incorporating drainage systems. The old road's alignment was also reused for a railway, intended to facilitate construction. By incorporating the logics of deltaic growth (Eizaguirre, 1994), water management became the structuring basis upon which mobility infrastructures were established.

Although technically ambitious and ecologically disruptive, the project was justified by the arrival of new water flows from Barcelona. This was no longer sediment-laden water descending from Castellar de n'Hug, but rather urban wastewater, signalling a shift from the traditional mountain-to-sea circulation to a new city-to-territory dynamic. The two projects were thus intrinsically linked, mutually dependent, and proposed a new way of conceptualising the role and structure of the Llobregat Delta (Queralt & Isla, 2018).

Towards a systemic and circular vision

Garcia Fària's work thus encapsulated the major urban and territorial debates of late-nineteenth-century Europe, while at the same time anticipating themes central to contemporary urbanism: the circular management of flows, interdependence across scales, and the need to understand infrastructure not merely as technical devices but as territorial projects with ecological and social potential.

Although neither project was realised,[10] their importance lies in the establishment of a design principle that continues to resonate strongly in contemporary urban experiences. Many of the principles Garcia Fària anticipated have since been reinterpreted in subsequent projects, both international and local, evidencing the continuity and relevance of his integrative vision.

CONTINUITIES AND CONTEMPORARY RESONANCES

Within this framework, the most direct heir to Garcia Fària's thinking is the construction of the complex system of water treatment facilities in the final stretch of the Llobregat. From the second half of the twentieth century, with the construction of the first wastewater treatment plants, through to the desalination plant built in 2009, the river's lower course has become a sophisticated network where water is treated, regenerated, recycled and reintroduced into an assemblage of plants, pumping stations, irrigation networks and infiltration ponds.[11] This system both improves the efficiency of water use (alleviating pressure from metropolitan Barcelona) and ensures the viability of the Llobregat Agrarian Park, an agricultural plain embedded within the metropolitan territory with both productive and recreational functions (CUADLL, 2004; Ferret, 1985). Where Garcia Fària envisioned collectors conveying wastewater to the delta, a highly complex network now distributes regenerated water to sustain agricultural productivity and ecological balance, thereby mitigating urbanisation pressures (Figure 6).[12] The fragile equilibrium between city and delta is today maintained through the feedback and recirculation of urban flows into the territory (Queralt & Isla, 2018).

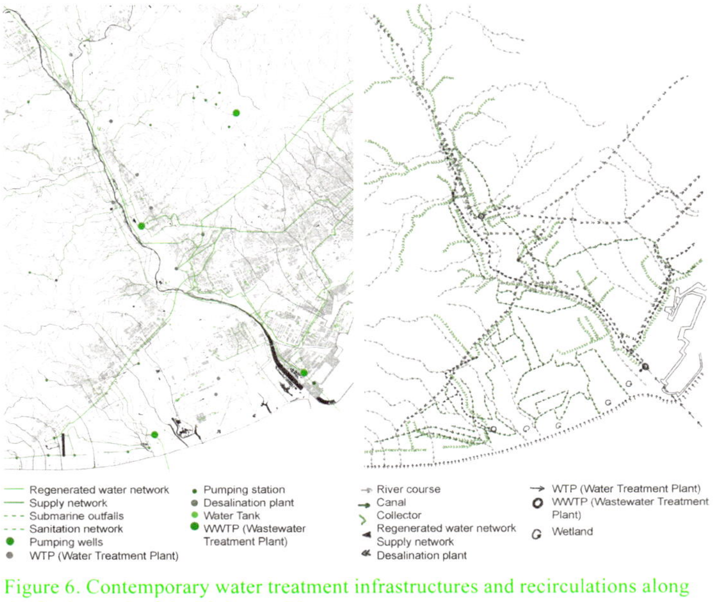

Figure 6. Contemporary water treatment infrastructures and recirculations along the final stretch of the Llobregat River.

Other contemporary projects, beyond the Llobregat, also embody these principles. These are long-term processes in which territorial transformation is grounded in principles of circularity through water treatment. A paradigmatic case is the Emscher Landschaftspark in

9 The old Valencia Road, historically known as the *Camí Ral*, constituted a fundamental artery crossing the Llobregat Delta, linking Barcelona with the southern Iberian Peninsula through settlements such as El Prat de Llobregat, Viladecans and Gavà. This historical route played a structuring role in the organisation of the delta's agricultural landscape and in the subsequent development of its urban settlements.

10 The Proyecto de Saneamiento, as he himself explained in the publication *Anarquía o Caciquismo?* in 1902, was not carried out due to a conflict of interests stemming from the refusal of the architect and engineer to award the works in an illicit manner (Garcia Fària, 1902). Garcia Fària's relationship with the Barcelona City Council gradually deteriorated to the point of a legal dispute over the payment of his professional fees, and it was not until 1901 that the Council – this time under the regenerational influence of the Catalanist conservative party Lliga Regionalista – relaunched the project, but under the direction of Jaume Gustà i Bondia (Tarragó Cid, 1974), with a less ambitious result.

In any case, the disagreements with the City Council do not explain the failure to implement the rectification of the final stretch of the Llobregat. In this regard, Garcia Fària makes no mention of it in his later writings, and it may be concluded that the complexity of the proposal was such that it met the same fate as the earlier projects analysed.

11 It is not a project of single authorship, but rather a territory consolidated through various plans and projects: from the Pla Comarcal (1953), the Pla General Metropolità (1976), the Proposta Marc per a la recuperació dels espais Fluvials (1995) and the Pla Especial del Parc Agrícola del Baix Llobregat (1994).

12 It is important to note that, although for reasons different from those expressed by Garcia Fària, the final stretch of the Llobregat River was diverted westward in the early 2000s in order to expand Barcelona's Zona Franca.

the Ruhrgebiet, Germany (1990–present), an industrialised river basin where wastewater circulating through existing canals is treated and reintegrated into the natural system (Reicher, 2017). Following a similar logic on a more domestic scale, the Swedish neighbourhood of Hammarby Sjöstad in Stockholm (1990–2000) incorporated wastewater treatment into its urban fabric, enabling both the fertilisation of the hinterland and energy production (Pandis Iveroth & Brandt, 2011; Pandis Iveroth et al., 2013).

At a much larger scale, the Dutch project Room for the River (2007–present) illustrates the transformative potential of river margins as fields of intervention (Rijke et al., 2012). By designating intermediate floodable zones, it has established a renewed cycle among river, soil and human activity while enhancing urban safety.

In all these cases, water functions as the vector linking city and territory, advancing an interpretation that transcends linear and extractive systems. They demonstrate that the concern with the circular management of flows is a historical constant, evolving in parallel with the productive and reproductive models of society.

CONCLUSION: TOWARDS BECOMING CIRCULAR

The historical and projective trajectory analysed situates Garcia Fària within a broader genealogical context in which his projects (although never realised) formulated a clear hypothesis: that circular resource management is key to ensuring balance between city and territory. His vision shows that circularity extends far beyond a contemporary reading; rather, it constitutes a historical process in continuous evolution. Becoming circular therefore entails recognising this continuity and understanding that present practice is nourished by projective processes often neglected or forgotten.

In this sense, this legacy poses both a challenge and an opportunity. The challenge lies in overcoming the linear interpretation of infrastructures and embracing the complexity of hydrological and material cycles; the opportunity lies in understanding infrastructures as agents capable of generating positive effects beyond the interests of the human species, operating as mediating systems between the city, agricultural practices, soil conditions, hydrological dynamics and living ecologies. This reconceptualisation moves beyond a purely technical understanding of infrastructure, framing it instead as an instrument of spatial production grounded in readings of interdependence across species and scales. It therefore becomes necessary to overcome an urban-centric perspective and to rearticulate this reading from the delta towards the city. From this standpoint, the failure of Garcia Fària's project cannot be understood solely as the result of political disinterest; rather, it is inseparable from the contemporaneous discovery (1893) of the deep aquifer waters (Almera, 1894), which revealed a latent hydrological potential and a previously unrecognised equilibrium that profoundly transformed urban growth and the future of the delta (Queralt & Isla, 2018)). This third dimension opens new perspectives beyond surface-based dynamics, in which the city emerges as one component within a far more extensive system that exceeds strictly urban logics.

At the same time, this delta-oriented perspective, grounded in its historical processes of formation, reclaims the role of infrastructures as adaptive systems of negotiation between multiple realities. A constellation of paths, irrigation canals and floodable areas (Figure 7) weaves a dense network of 'silent infrastructures' that have historically mediated between hydrological dynamics, ecosystem balances and agricultural productivity across the territory. Although modest in scale, these elements have constituted the very rationale and underlying structure of the landscape, embodying an infrastructural logic rooted in proximity, circular cycles and long-term adaptation, in which urban and rural functions are inseparable from the ecosystemic equilibria in which they are embedded.

Figure 7. 'Silent infrastructures' at the Llobregat Delta, Autumn 2025.

Reinterpreting and re-situating the significance of these traces is essential to understanding how cities negotiate their hinterlands over time. Rather than imposing linear solutions, these infrastructures are established through dialogue. Between surface and subsurface. Between city and delta. Between human needs and ecological processes. They thus demonstrate that circularity is achieved not through closed systems or definitive solutions, but through practices capable of integrating variability, seasonality and coexistence among diverse ecosystemic components.

From this perspective, becoming circular cannot be understood as a static condition, but rather as a dynamic, situated and necessarily political practice. By revisiting Garcia Fària's unbuilt projects within this expanded framework (which integrates surface and subsurface dynamics alongside the delta's silent infrastructures), this essay highlights how historical inquiry can enrich contemporary debates on urban metabolism, post-anthropocentric infrastructures and ecological interdependencies. In this sense, history does not serve a merely instrumental role; instead, it becomes an operative form of critique through which more inclusive, resilient and ecologically balanced relationships between city and territory can be reformulated.

Acknowledgements

Writing this essay has offered an opportunity to further pursue a line of research initiated during the preparation of my doctoral dissertation. It would not have been possible without the support and encouragement of my director and research colleague, Professor Carles Crosas Armengol, who first introduced me to the figure of Pere Garcia Fària and opened a path of inquiry that we are still only beginning to explore.

References

Allen, R. C. (2004). *Revolución en los campo: la reinterpretación de la revolución agrícola inglesa.* Prensas Universitarias de Zaragoza.

Almera, J. (1894). *Los terrenos pliocénicos del Bajo Llobregat y Llano de Barcelona.* Imprenta de Henrich y Ca.

Atkinson, G. (1997). Eugène Belgrand (1810–1878): Civil engineer, geologist and pioneer hydrologist. *Transactions of the Newcomen Society, 69*(1), 97–127.

Belgrand, E. (1887). *Les travaux souterrains de Paris, Vol. 5.* Dunod.

Cerdà, I. (1867). *Teoría general de la urbanización y aplicacion de sus principios y doctrinas a la reforma y ensanche de Barcelona, Vol. 2.* Imprenta Española.

Corominas, M. (1986). *Suelo, técnica e iniciativa en los orígenes del ensanche de Barcelona.* Universitat Politècnica de Catalunya.

Crossley, C. (2008). Pierre Leroux and the Circulus: Soil, socialism and salvation in nineteenth-century France. In *Histoires de la Terre* (pp. 105–118). BRILL.

CUADLL (2004). *Situació actual de la gestó de les aigües a l'àrea hidrogeológica del Baix Llobregat. La visió dels usuaris. Comunitat d'Usuaris d'Aigües de la Vall Baixa del Delta del Llobregat.* Comunitat d'Usuaris d'Aigües de la Vall Baixa del Delta del Llobregat.

Cuchí, A. (2011). La reconsideració de l'aigua a partir de la sostenibilitat. In Museu d'Història de Barcelona: Institut de Cultura (Ed.), *La revolució de l'aigua a Barcelona. De la ciutat preindustrial a la metròpoli moderna, 1867–1967* (pp. 166–170). Ajuntament de Barcelona.

Eizaguirre, X. (1994). El Baix Llobregat: espais oberts, territoris de la ciutat. *Papers Regió Metropolitana de Barcelona Territori, Estratègies, Planejament, 19*, 59–73.

Esteve, A. & Recaño, J. (2006). (Re-)visitando Garcia Fària Un estudio de los factores espaciales y medioambientales de la mortalidad en la Barcelona de finales del siglo XIX. *Revista de Demografía Histórica-Journal of Iberoamerican Population Studies, 24*, 121–180.

Ferret, J. (1985). *L'Aprofitament de les aigües subterrànies del Delta del Llobregat, 1933 –1983.* Centre d'Estudis Comarcals del Baix Llobregat.

Finlay, M. R. (1991). The Rehabilitation of an agricultural chemist: Justus Von Liebig and the Seventh Edition. *Ambix, 38*(3), 155–167.

Gandy, M. (1999). The Paris sewers and the rationalization of urban space. *Transactions of the Institute of British Geographers, 24*(1), 23–44.

Garcia Fària, P. (1898). Proyecto de rectificación del río Llobregat. *Revista de Obras Públicas, 1170*, 137–39.

Garcia Fària, P. (1902). *Anarquía o Caciquismo?* Imprenta de Henrich y Ca.

Gómez Ordóñez, J. L. (1982). *El urbanismo de las obras públicas.* Universitat Politècnica de Catalunya.

Gorostiza, J. L. R. (2014). Edwin Chadwick, el movimiento británico de salud pública y el higienismo español. *Revista de Historia Industrial, 0*(55), 11–38. https://raco.cat/index.php/HistoriaIndustrial/article/view/280098

Kaika, M. & Swyngedouw, E. (2000). Fetishizing the modern city: the phantasmagoria of urban technological networks. *International Journal of Urban and Regional Research, 24*(1), 120–38.

Lewis, R. A. (1952). *Edwin Chadwick and the Public Health Movement, 1832–1854.* Longmans, Green & Co.

Llop, C. (2017). *Ciudades, territorios metropolitanos y regiones urbanas eficientes: estrategias y propuestas de proyecto para la regeneración de la ciudad mosaico territorial después de la explosión de la ciudad: la Región metropolitana de Barcelona como laboratorio* (Vol. 2). Universitat Politècnica de Catalunya.

Magrinyà Torner, F. (1995). La propuesta de saneamiento de Cerdà para Barcelona. *Revista Del Colegio de Ingenieros de Caminos, Canales y Puertos, Saneamiento, 2*(33), 98–111.

Martí, J. & Crosas, C. (2023). Salud, agua y territorio: infraestructuras hídricas y salud pública en el urbanismo del siglo XIX. *SUF-H 2023: VII Congreso ISUF-H Chile: Forma Urbana Para Un Buen Vivir – International Seminar on Urban Form, Santiago, Chile*, 36–42.

Miranda, M. Á. (2006). Pedro Garcia Fària, ingeniero de caminos (y arquitecto). *Scripta Nova: Revista Electrónica de Geografía y Ciencias Sociales, 10*(221), 205–28.

Monlau, P. F. (1841). *Abajo las Murallas!* (Imprenta del Consti-tu-cional, Ed.). Ayuntamiento Constitucional de Barcelona.

O'Neil-Henry, A. (2016). Hugo's guano: Sustainable sewage in *Les Misérables. Nineteenth-Century Contexts, 38*(5), 333–41.

Pandis Iveroth, S. & Brandt, N. (2011). The development of a sustainable urban district in Hammarby Sjöstad, Stockholm, Sweden? *Environment, Development and Sustainability, 13*(6), 1043–64.

Pandis Iveroth, S., Vernay, A.-L., Mulder, K. F. & Brandt, N. (2013). Implications of systems integration at the urban level: The case of Hammarby Sjöstad, Stockholm. *Journal of Cleaner Production, 48*, 220–31.

Perich, L. S. i. (1996). El Risc d'inundacions al delta del Llobregat: Viure contra l'aigua? *Treballs de La Societat Catalana de Geografia, 42*, 223–64. https://raco.cat/index.php/TreballsSCGeografia/article/view/157097

Queralt, E. & Isla, E. (2018). L'aigua al Delta. In *Els sistemes naturals del delta del Llobregat* (pp. 43–70). Institució Catalana d'Història Natural.

Reicher, C. (2017). STÄDTEBAULICHES ENTWERFEN. In *Städtebauliches Entwerfen* (pp. 172–209). Springer Fachmedien Wiesbaden.

Reid, D. (1991). *Paris Sewers and Sewermen: Realities and Representations.* Harvard University Press.

Rijke, J., van Herk, S., Zevenbergen, C. & Ashley, R. (2012). Room for the river: delivering integrated river basin management in the Netherlands. *International Journal of River Basin Management, 10*(4), 369–382.

Ringen, K. (1979). Edwin Chadwick, the market ideology, and sanitary reform: On the nature of the 19th-century public health movement. *International Journal of Health Services, 9*(1), 107–20.

Rosen, G. (1975). Health in the city: A comparative analysis. *Ethics in Science and Medicine, 2*, 89–95.

Sabaté i Casellas, F. (1994). Pere Garcia Fària i els Origens de l'Enginyeria Sanitaria. *Gimbernat: Revista d'Història de La Medicina i de Les Ciències de La Salut, 22*, 227–36.

Simmons, D. (2006). Waste not, want not: Excrement and economy in nineteenth-century France. *Representations, 96*(1), 73–98.

Simo, T., Duran, J.-M., Vázquez-Suñé, E., Ramírez, J., Barnolas, A., Alcalá, F. & Gàmez, D. (2005). Arquitectura de facies de los deltas cuaternarios del Río Llobregat, Barcelona, España. *Geogaceta, 38*, 171–74.

Sturge, A. (1879). Sewage irrigation in Paris. *Journal of the Society of Arts*, 980–81.

Tarragó Cid, S. (1974). Un continuador de la obra de Cerdà: Pere Garcia Fària. *Cuadernos de Arquitectura y Urbanismo, 100*, 45–49.

Vandenput, B. (2019). Victor Hugo's Paris of sewers. *OASE Journal for Architecture: The Urban Household of Metabolism, 104*, 32–37.

Valentina Morales Puebla, Ayami Nakamura and Constanza Ipinza
Universidad de Santiago de Chile, Facultad de Arquitectura y Ambiente Construido

LITHIUM EXTRACTION AND ECOLOGICAL RESISTANCE IN THE ANDEAN ALTIPLANO

INTRODUCTION

The research presented here offers a critical reflection on the role of architecture and territorial planning in contexts of lithium extractivism, using the case of the Maricunga Salt Flat (Salar de Maricunga) located in the altiplano of northern Chile. These territories, regarded as sacred by Andean communities, form a high-mountain ecosystem that hosts a unique ecological, geological and cultural assemblage. However, the increasing extractive pressure in the altiplano has triggered profound transformations, particularly in the hydrological processes of salt flats. The extraction of groundwater for lithium mining has drastically reduced water recharge, fragmenting habitats essential to various endemic species that have inhabited this place for centuries. In addition, these activities are altering the historical relationship between local communities and their territory, whose identity bond has been forged over generations around a worldview that recognises the spiritual agency of bodies of water, animals and high mountains.

Paradoxically, the so-called 'lithium triangle' comprising Chile, Argentina and Bolivia, which together concentrate around 50 per cent of the world's known lithium resources, are framed in international discourse as a green and sustainable 'dream' (Bonelli & Pavez, 2025) due to their strategic role in supplying the lithium battery industry in the era of decarbonisation. However, this energy transition merely disguises the ecological and social costs imposed on the periphery of the world system as a promise of a low-carbon future. In the case of Maricunga, this threat materialised in the disruption of hydrological balance, loss of biodiversity, and the severing of ritual practices that connect communities to water bodies and mountains. Thus, the conflict is not only ecological and economic, but ontological – it confronts two worldviews and two ways of relating to the land.

From a posthumanist perspective (Braidotti, 2013), this essay articulates a critique of the anthropocentric paradigm that has legitimised the expansion of extractive models in the region, obscuring ecological impacts that extend beyond the human. It calls for the destabilisation of human and colonial supremacy embedded in prevailing knowledge systems. In contrast, it vindicates the ancestral knowledge of the Andean worldview as a foundation for new design epistemologies. Architecture and planning, in this sense, face the challenge of integrating multiple forms of life, which requires attending to complex territorial assemblages and ethical-material dilemmas. The discipline must therefore reorient itself towards a critical practice that questions the logic of nature's instrumentalisation, opening itself to an ecosophical vision (Guattari, 2014), where care, reciprocity and interdependence become structuring principles of design thought.

ALTIPLANO SALT FLATS AS HYDROLOGICAL AND ECOLOGICAL BALANCE

From a historical perspective, the salt flats of the Andean represent a living memory of ancient landscapes in which large bodies of water once dominated. However, in a process linked to physical and environmental factors, increasing aridity led to their evaporation, reconfiguring them into the salt flat forms we know today (Moreno et al., 2007). In this context, salt flats can be understood as the terminal phase of ancient lacustrine systems that still preserve the legacy of extensive geological periods of water accumulation, where salts and minerals are concentrated, forming an active hydrogeological network that regulates groundwater recharge, surface water dynamics and atmospheric processes (Risacher et al., 1999).

Today, Andean salt flats are unique and fragile ecosystems that thrive under extreme conditions of altitude, temperature, solar radiation and very little rainfall. At the same time they are complex hydrological regulators where water – scarce, precious and cyclical – sustains life in its broad spectrum, from microbial mats to flamingos, vicuñas and humans. This interdependence supports a biodiversity composed largely of highly specialised species adapted to extreme environmental conditions, making these ecosystems both ecologically distinctive and particularly sensitive to disturbance. High-altitude hypersaline lagoons such as Santa Rosa in the Maricunga Salt Flat exemplify the delicate ecological balance of Andean wetland systems, where water bodies function as key ecological niches (Figure 1). They also harbour microbial communities essential to the existence of other organisms, serving as the foundation of the food chain and preserving characteristics analogous to primitive microbial ecosystems linked to the origin of life on Earth (Dorador, 2021).

Figure 1. The Santa Rosa lagoon, Nevado de Tres Cruces National Park, Atacama, Chile. *Source*: Vicencio Campos (2020).

In Chile, around 63 high-Andean salt flats have been reported, 14 of which were incorporated into a network of protected salt flats created in 2024 under the framework of the National Lithium Strategy (Government of Chile, 2023). Among them, the Maricunga Salt Flat is the southernmost high-Andean wetland in Chile and harbours unique biodiversity that remains only partially protected, since only one sector lies within the Nevado de Tres Cruces National Park, while other parts are concessioned for lithium mining (Figure 2). Maricunga also includes a flamingo nesting area (Figure 3) recently recognised by the Chilean National Forest Corporation (CONAF), and hosts a microscopic world of cyanobacteria and microorganisms whose properties are still under scientific study (Dorador, 2021). Its ecosystem value, however, is caught between regulatory and environmental tensions that result in only partial protection of its hydrological system.

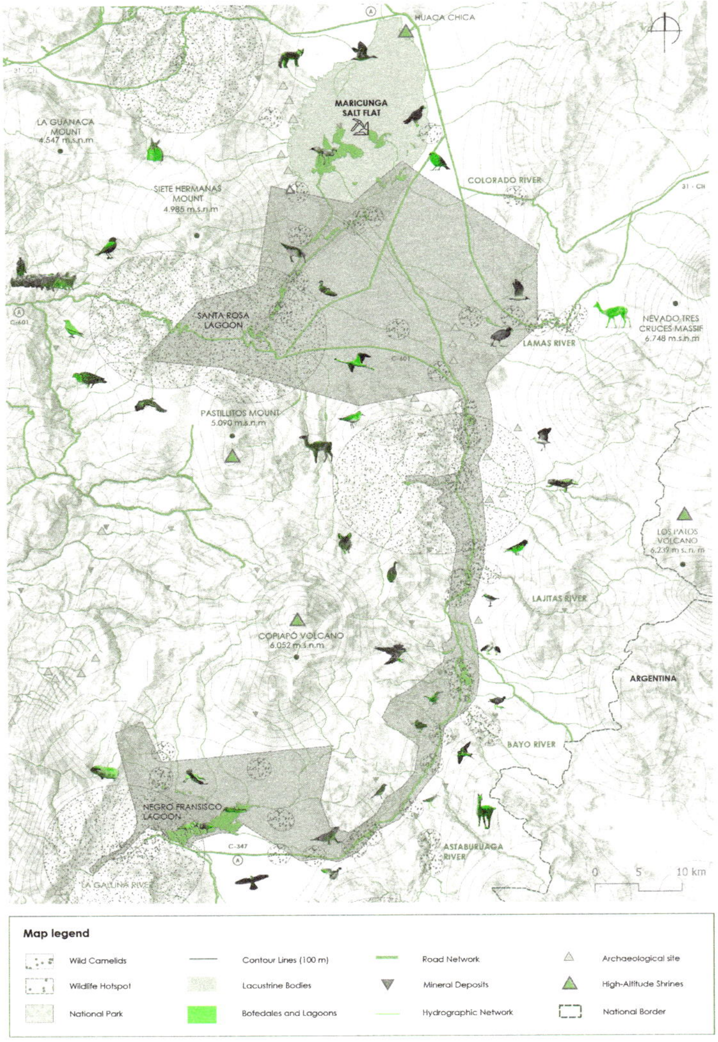

Figure 2. Location map of the Nevado de Tres Cruces National Park and Maricunga Salt Flat. Map elaborated by the author using QGIS and publicly available geospatial datasets.

Figure 3. A nesting colony of flamingos in the Nevado de Tres Cruces National Park. *Source*: Cerda & Cornejo (2022).

As illustrated in Figure 4, Maricunga exemplifies the intricate networks that define salt flat ecologies. Every organism plays a role that extends beyond its place in the food chain. Microorganisms act as primary producers (some perform photosynthesis) and nutrient recyclers, transforming organic matter into energy available for other species. Brine shrimp (*Artemia salina*), as filter-feeding crustaceans, transfer that energy to higher levels by becoming biomass consumed by larger birds. Flamingos act as ecosystem engineers by stirring sediments, oxygenating water and redistributing nutrients, thus creating conditions for microbial communities to flourish. The Andean fox contributes to seed dispersal while moving across the territory, connecting animal and plant dynamics. And the Andean condor closes the cycle by cleaning carcasses and returning nutrients to the soil, preventing the spread of disease. These intertwined relationships show that the survival of each species depends not only on direct feeding interactions but also on complementary ecological roles that sustain the integrity and resilience of the salt flat ecosystem.

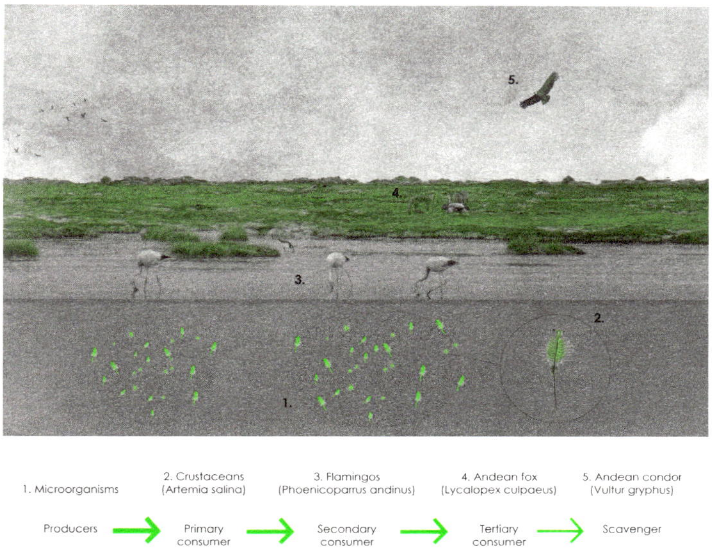

Figure 4. Conceptual diagram of energy flows in the high-Andean ecosystem of the Nevado de Tres Cruces. Author's elaboration.

In such extreme environments, the boundaries between what is considered life and what is not become blurred. Bacteria induce mineral crystallisation, while salts host living structures that metabolise light and carbon. Salt flats thus embody a lesson in relationality. For design disciplines, this is not a poetic metaphor but a methodological challenge. Designing with the territory requires recognising that salt flats are not landscapes to be occupied but infrastructures of life. From this recognition emerges the possibility of conceiving architecture and planning as reparative practices capable of translating invisible thresholds into visible, tangible and governable forms that support coexistence.

THE SACRALITY OF TERRITORY IN THE ANDEAN COSMOLOGY

Human settlement in the high Andean region dates back thousands of years (*c.* 13,000 BCE), with Indigenous peoples currently distributed across more than two hundred communities. For these communities, territory is inseparably bound to the sacred environment, where culture is practised and memory is embodied. Within this ontology, nature, climatic phenomena and even the cosmos are understood as possessing life and personhood. At the heart of this vision lies Pachamama – Mother Earth in the Quechua language – revered as the source of fertility and balance. This bond is sustained through rituals of reciprocity (Fernández Juárez, 1994; Cavalcanti-Schiel, 2007). The etymology of 'pacha' connotes cosmos, time, space and earth, while 'mama' signifies mother, expressing a relational conception of the world still honoured by Indigenous communities.

From this worldview arise the principles of *sumak kawsay* (Kichwa) and *suma aamaña* (Aymara), translated as 'living well'. These philosophies reject extractivist logics that maximise individual gain, instead foregrounding collective flourishing through reciprocity, complementarity and balance. At their core is radical relationality: nothing exists in isolation but through bonds among humans, animals, mountains, waters and ancestors, all constituting the *ayllu* as an expanded community (De la Cadena, 2015). For spatial practice, this means conceiving territory not as an inert resource but as a living fabric where cyclical use, thresholds and obligations sustain harmony.

Sacred mountains exemplify this ontology. In many civilisations, mountains have symbolised transcendence and cosmic order, serving as *axes mundi*, bridges between earth and sky (Eliade, 1959). In the Andes, the *mallkus* or *apus* are tutelary beings, protectors and givers of life. They are living entities with will and agency, maintaining an intimate relationship with water, fertility and memory. From their bodies flow rivers that sustain human and non-human life, integrating into a relational fabric where rituals ensure reciprocity (Gil & Fernández, 2008). The *apus* embody both protection and discipline: they are grandparents with whom one converses, offers thanks or seeks counsel. This everyday dialogue reveals cosmology as a constant negotiation of care with the more-than-human world.

In the case of Maricunga, these sacred relations are embodied by the Colla people, whose ancestral territory includes the salt flat as part of their migratory routes and ritual landscapes (Figure 5). Officially recognised in Chile in 1976 (FUCOA, 2012), the Colla practice of transhumance, a cyclical movement of families and herds, has not only guaranteed subsistence but also consolidated territorial knowledge based on ecological balance (Gil & Fernández, 2008). For the Colla, reciprocity and stewardship are principles that extend to human, animal, plant, geological and cosmic dimensions (Rueda, 2015). Rituals performed in the mountains reaffirm belonging, memory and continuity, integrating spiritual and ecological care.

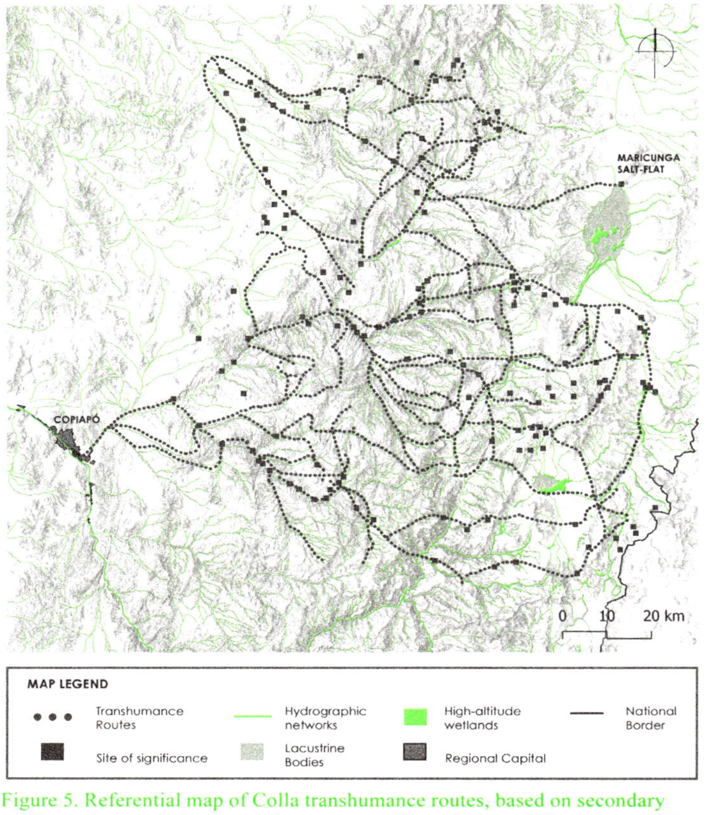

Figure 5. Referential map of Colla transhumance routes, based on secondary studies and representing approximate seasonally variable mobility patterns. Map elaborated by the author using QGIS and publicly available geospatial datasets.

Lithium extraction threatens these equilibria. Mining expansion, combined with the privatisation of water, has displaced families, fragmented communities and reduced access to sacred resources. In Maricunga, depriving Colla communities of water is more than an environmental issue, because it silences a sacred entity and disrupts reciprocity with Pachamama. Yet resistance here is not merely defensive. The Colla propose alternatives grounded in transhumance as a system of restoration and regeneration: mobility prevents overexploitation, rest periods allow ecological recovery, and ancestral water management secures continuity of ecosystems (FUCOA, 2012).

For design and planning disciplines, acknowledging these practices is not symbolic but methodological. Transhumance offers a paradigm of cyclical territorial use, contrasting sharply with extractivist logics of permanent depletion. Incorporating this worldview into planning implies conceiving infrastructures that regenerate rather than exhaust, and spaces that honour ritual thresholds rather than erase them. In this sense, the Colla are not only defending Maricunga but also proposing a way to reimagine territorial planning as an act of guardianship – where justice is simultaneously environmental, cultural and spiritual.

IMPACTS OF LITHIUM MINING AND ITS INFRASTRUCTURES

The energy transition has unleashed an extractive rush for lithium, placing countries with the largest lithium reserves at the centre of a geopolitical struggle for strategic control. In Chile, unlike metallic mining, lithium is extracted from salt flats, obscuring the fragile and unique character of these wetlands. The process consists of pumping groundwater into evaporation ponds of up to 300 × 1,000 metres, equivalent to 66 football fields (Nodo Salares Laboratorios Naturales, n.d.). Replicated across the desert, they form an industrial mosaic covering the area of a medium-sized city (Figure 6). It is estimated that for every ton of lithium, more than two million litres of water evaporate in the driest desert in the world (Marinova et al., 2025), severely straining territorial water balances.

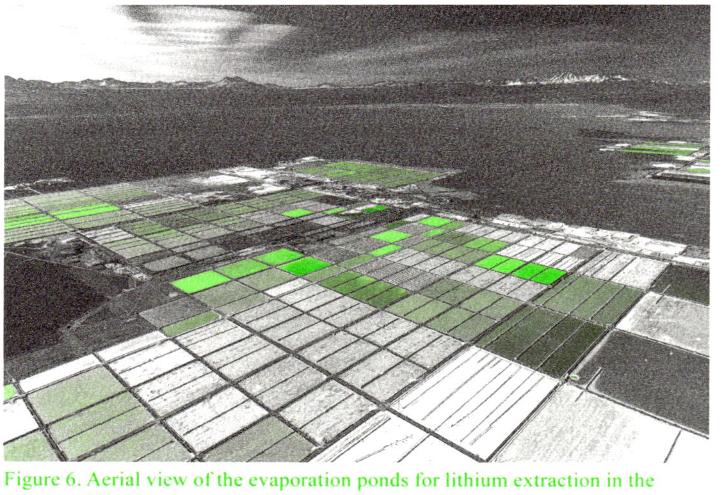

Figure 6. Aerial view of the evaporation ponds for lithium extraction in the Atacama Salt Flat. *Source*: Ladera Sur.

This large-scale 'mining of water' produces cascading effects. Excessive groundwater extraction lowers aquifer levels, drying surface water sources and degrading high-Andean wetlands that sustain specialised biodiversity, including flamingo populations that depend on salt lakes and lagoons as key breeding habitats (Sticco et al., 2021; Caziani et al., 2007). Groundwater depletion can also alter soil moisture and surface energy balances, producing measurable local climate changes at the basin scale (Scheihing & Tröger, 2017). In the Atacama Salt Flat, satellite-based studies indicate that intensive brine extraction has caused surface subsidence of approximately 1–2 centimetres per year, reflecting progressive aquifer depletion (Aylwin et al., 2025). Mining infrastructures such as roads, pipelines and temporary worker camps can further disrupt salt-flat hydrology through earthworks and minor topographic barriers, causing upstream flooding, downstream desiccation and the salinisation of soils and freshwater aquifers (Sticco et al., 2021).

For local communities, this overexploitation of water creates more than ecological damage. It threatens the very possibility of life in the desert (Aylwin et al., 2025), deepens territorial fragmentation and undermines participation in decision-making. Indigenous consultation processes often operate as bureaucratic formalities, legitimising pre-decided projects rather than ensuring self-determination. This exclusion fractures community cohesion, forcing residents into legal struggles to defend basic rights. Yet the deepest impact is ontological. For Indigenous peoples, salt flats are not inert deposits but living relatives, where rituals of reciprocity sustain bonds with ancestors, mountains and waters. To drain their aquifers is not only an environmental loss but a spiritual wound: it silences sacred beings, disrupts rituals, and fractures community life that has endured for centuries.

The risk of irreversible degradation is evident. The Punta Negra Salt Flat, exploited for decades to supply copper operations, lost in just 24 years aquifer reserves formed over millennia, leading to its ecological collapse (Dorador, 2021). The First Environmental Tribunal of Chile described the damage as 'permanent and irreparable' (Primer Tribunal Ambiental de Chile, 2023). With its desiccation, wetlands, birds, mammals and plants disappeared, alongside cultural practices tied to its waters.

Despite these lessons, Chile's National Lithium Strategy (ENL) (Gobierno de Chile, 2023) designated several salt flats for exploitation, including Maricunga (Figure 7). This decision reveals a profound contradiction: Maricunga is hydrologically linked to the Santa Rosa lagoon, protected as a Ramsar site within the Nevado de Tres Cruces National Park. In other words, it is a wetland of international importance, recognised for its high ecological value, biodiversity, and ecosystem services such as water regulation (Ramsar Convention Secretariat, n.d.) Exploiting it thus undermines the integrity of legally safeguarded water bodies, exposing the paradox of conservation and extraction coexisting in the same basin (Figure 8). The paradox deepens considering that the ENL also announced the creation of a Network of Protected Salt Flats to fulfil international biodiversity targets, while omitting Maricunga from such protection, even though its ecological fragility is undeniable.

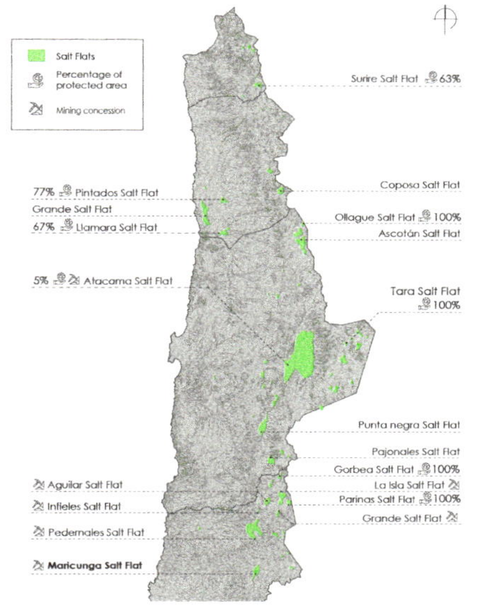

Figure 7. Main salt flats in Chile for extraction and conservation, based on the National Lithium Strategy (Gobierno de Chile, 2023). Map elaborated by the author using QGIS and publicly available geospatial datasets.

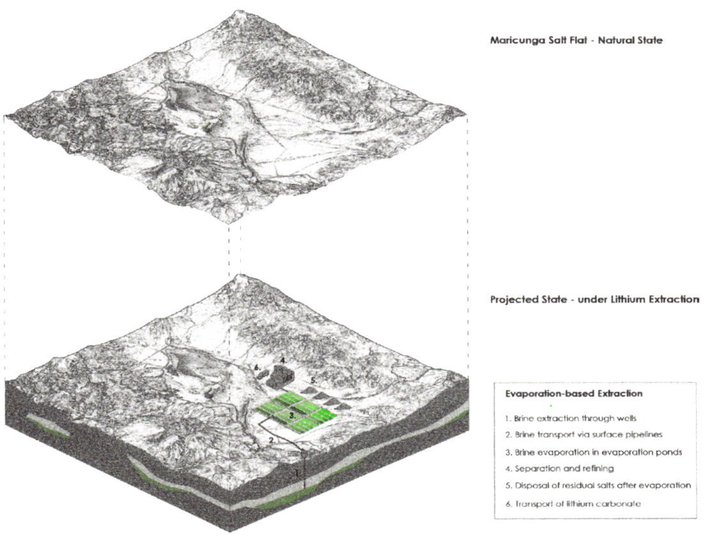

Figure 8. Schematic 3D representation of the Maricunga Salt Flat in its natural state (top) and under projected lithium extraction (bottom). The diagram is conceptual and does not represent actual mining infrastructure. Topographic base model generated by the author using QGIS and satellite imagery.

Proposed technological fixes, such as direct lithium extraction (DLE), do not resolve the issue. By reinjecting brine, DLE alters subterranean flows and chemical balances, placing interconnected lagoons and wetlands at equal risk. As Cristina Dorador warns, high-Andean salt flats are extremely fragile, precisely because such interventions can alter subterranean flows and hydrochemical equilibrium, potentially destabilising ecosystems (Delfino, 2025). Any disruption of water reverberates throughout the system. For design disciplines, this reveals how infrastructures – evaporation ponds, pipelines, temporary worker camps – are not neutral: they redraw the desert into geometric grids, overwrite subterranean circulations and inscribe new forms of inhabitation. What is at stake is the very design of territory: whether it is conceived as a living fabric of reciprocity or as a surface for extraction.

ALTERNATIVE HORIZON: THE LOVING DIALOGUE WITH THE NON-HUMAN DIMENSION

To avoid a future of depletion and collapse, there is now an urgent need to abandon the logic of separation and domination, and move towards a holistic approach that learns from ecosystems, their organisation and their resilience. From a territorial perspective, this essay raises the calls for an ethical rethinking of how space is inhabited and conceived, imagining alternatives based on justice and ecological balance. Rather than seeing the salt flat as a 'resource in crisis' to be managed, we must understand it as a socio-natural and spiritual fabric that sustains life, memory and community. The salt flat is not an inert object but a living interlocutor within the *ayllu*, with which relations of care, reciprocity and responsibility are forged. From this relational perspective, extraction cannot be understood as a loving practice, as it strips the salt flat of its life and reduces it to mere productivity. The only coherent dialogue is one that respects its integrity by refusing to exploit it.

This perspective calls for a profound reorientation of territorial planning and design. Conventional planning tools tend to overlook the ecological continuity of wetlands, transhumance routes and hydrological flows, fragmenting living systems into separate administrative units that fail to protect them effectively. The contemporary crisis, then, is fundamentally ontological (Escobar, 2018) and exposes the limitations of static planning frameworks when ecosystems are sustained by flows, movements and relationships that transcend administrative boundaries. Water does not follow zoning lines, animals do not recognise property lines, and ecological processes unfold through interconnected systems rather than isolated units.

In contrast, a territorially coherent zoning approach should incorporate multiple dimensions by integrating the sacred, the ecological and the communal into new forms of sovereignty that respond to life beyond the human. Planning that fails to acknowledge this relational condition risks undermining the very systems it seeks to manage. In this sense, the Andean practice of transhumance emerges as a counter-model of territorial co-production in which humans and non-humans jointly determine routes, times and modes of occupation based on regeneration, reciprocity and climatic conditions. Transhumance challenges modern territorial logics that seek to fix and stabilise living landscapes, offering instead a dynamic and adaptive model that could inform relational futures. Making and mapping these seasonal movements visible becomes a way of recognising territory as process rather than object.

Imagining an alternative future requires confronting the accelerated and sustained growth in demand for technological resources. As the global development of digital infrastructure and lithium consumption continue to increase, it becomes more difficult to counteract the economic pressures exerted on salt flats and other fragile ecosystems. The paradox of the energy transition lies in the ecological and ontological impacts analysed in this essay, where lithium emerges as an element mobilised by organisms and systems obsessed with energy accumulation and storage (Weinberg & Bonelli, 2021).

In this context, the concept of ecological resistance takes on particular relevance when the invitation also involves debating our lifestyles (Otero, 2024), and reducing dependence on lithium and limiting its consumption implies a shared responsibility between governments, industries and individuals. For ecosystems like the high Andean salt flats, which hold millennia of ecological information, recovery may not be possible once certain thresholds are exceeded. Instead of assuming resilience as the capacity to recover after a disturbance, ecological resistance emphasises a system's ability to withstand the disturbance without losing integrity or function. This raises a crucial question. Recognising natural phenomena as dynamic and interrelated processes, rather than static resources, becomes essential for any practice committed to sustaining life.

The Maricunga Salt Flat, as the southernmost high-altitude wetland in Chile and sacred Colla territory, embodies this alternative horizon. Protecting this place is not just a matter of biodiversity conservation; it entails safeguarding a relational ontology where justice encompasses the environmental, cultural and spiritual dimensions. In this sense, recent legal precedents such as the recognition of rights granted to the Mar Menor, a highly endangered saltwater lagoon in Spain, demonstrate that acknowledging ecosystems and bodies of water as legal subjects is not merely symbolic, but a concrete mechanism for territorial protection. Granting rights to water bodies that play a central role in the ecology and cosmology of a place offers a way to translate relational ontologies into operative frameworks for planning, governance and design.

As Escobar (2018) suggests, defending territory is also defending the right of worlds to exist differently. Extractivism is not only the act of extracting resources; it is also a form of ontological occupation that systematically negates existing worlds, their temporalities and their relations of care. In this sense, the pluriverse is not an ethical ideal but a political condition, one that demands the coexistence of multiple worlds without reducing them to a single developmental logic. Ecosystem-inspired design – cyclical, regenerative and reciprocal – offers a path to restructuring these relationships and strengthening the bonds between human beings, mountains, water and the more-than-human world. Finally, reconceptualising our relationship with the world by recognising vulnerability, interdependence and relational responsibility is an ethical and political imperative. Only from this perspective can architecture and land-use planning contribute meaningfully to the future of the planet. As Donna Haraway (2016) writes, it is 'still possible if we render each other capable of worlding and reworlding for flourishing' (p. 96). However, the time for repair is not in the future – it is now.

Declaration

ChatGPT-5 was used to review the grammar and English language.

Acknowledgement

The authors would like to thank the School of Architecture at the University of Santiago for its support.

References

Aylwin, J., Cayo, J. C., Feierabend, S., del Pino, S., Olivera, M. & Tufró, M. (2025). *Litio y derechos humanos en los salares altoandinos de Argentina, Bolivia y Chile*. Observatorio Ciudadano.

Bonelli, C. & Pavez, A. (2025). White mining's green dream: Entropy and the mirage of sustainability in Northern Chile. *The Extractive Industries and Society*, *23*, 101683.

Braidotti, R. (2013). *The Posthuman*. Polity Press.

Cavalcanti-Schiel, R. (2007). Las muchas naturalezas en los Andes. *Perifèria, Revista de Recerca i Formació en Antropologia*, 7.

Caziani, S. M., Rocha Olivio, O., Rodríguez Ramírez, E., Romano, M., Derlindati, E., Tálamo, A., Ricalde, D., Quiroga, C., Contreras, J. P., Valqui, M. & Sosa, H. (2007). Seasonal distribution, abundance, and nesting of Puna, Andean, and Chilean flamingos. *The Condor*, 109(2), 276–87.

Cerda, I. & Cornejo, A. (2022). *Huellas altoandinas de la Región de Atacama*. Masatierra Ediciones.

De la Cadena, M. (2015). *Earth Beings: Ecologies of Practice Across Andean Worlds*. Duke University Press.

Dorador, C. (2021). Conservación de salares: Aprendizajes desde los microorganismos. In Observatorio Plurinacional de Salares Andinos (Ed.), *Salares Andinos: ecología de saberes por la protección de nuestros salares y humedales* (pp. 162–69). Fundación Tanti.

Delfino, E. (2025). Cristina Dorador: 'Se está tratando de obtener la mayor cantidad de litio en el menor tiempo posible y los efectos son muy grandes' Entrevista en Mongabay Latam, 9 February. https://es.mongabay.com/2025/02/cristina-dorador-grave-impacto-extraccion-litio-salares-extincion-entrevista/

Escobar, A. (2018). *Designs for the Pluriverse: Radical Interdependence, Autonomy, and the Making of Worlds*. Duke University Press.

Eliade, M. (1959). *The Sacred and the Profane: The Nature of Religion*. Harcourt.

Fernández Juárez, G. (1995). *El banquete aymara: mesas y yatiris*. Hisbol.

FUCOA (2012). *Colla: Serie Introducción Histórica y Relatos de los Pueblos Originarios de Chile*. Ministerio de Agricultura, Fundación de Comunicaciones, Capacitación y Cultura del Agro.

Gil, A. & Fernández, M. (2008). Trashumancia en los Andes: movilidad, territorio y cultura. *Revista de Estudios Andinos*, *40*(2), 215–34.

Gobierno de Chile (2023). *Estrategia Nacional del Litio* [National Lithium Strategy]. https://www.gob.cl/litioporchile/

Guattari, F. (2014). *The Three Ecologies* (trans. I. Pindar & P. Sutton). Bloomsbury Academic. (Original work published 1989).

Haraway, D. J. (2016). *Staying with the Trouble: Making Kin in the Chthulucene*. Duke University Press.

Marinova, S., Roche, L., Link, A. & Finkbeiner, M. (2025). Water footprint of battery-grade lithium production in the Salar de Atacama, Chile. *Journal of Cleaner Production, 487*.

Moreno, A. S., Giralt, S., Valero-Garcés, B., Sáez, A., Bao, R., Prego, R., Pueyo, J. J., González-Sampériz, P. & Taberner, C. (2007). A 14 kyr record of the tropical Andes: The Lago Chungará sequence (18°S, northern Chilean Altiplano). *Quaternary International, 161*(1), 4–21.

Nodo Salares Laboratorios Naturales (n.d.). Cápsula informativa 2. Salares Lab – Laboratorios Naturales de Salares. https://salareslab.cl/capsula/

Otero, M. (2024). *Marina Otero, académica de Harvard experta en infraestructura digital y datos | El Chile Que Viene*, Súbela News, YouTube video. https://www.youtube.com/watch?v=pi4vyUt1wmo.

Primer Tribunal Ambiental de Chile (2023). Sentencia R-86-2023. https://www.1ta.cl/primer-tribunal-ambiental-sentencia-r-86-2023/

Páez, M. C., Alé Marinangeli, G., Maidana, C. & Plastiné Pujadas, I. (2023). La Pachamama, memorias de un tiempo pasado y rituales vigentes en el Valle Calchaquí Norte (Salta, Argentina). *Runa, 44*(1), 91–107.

Ramsar Convention Secretariat (n.d.). Negro Francisco and Santa Rosa Lagoon Complex (Ramsar Site No. 877). Ramsar Sites Information Service.

Risacher, F., Alonso, H. and Salazar, C. (1999). Geoquímica de aguas en cuencas cerradas: I, II y III Regiones – Chile, Technical Report S.I.T. 51, Conv. de Coop. DGA-UCN-IRD, Santiago.

Rueda, J. (2015). Diálogo amoroso-ritual con los cerros. *Chasqui: Revista de literatura latinoamericana, 44*(1), 159–79.

Scheihing, K. & Tröger, U. (2017). Local climate change induced by groundwater overexploitation in a high Andean arid watershed, Laguna Lagunillas basin, northern Chile. *Hydrogeology Journal*, 26, 705–19.

Sticco, M., et al. (2021). *Impactos ambientales de la explotación de litio en los humedales y recursos hídricos del Altiplano*. Fundación para la Conservación y el Uso Sustentable de los Humedales.

Vicencio Campos, O. (2020). *Paisaje y geología del Parque Nacional Nevado de Tres Cruces*. Ministerio de las Culturas, las Artes y el Patrimonio de Chile.

Weinberg, M. & Bonelli, C. (2021). Litio: hacia una teoría de las transiciones bipolares. In F. Díaz, A. Kubrak & M. Otero Verzier (Eds.), *Lithium: Estados de agotamiento* (pp. 88–95). Ediciones ARQ, Pontificia Universidad Católica de Chile.

Carlos Zeballos-Velarde
Universidad Nacional de San Agustín

BECOMING MORE-THAN-HUMAN: ECOLOGICAL COEXISTENCE IN THE URBAN LINKAGES PROJECT

INTRODUCTION

Informal urbanisation processes have had a significant impact on Latin American cities, as the fast growth of cities into ecologically vulnerable areas frequently surpasses the rate of official infrastructure development and institutional planning. According to Inostroza (2017), informality is a structural element of urban growth in Latin America, especially in the Andes, rather than just a phase of transition. This phenomenon has exacerbated socio-spatial fragmentation and environmental vulnerability in Peru by causing a proliferation of peripheral urban communities on unstable slopes, dry riverbeds and flood-prone ravines (Calderón Cockburn, 2017; Dammert-Guardia et al., 2024).

The second-largest city in Peru, Arequipa is a prime example of this state. Informal settlements have grown along the steep sides of seasonal ravines near the dormant Misti volcano on its outskirts, in the districts of Mariana Melgar, Alto Selva Alegre and Miraflores (Figure 1). These ravines are extremely dynamic habitats that are vulnerable to ecological degradation in the dry season and heavy floods during the rainy season (Mazer et al., 2021). Yet, rather than being treated as complex socio-natural systems, they are often approached as infrastructural voids or hazards to be controlled through rigid canalisations or fencing, reinforcing a logic of urban exclusion. Informal settlements, meanwhile, are routinely stigmatised as 'illegal' or 'precarious', despite their embeddedness in local livelihoods, spatial practices and ecological relations (Zeballos-Velarde, 2024).

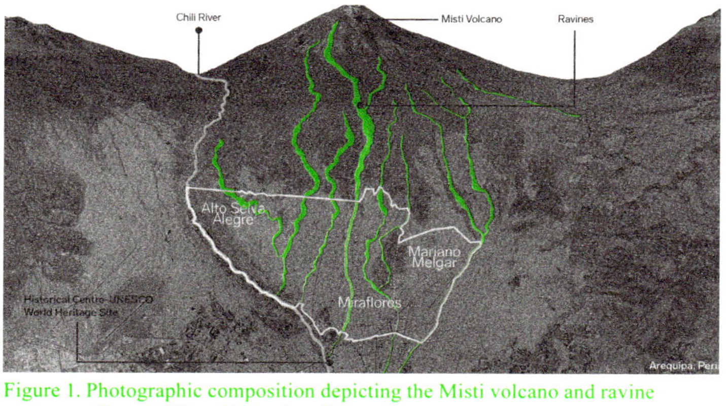

Figure 1. Photographic composition depicting the Misti volcano and ravine system on the outskirts of Arequipa, Peru.

The Urban Linkages project was conceived as a response to these interwoven challenges of risk, exclusion and ecological neglect. An interdisciplinary and participatory initiative, it reimagines these ravines not as threats to be contained, but as socio-ecological corridors capable of fostering biodiversity, social cohesion and climate resilience. The project frames architecture as a medium for more-than-human coexistence, drawing on ecological design and critical urban theory. Non-human life, including native plants, soil dynamics and hydrological cycles, are regarded as essential co-authors of urban form (Zeballos-Velarde et al., 2022).

Instead of using top-down planning and traditional 'grey' infrastructure, the initiative suggests multi-scalar place-building techniques based on environmental restoration, community involvement and spatial diagnostics. Its central premise is the idea of shared agency – a relational framework in which both communities and ecosystems shape the urban landscape through dialogic and adaptive interactions (Bratman, 2014). This move from anthropocentric control to ecological stewardship challenges the dominant 'man over nature' paradigm and aligns with calls for a radical rethinking of spatial practice in the context of climate collapse and socio-environmental justice.

Historically, built environments have emerged from an anthropocentric paradigm that sees humans as the sole actors shaping space. This dualism, rooted in Western thought, separates culture from nature and reinforces the idea that non-human life is passive. In the face of accelerating climate crises and urban inequality, 'becoming more-than-human' calls for a fundamental rethinking of architectural practice – towards ecosystems that centre cooperation, resilience and multispecies interdependence.

ARGUMENT

The main argument of the Urban Linkages project is that the peripheral fragmentation of Arequipa is caused by a combination of institutional, socioeconomic, ecological and geographical issues rather than just population growth. Mariano Melgar, Alto Selva Alegre and Miraflores are examples of peripheral neighbourhoods that lack proper urban integration and proper infrastructure. They are located on steep slopes and along *torrenteras* – seasonal ravines that are prone to flash floods (Dammert-Guardia et al., 2024). Despite their high population density, these regions continue to be institutionally excluded and geographically disjointed. This state of disarray is similar to what Roy (2005) refers to as 'urban informality' – not just a lack of planning, but a kind of government in which selective enforcement and institutional absences deliberately create exclusion.

Conventional solutions have prioritised centralised, engineering-led interventions: informal neighbourhoods are targeted for top-down regularisation or removal, and ravines are canalised with concrete walls. In these methods, urban risks are managed through control rather than collaboration, reflecting a technocratic mindset that views resilience as resistance – an attitude of 'man over nature' (Vale, 2013). These interventions frequently perpetuate cycles of vulnerability and mistrust by ignoring the lived realities, abilities and expertise of local people (Watson, 2009).

Urban Linkages, on the other hand, promotes the idea of shared agency, according to which natural systems and communities co-author urban territory. This is consistent with new discourses in adaptive planning and landscape urbanism that support adaptable, multispecies and participatory approaches to resilience (Corner, 2006). Because locals have first-hand knowledge of flood patterns, transportation routes and social gathering places, shared agency is not just a moral idea but also a practical tactic that is necessary for context-sensitive planning (Chambers, 1994).

The initiative reframes involvement as co-production, where communities work with professionals to identify risks, define visions and create interventions. This is different from consultation after design decisions are made. It is in line with the tenets of participatory government that prioritise democratic legitimacy, inclusivity and the development of trust (Fung, 2006). Alongside the environmental, social and economic pillars of sutainability, it also represents the cultural dimension known as the 'fourth pillar' that is crucial to long-term urban viability due to the importance of cultural identity, local knowledge and community agency (UNESCO, 2016).

To operationalise this vision, Urban Linkages introduces three interdependent concepts:

1. Landscape urbanism: By reforesting the volcanic slopes and revegetating dry ravines, the project reduces erosion, slows flash floods and enhances biodiversity. These landscape interventions transform hazardous terrains into ecological assets, echoing theories that see landscape as infrastructure (Waldheim, 2006).
2. Urban linkages: These are infrastructural and ecological elements that connect fragmented areas – pedestrian bridges, transverse roads and green corridors. Rather than isolating risk-prone zones, linkages integrate them into the broader urban fabric, enhancing connectivity and socio-ecological function (Ahern, 2011).
3. Barrial centralities: Localised service hubs – schools, markets, clinics, cultural centres – embedded within neighbourhoods to reduce dependency on distant centralities. These anchors enhance walkability, neighbourhood identity and collective capacity to respond to crises, in line with the logic of the '15-minute city' (Moreno et al., 2011).

These tactics come together to provide a new definition of resilience that goes beyond physical defence and includes social cohesiveness, ecological restoration and institutional empowerment. This idea is in line with Folke et al. (2010), who define resilience as the ability to change via education, adaptation and teamwork rather than returning to a pre-existing state.

The project also challenges the dominance philosophy ingrained in traditional infrastructure operations. Urban Linkages' support of more-than-human urbanism places it in line with an expanding corpus of research that demands ecological coexistence and multispecies justice (Whatmore, 2006). Ravines are intricate living systems – corridors for water, soil, plants, and both human and non-human life – rather than empty spaces that need to be filled or hazards that need to be enclosed.

Urban Linkages recognises ravines as potential linear parks and ecological infrastructures. It shifts from an extractive model of protection to one of coexistence. Flood-prone areas are treated not as voids or hazards, but as shared commons that nurture biodiversity, enable water flows and host public life. Architecture is reframed as a dynamic act of care – responsive to terrain, time, and the interrelations of human and more-than-human actors.

METHODOLOGY

In line with modern theories of socio-ecological resilience and inclusive planning, the Urban Linkages project uses a methodology that combines participatory and transdisciplinary procedures with rigorous technological diagnostics (Healey, 1997). The following five interconnected dimensions make up its design.

Community-based workshops

Participatory workshops were conducted in the districts of Mariano Melgar, Alto Selva Alegre and Miraflores (Figure 2). Using participatory mapping techniques – including drawings, symbols and group discussions – residents identified flood-prone areas, informal paths and sites of cultural significance. This strategy is in line with methods established by Chambers (1994) and extended by Cornwall (2008), who contend that equitable and successful planning requires local knowledge systems. Data and narratives collected during fieldwork were analysed using tools such as ATLAS.ti, allowing for thematic coding that surfaced patterns of risk perception, ecological value and social aspiration. The workshops went beyond extractive consultation, enabling residents to become co-designers in risk-sensitive planning (Zeballos-Velarde, 2021).

Figure 2. One of the participatory workshops conducted with community members, university students and municipal technical staff.

Expert and interdisciplinary collaboration

Experts from a variety of disciplines, including landscape architecture, environmental science, urban planning and disaster risk management, were also brought together in workshops. The scientific validity and creative resilience of the proposals were guaranteed by this interdisciplinary approach. International experts like Jan Turkstra of the United Nations Human Settlements Programme (UN-Habitat) and Susan Herrington, who conceptualises landscape as both ecological and cultural infrastructure (Herrington, 2016), enhanced the project's conceptual underpinnings. Best practices in transdisciplinary urban research, which stress knowledge co-creation across sectors and scales, are reflected in this integration (Lang et al., 2012).

Becoming

Systemic diagnostic framework

A four-pillar framework guided the territorial diagnosis:

1. Physical-spatial: assessing geomorphology, land use, spatial fragmentation and infrastructure deficits.
2. Socio-economic: evaluating demographic trends, income disparities and access to services.
3. Environmental: mapping degradation, biodiversity loss and exposure to hydro-meteorological risks.
4. Institutional: examining governance gaps, planning instruments and inter-municipal coordination.

This multifaceted approach enables a detailed understanding of the interdependencies influencing risk in peripheral urban settings, and is consistent with complexity-based planning models and urban systems theory (Davoudi, 2012).

Cartographic and visual tools

Drone photography, space syntax analysis and geographic information systems (GIS) were used to create layered spatial diagnostics. GIS mapping made it possible to visualise topography (Figure 3), land use and flood zones (Goodchild, 2007), while drone technology allowed for the validation of ground conditions by providing high-resolution imagery. The development of space syntax by Hillier (2015) made it possible to analyse mobility flows and spatial integration across dispersed communities, indicating the areas where urban connections could have the biggest effects. By creating a common language between communities and specialists, these visual aids facilitated both technical design and interactive discussion.

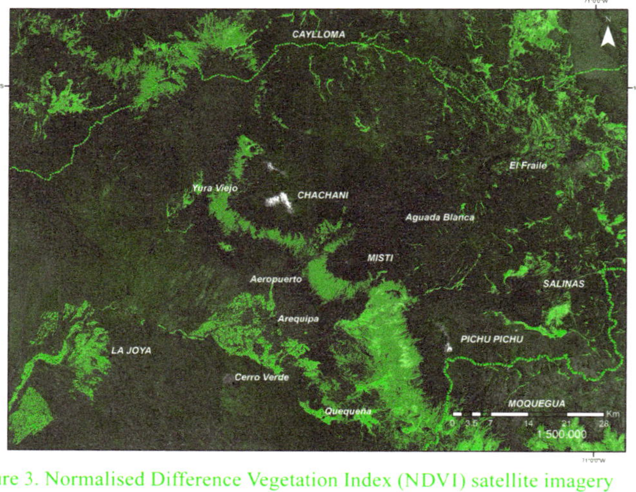

Figure 3. Normalised Difference Vegetation Index (NDVI) satellite imagery illustrating native vegetation patterns concentrated along the volcanic foothills. *Source*: Zeballos-Velarde (2024).

Institutional embedding in urban planning instruments

The results of Urban Linkages were integrated into Arequipa's official planning frameworks. Large-scale ecological restoration initiatives, like reforestation of volcanic bases and treatment of ravine ecosystems, were among the provincial contributions to the Plan de Acondicionamiento Territorial (Territorial Development Plan) (Figure 4). The Plan de Desarrollo Metropolitano (Metropolitan Development Plan) included design ideas for roadways, cross-bridges and linear parks that would connect disjointed districts at the metropolitan level. To guarantee reproducibility and long-term effects, appeals for the 'institutional anchoring' of participatory processes are echoed by this integration into official policy tools (UN-Habitat, 2019).

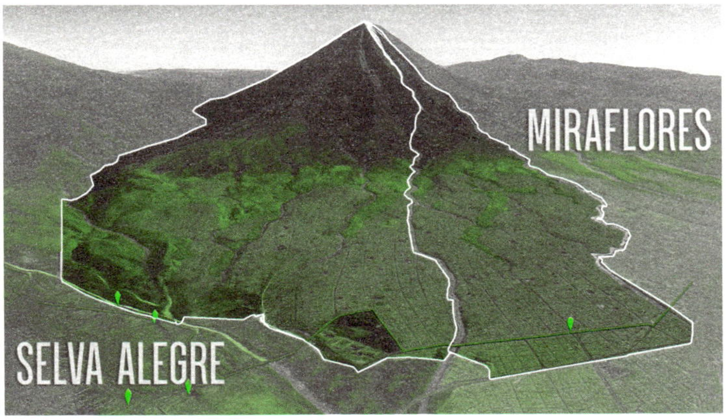

Figure 4. The reforestation of volcanic foothills through the Urban Linkages project has been established as a strategic priority within the proposed Territorial Development Plan for Arequipa 2026–2045.

Urban Linkages provides a reproducible approach to resilience planning in vulnerable urban settings by fusing systemic analysis, spatial technology and grassroots engagement. In addition to validating community inputs, its incorporation into official urban plans shows that environmental justice and participatory governance can come together to create revolutionary planning models (Swyngedouw & Moulaert, 2010). The concept shifts from technocratic fixes to long-term urban management, ecological ethics and shared action.

DISCUSSION

The Urban Linkages project makes several contributions to urban planning theory and practice.

Reframing risk and ecology

One of the most significant contributions of the project lies in its critique of dominant, top-down disaster risk management strategies, which often reinforce dualistic separations between humans and their ecological contexts. Conventional flood defences in Arequipa – such as concrete walls and canalised ravines – embody what Pelling (2011) terms a 'resistance paradigm', aiming to control or suppress natural systems rather than coexisting with them. These hard infrastructures frequently sterilise public space, disconnect communities from riverine landscapes, and marginalise urban nature (UNESCO, 2018).

The transformation of ravines from dangerous voids into socio-ecological infrastructures is a key innovation of the Urban Linkages project. Instead of enclosing these areas with inflexible 'grey' engineering solutions, the initiative aims to create green-blue corridors that can act as public amenities, buffer flooding and restore wildlife (Figure 5). The ideas of landscape urbanism, which sees the landscape as a fundamental medium for urban organisation and ecological performance, are echoed in this reinterpretation (Waldheim, 2006; Corner, 2006). In addition to reducing erosion and controlling hydrology, native reforestation of Arequipa's ravines improves ecological connections and microclimates. The literature on climate adaptation is increasingly supporting such integrated methods (Ahern, 2011), particularly in cities in the Global South that are confronting escalating hydro-meteorological hazards.

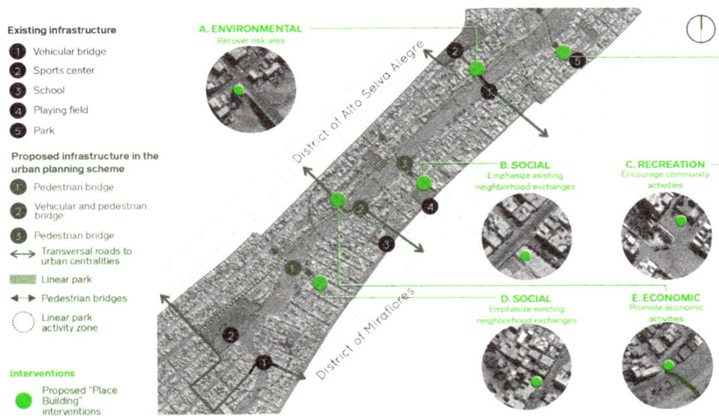

Figure 5. Example of an intervention area showing the critical transition zone between the ravine system and adjacent urban development.

Democratising planning through participation

Participation in Urban Linkages goes beyond traditional stakeholder engagement; rather, it is presented as a shared agency and co-production process in which communities actively co-design spatial transformation and risk mitigation. This supports the long-standing claims that procedural justice and empowerment can be achieved through participatory planning (Healey, 1997). The incorporation of indigenous knowledge contested the technocratic domination of planning in Arequipa's underprivileged districts, which are sometimes labelled as 'informal'. Sandercock (2003) points out that when tales and lived experiences are included in democratic discourse, they become legitimate sources of planning intelligence.

Residents develop tangible and emotional connections with the landscapes they live in through workshops and local implementation, in addition to expressing their risk perceptions (Ernstson et al., 2008). Here, risk becomes an ecological rhythm to be comprehended and incorporated rather than a hazard to be eliminated, a process Ahern (2011) refers to as 'safe-to-fail' planning.

Additionally, local participants pointed out certain spatial and social dynamics that are not depicted on official maps, such as alleys that are prone to flooding, unofficial marketplaces, and culturally significant areas, supporting the idea that effective urban resilience solutions require bottom-up spatial information (Goodchild, 2007). Another important result was the development of trust; collaborative approaches promote legitimacy and ownership in situations where planning institutions are frequently viewed with suspicion (Cornwall, 2008).

Importantly, Urban Linkages highlights the innovative potential of inclusive procedures by showing how new planning categories, such as barrial centralities, might arise from participatory debate.

Enhancing connectivity through urban linkages

Arequipa's urban fragmentation is multifaceted, encompassing social, institutional and spatial aspects. To remedy this, the concept designs urban links that use natural corridors, transversal highways and pedestrian bridges to reunite disjointed areas (Figure 6). UN-Habitat (2019) emphasises that integrated urban connection is essential for inclusive, sustainable cities, especially in post-informal settings.

This strategy is in line with Soja's (2010) concept for spatial justice, which holds that democratic urbanism is predicated on fair access to urban space and infrastructure.

Multi-scalar design and barrial centralities

The concept of barrial centralities introduces a tactical response to peripheral vulnerability by reinforcing local nodes – markets, schools, health centres – that reduce dependence on the congested urban core. This approach is consistent with the '15-minute city' paradigm (Moreno et al., 2011), which prioritises spatial proximity and polycentrism to enhance urban resilience and equity. Importantly, these centralities support both everyday life and emergency response, acting as hubs for social cohesion and resource distribution in crisis scenarios (Vale, 2013).

Seasonal water flows are now seen as temporal indicators that direct adaptive architecture responses rather than as disturbances. According to Shannon & Smets (2010), ecohydrological urbanisation is becoming popular, and post-anthropocentric planning is including multispecies design principles. In this context, architecture takes on the role of an interface, acting as a mediator between environmental change and human use. This reasoning is demonstrated by the project's usage of modular community infrastructures. These buildings, which are inexpensive, adaptable, and can be constructed gradually, provide shade, access to water, recreational opportunities and environmental monitoring. They provide a robust morphology that is ideal for unofficial, biologically dynamic urban margins because of their amphibious nature, which allows them to adapt to both dry and flood-prone environments (Zeballos-Velarde & Chevarría-Aredo, 2024) (Figure 7). Their presence 'stitches' the broken borders of cities over time, establishing areas for shared use, connection and remembrance. This strategy mirrors urban acupuncture approaches, in which small-scale interventions catalyse broader systemic transformations (Madeddu, 2016).

Figure 6. Comparative views of the ravine area prior to and following the implementation proposal of Urban Linkages, now integrated into the city's official masterplan.

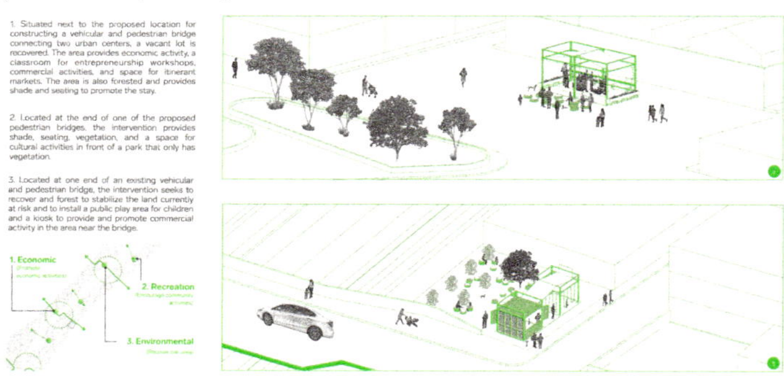

Figure 7. 'Place-building' through non-ephemeral public space interventions. Flexible modular structures proposed for targeted areas of intervention.

By linking these nodes through ecological and infrastructural linkages, Urban Linkages delivers a truly multi-scalar design, bridging localised needs with metropolitan systems.

Contribution to sustainability debates

Instead of emphasising technology or 'smart cities', the programme highlights social practices, place-based knowledge and multispecies ethics to promote ecological and cultural sustainability. This is consistent with the growing recognition that culture represents a fourth pillar of sustainability, alongside environmental, social and economic factors (Bchir & Zeballos, 2024). It also responds to critiques of dominant urban resilience narratives that significantly emphasise control and dominion over nature. The programme encourages a more symbiotic approach, based on what Escobar (2018) calls 'relational design' – an ontological shift towards living with, rather than against, the environment.

Replicability and systemic impact

The Urban Linkages methodology has proven adaptable, adopted both by Arequipa's Plan de Acondicionamiento Territorial and Plan de Desarrollo Metropolitano. This is particularly significant given that Peruvian planning regulations have traditionally prioritised technical and territorial dimensions over a landscape perspective. The integration of landscape and participatory diagnostics into formal planning frameworks represents a paradigmatic shift in Peruvian urbanism.

Nevertheless, the project acknowledges its limitations. As with many urban innovations in the Global South, implementation hinges on political will, institutional coordination and long-term funding. Without these enablers, even the most socially embedded and ecologically sound proposals risk remaining unrealised. This reflects broader challenges in translating experimental planning into durable governance structures (Pieterse, 2008).

CONCLUSION

Urban Linkages offers a transformative contribution to sustainable urbanism by reframing peripheries as laboratories, ravines as infrastructures, and culture as a core dimension of resilience. Its participatory and technical methodology demonstrates how hybrid knowledge can generate strategies that are both socially legitimate and scientifically rigorous.

At a theoretical level, the project enriches debates on resilience, landscape urbanism and cultural sustainability; at a practical level, it provides a replicable framework for cities confronting informality, risk and fragmentation. By bridging local realities with global concerns, it situates Arequipa as a reference point for worldwide urban challenges.

The project's true value lies in its paradigm shift. It calls for collaborative stewardship between communities and ecosystems, positioning culture and participation as foundations of sustainability. Its acknowledgement of becoming more-than-human recognises that architecture must work alongside natural processes, embracing transition, coexistence and mutual care.

In a time of planetary crisis, Urban Linkages affirms that sustainability is ultimately about relationships: between people, places and the more-than-human worlds they co-create.

Acknowledgement

Many thanks to the Universidad Nacional de San Agustín de Arequipa for funding the project Costuras Urbanas (Urban Linkages) from 2017 to 2021. Although this article is not formally part of that project, the research carried out there laid the foundations for the ideas discussed here.

References

Ahern, J. (2011). From fail-safe to safe-to-fail: Sustainability and resilience in the new urban world. *Landscape and Urban Planning, 100*(4), 341–43.

Bchir, E. & Zeballos, C. (2024). The human dimension at the heart of the scientific sustainable approach. Union International d'Architectes MAG, 22 May. https://www.uia-architectes.org/en/mag/the-human-dimension-at-the-heart-of-the-scientific-sustainable-approach/.

Bratman, M. E. (2014). *Shared Agency: A Planning Theory of Acting Together.* Oxford University Press.

Calderón Cockburn, J. (2017). *La ciudad ilegal: Lima en el siglo XX.* DESCO.

Chambers, R. (1994). Participatory rural appraisal (PRA): Challenges, potentials and paradigm. *World Development, 22*(10), 1437–54.

Corner, J. (2006). Terra fluxus. In C. Waldheim (Ed.), *The Landscape Urbanism Reader* (pp. 21–33). Princeton Architectural Press.

Cornwall, A. (2008). Unpacking 'participation': models, meanings and practices. *Community Development Journal, 43*(3), 269–83.

Dammert-Guardia, M., Torres-Obregón, D., Aiquipa-Zavala, A., Jiménez-Palacios, R., Zeballos-Velarde, C. & Martínez-Valdivia, A. (2024). De la informalidad urbana al régimen urbano especulativo: análisis comparativo de tres ciudades del Perú. *Ciudad Y Territorio Estudios Territoriales, 56*(222), 1371–88.

Davoudi, S. (2012). Resilience: A bridging concept or a dead end? *Planning Theory & Practice, 13*(2), 299–333.

Ernstson, H., Sörlin, S. & Elmqvist, T. (2008). Social movements and ecosystem services: The role of social network structure in protecting and managing urban green areas in Stockholm. *Ecology and Society, 13*(2).

Escobar, A. (. (2018). *Designs for the Pluriverse: Radical Interdependence, Autonomy, and the Making of Worlds.* Duke University Press.

Folke, C., Carpenter, S. R., Walker, B., Scheffer, M., Chapin, T. & Rockström, J. (2010). Resilience thinking: Integrating resilience, adaptability and transformability. *Ecology and Society, 15*(4), 20.

Fung, A. (2006). Varieties of participation in complex governance. *Public Administration Review, 66*, 66–75.

Goodchild, M. (2007). Citizens as sensors: The world of volunteered geography. *GeoJournal, 69*, 211–21.

Healey, P. (1997). *Collaborative Planning: Shaping Places in Fragmented Societies.* Macmillan.

Herrington, S. (2016). *Landscape Theory in Design.* Routledge.

Hillier, B. (2015). *Space is the Machine: A Configurational Theory of Architecture.* CreateSpace Independent Publishing Platform.

Inostroza, L. (2017). Informal urban development in Latin American urban peripheries: Spatial assessment in Bogotá, Lima and Santiago de Chile. *Landscape and Urban Planning, 165*, 267–79.

Lang, D. J., Wiek, A., Bergmann, M., Stauffacher, M., Martens, P., Swilling, M. & Thomas, C. J. (2012). Transdisciplinary research in sustainability science: practice, principles, and challenges. *Sustainability Science 7*, 25–43.

Madeddu, M. (2016). Urban acupuncture: Celebrating pinpricks of change that enrich city life. *Journal of Urban Design, 21*(4), 533–34.

Mazer, K. E., Tomasek, A. A., Daneshvar, F., Frankenberger, L. C., McMillan, S. K., Novoa, H. M. & Zeballos-Velarde, C. (2021). Integrated hydrologic and hydraulic analysis of torrential flood hazard in Arequipa, Peru. *Journal of Contemporary Water Research & Educaation, 171*(1), 93–110.

Moreno, C., Allam, Z., Chabaud, D., Gall, C. & Pratlong, F. (2011). Introducing the '15-minute city': Sustainability, resilience and place identity in future post-pandemic cities. *Smart Cities, 4*(1), 93–111.

Pelling, M. (2011). *Adaptation to Climate Change: From Resilience to Transformation.* Routledge.

Pieterse, E. (2008). *City Futures: Confronting the Crisis of Urban Development.* Zed Books.

Roy, A. (2005). Urban informality: Toward an epistemology of planning. *Journal of the American Planning Association, 71*(2), 147–58.

Sandercock, L. (2003). *Cosmopolis II: Mongrel Cities of the 21st Century.* Continuum.

Shannon, K. & Smets, M. (2010). *The Landscape of Contemporary Infrastructure.* NAi Publishers.

Soja, E. W. (2010). *Seeking Spatial Justice.* University of Minnesota Press.

Swyngedouw, E. & Moulaert, F. (2010). Socially innovative projects, governance dynamics and urban change: Between state and self-organisation. In F. Moulaert, F. Martinelli, E. Swyngedouw & S. González (Eds.), *Can Neighbourhoods Save the City?* (pp. 63–80). Routledge.

UNESCO (2016). Culture: Urban future; Global report on culture for sustainable urban development. UNESCO. https://unesdoc.unesco.org/ark:/48223/pf0000246291

UNESCO (2018). The United Nations world water development report 2018: Nature-based solutions for water. UNESCO World Water Assessment Programme. https://unesdoc.unesco.org/ark:/48223/pf0000261424.locale=en

UN-Habitat (2019). *Social Resilience Guide.* United Nations Human Settlements Programme.

Vale, L. J. (2013). The politics of resilient cities: Whose resilience and whose city? *Building Research & Information, 42*(2), 191–201.

Waldheim, C. (2006). *The Landscape Urbanism Reader.* Princeton Architectural Press.

Watson, V. (2009). 'The planned city sweeps the poor away…': Urban planning and 21st century urbanisation. *Progress in Planning, 72*(3), 151–93.

Whatmore, S. (2006). Materialist returns: Practising cultural geography in and for a more-than-human world. *Cultural Geographies, 13*(4), 600–09.

Zeballos-Velarde, C. (2021). Urban Linkages: A methodological framework for improving resilience in peripheral areas – The Case of Arequipa, Peru. In J. Martinez, C. Mikkelsen & R. Phillips (Eds.), *Handbook of Quality of Life and Sustainability* (pp. 533–50). Springer.

Zeballos-Velarde, C. (2024). *Atlas Ambiental de Arequipa* (2nd edn.). Universidad Católica de Santa María.

Zeballos-Velarde, C. & Chevarría-Aredo, S. (2024). Place building: Enhancing urban resilience in hazard prone areas' public spaces – The case of Arequipa, Peru. In C. Blanco Jr. & I. Gawad (Eds.), *UIA Guidebook for the 2030 Agenda* (pp. 358–59). Union International d'Architectes.

Zeballos-Velarde, C., Yory García, C. M., Chui Choque, E. & Zuluaga, L. (2022). Acupuntura urbana en bordes de ciudad: ejercicios en Arequipa y Bogotá. *Estudios demográficos y urbanos, 109*(1), 265–305.

Blanca Pujals

DESIGNING WITH RARE EARTHS: UNVEILING MATERIAL GEOPOLITICS

INTRODUCTION

We tend to regard technologies and design elements as neutral technical artefacts, and therefore to assume that political questions relate exclusively to how they are used. Yet these artefacts are often, by their very design and material configuration, capable of enabling or constraining particular actions and behaviours, and of favouring certain interests over others.

Understanding the material reality of our technology (Figure 1) helps us respond to contemporary technological and ecological needs. The surfaces of our technologies are neither immaterial nor neutral; rather, they are the sedimented layers and stratigraphic records of global geopolitics.

Figure 1. Bastnaesite rare earth mineral (the green parts – reddish-brown in reality) found in the Paleoproterozoic carbonatite deposit in Mountain Pass, California.

Following their traces across landscapes and history reveals multiple layers interconnected through a timeless resonance of what Rob Nixon (2011) has coined 'slow violence', a violence that is invisible, gradual and relentless, affecting territories, communities and ecosystems across vast geographies and timescales, which, precisely because it is not a spectacular, isolated event, has often passed unnoticed within the accelerated system of progress we inhabit.

The Western epistemology of management and control, which decides what is allowed to live and what may be left to die, as Achille Mbembe (2003) explains with his concept of 'necropolitics', treats both context and beings as matter to be extracted, produced and manipulated, often to the point of exhaustion. This unveils different forms of possession, property, rights and conflict.

In 2018, the Maya K'iche' Indigenous leader and Guatemalan activist Lolita Chávez Ixcaquic, then living in refuge in the Basque Country, Spain, due to threats against her life, took part in the architecture programme 'Geographies and Forms of Power'[1] at the Tabakalera international centre for contemporary culture in Donostia/San Sebastián (Figure 2). There, she denounced the destructive impact of extractive mining on Indigenous territories in Guatemala, particularly in the Quiché region, highlighting how the pursuit of minerals threatens both the environment and the rights of local communities.

Figure 2. Maya K'iche' Indigenous leader and Guatemalan activist Lolita Chávez Ixcaquic delivering a lecture as part of the 'Geographies and Forms of Power' programme at the Tabakalera international centre for contemporary culture, Donostia/San Sebastián, Basque Country, Spain, 2018.

In *A Geology of Media*, Jussi Parikka (2015) argues that digital media cannot be understood solely as cultural technologies, but also as geological phenomena, shaped and built by minerals and extractive processes. Similarly, in the context of architecture and urbanism, climate change mitigation and energy transition technologies bring sociomaterial transformations into the design process itself, intertwining human, cultural and political relationships with the objects, spaces, infrastructures and materials that make them possible. This inextricably entangles contemporary sustainable technologies with environmental exploitation and the toxicity of electronic waste.

1 The programme was a series of talks held at the Tabakalera centre between 2017 and 2018. Guest curated by the author in collaboration with Ula Iruretagoiena and Ibon Salaberria, the directors of the centre's 'Cities and Other Policies' programme of which it was a part, it explored architecture as a tool for producing and exercising violence, and its role as a witness, agent or apparatus revealing the geographies of power in contemporary conflicts.

In recent years, architects and researchers have increasingly focused on the environmental and social impacts of extractive practices. Godofredo Enes Pereira, architect and environmental activist, has spent the past decade, both independently and with the action-research agency GIT/Territorial Research Group, researching community resistance and collaborating internationally to map and make visible territorial voices opposing lithium mining (LIQUIT: Voices of the Territories, n.d; Pereira, 2015). Design and materials researcher Michaela Büsse (2025) examines sand, a material whose escalating use in urbanisation, infrastructure and construction reveals the profound economic, environmental and social consequences of its scarcity.

What configures our designs, buildings, cities and infrastructures is inextricably linked to their material dimensions throughout the entire chain of extraction, production and disposal. In this context, rare earth elements (REEs), essential for technological development and the transition to renewable energy, are also active agents in contemporary global geopolitics and environmental conflicts.

Tracing the materiality of REEs, or 'rare earths', to expose the infrastructures and policies of the digital and ecological transition connects abstract technological consumption and deferred toxicities, geopolitical control and contested ecosystems.

RARE EARTHS

The development of today's technology has generated unprecedented demand for so-called 'transition minerals' or 'critical minerals': lithium, cobalt, coltan, copper and rare earth elements.[2] They are spatially ubiquitous but structurally invisible.

Figure 3. The Baogang Tailings Dam in the city of Baotou, Inner Mongolia, China, is a new, anthropogenic lake of toxic sludge created by the world's largest rare-earth mine, Bayan Obo.

Discovered in Sweden over two hundred years ago, REEs are particularly strategic materials in the current and future global geopolitical arena. They are a series of 17 metals that are irreplaceable in today's tech industry due to their fundamental role in improving the screens and speed of electronic devices, and they are also essential for advances in military technology, semiconductors, batteries and renewable energy technologies.[3]

These elements are actually relatively abundant in the Earth's crust, but are deemed 'rare' because it is difficult to find them in their pure form and to mine them without significant environmental and social costs (Figure 3). Extracting them from their ores often requires the use of acids, which is how they came to be known as 'earths'; seventeenth-century chemists used the term to describe earthy-looking metal oxides that, despite being seemingly unalterable, were found to be soluble in acids. Their extraction and processing activities can cause habitat destruction, soil erosion and contamination of water and subsoil with heavy metals and radioactive waste.

In addition to their industrial use, they are employed in varying concentrations in agriculture as phosphate fertilisers, contributing to the progressive accumulation of REEs in agricultural soils. They are also found in high concentrations in rivers in densely populated urban areas, especially in Europe and the United States. This is the case with gadolinium, used as a contrast agent in magnetic resonance imaging, which passes almost unaltered through wastewater treatment plants.

In contemporary architecture and urban planning, REEs are integral to sustainability and energy efficiency. They are embedded in lighting, technology, energy systems and advanced material finishes in buildings, cities and infrastructures. While there is no precise figure for the percentage of REEs used in construction, they are widely distributed in building materials and processes.

Concrete, for example, one of the world's most widely used construction materials, can be strengthened and made more durable with REEs such as cerium oxide. Their use improves resistance to chemical damage, for example in nuclear waste storage or undersea structures. Yttrium, Europium and terbium are essential for energy-efficient LEDs in building and public lighting, covering red, green and white light, as well as for phosphors, lasers in fibre optics, and fluorescent lamps. Lanthanum and cerium enhance architectural glass and ceramics, providing high refractive index, polish and UV protection.

2 Lithium, sourced mainly from the South American 'lithium triangle' (Argentina, Bolivia and Chile), is vital for batteries and electric vehicles, yet its extraction threatens scarce water supplies in some of the driest regions on the planet, laying bare the contradictions of a 'clean energy' that undermines fragile ecosystems. Coltan, tied to the production of tantalum for electronic devices, is often mined by hand in the Democratic Republic of the Congo, where the trade has been linked to armed conflict, labour exploitation and cycles of violence that affect entire communities. Cobalt, another key element for electric vehicle batteries, is also largely mined in the Congo, where dangerous and exploitative conditions, including child labour and severe pollution, make visible the human and environmental cost of technologies marketed as sustainable.

3 For example, production of high-power magnets for electric motors, wind turbines and hybrid and electric vehicles; manufacturing of LED screens, TV screens and mobile devices; components in fluorescent lights, LED lamps and efficient lighting; catalysts in the automotive, petrochemical and oil-refining industries; applications in rechargeable batteries, especially lithium-ion batteries and batteries for electric vehicles; use in optical fibres, laser communications and data-transmission technologies; essential for night-vision devices, radar systems, sonar and military communications; components for guidance and precision systems in weaponry and defence technology; materials for helmet-mounted displays, headphones and augmented-reality devices; use in quantum computing, spintronics and neuromorphic technologies; elements in advanced sensors for AI and data analysis systems; applications in hard-drive and storage-device magnets; special treatments in glass, ceramics and superconductors; contrast agents and diagnosis and treatment materials in medicine and magnetic resonance imaging; additives in the manufacture of ultraviolet-resistant glass and for precision optics; uses in industrial processes such as metal purification and the manufacture of speciality glass.

Praseodymium and neodymium are used as colourants in glass, enamels and ceramics, and can filter specific wavelengths such as ultraviolet and infrared radiation that can contribute to a building's energy performance. They are also critical in alloys, magnets, lasers and compact motors found in lifts, fans, automatic curtains, wind turbines and electric transport. Dysprosium, in turn, improves the high-temperature performance of permanent magnets in motors, HVAC systems, wind turbines and electric trains and trams.

Due to their vast, temporally dispersed and structurally elusive material entanglements, REEs can be considered 'hyperobjects' in the sense described by Timothy Morton (2013), their impacts accumulating both physically and symbolically across technological and political strata, and their vast spatial distribution and temporal delayed effects conditioning human and other-than-human life while eluding direct perception.

REES GEOPOLITICS

China's dominant role as the world's leading producer and exporter of REEs – accounting for more than 80 per cent of global production (US Geological Survey, 2023) – began in the early 1980s, although experts from the state-run Chinese Academy of Sciences have recently warned that this long period of almost complete global dominance could be coming to an end due to the opening of new mines in Australia, South Africa and Greenland (Darabshaw, 2025). The fact that the processing and mining of these materials is concentrated in just a few countries makes their supply chains highly vulnerable from a geopolitical point of view, creating a dependency on the part of the technology and defence sectors of other nations.

It is this situation that explains the United States' strategic interest in Greenland (Perkins, 2025). According to recent data from the US Geological Survey, there are around 85 million metric tonnes of REEs deposits worldwide, with some 44 million in China, 21 million in Brazil, 6.9 million in India, 6.3 million in Australia, 3.8 million in Russia, 3.5 million in Vietnam, and only 1.9 million in the United States. The Kvanefjeld deposit in Greenland is thought to be the world's second-largest, and it also contains significant reserves of uranium and sodium fluoride, making it one of the most important polyelemental deposits globally.

Ukraine also has several REEs deposits and other reserves of strategic elements such as lithium, graphite and uranium, which, in this new map of global interests, has put its natural resources in the crosshairs of powers such as the US and Russia. On 3 February 2025, US President Donald Trump said that he wanted Ukraine to supply REEs to the United States in exchange for financial support for Kyiv's defence against Russia (Guardian & Agence France-Presse, 2025). According to statements by Ukrainian President Volodymyr Zelenskyy (Balmforth & Harmash, 2025), Russia has occupied approximately half of his country's rare-earth deposits.

REEs are therefore becoming a source of political pressure and foreign intervention, reshaping global alliances and disputes.[4]

Europe

These conflicts are intertwined with local struggles, where the discourse of 'strategic necessity' often conceals long-term environmental risks and socio-territorial dispossession.

In 2015, environmental lawyer Elena Solís[5] presented the case of Campo de Montiel in La Mancha, Spain, at the Centre for Research Architecture (Goldsmiths, University of London), in response to Spanish company Quantum Minería's proposed plan to extract monazite, a mineral rich in REEs, in the area. The project was immediately met with resistance from local communities, environmental scientists, the neighbourhood association Sí a la Tierra Viva (Yes to Living Earth) (Figure 4) and civil society due to threats to protected ecosystems, water resources and agricultural land. The platform submitted formal allegations, highlighting deficiencies in the existing hydrological data and calling for rigorous technical evaluations of water resources, and stating that the project omitted detailed assessments of threatened species and biodiversity in protected areas such as EU Natura 2000 sites and Zona de Especial Protección para las Aves (Special Protection Areas for Birds – ZEPA)

Figure 4. The Sí a la Tierra Viva (Yes to Living Earth) activist platform demonstration against rare-earth mining in Valdepeñas, Spain.

4 Research by the organisation Global Witness (Hammond & Matijevic, 2025) reveals that some of the world's poorest countries (including Somalia, Haiti, the Democratic Republic of the Congo and Yemen) have also been forced to sign agreements with lobbyists linked to Donald Trump, exchanging their minerals and other natural resources for humanitarian or military support from the United States.

5 Elena Solís is a Spanish environmental lawyer whose work focuses on the social and legal impacts of mining in Spain. As a leading figure within Ecologistas en Acción, a Spanish grassroots confederation consisting of 300 environmental groups, founded in 1998, she has actively opposed REEs and other critical mineral extraction projects, leading public awareness campaigns on terrestrial and deep-sea mining and pursuing legal action against environmental violations in both Spanish and European contexts.

(Plataforma Sí a la Tierra Viva, 2024). Although in 2017, following public protests and negative environmental reports, the Regional Government of Castilla-La Mancha rejected the project, in early 2024 Quantum Minería reapplied for new exploration permits, arguing the strategic need to secure Europe's supply of REEs given trade tensions with China.

Likewise, in the Canary Islands, particularly Fuerteventura, there are significant deposits of REEs and strategic metals both on land and in the submarine mountains, especially around areas such as the Tropic Seamount. While these resources could make the archipelago a strategic supplier for Europe's technological industry, local councils and communities have consistently opposed prospecting, warning of the risks to fragile ecosystems, landscapes and tourism-dependent livelihoods, and calling for thorough environmental studies before any action. The Government of the Canary Islands has likewise affirmed its commitment not to authorise research or exploitation, prioritising the protection of marine biodiversity and the local environment (EFE, 2025).[6]

In 2023, and possibly influenced by Spain's refusals to exploit its own deposits, Sweden announced that the mining company LKAB had discovered one of Europe's largest REEs deposits at the Per Geijer site near the Kiruna region in the north of the country (LKAB, 2023). However, LKAB also faced opposition from Sámi leaders,[7] such as LarsMarcus Kuhmunen, head of the Gábna Sámi community,[8] who warned that the project could fragment territories and disrupt reindeer migration routes used for generations, threatening both economic subsistence and cultural survival, while endangering the protection of indigenous land rights and traditional practices.

Extractive projects are often framed as strategic necessities, yet local and rural communities are rarely given meaningful opportunities to participate, even though they respond through protests, legal challenges, formal complaints and political advocacy. The reopening of mining projects to support digital and 'green' development implies a paradoxical situation that embodies a clear contradiction. These projects take place in peripheral regions, where livelihoods and cultural practices are deeply connected to the land and communities face not only water and ecological vulnerabilities but also broader social and territorial impacts.

Remote lands: deep sea and Outer Space

Global demand for REEs continues to grow and is expected to double every decade, placing unattainable demands on terrestrial reserves. As a result, marine deposits[9] (Figure 5), along with extraterrestrial exploration,[10] are emerging as an alternative, especially in the Pacific and Indian oceans and in underwater hydrothermal vents, which are vulnerable ecosystems with unique and fragile biodiversity.

Figure 5. A Parapagurus sp. crab carrying a coral (genus *Epizoanthus*) on its back makes its way across a field of ferromanganese nodules blanketing the seafloor of the Gosnold Seamount. Captured during Dive 16 of the 2021 North Atlantic Stepping Stones expedition.

ECOLOGICAL TRANSITION IN ARCHITECTURE

Moving towards an architecture less reliant on REEs and other critical minerals calls for recyclable technologies, circular economy strategies, passive design and alternative energy storage solutions.

Alternative ways to reduce dependence on REEs combine established practices with emerging approaches. In concrete and cement, supplementary materials such as fly ash, slag or natural pozzolans have long improved durability and chemical resistance without cerium or other REEs. Advanced surface treatments, including self-cleaning titanium dioxide coatings or high-performance polymer sealants, are technically proven but remain unevenly adopted due to cost, long-term performance and site-specific conditions.

In lighting and display technologies, more efficient phosphor systems and LED designs increasingly rely on abundant or recycled materials, reducing the use of yttrium, Europium and terbium. Similarly, architectural glass and ceramics can achieve UV filtering, solar control, colour effects and self-cleaning properties with nanostructured coatings, multilayer films or laminated composites, though these solutions are not yet standard.

6 The Galician Sea has also been in the news recently because the United Nations provisionally approved the request the Spanish government submitted in 2009 to extend Spain's Exclusive Economic Zone westward, beyond the 200 nautical miles established under the United Nations Convention on the Law of the Sea (UNCLOS), and it is now awaiting final ratification. This would grant Spain rights over seabed resources in the expanded area off the Galician coast, where scientific studies have identified metals such as cobalt, nickel, copper, manganese and REEs (Pardo, 2025). Galicia has a long-standing tradition of environmental advocacy, with local organisations such as the Galiza Non Se Vende, Asociación para a Defensa Ecolóxica de Galiza (ADEGA), Ecoloxistas en Acción, fishing communities and Asociación Pola Defensa da Ría (APDR) actively engaged in the protection of natural ecosystems and territorial resources. The Comuneros de Vincios has also raised concerns about developments concerning the potential future mining of REEs in the Serra do Galiñeiro mountain range in Pontevedra (Redacción, 2025).

7 The Sámi are the indigenous people of Sápmi, a region which today spans northern parts of Norway, Sweden, Finland and Russia's Kola Peninsula.

8 Gabna Sameby is a mountain Sámi village in Norrboeen County, located south of the Torne River and Talma Sameby and north of Laevas Sameby.

9 Countries such as China, India and Russia already hold several offshore exploration contracts for seabed minerals through the International Seabed Authority (ISA). In the case of the United States, its failure to ratify the United Nations Convention on the Law of the Sea (UNCLOS), established in 1982 to regulate activities in international waters, prevents its companies from participating directly in deep-sea mining, which is why former US political and military leaders have urged the Senate to ratify the treaty. In April 2025, President Trump issued an executive order instructing federal agencies to accelerate the approval of permits for deep-sea mining under the 1980 Deep Seabed Hard Mineral Resources Act (DSHMRA), a US law that predates the establishment of ISA. https://www.whitehouse.gov/presidential-actions/2025/04/unleashing-americas-offshore-critical-minerals-and-resources/

10 In the case of extraterrestrial mining, first Barack Obama in 2015 (Griffin, 2015) and later the Trump administration (Wall, 2020) paved the way by signing an executive order formally recognising the rights of private interests to claim resources in Space, disregarding the decades-long debate that began with the signing of the Outer Space Treaty during the Cold War in 1967.

Renewable energy generation increasingly uses abundant materials such as crystalline silicon photovoltaics, solar thermal systems, and turbines with conventional mechanical transmission, avoiding permanent magnets containing neodymium or dysprosium. Moreover, biomass and biogas from agricultural, forest and urban residues can further complement energy supply. Energy storage solutions for non-fossil sources, such as sodium-ion and iron-air batteries, thermal storage with hot water or molten salts, and mechanical systems including flywheels, compressed air and pumped hydro, offer alternatives but still remain at early stages of development.

Energy performance can also be improved through natural insulation materials like cork, wool, cellulose or plant fibres alongside efficient system design and passive strategies such as daylighting, natural ventilation and façade orientation.

Alongside these, there is growing potential in recovering materials from demolition and renovation through urban mining,[11] which reimagines cities not merely as consumers of resources but as 'deposits' of materials that have already been extracted, processed and used in products, infrastructures and buildings, and could re-enter the production cycle.[12]

Urban mining has been implemented in several countries, reflecting diverse approaches to recovering critical materials. In Africa, the unidirectional flow of e-waste from the Global North has long driven informal urban mining. Near Old Fadama in Accra, Ghana, one of the world's largest e-waste sites, communities manually dismantle electronics, perform repairs, and engage in DIY digital fabrication. While these activities provide economic opportunities, they also pose significant environmental and health risks.

In South Korea, government support through funding and policy incentives has facilitated the establishment of industrial-scale recycling facilities, enabling the efficient and economically viable recovery of lithium, cobalt and nickel from end-of-life electric-vehicle batteries (Chung & Park, 2018), reducing reliance on imported ores while supporting a rapidly growing domestic industry.

The Urban Mining Demonstration Base Programme in China has established forty-nine integrated sites combining collection, sorting and processing, where coordinated infrastructure and policies enable large-scale recovery of secondary resources.

In the European Union, platforms such as ProSUM[13] map the stocks of valuable metals hidden in old devices and end-of-life vehicles, enabling planners to identify and prioritise opportunities for resource recovery. In Germany and Belgium, specialised facilities dismantle and process e-waste to recover metals such as copper, gold and REEs for reuse in new electronics. At a local level, cities such as Amsterdam and Copenhagen demonstrate how municipal collection and sorting schemes can feed into urban mining processes. Furthermore, EU-funded projects such as Buildings As Material Banks (BAMB)[14] and SUM4Re[15] support the development of digital tools, material passports and automated sorting technologies to enhance the efficiency and traceability of e-waste recovery.

Although still underdeveloped and facing persistent challenges, including high dismantling costs, regulatory differences and uneven secondary processing capacity, this approach could ease pressure on primary extraction and fragile ecosystems, decrease waste, and strengthen local autonomy over raw materials, contributing to a more circular and sustainable economy.

Figure 6. Urban mining: e-waste at a recycling facility.

11 The term 'urban mining' was introduced in the 1980s by Professor Hideo Nanjyo of the Research Institute of Mineral Dressing and Metallurgy at Tohoku University (Nanjyo, 1988), and the concept has since become increasingly influential in Japan and other parts of Asia.

12 This approach seeks to reclaim metals from electronic waste (mobile phones, computers, batteries, appliances), end-of-life vehicles (steel, aluminium, copper, plastics, catalytic converters containing precious metals), buildings and infrastructures (copper wiring, steel frameworks, aluminium windows, glass, recycled cement), as well as from general urban waste streams, including cables, pipes and street furniture.

13 The ProSUM platform (European Urban Mine Platform, 2024) is a publicly funded EU research consortium under Horizon 2020, involving universities, geological surveys and industry partners.

14 BAMB is a publicly financed European Commission Horizon 2020 research project that unites 15 partners from multiple countries to develop circular building tools.

15 SUM4Re is a publicly funded Horizon Europe research and innovation project that combines digital urban mining with advanced data acquisition and analysis to create materials banks from buildings, involving a consortium of public and private partners across several European countries.

Beyond individual technologies, it remains essential to rethink and implement systemic strategies. Fostering a transition towards sustainable architecture requires approaches that involve reducing energy demand through passive design, maximising orientation, cross-ventilation, shading and other bioclimatic features, promoting circular economy principles that prioritise recycling and expand urban mining, and pursuing technological diversification by combining abundant, low-impact systems.

CONCLUSION

The geographies of REEs are integral, not peripheral, to architectural design discourse and future spatial-technological imaginaries. Digital and green technologies are not neutral interfaces but sedimented surfaces of planetary conflicts.

The impacts of REEs manifest in both physical and symbolic terms across technological and political strata. Although promoted as essential to sustainability, they are often used as tools for political and economic pressure, and their mining deepens historical geographical asymmetries, displaces communities, generates deferred toxicity, and heightens tensions between environmental protection and dominant economic narratives of progress. REEs are not simply resources; they mediate spatial, environmental and political transformations. Despite growing interest in recycling and alternative supply chains, the discourse of 'strategic necessity' often conceals long-term environmental risks and socio-territorial dispossession.

An ecological and digital transition cannot be measured by efficiency alone; it requires deeper, multidimensional consideration based on material justice, territorial accountability and political responsibility. Architects and spatial practitioners can embed this awareness within the design process itself, integrating material, ecological and geopolitical insights from the outset to mitigate the reproduction of harmful cycles of extraction, pollution and inequality. Integrating the ecological transition into architecture requires a systemic approach that considers materials, design strategies and the resources flow network as interconnected, from extraction to disposal. Circular economy strategies, urban mining, passive design, and the use of abundant or recycled materials instead of critical minerals such as REEs offer possible avenues for achieving this shift.

Cultivating material knowledge in architectural practices shifts the focus from isolated objects to systemic relations and recognises that design begins not at the first drawings but at the mine, not in the studio but in contested landscapes. It involves examining the infrastructural level of contemporary material flow dynamics, where materials are agents and narrators of political and ecological transformations. This form of hyper-consciousness encourages spatial ethics that resist extractivist practices and work towards sustainable futures.

Acknowledgements

This text forms part of the long-term project Geopolitics of Materials (2018–present). I am grateful to the institutions that have supported its presentation until now: the Centre de Cultura Contemporània de Barcelona (CCCB); the Oslo National Academy of the Arts (KHiO), Norway; KTH Royal Institute of Technology, Stockholm; the Graduate School of Architecture, Planning and Preservation (GSAPP), Columbia University; the Vallès School of Architecture (ETSAV-UPC); and the Spanish Academy in Rome.

References

Balmforth, T. & Harmash, O. (2025). Zelenskiy says 'Let's do a deal', offering Trump mineral partnership, seeking security. Reuters.com, 7 February. https://www.reuters.com/world/zelenskiy-says-lets-do-deal-offering-trump-mineral-partnership-seeking-security-2025-02-07/

Büsse, M. (2025). Granular power: The gritty politics of sand. e-flux Architecture, 26 March. https://www.e-flux.com/architecture/intensification/657582/granular-power-the-gritty-politics-of-sand

Campo de Montiel Info (2025). El Seprona denuncia a Quantum Minería. 5 May. https://campodemontielinfo.com/seprona-denuncia-a-quantum-mineria/

Chung, J. & Park, J. (2018). 'Urban mining' in South Korea pulls rare battery materials from recycled tech. Reuters, 12 April. https://www.reuters.com/article/us-southkorea-mining/urban-mining-in-south-korea-pulls-rare-battery-materials-from-recycled-tech-idUSKBN1HJ14T

Darabshaw, S. (2025). Chinese agency admits rare earth rule may end, will the U.S. seize the throne? MetalMiner, 27 March. https://agmetalminer.com/2025/03/27/china-rare-earth-metals-rule-may-end/

EFE (2025). El Gobierno de Canarias reitera que no va a autorizar la búsqueda de tierras raras. elDiario.es, 13 February. https://www.eldiario.es/canariasahora/politica/gobierno-canarias-reitera-no-autorizar-busqueda-tierras-raras_1_12052003.html

European Urban Mine Platform (2024). Unlocking value: EU's urban mining tools to harness resources from waste. Mining South East Europe, 11 May. https://www.miningsee.eu/unlocking-value-eus-urban-mining-tools-to-harness-resources-from-waste/

Griffin, A. (2015). Asteroid mining made legal after Barack Obama gives US citizens the right to own parts of celestial bodies. *The Independent*, 26 November. https://www.independent.co.uk/tech/asteroid-mining-made-legal-after-barack-obama-gives-us-citizens-the-right-to-own-parts-of-celestial-bodies-a6750046.html

Guardian & Agence France-Presse (2025). What are rare earth elements, and why does Trump want them from Ukraine? *The Guardian*, 5 February. https://www.theguardian.com/us-news/2025/feb/05/donald-trump-rare-earths-ukraine-us-trade-deal-aid-russia

Hammond, C. & Matijevic, P. (2025). Revealed: Trump-linked firms cash in on mineral lobbying deals as US cuts aid. Global Witness, 9 July. https://globalwitness.org/en/campaigns/transition-minerals/revealed-trump-linked-firms-cash-in-on-mineral-lobbying-deals-as-us-cuts-aid

LIQUIT: Voices of the Territories (n.d.). The project. https://liquitvoices.org/en/the-project/

LKAB (2023). Europe's largest deposit of rare earth metals located in Kiruna area. LKAB, 12 January. https://lkab.com/en/press/europes-largest-deposit-of-rare-earth-metals-is-located-in-the-kiruna-area/

Mbembe, A. (2019). *Necropolitics*. Duke University Press.

Morton, T. (2013). *Hyperobjects: Philosophy and Ecology after the End of the World*. University of Minnesota Press.

Nanjyo, H. (1988). Urban mine: New resources for the year 2,000 and beyond. *Bulletin of the Research Institute of Mineral Dressing and Metallurgy*, *43*(2), 239–51.

Nixon, R. (2011). *Slow Violence and the Environmentalism of the Poor*. Harvard University Press.

Pardo, L. (2025). Galicia gana bajo el océano un territorio del tamaño de Extremadura con metales, tierras raras y bidones radiactivos. elDiario.es, 1 September. https://www.eldiario.es/galicia/galicia-gana-oceano-territorio-tamano-extremadura-metales-tierras-raras-bidones-radiactivos_1_12570533.html

Parikka, J. (2015). *A Geology of Media*. University of Minnesota Press.

Pereira, G. (2015). The underground frontier, *Continent CC*, *4*(4), 4–10.

Perkins, T. (2025). Trump donors eye potential bonanza if US succeeds with Greenland land-grab. *The Guardian*, 15 April. https://www.theguardian.com/us-news/2025/apr/15/trump-greenland-donors-investors-finance

Plataforma Sí a la Tierra Viva (2024). El proyecto de Quantum Minería para explorar tierras raras en Ciudad Real es incompatible con la protección del medioambiente y carece de licencia social, 6 March. https://www.sialatierraviva.org/2024/03/el-proyecto-de-quantum-mineria-para-explorar-tierras-raras-en-ciudad-real-es-incompatible-con-la-proteccion-del-medio-ambiente-y-carece-de-licencia-social.html

Redacción (2025). La Serra do Galiñeiro, blindada contra la minería de tierras raras y los parques eólicos. Cadena SER, 29 October. https://cadenaser.com/galicia/2025/10/29/la-serra-do-galineiro-blindada-contra-la-mineria-de-tierras-raras-y-los-parques-eolicos-radio-vigo/

US Geological Survey (2023). Mineral commodity summaries 2023: Rare earths. US Department of the Interior. https://www.usgs.gov/centers/nmic/rare-earths-statistics-and-information

Wall, M. (2020). Trump signs executive order to support moon mining, tap asteroid resources. Space.com, 7 April. https://www.space.com/trump-moon-mining-space-resources-executive-order.html

EDITORS' AND CONTRIBUTORS' BIOGRAPHIES

EDITORS

PAU BAJET is an architect who graduated from the Escola Tècnica Superior d'Arquitectura de Barcelona, Universitat Politècnica de Catalunya (ETSAB-UPC) in 2013. He was awarded a PhD 'by design' in 2023 by the School of Art, Architecture and Design at London Metropolitan University, supported by a La Caixa fellowship. He is a Lecturer in Architectural Design at ETSAB-UPC, where he has taught since 2017. He co-founded Bajet Giramé with Maria Giramé in 2017, a studio that develops architectural projects, built prototypes, exhibitions and publications, exploring material, social and ecological interrelations. Their work was awarded the FAD 2024 'City and Landscape' Prize and the studio was also a finalist for the AR Emerging Award 2024.

MARIONA BENEDITO is an architect who graduated from ETSAB-UPC in 2000. She is an Associate Lecturer of Architectural Design at the UPC, where she has taught since 2003. She is also Associate Professor and Coordinator at the IE School of Architecture and Design, and teaches the Social Logics master's course at Escola Tècnica Superior d'Arquitectura La Salle at Ramon Llull University (ETSALS-URL). Her practice is conceived in open terms and developed through collaboration with offices and professionals from other disciplines. She was the founder of Estudi d'Arquitectura MIM-A, and has led her own studio since 2020. Her work was awarded, among others, the FAD Prize in 2020 and 2015, and she was a finalist of the EU Mies van der Rohe Award.

MARIA GIRAMÉ is an architect who graduated from ETSAB-UPC in 2013. She has been Associate Lecturer of Architectural Design at ETSALS-URL since 2020. After four years at David Chipperfield Architects in London, she co-founded Bajet Giramé with Pau Bajet in 2017. The studio develops architectural projects, built prototypes, exhibitions and publications, exploring material, social and ecological interrelations. Their work was awarded the FAD 2024 'City and Landscape' Prize and the studio was also a finalist for the AR Emerging Award 2024.

TOMEU RAMIS is an architect who graduated from ETSAB-UPC in 2002. He is Associate Lecturer of Architectural Design at UPC where he has taught since 2003. He is currently also Associate Professor at ETSALS-URL. In 2002 he co-founded FLEXOarquitectura, a Barcelona-based studio working across housing, public buildings, urban projects, exhibitions and installations. The practice is grounded in the capacity of each project to make sense within a specific context, using conceptual and narrative resources together with technical, economic and material conditions. The studio's work was awarded the FAD 2025 'City and Landscape' Opinion Prize, was showcased at the Venice Architecture Biennale in 2012 and 2016, and nominated for the EU Mies van der Rohe Award in 2013.

PAU SARQUELLA is an architect who graduated from ETSAB-UPC in 2011. He has been Associate Lecturer of Architectural Design at Escola Politècnica Superior, Grau en Arquitectura, Universitat de Girona (EPSARQ-UdG) and ETSALS-URL since 2020, and previously taught at Chulalongkorn University, Bangkok. In 2019 he co-founded Sarquella Torres with Carmen Torres. Based in Banyoles, the studio works across scales, with projects shaped by context, use and time rather than a fixed formal language. The practice was awarded the FAD International 2019 Opinion Prize as well as a jury mention, and the Bauwelt Prize, Arquia Próxima and Europan17. Beyond the studio, in 2014 he co-founded Persiana Barcelona, a company that redesigned the traditional roller blind, a project that won the Silver Delta (ADI FAD) and Arquia Próxima awards.

CARMEN TORRES is an architect who graduated from ETSAB-UPC in 2011. She has been Associate Lecturer of Architectural Design at the Escola Tècnica Superior d'Arquitectura del Vallès, Universitat Politècnica de Catalunya (ETSAV-UPC) since 2019, where her teaching and research activity has received academic recognition. She previously taught at Chulalongkorn University, Bangkok. In 2019 she co-founded Sarquella Torres with Pau Sarquella. Based in Banyoles, the studio works across scales, with projects shaped by context, use and time rather than a fixed formal language. The practice was awarded the FAD International 2019 Opinion Prize as well as a jury mention, and the Bauwelt Prize, Arquia Próxima and Europan17.

In 2023, the editors joined forces with Chechu Zábala to conceive 'Becoming. Architectures for a Planet in Transition', the winning proposal of the international competition to curate the UIA World Congress of Architects 2026 Barcelona.

CONTRIBUTORS

ARCHITECTEN JAN DE VYLDER INGE VINCK is a practice in which making and the thinking are deeply imbedded. The baselines UNIVERSUM CAROUSEL JOURNEY and also FORM LIFE URGE give image to this. Inge Vinck is Professor at the Baukunstklasse Kunstakademie Düsseldorf and Jan De Vylder holds the Chair of Share of Architecture an(d) Attitude at ETH Zürich. Their practice has exhibited and has been published worldwide and has been awarded multiples times. Their portfolio includes the Palais des Expositions, Lieve Bloemen Lus house and the housing project Vos Bloei Bos.

ASSEMBLE is a London-based organisation founded in 2010. They design and make buildings, artworks, gardens, playgrounds, furniture, exhibitions and events, as well as developing business plans and project strategies, creating organisations, designing, constructing and managing workspaces, and curating, teaching, writing books, publishing research and lecturing publicly. Each of these activities form an interconnected body of work. COMMON TREASURES is a new, independent organisation established by members of Assemble and a community of collaborators in 2025 to develop models of architecture practice that equip organisations and communities that are largely excluded from architectural design services with the tools, resources and capacity to design for better outcomes in rural parts of the UK.

ATELIER BOW-WOW is based in Tokyo and was founded in 1992 by Momoyo Kaijima and Yoshiharu Tsukamoto. Yoichi Tamai was appointed partner in 2015. Atelier Bow-Wow is an acclaimed international practice with an extensive portfolio of work, as well as exhibitions and publications. The firm's projects span from residential buildings to public spaces and are characterised by a commitment to sustainability, social impact and an understanding of human behaviour in the built environment. In 2012 Tsukamoto and Kaijima received the RIBA International Fellowship, and the Wolf Prize Laureate in Architecture in 2022.

BANGKOK TOKYO ARCHITECTURE is an architectural studio founded by Wtanya Chanvitan and Takahiro Kume in 2017. The studio is fascinated by open-ended structures and the thoughtful assembly of everyday elements, blurring the lines between the ordinary and the exceptional. Their practice explores ways to liberate architecture from the realm of experts and professionals, aiming to discover potential models of continuity.

BAUKUNST is an architectural office established in Brussels in 2010. Combining art and technology, dialoguing and interplaying various forms of knowledge, BAUKUNST is committed to explore architecture as a medium with which both to think about building (BAU) and build ways of thinking (KUNST).

BC ARCHITECTS & STUDIES & MATERIALS is a hybrid practice, designing and undertaking 'acts of building' towards systemic change in the construction sector. BC stands for Brussels Cooperation, and the office's practice is deeply embedded in place and people, striving for bioregional, low-tech, circular, beautiful and inclusive design. They work with their minds and their hands, undertaking activities such as design, community organisation, material production, teaching and prototyping.

BeAr is an architecture studio based in Bilbao that explores architecture as a discursive practice. It is led by Ane Arce and Iñigo Berasategui. Their work has received major recognition and has been widely published in national and international specialised media. Notable awards include the Peña Ganchegui Award 2019 for Best Young Basque Architects, the Egurtek Award 2020, and multiple COAVN Awards 2025, as well as distinctions from FAD, Arquia Próxima and BEAU.

GIOVANNA BORASI joined the Canadian Centre for Architecture (CCA) in 2005 and held various curatorial positions there before becoming Director and Chief Curator in 2020. Her work explores ways to challenge conventional definitions of architectural practice through societally oriented interdisciplinarity. Among her recent CCA projects are the exhibition and book *A Section of Now* (2021), the documentaries *What It Takes to Make a Home*, *When We Live Alone*, and *Where We Grow Older* (2019–23), and *The fortune of the city is that it has never been perfect* (2026), an exhibition and book about Álvaro Siza's urbanistic thinking.

BRANDLHUBER+ was founded in 2006 as a collaborative design practice. Since 2022 it has continued as the cooperative practice b+. Focusing on the reuse and transformation of existing buildings and neighbourhoods, the practice works with what already exists. Across buildings, research, films, publications and exhibitions, it treats legal, economic and regulatory frameworks as design material to develop built arguments and narratives for systemic change. HOUSEEUROPE! is a community-driven non-profit for the built environment, translating practical competency into policy and advocacy. Its work is rooted in direct experience within the building industry. HouseEurope! was founded in 2023 with one question: how to build without costing people and the planet? The goal is to make systemic changes in how we build and raise awareness of the social-ecological transformation of the built environment.

STÉPHANIE BRU AND ALEXANDRE THERIOT founded BRUTHER in Paris in 2007 and 2022 in Zurich. Their work balances strategy and form, rigour and freedom, and the specific with the generic. BRUTHER has been widely published (including in *2G*, *El Croquis* and *A+U*) and recognised with major awards such as the Équerre d'Argent, the Dejean Prize and the Swiss Architectural Award. Bru and Theriot lecture at various universities internationally. Bru currently teaches at USI Mendrisio and the Karlsruhe Institute of Technology, and Theriot teaches at ETH Zürich.

IBIYE CAMP is a British Nigerian artist based in London whose work investigates postcolonial conditions, technology and the built environment. Using architectural tools to produce film, sound, textiles and 3D objects, her practice examines landscapes shaped by industrial systems, critiquing technological and manufacturing biases. Her work has been presented at the Sharjah Architecture Triennial (2019), Istanbul Biennial (2020), Shanghai Biennale (2021), Venice Architecture Biennale (2023) and Wellcome Collection (2025), and in 2026 she had her first solo show at Bonnington Gallery, Nottingham.

MATILDE CASSANI is the founder and director of the eponymous Matilde Cassani Studio. The practice operates at the intersection of architecture, installations and event design. Its work finds roots in the spatial implications of human rituals in the contemporary urban setting. It deals with the spatial implications of cultural pluralism in the contemporary Western city. Cassani's works have been exhibited in many cultural institutions and biennales and widely published.

COLECTIVO C733 was established in 2019 for the development of public projects in Mexico. It brings together the studios of Gabriela Carrillo, Carlos Facio and José Amozurrutia (TO), Eric Valdez (labg) and Israel Espín. Throughout their trajectory as a collective they have developed over 30 urban equipment projects in all regions of the country, with a focus on projects integrated into the Urban Improvement Plan of the Ministry of Agrarian, Territorial, and Urban Development of Mexico.

COMMON ACCOUNTS is a research studio in architecture and spatial practice that operates between Madrid and Toronto. Run by Igor Bragado and Miles Gertler, the studio's work is driven by an interest in self-design and the human body's interface with its environment. The work of Common Accounts – often materialised as building, installation, image and text – was awarded with a 2023 League Prize from the Architectural League of New York and is in the collections of the National Museum of Modern and Contemporary Art (MMCA) in Seoul and MUDAC in Lausanne.

DESIGN EARTH is a research practice founded by Rania Ghosn and El Hadi Jazairy in 2010. Their work engages the medium of the speculative architectural project to make public the climate crisis. They are recipients of the United States Artist Fellowship, Architectural League Prize for Young Architects + Designers, Boghossian Foundation Prize, and ACSA Faculty Design Award for outstanding work in architecture and related environmental design fields as a critical endeavour.

FORENSIC ARCHITECTURE (FA) is a research agency based at Goldsmiths, University of London. Its mandate is to develop, employ and disseminate new techniques, methods and concepts for investigating state and corporate violence. The team includes architects, software developers, filmmakers, investigative journalists, scientists and lawyers. Eyal Weizman is the Founder and Director of FA, and also Professor of Spatial and Visual Cultures at Goldsmiths. FA is the recipient of The Right Livelihood Award, a Peabody Award for interactive media, the European Cultural Foundation Award for Culture, and the RIBA Charles Jencks Award.

EVA FRANCH I GILABERT is an architect, curator, researcher and educator working between Barcelona, Prague and New York. She co-founded FAST, teaches at the Academy of Arts, Architecture and Design in Prague (UMPRUM) and Columbia University Graduate School of Architecture, Planning and Preservation (GSAPP), and has led the Architectural Association (London) and Storefront for Art and Architecture (New York), curating major international exhibitions.

SANA FRINI is a Tunisian architect and co-founder of Locus. She earned a MArch in Architecture and Southern Urban Studies from the Technical University of Lisbon and an MSc in Globalisation and Environment from the Nova School of Business and Economics (SBE). Her work focuses on Global South architectural processes, neo-vernacular systems, local reintegration and climate resilience. She has led projects in social housing, post-reconstruction, installations and research across France, Mexico, Portugal, Spain, the US and Tunisia. Her work has been shown at the Venice Architecture Biennale, Versailles Biennale and Mexican Design Week. She has taught at Cornell, Kent and Columbus universities.

H ARQUITECTES is an architecture studio based in Sabadell, Barcelona, founded in 2000 by David Lorente, Josep Ricart, Xavier Ros and Roger Tudó. Their work explores the environmental, material and spatial intelligence of architecture, with a strong emphasis on construction processes, bioclimatic and thermodynamic strategies, local resources and structural clarity. Their experimental practice takes a grounded, direct, responsive and culturally rooted approach. They have taught at ETSAV-UPC, ETSAB-UPC, Harvard GSD and ETH Zürich. Their work has been widely published, exhibited and awarded.

JUAN HERREROS is a PhD architect, Professor at Columbia University, and Chair Professor at the Escuela Técnica Superior de Arquitectura de Madrid (ETSAM). He has carried out teaching and research activities at leading European and American institutions. He has received numerous distinctions, most notably the International Fellowship of the Royal Institute of British Architects (RIBA). Since 2017 he has directed the Constructing Practice symposiums at Columbia, which document the work of younger generations. Herreros and Jens Richter make up estudioHerreros, a highly awarded, exhibited and published architectural practice with professional and academic activity across four continents.

HOLES is an architectural practice led by Mio Tsuneyama and Fuminori Nousaku. Based on lived experimentation in their home/studio, Holes in the House, they explore multispecies habitability by reconnecting architecture within a complex ecological mesh through their philosophy of Urban Wild Ecology. Their work engages local resources and material flows, emphasising coexistence with healthy soil through breathable, biodegradable materials and independent foundations. They have taught at Columbia GSAPP, EPFL and TU Munich, and received a Special Mention at the 2016 Venice Architecture Biennale.

KK+N+S is an occasional combination between landscape architects Dirk Sijmons + Lodewijk van Nieuwenhuijze (H+N+S Landscape architects), architect Ro Koster (Ro&Ad architects) and exhibition architect Herman Kossmann (KdJ exhibition architects). All four share a fascination with the relationship between nature and culture and with the use of nature-based solutions in design practice. Alongside their regular professional work, they collaborate in a loose but ongoing manner on research-by-design projects, competitions and pilot studies that explore how water safety can be achieved through the deployment of abiotic and biotic natural processes.

MAIO is a Barcelona-based architectural office, led by Alfredo Lérida, Anna Puigjaner, Guillermo López and Maria Charneco, which develops spatial systems to challenge biased structures. POL ESTEVE CASTELLÓ is a PhD architect who investigates the relationship between body, space and technology, focusing on non-conforming bodies, non-canonical histories, and collective design. They teach at ETH Zürich's Chair of Architecture and Care and at the Architectural Association, London. CARE. is a research and educational project launched in 2023 at ETH Zürich's Department of Architecture. It explores non-conforming bodies to promote new forms of interdependent care through design and theory.

TIMOTHY MORTON is Rita Shea Guffey Chair in English at Rice University and Director of the Cool America Foundation. Morton is the author of 25 books, translated 51 times into 20 languages, and the author of the libretto for the opera *Time Time Time* by Jennifer Walshe. Morton co-wrote and appears in *Living in the Future's Past*, a 2018 film about global warming with Jeff Bridges. Morton has collaborated with Laurie Anderson, Björk, Andrew Melchior, Susan Kucera, Hrafnhildur Arnadottir, Sabrina Scott, Adam McKay, Jeff Bridges, Olafur Eliasson, Pharrell Williams and Justin Guariglia.

NICOLAS DORVAL-BORY ARCHITECTES is a Paris-based architecture office founded in 2008 by Nicolas Dorval-Bory, joined by long-time collaborator Hugo Taillardat as partner in 2025. The office was nominated for the Prix de la Première Œuvre in 2014 and won the AJAP in 2016. The practice is closely linked to academia, particularly the ÉNSA Versailles, where Nicolas Dorval-Bory has been extensively teaching since 2014 and acts as a director since 2025.

MARINA OTERO VERZIER is an architect and researcher, and a lecturer at Harvard GSD. At Columbia GSAPP she leads the Data Mourning clinic on digital infrastructures and climate catastrophe. A recipient of the 2022 Harvard Wheelwright Prize, she collaborates with scientific institutions on prototypes like *Computational Compost*. In Chile, she contributed to the first National Data Centers Plan. Her book *En las Profundidades de la Nube* (2024) proposes new paradigms and aesthetics for data storage. She previously directed the MA in Social Design at Design Academy Eindhoven (DAE) and was Director of Research at Nieuwe Instituut.

PLAN COMÚN was founded in 2012 and is based in Paris and Santiago de Chile. The studio provides strategies to maximise and reinforce public and collective space – understood as a key aspect of architecture, regardless of its scale or programme – by means of simple architecture tools, through critical discourse, research, design and building. Its strategic approach to briefs and commissions questions and transforms spatial hierarchy and uses.

MATTHIAS SCHULER is an internationally recognised visionary who introduced the concepts of integrated design and climate engineering to Germany. He is one of Transsolar's founders, an international engineering firm with offices in Stuttgart, Munich and New York, established in 1992. He is driven by the curiosity to find the optimum and most innovative solutions. His deep respect for and understanding of the architectural design process strongly influence his collaboration with architects. His goal is to create the most comfortable, ecological, economical and valuable living and working environments possible, and he sees climate engineering as an approach that respects both people and nature.

SIMULAA is an architectural practice established in Naarm by Andre Bonnice and Anna Jankovic. Their work is defined by considered analysis and a research-based approach that prioritises time-based design thinking. It spans a broad range of scales and contexts, exploring how architecture might respond and act in a world defined by environmental limits, interrelational systems and layered temporalities. Bonnice and Jankovic are lecturers in architecture at the University of Melbourne and RMIT University, respectively, where they also teach and undertake research.

BAS SMETS has a background in landscape architecture, civil engineering and architecture. He founded his Brussels-based firm in 2007 and has completed over 50 international projects with his team of 24 architects and landscape architects. His work ranges from territorial visions to parks and urban spaces, exploring 'Augmented Landscapes' that create new microclimates. In 2023 he was appointed Professor in Practice at Harvard University Graduate School of Design (GSD). In 2025 he represented Belgium at the Venice Architecture Biennale and was named Officer in the Order of Arts and Letters by the French Minister of Culture.

NUNO MELO SOUSA has lived and worked in Penafiel, northern Portugal, since 2012. He draws and sometimes paints too, but he mostly draws: on walls, on papers and on tables as the slowness of the act of building leaves him yearning for the immediate.

He has taught at the International Program in Design and Architecture (INDA) at Chulalongkorn University and at USI Mendrisio, and is currently teaching Projecto IV at the Faculty of Architecture of the University of Porto (FAUP). He has led multiple workshops and has lectured at several universities and venues. Nuno plays with Muay, and he likes to draw on-site rather than in CAD.

STRUCTURAL XPLORATION LAB (SXL) unites architecture and structural design. A research lab at the Swiss Federal Institute of Technology (EPFL), it paves the way for reuse of load-bearing components in buildings, developing design methods, construction processes, prototypes, assessment procedures and computational means. Its research and education activities are mission-oriented, driven by sustainability challenges, rooted in history and boosted by pragmatism. The lab has gained international recognition for its research and prototypes on the structural reuse of saw-cut concrete and concrete rubble.

MARINA TABASSUM is an acclaimed architect and educator, and founder of Marina Tabassum Architects (2005). A graduate of the Bangladesh University of Engineering and Technology (BUET), she previously co-founded the Dhaka-based firm URBANA. A professor at TU Delft, she has held chairs at Yale and Toronto universities and Harvard GSD. A two-time Aga Khan Award laureate (2016 and 2025), she has received major international honours and was named among TIME's 100 Most Influential People (2024).

TAKK (MIREIA LUZÁRRAGA AND ALEJANDRO MUIÑO) is an architecture studio based in Barcelona and New York, integrating ecological thinking into spatial production. They teach at Columbia GSAPP and have taught at the University of Tokyo. Their work is part of the collections of the Frac Centre, Museum of Contemporary Design and Applied Arts (MUDAC), Barcelona Design Museum (DHUB), Vitra Design Museum and others.

TEN is composed as a record label, providing new formats for interdependent work groups with emphasis on design by research. It aims to conceive, explore and produce ideas that both state and expand upon emerging practices in the built environment. Its focus lies on producing new realities by means of building prototypes, urban propositions, algorithmic design and materials research with a range of collaborators, colleagues, institutional partners and private clients. TEN forms three legal entities to fulfil its agency: INSTITUTE as a not-for-profit association, STUDIO as a collection of single companies, and WORKS as a limited share company.

PHILIP URSPRUNG is Professor for the History of Art and Architecture at the Department of Architecture at ETH Zürich and Head of the Institute of the History and Theory of Architecture. From 2017 to 2019 he served as Dean of the Department. Among his publications are *Herzog & de Meuron: Natural History* (2002), *Brechas y conexiones: Ensayos sobre arquitectura, arte y economía* (2016) and *Values and Surfaces: Art, Economy, Architecture* (2025). In 2023 he represented Switzerland, with Karin Sander, at the Venice Architecture Biennale with the exhibition 'Neighbours'.

ENRIQUE WALKER is an architect. He has taught at Columbia University where he directed the Master of Science programme in Advanced Architectural Design, as well as at the Tokyo Institute of Technology, Princeton University, MIT, University College Los Angeles (UCLA), Harvard University and USI Mendrisio. His publications include *The Ordinary: Recordings* (2018), *The Dictionary of Received Ideas + Under Constraint* (2017), *Lo ordinario* (2010) and *Tschumi on Architecture: Conversations with Enrique Walker* (2006). He is currently a professor at the Universidad de Chile.

MARK WIGLEY is Professor of Architecture and Dean Emeritus at Columbia University. He is a historian, theorist and critic who explores the intersection of architecture, art, philosophy, culture and technology. His recent books include *We the Bacteria: Notes Toward Biotic Architecture* (with Beatriz Colomina), *Konrad Wachsmann's Television: Post-Architectural Transmissions*, *Are We Human? Notes on an Archaeology of Design* (with Beatriz Colomina) and *Buckminster Fuller Inc.: Architecture in the Age of Radio*. He has curated numerous exhibitions at institutions including the Museum of Modern Art (MoMA) and the Triennale di Milano.

RESEARCH BY DESIGN CREDITS

SEA-LEVEL RISE? LAND-LEVEL RISE!

Authors
Dirk Sijmons (KK+N+S), Amersfoort, The Netherlands

Team
Dirk Sijmons, Lodewijk van Nieuwenhuijze (H+N+S Landscape architects) and Ro Koster (RO&AD architects)

Audiovisual production:
SHOSHO Amsterdam

Sixteen peeping boxes with support of:
Jim van Belzen (Netherlands Institute of Marine Research), Ziega van den Berg (MUST, Urbanism), Maud van den Beuken (artist), Roos Bol (ARK re-wilding), Tjeerd Bouman (Netherlands Institute of Marine Research) and Corine Steenwijk (EcoWende), Yttje Feddes + Rick Lensink (LOF Landscape Architects), Maarten Kleinhans (University of Utrecht), Ad Kil (RO&AD architects), Robbert de Koning (Landscape architect), John Körmeling (architect) + Marcel Stive (TU-Delft), Herman Kossmann (Kossmanndejong), Ro Koster (RO&AD architects), Thijs Middeldorp and Harpo 't Hart (Embassy of the North Sea), Valérie Reijers (University of Utrecht), Ronald Rietveld (artist, RAAAF), Peter Veenstra (LOLA landscape architects), Bregje van Weesenbeeck (Deltares), KossmanndeJong (Exhibition Architects), Jan Wilbers (H+N+S Landscape architects), Ester van de Wiel (artist), and Alphons van Winden (ARK Rewilding)

Funded by
UIA World Congress of Architects 2026 Barcelona; World Wildlife Fund Netherlands; Society for the Protection of Birds, Netherlands; Natuurmonumenten (Netherlands Society for Nature Conservation); Wadden Sea Association; Ecowende; Deltares; Royal BosKalis Westminster N.V.; DEME Group; Delta 2120; EFL Foundation; Stimuleringsfonds Creatieve Industrie (Creative Industries Fund); Municipality of Rotterdam; Province of Zeeland; H+N+S Landscape architects; Kossmanndejong exhibition architects; and RO&AD architects.

MANIFESTO FOR SEDIMENTARY FUTURES: PRACTICES OF CARE AND MORE-THAN-HUMAN COEXISTENCE

Authors
Eva Franch i Gilabert (FAST) and TAKK (Mireia Luzárraga and Alejandro Muiño), New York, USA and Barcelona, Spain

Team
Eva Franch i Gilabert, Mireia Luzárraga and Alejandro Muiño

With the support of
Water Parliaments was launched as the 2025 Catalonia in Venice representative, organised and commissioned by the Institut Ramon Llull, as an official event at the 19th Venice Architecture Biennale.

Funded by
UIA World Congress of Architects 2026 Barcelona and Institut Ramon Llull

FLOWS AND PROPORTIONS: RELATIONSHIPS BETWEEN THE DIRECTION OF SPACE AND ITS DEGREE OF CIRCULARITY

Author
H arquitectes, Barcelona, Spain

Team
Roger Tudó Galí, David Lorente Ibáñez, Josep Ricart Ulldemolins and Xavier Ros Majó

With the support of
EGOIN wood group

Funded by
UIA World Congress of Architects 2026 Barcelona

SPOLIA

Authors
BAUKUNST and the Structural Xploration Lab (SXL), Swiss Federal Institute of Technology in Lausanne (EPFL), Brussels, Belgium and Fribourg, Switzerland

Team
Mateo von Arx, Jan Brütting, Olivier Campagne, Maria Agustina Etcheverry, Justine Devergnies, Corentin Fivet, Enrique Goberna, Maxence Grangeot, Elena Hortigüela Páramo, Nataliya Kotova, Célia Küpfer, Xavier Llopis Raja, Simone Marcolin, Andries Merckx, Maryline Misselyn, Vincent Prévost, Florian Thys, Philipp Schmitz and Adrien Verschuere

With the support of
Technical Partner: schlaich bergermann partner (sbp), Sorigué, Wallonie-Bruxelles Architectures (WBA)

Funded by
BitHabitat Foundation, DIBA and Barcelona City Council

LIGHT FEVER

Author
BRUTHER (Stéphanie Bru and Alexandre Theriot), with Studio Theriot ETHZ, Paris, France and Zurich, Switzerland

Team
Development and coordination:
Alice Fenwick and Leslie Majer

Contributors:
Arnaud Bostelmann, Philippe Buchs, Marta Cassany, Blanka Major, Oliviero Vitali, Gustav Ingold, François Beuchot, Reto Lui Jung and Toby Büchel

Student contributors:
Leander Areni, Linda Arnaboldi, Adriana Balagué Reventos, Giacomo Botteon, Xiaohan Chen, Ethan Drodge, Benjamin Frei, Maria Gisler, Lukas Haas, Noah Kaiser, Lukas Kistler, Santiago Madueno, Aris Marsanich, Cecile Mathieu, Sofia Ortelli, Timon Rajmon, Justus Rumpf, Janis Sua, Jonathan Troger, Marie-Lou Vocke, Valentin Wegenstein, Leo Yuan and Analisa Zwahlen

With the support of
ETH Zürich and Karlsruhe Institute of Technology

Funded by
UIA World Congress of Architects 2026 Barcelona

GROUNDED FUTURES

Author
BC architects & studies & materials, Brussels, Belgium

Team
Laurens Bekemans, Antoine Biotteau, Ken De Cooman, Elise Duchêne, Ella Peeters, Henri Uijtterhaegen, students and chair Act of Building at RWTH Aachen

Project partners
Alginate Resource Partner:
CEAMSA, Porriño, Spain

CDW Resource Partners:
Hercal Diggers, Terrassa, Spain

Excavation Resource Partners:
Benjumea, Puigfel, GRC, Barcelona, Spain

Cyanobacteria Resource Partner:
Microalgae lab, Tarragona, Spain

Vibrocompaction Production Partner:
Fetdeterra in Lleida, Spain

Extrusion and Moulding Production Partner and Co-developer:
Piera Ecoceramica, Barcelona, Spain

Knowledge Partner:
UPC, Barcelona, Spain

Videographer:
Alexandre Humbert

Funded by	BitHabitat Foundation, DIBA and Barcelona City Council

PUBLIC PLEASURES:
THE ARCHITECTURES OF CARE AND DESIRE

Authors	MAIO and Care., ETHZ (Ethel Baraona Pohl, Pol Esteve Castelló, Anna Puigjaner), Zurich, Switzerland and Barcelona, Spain
Team	*Research:* Care. and ETH Zürich (Anna Puigjaner, Ethel Baraona Pohl, Pol Esteve Castelló, Laura Bravo and Pau Gelpí Roig) *Design:* MAIO and Pol Esteve Castelló
With the support of	The Chair of Architecture and Care (ETH Zürich) and the Stavros Niarchos Foundation
Funded by	UIA World Congress of Architects 2026 Barcelona

JAGÜEY: WATER COMMONS

Author	Colectivo C733 (Eric Valdez, Israel Espín, Carlos Facio, Gabriela Carrillo and José Amozurrutia), Mexico City, Mexico
Team	*Colectivo C733 team:* Joyce Meneses, Sofía Gaytan, Fred Ardila, Alfredo Reyes, Axayacatl Campos and Maestro Juan Manuel Escobar. *Riparia team:* Giordana Rojas, Laurent Herbiet, Rubén Esparza, Diego Ramírez, Mariel Vega,Maestro Triniberto Garrido and Pedro Alvarado. *Communications team:* Bea Bea and Pablo Cruz
With the support of	The community of Yuguelito, Iztapalapa, Ciudad de Mexico *Interdependance consultants:* Johanna Lozoya, Andrés Cota, Daniel Giménez Cacho, Daniela Rea, Iván Flores, Maya Goded, Verónica Delgado, Jachen Schleich, Carina Arvizu, Enrique Lomnitz, Ximena de Gortari, Cecilia Barraza, Héctor Zamora, Valeria Hamel, Alejandra Chavez, Maleina Gastelum and Juan Manuel Arguelles.
Funded by	UIA World Congress of Architects 2026 Barcelona, Colectivo C733, Riparia, Gerdau Corsa, Geotecnomex, Rotoplás, Ladrillos de México and Huguet Mallorca.

EARTHWORKS

Author	Forensic Architecture (Eyal Weizman, Elizabeth Breiner and Júlia Nueno Guitart)
Team	*Project design and curation:* Eyal Weizman, Elizabeth Breiner and Júlia Nueno Guitart *Project support:* Elpida Giannakou *Forensic Architecture team:* Eyal Weizman, Samaneh Moafi, Robert Trafford, Angela Mehta, Elizabeth Breiner, Omar Ferwati, Nour Abuzaid, Kishan San, Lola Conte, Davide Piscitelli, Stafford Scott, Agata Nguyen Chuong, Nicholas Masterton, Natalia Sliwinska, Elliot Bourne, Lucia Rebolino, Joshua Richards, Madeleine Griffiths, Ray Adams Row Farr, Isabella Parlamis, Júlia Nueno Guitart, Tobechukwu Onwukeme, Ashraf Hamdan, Jack Parker, Thomas Simon Matta and Tobi Ajiwe
Funded by	UIA World Congress of Architects 2026 Barcelona

FROM BUILDING TO POLICY – THE RIGHT TO HOUSING

Author	Brandlhuber+, b+ and HouseEurope!, Berlin, Germany
Team	Severin Bärenbold, Arno Brandlhuber, Ludwig Engel, Olaf Grawert, Jonas Janke, Roberta Jurčić, Anastasiia Kalyta, Alina Kolar, Maximilian Lewark, Jackie Orner, Hannah Rettl, Josiane Schmidt, Rosa Schuster and Alexander Throm
With the support of	CCA – Canadian Centre for Architecture, s+ Chair for Architecture and Storytelling (station.plus, D-ARCH, ETH Zürich) and Studio CNP
Funded by	UIA World Congress of Architects 2026 Barcelona

ENTR'ACTE ATTI'TUDE ATTU'NE

Authors	Architecten Jan de Vylder Inge Vinck with ETHZ D ARCH IEA. CHAIR/ SHARE OF JDV ON ARCHITECTURE AN(D) ATTITUDE, Zurich, Switzerland; and KADUS KUNSTAKADEMIE, DÜSSELDORF. BAUKUNSTKLASSE INGE VINCK, Ghent, Belgium
Team	Jan de Vylder and Inge Vinck. *Assistant:* Justinas Žuklys
With the support of	ETH Zürich and Kunstakademie Düsseldorf
Funded by	UIA World Congress of Architects 2026 Barcelona

NOCTURNAL BEHAVIOUROLOGY:
TRANSITIONING TOWARDS A NOCTURNAL URBANISM AS CLIMATE CHANGE ADAPTATION

Authors	Atelier Bow-Wow (Momoyo Kaijima and Yoshiharu Tsukamoto) and Tsukamoto Lab, Institute of Science Tokyo, Tokyo, Japan
Team	Yoshiharu Tsukamoto, Momoyo Kaijima, Yoichi Tamai, Abir Ezzedine, Tim Hornung and JaeJin Kim
With the support of	Tsukamoto Lab Members
Funded by	UIA World Congress of Architects 2026 Barcelona

EMERGING WORKSHOPS CREDITS

BRAVA!

Author DESIGN EARTH (Rania Ghosn and El Hadi Jazairy), Cambridge, Massachusetts and Ann Arbor, Michigan, USA

Team *Workshop Leaders:*
Rania Ghosn and El Hadi Jazairy

Assistant:
Helena Armengol

Workshop participants:
Gauri Bahuguna, Mario Beltrame, Nafisah Binti Ezam, Margareth Chavez Cutti, Daniel Eslava, Ebru Evin, Ralf Hinrichs, Erdem Karaçay, Luke Shimon Lee, Ilaria Maurelli, Sevin Ozuguz, Jana Sami Ashraf, Álvaro Sánchez González, Aya Sellami and Irene Valdés Martín

Funded by UIA World Congress of Architects 2026 Barcelona

ADDITIONS AND ADAPTATIONS

Author Simulaa (Andre Bonnice and Anna Jankovic), Naarm, Australia

Team *Workshop Leaders:*
Anna Jankovic and Andre Bonnice

Assistant:
Pol Mensa

Workshop participants:
Guillermo Arana, Cornelius Boateng, Albera Bonet Colom, Sima Bucar Fiskin, Cheuk Tung Chan, Silje Ekornrud Seim, Mehmet Derin Incekas, Janka Kalmár, David Raül Lillo Abad, Zhi Xing Lim, Kliment Maikov, Belen Perdiguer, Belinda Rodríguez Weiss, Mariya Romanosova and Wanfeng Si

Funded by UIA World Congress of Architects 2026 Barcelona

MAKING KNOTS, WEAVING SHED

Author HOLES (Mio Tsuneyama and Fuminori Nousaku), Tokyo, Japan

Team *Workshop Leaders:*
Mio Tsuneyama and Fuminori Nousaku

Assistant:
Cristina Vilaró

Workshop participants:
Andreas Borgers, Baptiste Dintilhac, Rim El Mechti, Florencia Galecio, Talin Kış, Ivan Le Hir, Margaux Lomax, Giacomo Oldfield, Inès Penneron, Gabriela Pérez Viñoly, Oliver Ray-Chaudhuri, Dali Salamova, Clément Taulelle and Sebastian Vella

Funded by UIA World Congress of Architects 2026 Barcelona

THE COOLEST SUMMER OF THE REST OF OUR LIVES

Author Nicolas Dorval-Bory Architectes (Nicolas Dorval-Bory and Hugo Taillardat), Paris, France

Team *Workshop Leaders:*
Nicolas Dorval-Bory and Hugo Taillardat

Assistant:
Araitz Villalba

Workshop participants:
Utsav Adhikari, Enrico Berta, Stav Bouzaglo, Gina Dahl, Axel Decat, Eva Erny, Philippe Finn Fleischmann, Ela Grasselli, Yung Jian Hwang, Mariami Kurtishvili, Corinne Leclerc, Anna Levedag, Mariana López Ulloa, Giovanni Stoppoloni and Barbora Svobodová

Funded by UIA World Congress of Architects 2026 Barcelona

TRY AGAIN. FAIL AGAIN. FAIL BETTER

Author TEN, Zurich, Switzerland and Belgrade, Serbia

Team *Workshop Leaders:*
Nemanja Zimnojic, Ognjen Krasna, Lukas Burkhart and Scott Lloyd

Assistant:
Meritxell Compte

Workshop participants:
Valentina Aguilar, Lenart Berdon, Fiorella Vanessa Calderon Martinez, Santiago Castillo Reina, Ioanna Karampetsou, David Kirchmann, Carla López Arnau, Gia Cat Luong, Luke McDonell, Guillem Prior Carregui, Javier Rubio, Bara Shatnawi, Ruilong Wang, Güneş Yazar and Ahmad Zeidan

Funded by UIA World Congress of Architects 2026 Barcelona

ONE, TWO, THREE, MORE, MANY TABLES

Author Nuno Melo Sousa, Penafiel, Portugal

Team *Workshop Leader:*
Nuno Melo Sousa

Assistant:
Bárbara Fonseca

Workshop participants:
Sebastián Arancibia Caballero, Valerie Bach, Rareş David, Marios Gerontas, Benjamín Grove González, Riku Hara, Maria Malecka, Juan Manuel Pachué, Lucía Prieto Heras, Arthur Priso Malolo, Andres Quiroz, Maite Santos Alcocer, Silvia Sierra Maestro, Olímpia Solà Inaraja and Agnieszka Wiecha

Funded by UIA World Congress of Architects 2026 Barcelona

A HOME FOR US

Author Plan Común (Kim Courréges, Felipe De Ferrari, Nissim Haguenauer and Marcelo Cox), Paris, France and Santiago, Chile

Team *Workshop Leaders:*
Felipe De Ferrari and Kim Courréges.

Team members:
Kim Courrèges, Nissim Haguenauer and Marcelo Cox

Assistant:
Elena Roig

Workshop participants:
Aristodimos Antimissaris Castro, Carlos David Arcos Jácome, Malak Atwi, Chaemi Bang, Andrea Cascaval, Martín Diez Dojorti, Julia García Sanjuán, Lara Grefer, Daphne Mesochoriti, Nathan Oriou, Marianthi Papageorgiou, Lukas Raabe, Emma Saavedra Sarget, Kiara Valeria Sandoval Montalvo and Eloy Tenza

Funded by UIA World Congress of Architects 2026 Barcelona

MERCHANTS & WARRIORS

Author Assemble (James Binning) and Common Treasures (Camille Sineau), London, UK

Team	*Workshop Leaders:* James Binning, Camille Sineau, Emily Mason and Antoine Plouzen Morvan *Audiovisual production:* Antoine Plouzen Morvan *Assistant:* Xavier Ruiz Safont *Workshop participants:* Hanon Emmanuel Beugré, Nippit Cheybumroong, Talya Derya, Antar Ghazoul, Ana Gilmet, Ignacio González Rebaque, Angelica Lindoso Piedra, Frida Lomholt, Agata Mrozowski, Madita Müller, Murtaza Mustafa, Milena Rakocevic, Robin Ringel, Helene Stüben and Mee-Linn Swartz
Funded by	UIA World Congress of Architects 2026 Barcelona

REVISED CARTOGRAPHIES

Author	Ibiye Camp, London, UK
Team	*Workshop Leaders:* Ibiye Camp, Sofia Yanez Perteagudo and Lauren-Loïs Duah *Assistant:* María Campos *Workshop participants:* Danielle Marie Caballero, Sara Cruz Francos. Dieudonné Elohym da Costa, Bastián Arnaldo Gabriel Espinoza Pino, Camilo Garcia, Luis Enrique García Guevara, Inam Kula, Verónica Lee, Maria Pia Milesi, Mercy Moturi, Meral Nabulsi, Sandra Revuelta Albero, Henry Ronoh, Gretta Valeria Toala Moreira and Brianna Westbrook
Funded by	UIA World Congress of Architects 2026 Barcelona

PARADE!

Author	Common Accounts (Igor Bragado and Miles Gertler), Madrid, Spain and Toronto, Canada
Team	*Workshop Leaders:* Igor Bragado and Miles Gertler *Assistant:* Clara Alsedà *Workshop participants:* Artur Akhunov, Gabriela Amstalden Martins, Guillermo Basso, William Bennie, Marta Finotti, Helena Keh, Martina Lopez, Natalia Lvova, Petr Malásek, Rosalía Martínez Pérez, Lemmy Nuijens Fontanals, Mariona Pons Bartrolí, Georgia Rumble, Georgy Salko and Ewa Tokarska
With the support of	The University of Toronto John H. Daniels Faculty of Architecture, Landscape, and Design, 2025 Associate Dean Research Discretionary Fund
Funded by	UIA World Congress of Architects 2026 Barcelona

COLLECTIVE COMPLETIONS

Author	Bangkok Tokyo Architecture (Wtanya Chanvitan and Takahiro Kume), Bangkok, Thailand and Tokyo, Japan
Team	*Workshop Leaders:* Wtanya Chanvitan and Takahiro Kume *Assistant:* Jep Sayós *Workshop participants:* Anastasia Bastrygina, María Bazaco González, Chaima Belhassen, Maria Luciana Franchetti, Florian Fuchs, Pau Garrofé Montoliu, Leonardo Grohmann, Mai Jaureguizar Furukubo, Lelissa Erkissa Kasim, Paula Navarro Pinin, Wai Kwan Ng, Gonçalo Queirós, Andrea Raos, Miya Richir and Chuanjie Yan
Funded by	UIA World Congress of Architects 2026 Barcelona

ELEMENTS OF DISSIDENCE:
NEW POETICS OF RESISTANCE

Author	BeAr (Iñigo Berasategui and Ane Arce), Bilbao, Spain
Team	*Workshop Leaders:* Iñigo Berasategui and Ane Arce *Assistant:* Julia Dubois *Workshop participants:* Zain Abuolaim, Mafalda Albano, Oriol Aparicio, Cristobal Araujo, Sinai Alejandra Blanco Pérez, Lucia Castellanos Cervantes, Federico Forner, Michael Lagos, Edouard Michel, Aratz Mora, Nicola Reeves, Marlon Brando Rueda, Valeria Torres, Ismael Villar Trujillo and Ryohei Mikami
Funded by	UIA World Congress of Architects 2026 Barcelona

The UIA World Congress of Architects 2026 Barcelona

A SITUATED EVENT

With its epicentre at the Tres Xemeneies (Three Chimneys) abandoned turbine hall, the UIA World Congress of Architects 2026 Barcelona takes place along the city's peripheral seafront, a territory marked by conflicting and evolving rhythms grounded in social and ecological pasts. The Congress – its discussions and investigations – engages with these physical and cultural traits, rather than adopting the site as merely a distant backdrop. Home to more than three million inhabitants, the metropolitan region of Barcelona condenses many of the tensions addressed in this book: housing emergency, biodiversity loss, resource scarcity, welfare decline, colonial wounds, mass tourism and mobility stress. These localised imbalances echo global concerns experienced from within, where local actions reverberate across planetary networks.

Barcelona therefore becomes an open laboratory, embedded in a specific site: an opportunity to situate, test, discuss and exhibit the themes of Becoming. Beyond engaging the city as an idealised model to be replicated, this approach aims to critically learn from it, inhabiting its goods and evils. It avoids the illusion of a clean, predictable laboratory, rather connecting with an array of earthy, broken yet hopeful situations. Its layered histories – from agricultural landscapes to industrial expansion, from Olympic transformation to post-industrial transition – coexist with uncertain futures shaped by climate change, demographic shifts and geopolitical realities. The programme of talks, open-air celebrations, exhibitions and investigations is grounded in the multiplicity of this vivid, Mediterranean laboratory, from which new ways of imagining and making architecture may depart.

The programme as friction

Over three days, diverse sessions bring together renowned architects, researchers and influential figures from various disciplines. Hundreds of speakers participate in parallel across eight adjacent stages at the International Barcelona Convention Centre (CCIB) – much like a music festival where visitors can design their own trajectories by moving between them. Each half-day focuses on one thematic line, with the six Becomings unfolding across a three-day structure that establishes a shifting conceptual framework through which different positions are articulated and confronted.

The programme places a primary focus on dialogue and exchange as a vehicle for discovering new meanings and potentials. In this sense, the Congress is designed to offer productive frictions and shared narratives framed by a collective awareness of Becoming. In most cases, architects do not present alone, but are brought together in small groups of three or four, offering overlapping talks and discussions. The sessions are always introduced and guided by local moderators, ensuring that conversations remain situated within the broader framework.

Similarly, the six plenary sessions, one for each Becoming, avoid centring on a singular or 'star' figure, which often over-represents a single perspective. Instead, they are composed of a cohort of six guests in a shared dialogue, representing different generations, forms of practice and theoretical positions, whose Research by Design essays are featured in this book. Above individual voices, this structure is designed to signify a plurality of meanings and findings, embodying a diversity of architectural prospects.

The Tres Xemeneies (Three Chimneys) site on the Barcelona seafront.

The Three Chimneys: A transitional site

Within the territorial continuum of the city's seafront, the former thermal power station of Sant Adrià de Besòs – the Three Chimneys – emerges as the representative site of the Congress. Once part of a controversial energy infrastructure built in the 1970s, it stands today as one of the most charged post-industrial sites in the metropolitan area. Originally conceived to respond to growing energy demands, the plant quickly became a focal point for environmental concerns and urban conflict; tensions that resonate with the questions the Congress aims to address.

Interior of the turbine hall where the central exhibition takes place.

Decommissioned in 2011 and partially reactivated in 2024 for the Manifesta 15 temporary art installation, the structure remains suspended between past and future. Manifesta's minimal interventions opened the turbine hall to public use while preserving its monumental and raw condition, establishing the basis for its future transformation. The building therefore hosts the Congress in a transitional state: rather than a 'finished' venue, it is conceived as a space in motion, open to occupation, improvisation and celebration. The turbine hall houses the central exhibition and the Emerging Workshops, while the vast outdoor yard congregates institutional celebrations and open-air discussions.

The exhibition as material practice

The investigations presented in this book take spatial form through the central exhibition of the Congress. At its centre, twelve Research by Design teams present year-long inquiries through models, prototypes, audiovisual pieces and full-scale installations that expose architecture as a form of situated research. It also incorporates the outputs of the international Emerging Workshops (in which more than 180 young architects and students participated) and a selection of projects from the UIA student competition.

The exhibition is conceived as a dialogue between process and realisation – speculation and built work – bringing these forward-looking installations into contrast with completed projects that point towards emerging architectural trajectories. While the centre of the space is occupied by mock-ups and prototypes, it is surrounded by a parallel narrative in the form of a visual archive of built projects and published work by the speakers of each Becoming. These architectures emerge through a site-specific constellation of wall-mounted photography and original documents.

An open field for assembly

A system of lightweight structures reconfigures the Three Chimneys site into a space of collective use and performance. This ensemble of elements operates as an adaptable and reversible framework: an array of platforms, seating devices and service infrastructures assembled through standardised components, rented for a few days prior to its disassembly and return, following zero-waste principles. Suspended industrial textile enclosures modulate the light and atmosphere, defining temporary spaces while mediating with climatic conditions.

Attached to the turbine hall seafront façade, a grandstand structure acts simultaneously as seating, a connective device and an evacuation route, linking the ground level with the interior top level, and accommodating up to 1,500 people. Around it, dispersed elements – screens, sound systems, shades and service modules – support multiple forms of use, from presentations to informal gatherings. Within this spatial system, an informal exchange occurs every evening after the all-day parallel sessions. In this Open Forum, all the speakers

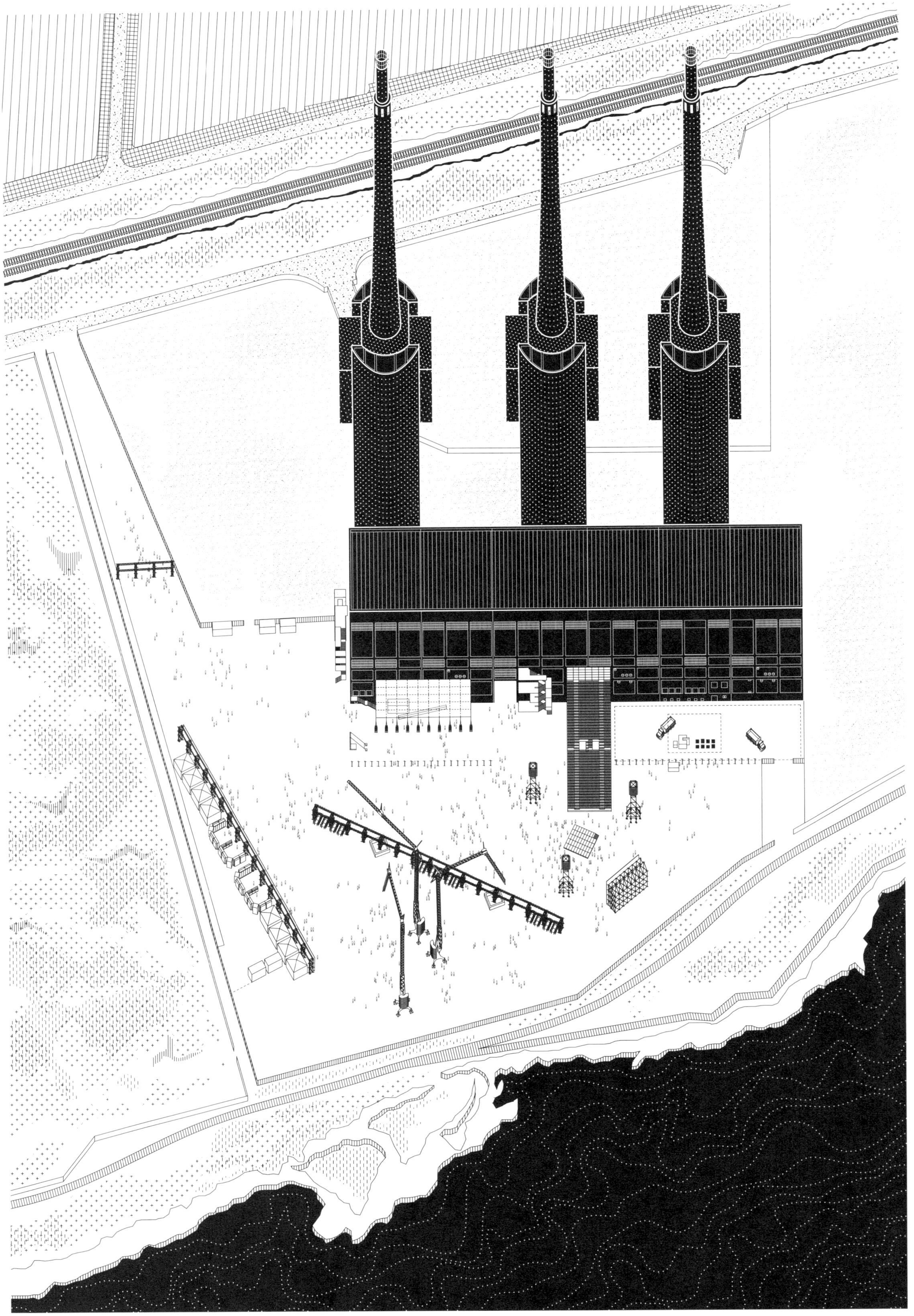

A reversible system of lightweight structures transforms the Three Chimneys site into an open field for assembly, exchange and collective use during the Congress days.

of the day come together in a shared arena where discussions continue and the boundaries between speakers and audience dissolve.

In sum, site, programme and exhibition operate together as an interrelated framework through which the investigations gathered in this book are spatially enacted and collectively engaged. It moves beyond disseminating architecture in predictable congress formats to provide conditions for more direct and deeper modes of awareness: it allows knowledge (and tacit knowledge) to emerge through the experience of shared encounters, productive frictions and material embodiment. In this sense, the Congress becomes a situated interval within an ongoing process: a collective rehearsal for inhabiting and activating transitions towards planetary betterment.

THREE-DAY SESSIONS

Monday 29 June

Stage 1

09:00 – 10:30
Plenary Session Becoming More-than-human

Mark Wigley, Bas Smets, Dirk Sijmons (KK+N+S), Eva Franch i Gilabert + TAKK, DESIGN EARTH, Simulaa
Moderated by Tomeu Ramis and Mariona Benedito

10:45 – 12:00
Radical Ecologies: Architecture as Political Engagement

Petra Blaisse, Andrés Jaque
Moderated by Albena Yaneva

12:15 – 13:30
Amid Landscape, Matter and Atmosphere

Junya Ishigami
Moderated by Guillermo Santomà

13:45 – 14:50
Economies of Means: Architecture between Efficiency and Generosity

Lacaton Vassal, H arquitectes
Moderated by Albert Ferré

15:05 – 16:30
The Politics of Reuse: Housing, Policy and Urban Strategy

Charlotte M. Barthes, HouseEurope!, Iñaqui Carnicero, Ann Pettifor
Moderated by Ana Méndez de Andés

16:45 – 18:15
Plenary Session Becoming Circular

BAUKUNST + SXL, H arquitectes, Nicolas Dorval-Bory, HOLES, Matthias Schuler, Sana Frini
Moderated by Carmen Torres and Pau Sarquella

Stage 2

10:45 – 12:15
Post Extractivism Urbanism

Chris Kennedy-Urban Systems lab, Paola Viganò, 51N4E
Moderated by Marc Montlleó

12:30 – 13:30
Territorial Frameworks: Landscape, Infrastructure and Time

Michel Desvinge
Moderated by Joan Busquets

13:45 – 14:50
From Salvage to Systems: Infrastructures of Reuse

Rotor, Zirkular
Moderated by Martí Riera (Socotec)

15:05 – 16:30
Structures in Transition: From Demolition to Reassembly

BAUKUNST, Søren Pihlmann, PARABASE
Moderated by Maria Rius Ruiz

Stage 3

10:45 – 12:15
Architecture in Multispecies Landscapes

Elii, Lydia Kallipoliti, Institute for Postnatural Studies
Moderated by Antonio Bernacchi (Animali Domestici)

12:30 – 13:30
Invisible Ecologies: Architecture in the Age of Microbial Life

Beatriz Colomina
Moderated by Ivan Lopez Munuera

13:45 – 15:00
Collage as Construction: Reuse as Design Intelligence

Jo Taillieu, Flores & Prats
Moderated by Alejandro Martínez del Río (Bona fide atelier)

15:15 – 16:30
Interventions in the Everyday

BURR Studio, SO? Architecture and Ideas
Moderated by Clàudia Raurell

Stage 4

10:45 – 12:15
Architecture, Territory and Practices of Care

Al Borde, Boonserm Premthada, Gustavo Utrabo
Moderated by Ferran Grau

12:30 – 13:30
Atmospheric Territories: Reclaiming Climate through Design

Bas Smets
Moderated by Hans Ibelings

13:45 – 15:00
Post-Extractivist Territories: Justice, Waste and Urban Cycles

Lara Almarcegui, Imani Jacq. Brown
Moderated by Manuel Bouzas

15:15 – 16:30
Reclaiming Local Cycles: Material, Structure and Climate

Carles Oliver, Solano Benitez
Moderated by Toni Gironés

Programme as of 30 April 2026

Stage 5

10:45 – 12:10
Rivers as Commons

Taller Capital, Turenscape, Margarita Jover
Moderated by Carme Ribas

12:25 – 13:30
Ecologies in Process: Between Land and Water

Kate Orff, Dirk Sijmons
Moderated by Miriam García (LandLab)

13:45 – 14:50
The Renewal of Building Materials

Amateur Architecture Studio
Moderated by Arturo Franco

15:05 – 16:30
Earthly Cycles: Bio-based Materials and Territorial Networks

Anupama Kundoo, Worofila, Natura Futura
Moderated by Laura Reus (Societat Orgànica)

Stage 6

10:45 – 12:00
Soil as Living Matter

Charles Waldheim, Catherine Mosbach
Moderated by Beatriz Borque

12:25 – 13:30
Designing with Climate and Energy

Philippe Rahm, TAKK
Moderated by Pablo Ibáñez Ferrera (Bartlebooth)

13:45 – 15:10
Thermodynamic Architectures: Energetic Circularity and Environmental Design

Javier García-Germán, Transsolar, Atmoslab
Moderated by Ferran Vizoso

15:25 – 16:30
Building Thought, Thinking Building

Barbara Buser, Curro Claret
Moderated by Bet Capdeferro (Bosch Capdeferro)

Stage 7

10:45 – 12:00
Green Corridors as Living Infrastructure

OESST + MARBORIS, Openact architecture, TAV, Carlos Zeballos-Velarde
Moderated by Maria Fandiño

12:15 – 13:30
Water as Common Infrastructure

A Gang of Three, Arsomsilp Community and Environmental Architects + Turenscape, Carles Enrich + Adriana Campmany, Milena Villalba
Moderated by Elena Albareda

13:45 – 14:45
Practices of Care: Cycles of Inhabitation

Anne Gross + Luna Bucherer, Adrià Goula, Caroline Stokholm + Jenny Amdi Sørensen
Moderated by Josep Garriga

14:55 – 15:40
Groundwork: Soil Ecologies in Urban Transformation

Edgar Mazo, Beatriz Borque + Jorge Vidal
Moderated by Rocio Pina Isla

15:45 – 16:30
Urbanisms of Reuse: Mapping Material Flows

Tosin Oshinowo, Daniel Torrego
Moderated by Rocio Pina Isla (Enorme Studio)

Stage 8

10:45 – 12:00
Architectures of Co-evolution

Manuela Valtchanova, A. Frediani + L. Barham, Sophie Falkeis
Moderated by Enric Pol

12:15 – 13:30
Ecologies of Food Production

Courage Kpodo, Office for Roundtable + JXY Studio, Sebastián Carvajal, FAST
Moderated by Cristina Goberna

13:45 – 15:00
Housing Futures and the Right to Remain

Docar Films, Rocio Calzado, Pere Joan Ravetllat + Rearq- UPC
Moderated by Ana Herreros (Solar xyz)

15:15 – 16:30
Rewriting Territorial Metabolisms

Kathy Velikov + Geoffrey Thün, Fernanda Córdova + Rolando Biere, Joan Maria Martí Elias
Moderated by Manuel Julià (JAAS)

Tuesday 30 June

Stage 1	Stage 2	Stage 3	Stage 4
9:00 – 10:30 **Plenary Session Becoming Embodied** BC architects & studies & materials, BRUTHER, TEN, Nuno Melo Sousa, Marina Tabassum, Philip Ursprung *Moderated by Pau Bajet and Maria Giramé*			
10:45 – 11:50 **Locally Grounded: Material, Climate and Community** Marina Tabassum, Palinda Kannangara *Moderated by Marta Thorne*	10:45 – 12:10 **Experimental Tectonics: Embodied Techniques for Everyday Spaces** Adamo Faiden, Arrov Frick, Josep Ferrando *Moderated by Ariadna Perich (Perich Such)*	10:45 – 11:50 **Relational Architecture: Proportion, Enclosure Openness** Go Hasegawa, Arquitectura G *Moderated by José Zabala (GHZ)*	10:45 – 12:10 **Earth Futures: From Craft Traditions to Technological Innovations** BC architects & studies & materials, Hive Earth, Lehm Ton Erde *Moderated by Sara Ferran (Taller 11)*
12:05 – 13:30 **Material as Time: Structure, Economy and Emergency Architecture** Shigeru Ban *Moderated by Jordi Badia (BAAS)*	12:25 – 13:30 **Technological Vernacular: Paradoxical Hybrids of Expression** BRUTHER *Moderated by Jorge Vidal*	12:05 – 13:30 **Situated Structures: on Topography, Gravity, Matter and Form** Manthey Kula, gru.a, Max Núñez *Moderated by Alberto Sánchez (Feina)*	12:25 – 13:30 **Rediscovering Stone: Ecological Continuities and Tectonic Invention** Roger Boltshauser, AAU Anastas *Moderated by Claudi Aguiló (Data AE)*
13:45 – 15:10 **Spatial Politics, Memory, and Resistance** Samia Henni, Malkit Shoshan, Estudio Teddy Cruz + Fonna Forman *Moderated by Ramon Faura*	13:45 – 14:50 **Domestic Space as Social Project: Architectural Strategies for Shared Living** Peris + Toral Arquitectes, Elli Mosayebi_EMI Architekt*innen *Moderated by Alvaro Martín Fidalgo (Oazeta Fidalgo)*	13:45 – 14:50 **Care and Systemic Transformation** Yasmeen Lari, Anna Puigjaner – MAIO *Moderated by Atxu Amman (temperaturasextremas)*	13:45 – 15:00 **Reframing Urban Infrastructures, Care, Gender and Inequality** Colectivo C733, Roman Meyer Falcón *Moderated by Zaida Muxí*
15:25 – 16:30 **A Common Good Approach to the Economy (Implications for Housing and the Built Environment)** Mariana Mazzucato *Moderated by Javier Burón*	15:05 – 16:30 **Beyond the Household: Collective Futures of Housing** Lacol, Clauss Kahl Merz Atelier *Moderated by Xavier Bustos*	15:05 – 16:30 **Housing as Commoning: Administration and Innovation in Sustainable Living** Josep M. Borrell, Silvia Hofer, Andreas Hofer *Moderated by Pablo García Astrain*	15:15 – 16:30 **Housing, Care and the Right to the City: Towards an Ethics of Urban Co-existence** Raquel Rolnik, Elizabeth Añaños *Moderated by Josep Bohigas*
16:45 – 18:15 **Plenary Session Becoming Interdependent** MAIO + Care., Colectivo C733, Assemble + Common Treasures, Plan Común, Giovanna Borasi, Juan Herreros *Moderated by Mariona Benedito and Tomeu Ramis*			

Stage 5

10:45 – 11:50
Architectural Acupuncture: Enhancing Rural Territories

Xu Tiantian
Moderated by Fuensanta Nieto

12:05 – 13:30
Wood Metabolisms: Ecologies of Timber Technology

Tomoaki Uno, Unai Gorroño, Enric Vadell Guiral
Moderated by David Tapias (Aixopluc)

13:45 – 15:00
Architectures of Resilience: Communities Between Rural and Urban Frontiers

Rural Urban Framework, Rahul Mehrotra
Moderated by Alejandro Echeverri

15:15 – 16:30
Urban Design and the Architecture of Coexistence

Jan Gehl
Moderated by Itziar Gonzalez

Stage 6

10:45 – 11:50
Architecture as Structure: From Gravity to Matter, Form and Space

Jun Sato, Mario Monotti
Moderated by Alonso Atienza (Atienza Maure)

12:05 – 13:30
Support and Performance: Temporalities, Radical Collectives and Political Infrastructures of Living

Langarita Navarro, ZAV Architects, BeL
Moderated by Begoña de Abajo (de Abajo Garcia)

13:45 – 14:50
Reproductive Labor and the Politics of the Commons

Silvia Federici
Moderated by Ana Méndez de Andés

15:05 – 16:30
Practices of Engagement: Experimental Architectures for Collective Spaces

Raumlabor, Teco Studio
Moderated by Ethel Baraona

Stage 7

10:45 – 12:10
Structural Infrastructures in Productive Landscapes

Máximo Bertoia, AGENdA, Atelier Ars, Estudio ALA
Moderated by Eduardo Mediero (Hanghar)

12:25 – 13:30
Reconstructing Memory: Ruins, Interiors and the Politics of Preservation

Salima Naji, Elias Khuri, Buket Ergun
Moderated by Benji Iborra (Mesura)

13:45 – 15:00
Architecture as a Practice of Interdependence

Cristiane Muniz + Fernando Viegas, Estudio MMX, Vivas Arquitectos, Chacarita Moderna
Moderated by Lucia Millet (Cierto Estudio)

15:15 – 16:30
Territorial Politics

Chiara Oggioni + Yi Sun, Víctor Cano-Ciborro, Ilaria Iacconi Iambrenghi, Aga Kuś
Moderated by Cesar Reyes Nájera

Stage 8

10:45 – 11:40
Material Frameworks: Structure as Environmental Mediator

P + S Estudio de Arquitectura, CINARK - Center for Industrialised Architecture, PERCEIVE
Moderated by David Mayol

10:50 – 12:30
Timber Infrastructures: Industrial Scaling and Robotic Reuse

Mass Madera IAAC, Yalei Zhu + Tianyi Gao
Moderated by Edouard Cabay

12:35 – 13:30
Earthen Processes: From Material Culture to Computational Performance

Tina Gregoric, Juana Colombo, Younes Ben Slimane
Moderated by Edouard Cabay

13:45 – 15:00
Unfinished Territories: Reassembling Interdependence

María Isabel Paz Suaréz, Kathrin Golda-Pongratz, Solam Mkhabela, Isabella De Bonis
Moderated by Patricia Reus

15:15 – 16:30
Everyday Practices of Interdependence

CO53, Rojita Sharma + Sadichchha Shrestha, Huinan Zhang
Moderated by Eva Serrats

Wednesday 1 July

Stage 1

9:00 – 10:30
Plenary Session
Becoming Hyper-conscious

Brandlhuber, b+ and HouseEurope!, Forensic Architecture, Ibiye Camp, Common Accounts, Timothy Morton, Marina Otero Verzier
Moderated by Maria Giramé and Pau Bajet

10:45 – 12:10
Unveiled Ecologies: From Data to Spatial Awareness

Limbo Accra, shaā /SOC, 300.000km/s
Moderated by Roger Paez

12:25 – 13:30
Politics, Ecologies and Technologies of Spatial Practice

Marina Otero Verzier, Paulo Tavares
Moderated by Olga Subirós

13:45 – 15:00
Fragile Architectures: Radić and Walker in Dialogue

Smiljan Radić, Enrique Walker
Moderated by Moisés Puente

15:15 – 16:30
Radical Imaginaries: Brodsky and Ursprung in Dialogue

Alexander Brodsky, Philip Ursprung
Moderated by Ricardo Devesa

16:45 – 18:15
Plenary Session
Becoming Attuned

Architecten Jan de Vylder Inge Vinck, Atelier Bow-Wow, Bangkok Tokyo Architecture, BeAr, Matilde Cassani, Enrique Walker
Moderated by Pau Sarquella and Carmen Torres

Stage 2

10:45 – 11:35
From Algorithms to Artificial Intelligence: Histories of Digital Reason

Mario Carpo
Moderated by Lluís Nacenta

11:50 –12:35
Architectures of Intelligence: Systems, Media and Design Agency

Areti Markopoulou, Lluís Ortega
Moderated by Lluís Nacenta

12:40 – 13:30
Digital Intelligence: Carpo, Markopoulou and Ortega in Dialogue

Mario Carpo, Areti Markopoulou, Lluís Ortega
Moderated by Lluís Nacenta

13:45 – 15:10
In Sequence: Rooms, Rules, Transformations

MOS, OFFICE Kersten Geers David Van Severen, Pezo von Ellrichshausen
Moderated by Pedro Pitarch

15:25 – 16:30
Vernacular Frictions: Between Ancestral Knowledge and Contemporary Experiment

Ted'A, Leopold Banchini
Moderated by Ophélie Herranz (Nomos Arquitectura)

Stage 3

10:45 – 12:00
Regulation and Form: Designing within Systems

Hiroyuki Ito, XDGA
Moderated by Andy Peñuela (MHAP)

12:15 – 13:30
Law as a Design Tool: Spatial Potential and Architectural Policies

Arno Brandlhuber
Moderated by Ivan Blasi

13:45 – 14:50
Add Away, Take On

Architecten Jan de Vylder Inge Vinck
Moderated by Carles Muro

15:05 – 16:30
Slightly Tilted: Displacement, Irony and Narrative

Un Parell d'Arquitectes, Kosmos, Infraestudio
Moderated by Omar Ornaque (AMOO)

Stage 4

10:45 – 12:10
Entangled Landscapes: Culture, Food and Climate Ecologies

Cooking Sections, Lluís Alexandre, Afreetekture
Moderated by Laida Memba

12:25 – 13:30
Investigating Mass Violence: Architecture as Evidence

Forensic Architecture, Center for Spatial Technologies
Moderated by Judit Carrera

13:45 – 14:50
Tokyo Metabolising

Atelier Bow-Wow
Moderated by Javi Jiménez Iniesta (Studio Animal)

15:05 – 16:30
Ordinary Evidence: Imaging Territories

Maxime Delvaux, Takashi Homma
Moderated by Urtzi Grau (Fake Industries)

Stage 5

10:45 – 12:00

Image, Representation, Media: Architecture After the Screen

Lev Manovich, Javier Fernández Contreras, John May
Moderated by Laura Bonell (Bonell Doriga)

12:15 – 13:30

Editorial Infrastructures: Magazines, Politics and Cultural Agency

Real Review, *PLOT*, Quaderns d'Arquitectura i Urbanisme, Accattone
Moderated by Guillermo López (MAIO)

13:45 – 15:10

Ritual and the Choreography of Space

Matilde Cassani, Tatiana Bilbao, Bêka & Lemoine
Moderated by Amadeu Santacana

15:25 – 16:30

Entangled Belongings and Postcolonial Imaginaries

AD - WO, New South
Moderated by Elvira Dyangani Ose

Stage 6

10:45 – 11:50

Architectural Labour: Precarity, Fees and the Political Economy of Practice

The Architecture Lobby, Ruth Schagemann
Moderated by Albert Nogueras

12:05 – 13:30

Futures of Architectural Pedagogy: Knowledge, Practice and Emerging Contexts

S. Delhay (EPFL), Xiangning Li (Tongji University), C. Benimana (MASS Design Group + African Design Centre), A. Freear (Rural Studio)
Moderated by Eulàlia Gómez (ETSAB)

13:45 – 15:10

Working Within the Generic

Yanfei Architects, Éric Lapierre, Jean Jacques Balzac
Moderated by Anna Bach (Anna & Eugeni Bach)

15:25 – 16:30

Composed Quotations: Ornament as a Collage

Point Supreme, Fala Atelier
Moderated by Adrià Escolano (OESST)

Stage 7

10:45 – 12:00

Territories of Violence: Memory, Infrastructure and Spatial Justice

Ana Laura Bertero, Nadia Habash, Damien Greder + Javier Fernández Contreras, Yevheniia Berchul + Nabi Agzamov
Moderated by Marina Povedano

12:15 – 13:30

Architectures of Information: Systems, Visibility and Digital Territory

M. del Campo + S. Manninger, V. Ma + L. Cheng, A. Andueza + A. Ribot, A. Atollo + P. Swagerman
Moderated by Nil Brullet (Brullet de Luna)

13:30 – 14:45

Practices of Attention

Anne Gross, Luca Quagliato + Guglielmo Trupia, Aleksandra Redzisz, Simone Marcolin
Moderated by Irena Visa

15:00 – 16:00

Economy of Means

Atienza Maure, Connor Gravelle, Hanoi Ad hoc
Moderated by Andrea Arriola (Aramé Studio)

Stage 8

10:45 – 12:00

Extractive Territories: Material Geopolitics and Ecologies of Resistance

Marcos Zegers, Blanca Pujals, Constanza Ipinza + Ayami Nakamura, Elspeth Mary Lee + Donn Holohan
Moderated by Romea Muryn (The Locument)

12:15 – 13:30

Planetary Archives: Memory, Deep Time and Ecological Imagination

Valentina Labriola, José María Torres Nadal, Michel Kessler + David Oesch
Moderated by Miquel Ruiz (h3o)

13:45 – 15:10

Unremarked Landscapes

Francisco Felipe Muñoz + Sete Álvarez Barrena, Jose Lorenzo Belandres, Ella Fleri Soler + Andrew Darmanin, Nipun Prabhakar
Moderated by Natalia Vera (O-SH Studio)

15:25 – 16:30

Delight and Choreography

Poetics of Belonging, Pol Esteve Castelló, Natalia Figueredo + Victoria McKenzie
Moderated by Nacho Martin

CATALYSTS OF RESILIENCE: UIA INTERNATIONAL STUDENT COMPETITION

Under the title 'Catalysts of Resilience', the UIA International Student Competition invited architecture students worldwide to design spatial interventions capable of strengthening the resilience of vulnerable environments. Participants were asked to identify territories exposed to future habitability challenges – whether ecological, social or political – and to propose architectural strategies able to anticipate and transform these conditions over time. Central to the brief was the understanding of time as a design tool, encouraging proposals that unfold through phased transformations rather than fixed solutions.

The competition received 587 submissions from students across the five UIA regions, revealing a remarkable diversity of sites and design approaches. Projects engaged contexts ranging from coastal and deltaic territories threatened by climate change to rural landscapes affected by abandonment, metropolitan edges undergoing fragmentation, and dense urban fabrics facing environmental and social pressures.

The international jury – composed of Tatiana Bilbao, Josep Ferrando (Chair), Marianna Rentzou (Point Supreme), Sumayya Vally (Counterspace),and Wtanya Chanvitan (Bangkok Tokyo Architecture) – highlighted the strong coherence between the competition theme and the conceptual framework of Becoming. The jury particularly valued proposals that approached fragile territories not through scenarios of collapse, but through the identification of latent ecological, spatial and social potentials capable of activating processes of resilience and long-term adaptation.

Across the awarded projects, several shared strategies emerged. Many proposals worked through landscape-based interventions, foregrounding ecological systems as active agents in spatial transformation. These included the restoration of coastal wetlands through reversible infrastructures, the reconnection of fragmented agricultural territories through green corridors, and the reactivation of terraced landscapes through agro-cultural practices linking ecological repair with local economies.

Other projects addressed extreme environmental conditions, such as deltaic islands affected by erosion or alpine territories threatened by soil instability. In these cases, architecture operated as a mediator between human and more-than-human processes: floating agricultural systems adapting to fluctuating water levels, lightweight timber structures supporting ecological regeneration, or landscape devices designed to evolve gradually through sedimentation, reforestation and ecological succession.

In dense urban contexts, several proposals explored incremental and adaptable spatial frameworks capable of responding to housing pressures, social fragmentation and environmental degradation. Rather than advocating large-scale demolition, these strategies introduced catalytic elements – modular infrastructures, shared urban systems or adaptive spatial layers – designed to enable gradual transformation while working with existing urban fabrics.

Through these approaches, the competition demonstrated how architectural thinking can operate across multiple temporal and territorial scales, linking immediate interventions with long-term ecological and social processes. The selected proposals illustrate how design – when attentive to context, time and collective practices – can act as a catalyst for resilient futures on a planet in transition.

PRIZES

First Prize
Harvey Rupp
(University of Western Australia, Australia)

Second Prize
Hikmet Eda Akbas and Sevval Bayir
(RWTH Aachen University, Germany)

Third Prize
Manuel Alexander Fustamante Mori
(University of the Basque Country, Spain)

Fourth Prize
Sarah Levihn, with Cheng Yu Han and Levin Suresh
(Tsinghua University, China)

Fifth Prize
Armin Maierhofer
(Royal College of Art – School of Architecture, United Kingdom)

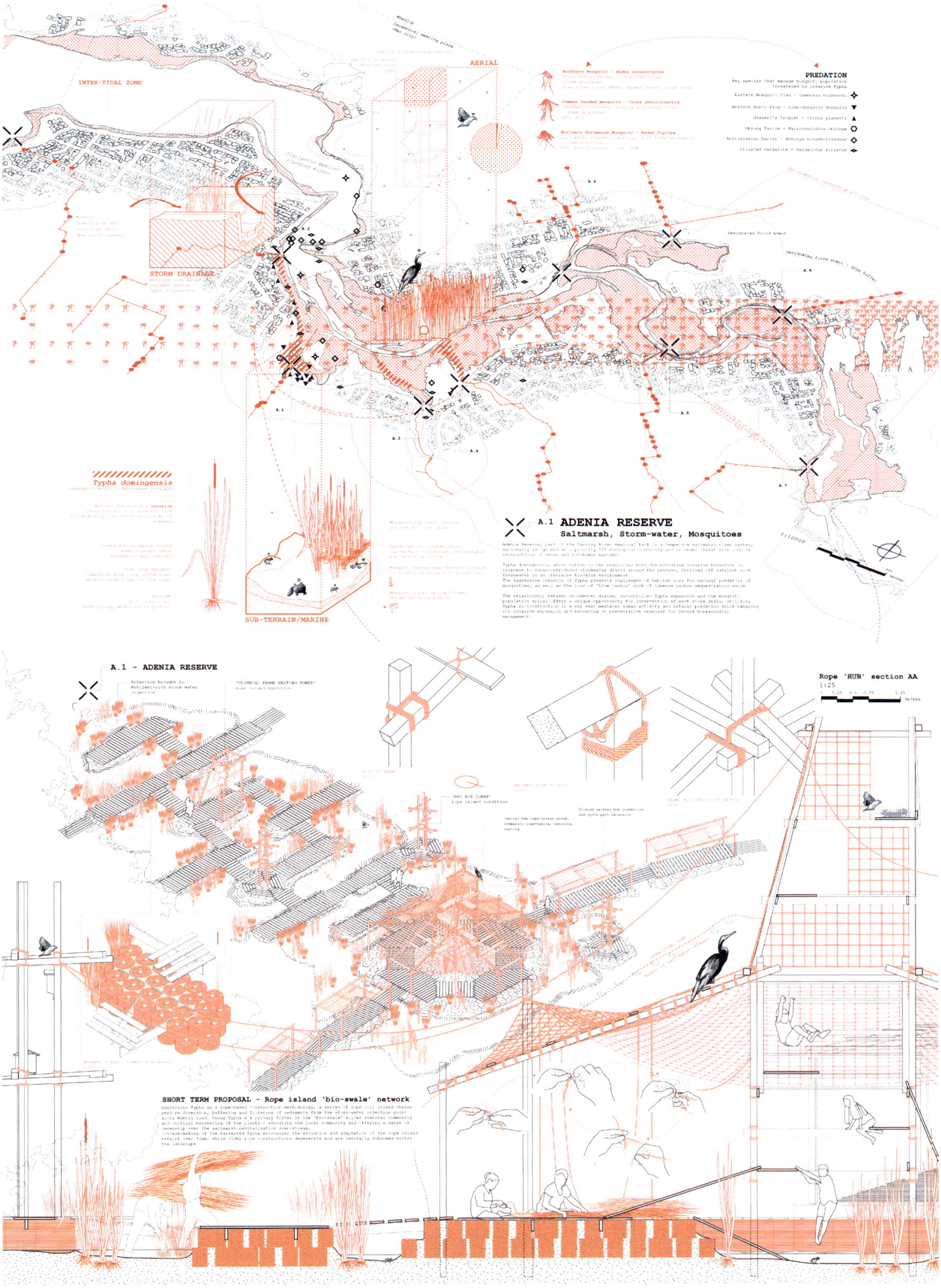

(Above and overleaf): Winning proposal panels by Harvey Rupp (University of Western Australia).

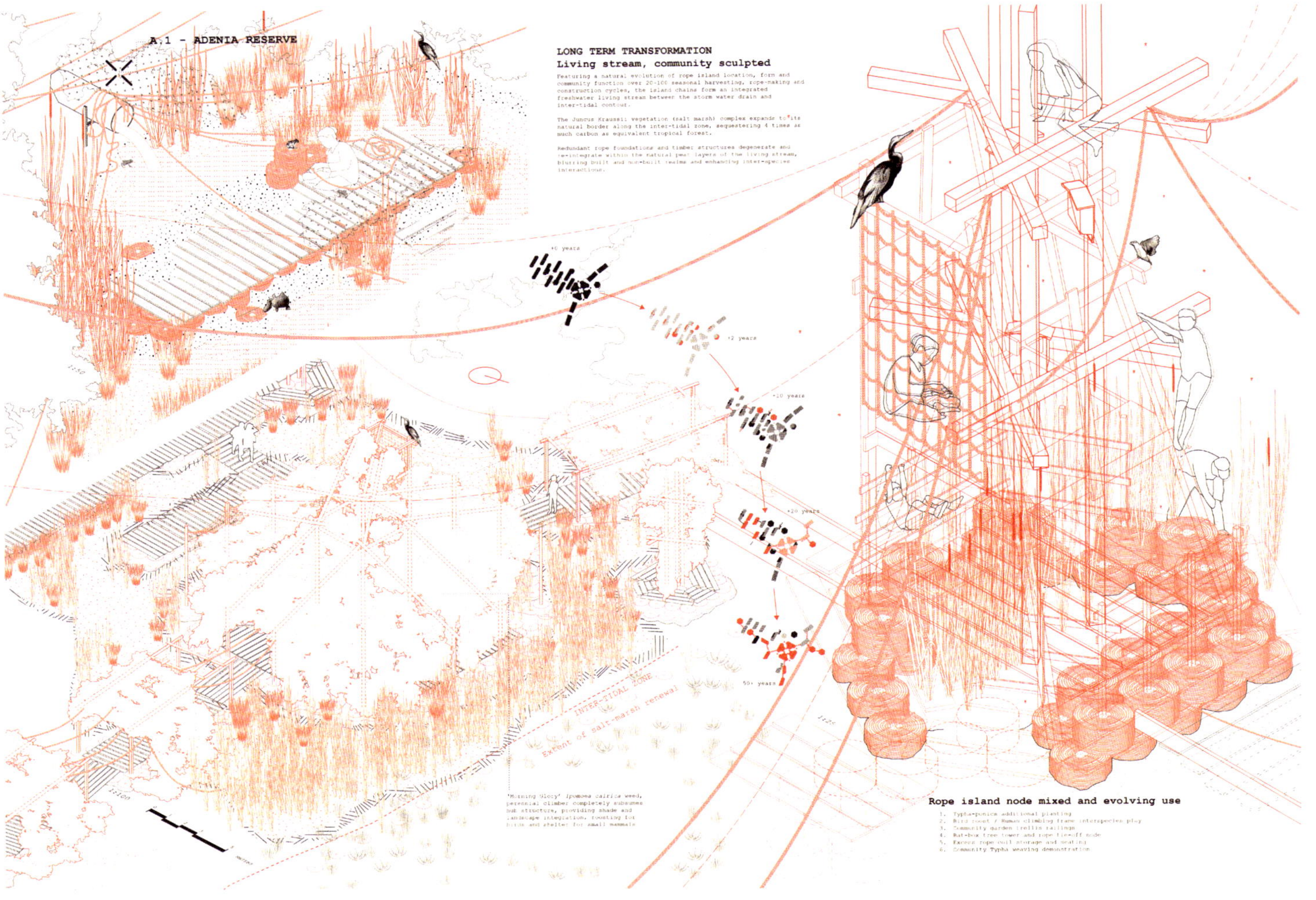
A.1 - ADENIA RESERVE
LONG TERM TRANSFORMATION
Living stream, community sculpted
Featuring a natural evolution of rope island location, form and community function over 20-100 seasonal harvesting, rope-making and construction cycles, the island chains form an integrated freshwater living stream between the storm water drain and inter-tidal contour.
The Juncus Kraussii vegetation (salt marsh) complex expands to its natural border along the inter-tidal zone, sequestering 4 times as much carbon as equivalent tropical forest.
Redundant rope foundations and timber structures degenerate and re-integrate within the natural peat layers of the living stream, blurring built and non-built realms and enhancing inter-species interactions.
+0 years
+2 years
+10 years
+20 years
50+ years
INTER-TIDAL ZONE
Extent of salt-marsh renewal
'Morning Glory' Ipomoea cairica weed, perennial climber completely subsumes hut structure, providing shade and landscape integration, roosting for birds and shelter for small mammals
Rope island node mixed and evolving use
1. Typha-punica additional planting
2. Bird roost / Human climbing frame interspecies play
3. Community garden trellis railings
4. Bat-box tree tower and rope tie-off node
5. Excess rope coil storage and seating
6. Community Typha weaving demonstration

HONOURABLE MENTIONS

Lim Zhi Xing and Mehmet Derin Incekas (Tsinghua University, China); Atsushi Yamaguchi, Ryuya Iijima, Rintaro Hirai and Yusuke Takabe (Waseda University Graduate School, Japan); Gabriela Pérez Viñoly and Sara Cruz Francos (Universidad Europea de Canarias, Spain); Zhang Moran, Wang Tianyi and Zhang Haimiao (Sichuan University, China); and Sanchit Agrawal (Harvard University Graduate School of Design, USA).

FINALISTS

Xiuming Cui and Xingyu Ye (Shanghai University, China); Thorbjørn Korshøj Bording Nielsen (Aarhus School of Architecture, Denmark); Javier Sepúlveda Carranza (Escola Tècnica Superior d'Arquitectura de Barcelona [ETSAB], Universitat Politècnica de Catalunya [UPC], Spain); Havva Nur Kurt (University of Western Australia, Australia); Fatima Najam and Lim Bao Chen (Tsinghua University, China); Nils Bonifay (ENSA Paris Val-de-Seine, France); Liu Yumeng, Chai Ziyue and Catalina Almendra Fuster Martínez (Xi'an University of Architecture and Technology, China); Oriol Aparicio, Marlon Brando Rueda and Kilian Valenciano de Mendiolaza (Escola Tècnica Superior d'Arquitectura de Barcelona [ETSAB], Universitat Politècnica de Catalunya [UPC], Spain); Mariya Romanosova and Tomas Martinez Garcia (TU Berlin, Germany); Liang An Yee (Tsinghua University, China); Toni Bosch Jerez, Guillermo Sanchez Cardenas and Matilde Serri Pini (Escuela Técnica Superior de Arquitectura del Vallès [ETSAV], Universitat Politècnica de Catalunya [UPC], Spain); Mateo Rodolfo Villada, Martin Vargas Robledo and Agustina Gallardo (Facultad de Arquitectura, Urbanismo y Diseño UNC, Argentina); Truong The Nguyen, Trinh Ho Minh Nhat and Vu Truc Ly (University of Architecture Ho Chi Minh City, Vietnam); Le Trung Tin and Nguyen Duc Duy (Ho Chi Minh City University of Technology and Education, Vietnam); Adriana de Salas Millán, Alba Capracci Aguirregómezcorta, Rosario Agulló Ruiz and Aya Himmi (Universidad Politécnica de Madrid, Spain); Aya Sellami and Adrien Morichon (ENSA Paris-Malaquais, France); Đồng Thùy Dung, Nguyễn Thế Quang, Vũ Tuấn Anh and Đỗ Hải Minh (Hanoi Architecture University, Vietnam); Cristian Manuel Pérez Rojas (Escola Tècnica Superior d'Arquitectura de Barcelona [ETSAB], Universitat Politècnica de Catalunya [UPC], Spain); Catalina Grand Browne (Pontificia Universidad Católica de Chile, Chile); Bastián Espinoza Pino, Esteban Barrientos Vargas, Tomás González Hidalgo and Edwin Vasquez Castillo (Universidad Mayor, Chile); Li Jiaqi, Yang Zheng and Chen Yujie (Xi'an University of Architecture and Technology, China); Paloma Echevarria (Pontificia Universidad Católica del Perú, Peru); Jiang Yutong, Liu Yikun and Shen Zijun (Xi'an University of Architecture and Technology, China); Mostafa Hussam Eldin, Malak ElKady, Habiba Haitham and Youssef Shawkat (Cairo University, Egypt); and Sarah Larsen (University of Western Australia, Australia).

CALL FOR PARTICIPANTS

CRITICAL DESIGN:
SELECTED CONTRIBUTIONS

P.A.R.C. – Previous Atmospheres Recovery Chapters
OESST (Adrià Escolano and David Steegmann) and MARBORIS (Mar Armengol)

Waycha Mayu Urban Biological Corridor
TAV

Bottling Warehouse and Offices for a Tequila Company
Atelier Ars

La Nave: Rehabilitation of an Old Industrial Warehouse
Atienza Maure

Rethinking Industrial Environments: Integrating Culture, Tradition and Sustainability
Estudio ALA

Regenerative Biogenic Façades for Extreme Climates
CINARK – Center for Industrialised Architecture

Farallones Coffee Wet Mill
AGENdA

Mass Madera: Advancing Industrialised Timber Construction in Spain
Mass Madera IAAC

Environmental Restoration of Rec Comtal in Vallbona
Carles Enrich

Shelter for Homeless Women: Architecture Serving Social Reintegration
Vivas Arquitectos

Benjakitti Forest Park
Arsomsilp Community and Environmental Architects and Turenscape

Land, Labour and Civic Ecology
Connor Gravelle

Ending Well
Courage Kpodo

The City of Indigenous Arts
Estudio MMX

Park in the Prado Neighbourhood: Life in a Garden
Connatural, Edgar Mazo

Khan Jaljulia Restoration
Elias Khuri

Rupgaon: A Paradigm for Climate Resilient Symbiotic Community Development
Fatiha Polin, PERCEIVE

Diadema Educational Block
Cristiane Muniz and Fernando Viegas, Bárbara Francelin and Thiago Augusto Zati, Escola da Cidade

Compluvium Pavilion
P + S Estudio de Arquitectura, Francisco Parada and Laura R. Salvador

Renaturalisation of Liconsa Parking
Beatriz Borque and Jorge Vidal

Your Greenhouse Is Your Kitchen
Office for Roundtable and JXY Studio

A Botanic LAB: Rethinking Educational Pedagogy through Productive Infrastructures
Máximo Bertoia

Tuzla Stream Co-habitat: Urban Regeneration through Waterscapes
Openact Architecture

Open Regeneration of Housing Estates in Barcelona
Pere Joan Ravetllat, Rearq – Universitat Politècnica de Catalunya (UPC)

Paleoinnovation in Agadir: Embodying Tomorrow
Salima Naji

Now That the Neighbourhood Is Nice, Why Do I Have to Move?
CO53, Sharona Cramer and Yotam Oron

Circular Building Cultures: 1:1 Design Research Methodology
Tina Gregoric, Institute of Architectural Design, TU Vienna

The Grid
Trung Mai, Ad hoc Practice

Alluvial Decoder (City of Raleigh Storm Memorial)
A Gang of Three

CRITICAL IMAGE:
SELECTED CONTRIBUTIONS

PALIMPEST: Overwriting Architecture
Adrià Goula

Supra-grounds
Aleksandra Redzisz

HOUSE-04: Reviving through Careful Inhabitation
Anne Gross and Luna Bucherer

The Invisible Hands
Caroline Stokholm and Jenny Amdi Sørensen

Datapolis+: The Materiality of Data
Atelier Atollo, Paul Swagerman, Negar Sanaan and Paul Cournet

One-Floor / One-Woman: Spatial Implications of Women's Labour
Wo-Men Work, Chiara Oggioni and Yi Sun

Humanitarian Imaginary
Damian Greder and Javier Fernández Contreras

Scrap Oriented Urbanism: Speculative Cartography for Socio-material Urbanism
Daniel Torrego

Documenting Difference
Text Catalogue, Ella Fleri Soler & Andrew Darmanin

The Storm: Architectures of Vernacular Geoengineering
FAST, Eva Franch i Gilabert and Jose Luís de Vicente

The Ecology Will Come and Welcome You in its Bosom
José María Torres Nadal

City Unfinished: Voices of El Ermitaño
Kathrin Golda-Pongratz

The Immortal, a Reflexion on the Sexto Pantéon Legacy
Chacarita Moderna

Antropia
Luca Quagliato and Guglielmo Trupia

The Mineral Landscape Has a Light Blue Sky
Marcos Zegers

Quito Fragmented
María Isabel Paz Suaréz

Under the Ice
Michel Kessler and David Oesch

Finsací (it ends here). Paiporta, Valencia, October 29, 2024
Milena Villalba

Tuned Territories: Water, Resistance and Decolonial Architecture
Natalia Figueredo and Victoria MacKenzie

Kutch's Living Birdhouse: Community Sanctuaries for Coexistence
Nipun Prabhakar

Alternative Urbanism: Self-organising Markets of Lagos
Oshinowo Tosin

The Great Together
Rocio Calzado and Jasper Meurer, Docar Films

Reviving Local Games, Reclaiming Public Spaces: Let's Play Initiative Nepal
Rojita Sharma and Sadichchha Shrestha

Food Architectures of Marine Cultivation for Ecological Production and Regeneration
Sebastian Carvajal

Watching the Grass Grow: Field Notes
Simone Marcolin

The Twilight Zone
Solam Mkhabela

Turning the Ecological Gears
Sophie Falkeis

All Come From Dust | من طين
Younes Ben Slimane

CRITICAL ESSAYS:
SELECTED CONTRIBUTIONS

Origin and Evolution of Architecture: On Human Architectural Ethology
Arturo Frediani, Lara Alcaina-Pozo, Larry Barham and Adriana Hernandez-Aguila

Counter-cartographies of Migrants to the Canary Islands
Víctor Cano-Ciborro

Designing Otherwise: Architecture Beyond the Human
Valentina Labriola

Learning from Garcia Faria: Circular Metabolism in the Late Nineteenth Century
Joan Maria Martí Elias

Lithium Extraction and Ecological Resistance in the Andean Altiplano
Valentina Morales Puebla, Ayami Nakamura and Constanza Ipinza

Becoming More-than-human: Ecological Coexistence in the Urban Linkages Project
Carlos Zeballos-Velarde

Designing with Rare Earths: Unveiling Material Geopolitics
Blanca Pujals

Spaces of Knowing: Co-creating Embedded Architectural Research Through Everyday Encounters
Aga Kuś

The Cloud is Burning! Cloud Architecture in the Spanish Context
Álvaro Andueza and Almudena Ribot

Subterranean Resonances: The Memory of the Air-Raid Shelters in Barcelona
Ana Laura Bertero

The Systemic Making of Space: Lucius Burckhardt's Architecture of Perception
Anne Gross

Erased from Within: Interior Loss and the Fiction of Preservation
Buket Ergun Kocaili

Re-Sourcing: Design, Extraction and Infrastructural Legacies in Western Australia
Elspeth Mary Lee and Donn Holohan

Brownfields
Fernanda Córdova

(A)esthetics of the Everyday: Environmental Poetics in Social Architecture
Francisco Felipe Muñoz

Spatial Interdependence: Hollowed Villages Becoming Sustainable Communities
Huinan Zhang, Shiyu Wei and Jun Shan

Intersectional Urbanism: Building Cities of Justice and Climate Resilience
Ilaria Iacconi Iambrenghi

Floating Manaus: Riverine Legacies and the Urban Utopia
Isabella de Bonis

Obscure Niches: Mapping Urban Becoming in Metro Manila's Interstices
Jose Lorenzo Belandres

Performative Earth Walls: Climate-responsive Geometry for 3D-printing
Juana Colombo, Farah Ali and Luca Owen Ring

Becoming Biomass: A Future History of Regional Biomaterial Transition
Kathy Velikov and Geoffrey Thun

Anarchaeological Practices for Radical Imagination
Manuela Valtchanova

Becoming Cybersyn Architecture and the Reassembly of Systemic Intelligence
Matias del Campo and Sandra Manninger

Architecture as Ethical Resistance to Colonial and Capitalist Violence
Nadia Habash

Discoteca de Playa: Mobilising Desire to Reimagine the Coast
Pol Esteve Castelló

Beyond Demolition, Architectures of Care: Sociotechnical Taxonomy of Housing Estates
Rocio Calzado

Marine Food Architectures for Ecological Regeneration in Chilean Patagonia
Sebastián Carvajal

Rethinking Competitions as Visibility Systems in the Digital Age
Vanessa Ma and Leroy Cheng

CO-POIESIS: Reused-Timber-Pavilion by Robotic Fabrication in Biennale Architettura 2025
Yalei Zhu, Tianyi Gao, Shitong Wang and Philip F. Yuan

Weaponisation of Water: Hydrological Infrastructure as a Battlefield in the Black Sea
Yevheniia Berchul and Nabi Agzamov

JURIES AND EVALUATING COMMITTEES

UIA INTERNATIONAL STUDENT COMPETITION

Jury
Tatiana Bilbao:
Founder of Tatiana Bilbao Estudio
Marianna Rentzou:
Co-founder of Point Supreme
Wtanya Chanvitan:
Co-founder of Bangkok Tokyo Architecture
Josep Ferrando (chair):
Founder of Josep Ferrando Architecture
Sumayya Vally:
Founder of Counterspace.
UIA representative

Alternate Jurors
Donn Holohan:
Co-founder of Superposition
Alejandro Vargas Marulanda:
Co-founder of Entropía.
UIA representative

Content Advisors
Maria Giramé:
Curator
Mariona Benedito:
Curator

INTERNATIONAL EMERGING WORKSHOPS

Selection Committee
Chrisna Du Plessis:
Delegate region V
Meritxell Inaraja:
Delegate COAC
Carmen Torres:
Curator
Tomeu Ramis:
Curator

Fellowships Selection Committee
Teresa Táboas:
Vice President Region I
Jerzy Grochulski:
Vice President Region II
Nivaldo Andrade:
Vice President Region III
Zhang Li:
Vice President Region IV
Vity Claude Nsalambi:
Vice President Region V

CALL FOR PARTICIPANTS: CRITICAL DESIGN

Jury
Carlos Facio:
Co-founder of Colectivo C733
Catherine Mosbach:
Founder of mosbach paysagistes
Kersten Geers:
Co-founder of OFFICE Kersten Geers David Van Severen
Xu Tian Tian:
Founder of DnA_Design and Architecture
Mariona Benedito:
Curator
Carmen Torres:
Curator

Preliminary evaluators
Nuno Melo Sousa:
Founder of Nuno Melo Sousa
Anadis Gonzalez + Fernando Martirena:
Co-founders of Infraestudio
Jorge Sobejano:
Co-founder of Burr Studio

CALL FOR PARTICIPANTS: CRITICAL IMAGE

Jury
Giovanna Borasi:
Director of the Canadian Centre for Architecture
Maxime Delvaux:
Architecture photographer
Louise Lemoine:
Co-founder of Bêka & Lemoine
Urtzi Grau:
Co-founder of Fake Industries Architectural Agonism
Maria Giramé:
Curator
Pau Sarquella:
Curator

Preliminary evaluators
Sonia Levy:
Associate Lecturer in Media Studies, Royal College of Art
Romea Muryn:
Co-founder and researcher at LOCUMENT
Zaickz Moz:
Visual artist and photographer, founder of MOS

CALL FOR PARTICIPANTS: CRITICAL ESSAYS

Jury
Keller Easterling:
Enid Storm Dwyer Professor at Yale University
Lydia Kallipoliti:
Associate Professor at Columbia University GSAPP
Marina Otero Verzier:
Professor at Columbia University GSAPP
Philip Ursprung:
Professor at ETH Zürich
Samia Henni:
Peter Guo-hua Fu School of Architecture, McGill University
Raquel Rolnik:
Professor at the University of São Paulo
Pau Bajet:
Curator
Tomeu Ramis:
Curator

Peer-review evaluators
Alba Arboix-Aliò, PhD, University of Barcelona (UB); Aldo Sollazzo, Noumena Group; Alex Mademochoritis, Université Gustave Eiffel; Álvaro Clua, PhD, Escola Tècnica Superior d'Arquitectura de Barcelona at Universitat Politècnica de Catalunya (ETSAB-UPC); Amadeu Santacana, PhD, ETSAB-UPC; Anastasios Floros, University of Ioannina; Andrea Iorio, PhD, Università Iuav di Venezia; Anna Sala, PhD, Escola Tècnica Superior d'Arquitectura del Vallès at Universitat Politècnica de Catalunya (ETSAV-UPC); Anthi Kosma, PhD, University of Thessaly; Ariane Harrison, PhD, Weitzman School, University of Pennsylvania; Arnau Pascual Carreras, ETSAB-UPC and Escola Tècnica Superior d'Arquitectura La Salle at Ramon Llull University (ETSALS-URL); Aspaso Kouzoupi, PhD, University of Thessaly; Avrokomi Zavitsanou, PhD, University of Ioannina; Ayesha Ghosh, Studio Ghosh; Calayde Davey, PhD, University of Pretoria; Carolina Dayer, PhD, Aarhus School of Architecture; Carson Chan; Caterina Viguera, Caterina Viguera Studio; Dana Cupkova, Carnegie Mellon University; De Peter Yi, University of Cincinnati; Deepika Raghu, PhD, ETH Zürich; Despoina Zavraka, PhD, Aristotle University Thessaloniki; Diego Rodríguez Lozano, PhD, Tecnológico de Monterrey; Dimitrios Giannisis, University of Patras; Dinorah Martínez Schulte, MANUFACTURA; Eduard Fernàndez Garcia, Self-office; Eduardo Rico Carranza, PhD, Institute for Advanced Architecture of Catalonia (IAAC); Eduardo Chamorro Martín, PhD, Tecnalia Research & Innovation; Fabiola Büchele, Studio NEiDA; Ferran Grau Valldosera, PhD, Escola Tècnica Superior d'Arquitectura Universitat Rovira i Virgili (ETSA-URV); Fiona Demeur, IAAC; Firas Safieddine, Spatial Forces; Gabriel Hernández, Escuela Técnica Superior de Arquitectura de Madrid, Universidad Politécnica de Madrid (ETSAM-UPM); Iacopo Neri, IAAC; Igor Bragado Fernández, IE University; Ionna Symeonidou, PhD, University of Thessaly; Jako-Albert Nice, PhD, Tshwane University of Technology, University of Pretoria; James Martin, Ithirlann; Jeanne Autran-Edorh, Studio NEiDA; Joaquim Moreno, PhD, University of Porto; Jordi Vivaldi, PhD, University of Innsbruck, Bartlett School of Architecture, University College London (UCL); José Carpio-Pinedo, PhD, ETSAM-UPM; Katerina Ritzouli, PhD, Democritus University of Thrace; Katherine Liapi, PhD,

University of Patras; Konstantinos Kostopoulos, National Technical University Athens; Laura Solsona Ramo, Self-office; Leon Guillermo Staines Diaz, PhD, Tecnológico de Monterrey; Leonidas Koutsoumpos, PhD, School of Architecture, National Technical University of Athens; Luís Ribeiro da Silva, PhD, Ursa Architecture; Macarena de la Vega León, PhD, ETSAM-UPM; Manuel Sánchez García, PhD, ETSAM-UPM; Maria Kuptsova, University of Innsbruck; Maria Rius Ruiz, PhD, Yale University and Columbia University; Maria de la Torre, PhD, Tecnológico de Monterrey; Maria Beni Ezquerro, ETSAB-UPC; Marilena Skavara, FABRICATE / Codica; Mariona Alcaraz Corbella, Synapcity Studio; Martina Fabré, ETSAV-UPC; Nico Botes, PhD, University of Pretoria; Nil Brullet, Brullet de Luna Architecture; Noelle The, Common Ground Landscapes; Nuria Ortigosa, PhD, ETSAV-UPC; Oriol Carrasco, PhD, IAAC; Pablo Villalonga, PhD, ETSAB-UPC; Peter Fisher, PhD, University of Sydney and University of New South Wales; Peter Stevens, University of Newcastle, Tom Farrell Institute for the Environment; Polyxeni Mantzou, PhD, University of Ioannina; Raül Avilla-Royo, PhD, ETSAB-UPC; Sara Vima Grau, PhD, ETSAB-UPC; Sergi Serrat Guillen, Tulane University; Sergio Castillo Hispán, PhD, Escuela Técnica Superior de Arquitectura de Granada, Universidad de Granada (ETSAG-UG); Sonsoles Vela Navarro, Tulane University of Architecture; Sorachai Kornkasem, PhD, Chulalongkorn University; Theodora Papidou, PhD, School of Architecture at Aristotle University of Thessaloniki; Vasileios Ntovros, School of Architecture at Technical University of Crete; Warisara Sudswong, Faculty of Architecture at Chulalongkorn University; Xavier Martín Tost, PhD, ETSALS-URL; Juana María Sánchez Gómez, PhD, Escuela Técnica Superior de Arquitectura Universidad de Málaga (ETSA-UM); Montserrat Solano-Rojo, PhD, ETSAG-UG; Nikolas Patsavos, University of Ioannina; and Patrick Donbeck, Chulalongkorn University.

CONGRESS CREDITS

CONVENED BY
UIA (International Union of Architects)

President
Regina Gonthier

Immediate Past President
José Luis Cortés

Secretary General
Rui Leao

Treasurer
Seif Alnaga

Region I Vice President
Teresa Táboas

Region II Vice President
Jerzy Grochulski

Region III Vice President
Nivaldo Andrade

Region IV Vice President
Zhang Li

Region V Vice President
Vity Claude Nsalambi

ORGANISED BY
The Higher Council of Professional Associations of Architects of Spain (CSCAE)

President of the CSCAE
Marta Vall-llossera Ferran

Architects' Association of Catalonia (COAC)

Dean of COAC
Guim Costa Calsamiglia

FUNDED BY

Government of Spain

President of the Government of Spain
Pedro Sánchez

Ministry of Housing and Urban Agenda (MIVAU)

Minister of Housing and Urban Agenda of the Government of Spain
Isabel Rodríguez

Secretary of State for Housing and Urban Agenda
David Lucas

General Secretary of Urban Agenda, Housing and Architecture
Iñaqui Carnicero

Government of Catalonia

President of Catalonia
Salvador Illa

Minister of Territory, Housing and Ecological Transition of the Government of Catalonia
Sílvia Paneque

Director General for Regional Planning, Urbanism and Architecture of Catalonia
Víctor Puga

Barcelona City Council

Major of Barcelona
Jaume Collboni

First Deputy Mayor
Laia Bonet

Chief Architect
Maria Buhigas

MAIN PARTNERS

ROCA
HP
HOLCIM

PARTNERS

VELUX
Kave Home

ORGANISATION OF THE CONGRESS

President of the Congress
Marta Vall-llossera Ferran

Director of the Congress
Guim Costa Calsamiglia

Honorary President of the Congress
Joan Busquets

Honorary President of the Scientific Committee
Fuensanta Nieto

Curators of the Congress and Presidents of the Scientific Committee
Pau Bajet
Mariona Benedito
Maria Giramé
Tomeu Ramis
Pau Sarquella
Carmen Torres

Collaborating Companies

Communication agency
Labóh

Press relations
Miriam Giordano

Art direction and graphic design
Principi

Technical Secretary
BARTER

Web development
No Somos Nada

Travel agency
Kuoni

Accreditation and Staff Company
Reed & Mackay

Curators' itineraries
AMOO Studio (Aureli Mora + Omar Ornaque)

Teamwork in Barcelona

Daniel Monfort (Executive Director)
Javier Rodríguez Ulibarri (Project Manager of the Congress)
Imanol Montero (Treasurer COAC)
Sònia Oliveras (General Manager COAC)
Jordi Cassadó (Financial Director COAC)
Cristina Guadalupe (Technical Secretary CSCAE, Workshop Coordinator and Translations)
Leonie Alessa Bremser (Assistant Curator, Editorial Project Manager and Event Manager Castell de Montjuïc)
Maria López (Assistant Curator)
Joana Ribeiro (Assistant Curator)
Leire Román (Assistant Curator)
Laura la Lueta Romero (Manager of Visitor Services Department and Official Itineraries Coordinator)

Clara Llensa (Director of Communications and Public Relations at COAC)
Xabier Artázcoz (Project Manager for 3X and Exhibition)
Marta Oller (Project Manager for CCIB)
Delfina Gronda (Project Manager Working Bodies)
Marina Deusedas (Project Manager UIA Member Sections)
Maria Ulacia (Project Manager UIA Awards)
Daniel Crespo (Sponsorship Manager)
Roser Badal (Head of the Dean's Office, COAC)
Claudia Agusto (Graphic Design)
Yolanda Rodríguez (Manager of Protocol)
Lili Herreros (Internship Visitor Services)

Teamwork in Madrid (CSCAE)

Daniel Monfort (Executive Director)
Elena Guijarro (Treasurer)
Arantxa Alonso (Head of the President's Office)
Almudena García (Head of the General Secretary's Office)
María Dolores Galán (Head of the Legal Advisory Department)
Miquel López (Legal Adviser)
Virginia Salinero (International Relations)
Nuria López (Head of Communications)
Leyre Salgado (Communication and Web Development)
Samuel González (Communication)
Natalia Bielsa (Head of the Technical Department)
José Antonio Roig (Architect of the Technical Department)
Raquel Reymondez (Manager of Protocol)
Juan José Rodríguez (Head of IT and Networks)
David Fernández (IT and Networks)
Macarena Concejal (Administration and Management)
Yolanda Espinosa (Registry Office and Accounting)
Mari Ángel López (Director of the Observatory)
Sergio García-Gasco (Deputy Director of the Observatory)
Enrique Ramírez (Head of the Observatory Office)

INSTITUTIONAL WORKING GROUP

Ministry of Housing and Urban Agenda (MIVAU), Government of Spain

Inmaculada Brugarolas
Héctor Jiménez
Sara León
Abraham Liébana
Víctor López-Rey
Carmen Moreno

Government of Catalonia

Elisabeth Tua
Ana Ruisánchez

Barcelona City Council

Pol Font

Team UIA

Carla Lima Vieira (Coordinator for International Relations and Working Bodies)
Olga Mihalikova (Executive Director)
Mwiyathi Wanjira (Head of Communications)
Michel Kaeppeli (Events Officer)
Sofia Salgueiro (Communications Assistant)
Célia Faria (Competitions and Awards Officer)
Anna Noonan (Executive Assistant)
Annäelle Casano (Executive Assistant)
Thibaud Hofer (UNESCO-UIA Validation Manager)
Erik Baron Vargas (Graphic Designer)

VENUES OF THE CONGRESS

Disseny Hub Barcelona
CCIB (Centre de Convencions Internacional de Barcelona)
Tres Xemeneies (Consorci del Besòs & FMB Endesa+Metrovacesa)
Castell de Montjuïc (Barcelona City Council)

ACKNOWLEDGEMENTS AND COLLABORATORS

Anna Ramos (Fundació Mies van der Rohe)
Bmotion
Cabosanroque
Cal Blay
CINESI
CIRCA Cultural Projects
Consorci del Besòs
Cube Studio
Marc López (Consorci del Besòs)
Ninoska Juan (World Capital of Architecture)
Nussli
OR Ingeniería
Relevance
Ribera García (Government of Catalonia)
Roger Subirà
Víctor Navarro (Department of Culture, Government of Catalonia)

and all those whose work, effort and knowledge have made this congress possible.

SCIENTIFIC COMMITTEE

Honorary Presidents
Joan Busquets – Honorary President of the Congress
Fuensanta Nieto – Honorary President of the Scientific Committee

Presidents of the Scientific Committee
Pau Bajet, Mariona Benedito, Maria Giramé, Tomeu Ramis, Pau Sarquella and Carmen Torres – General Reporters and Curators of the Congress

Committee Members
Alessandro Bonizzoni (UIA Delegate, Region I)
Ioannis Zavoleas (UIA Delegate, Region II)
Alejandro Echeverri (UIA Delegate, Region III)
George Kunihiro (UIA Delegate, Region IV)
Chrisna du Plessis (UIA Delegate, Region V)
Sara Topelson (UIA Past President)
Meritxell Inaraja (CSCAE/COAC Delegate)
Josep Lluís Mateo (CSCAE/COAC Delegate)
Mar Santamaria (CSCAE/COAC Delegate)
Elisa Valero (CSCAE/COAC Delegate)
Óscar Ares (CSCAE/COAC Delegate)

Observing Members
Regina Gonthier (President of the UIA)
Marta Vall-llossera Ferran (President of CSCAE and President of the UIA 2026 Congress)
Teresa Táboas (President of UIA Region I and Vice President of the UIA 2026 Congress)
Guim Costa Calsamiglia (Dean of COAC and Director of the UIA 2026 Congress)
Iñaqui Carnicero (Secretary General for Urban Agenda, Housing and Architecture of the Government of Spain)
Víctor Puga (Director General for Territorial Planning, Urbanism and Architecture of the Government of Catalonia)
Maria Buhigas (Chief Architect of Barcelona City Council)
Juan Antonio Ortiz (Vice-President of CSCAE)
Daniel Monfort (Scientific Committee Secretary)

The UIA World Congress of Architects 2026 Barcelona represents a key opportunity to place architecture at the forefront of contemporary debate, underscoring its capacity to address the complex challenges facing our societies and reaffirming its role as a true lever of transformation, capable of integrating environmental sustainability, social cohesion, technological innovation and cultural excellence.

Through its support for the Congress, the Ministry of Housing and Urban Agenda reaffirms its commitment to architectural quality as a matter of public interest, in line with the principles and values established in the Law on the Quality of Architecture.

This vision recognises and positions architecture at the heart of public policy, promoting initiatives that combine innovation, sustainability and social well-being, while advancing urban regeneration, accessibility, the rehabilitation of our built heritage and the right to adequate housing. Within this framework, architectural quality emerges as a fundamental pillar for the design and development of more equitable, resilient and liveable cities.

Iñaqui Carnicero Alonso-Colmenares
Secretary General for Urban Agenda,
Housing and Architecture
Ministry of Housing and Urban Agenda

Held in Barcelona, the UIA World Congress of Architects 2026 is also a recognition of Catalonia as a collective project in which human dignity is placed at the forefront in the city – the symbolic space in which we all live.

There is a long-standing definition of Catalonia as a city of cities, which also reflects a way of seeing life rooted in community, education, coexistence and hope. The bonds between people foster competitiveness and make us stronger as a society.

Dignity and opportunity are almost as indispensable as freedom in the city understood as a space for democratic coexistence. For this reason, it is paramount to reflect on collective life and on public and efficient mobility; on housing that is rational and economically accessible; and on our capacity to live, move and produce in a clean and sustainable way.

The major challenges facing Catalonia are closely linked to architecture as a way of thinking about building together in a more efficient, competitive and dignified manner.

Sílvia Paneque
Minister for Territory, Housing and
Ecological Transition
Government of Catalonia

The year 2026 is a landmark moment for Barcelona, with an extensive programme of activities reaching every neighbourhood, every corner and every resident. Architecture will transcend its traditional disciplinary boundaries, to be experienced in schools, in public squares and in museums, bringing it closer to citizens and inviting them to take an active part.

Being designated World Capital of Architecture represents an opportunity to demonstrate how, in Barcelona, architecture and urban planning are understood as tools to improve people's quality of life, strengthen social cohesion and build a more liveable, inclusive and sustainable city.

Thirty years after hosting it for the first time, the city again welcomes the UIA World Congress of Architects, thereby reaffirming the commitment of public institutions to both professionals and the city itself – promoting a people-centred urban model.

This publication brings together and preserves the best practices, research and experimental experiences in architecture, which remain as points of reference for addressing future challenges, while consolidating the international projection of Barcelona and Catalonia as benchmarks in contemporary architecture and urbanism.

Laia Bonet
First Deputy Mayor of Barcelona
Urban Planning, Ecological Transition,
Urban Services and Housing
Barcelona City Council

Organisers and Partners

This book and, by extension, the UIA World Congress of Architects 2026 Barcelona, have been made possible by a network of partner organisations that share the vision underpinning the Congress: an event that is international in scope, innovative, sustainable and open to the global architectural community. Each partner has contributed expertise, resources and an unwavering commitment, playing a decisive role in both the quality of the programme and its technical, logistical and exhibitory implementation.

To all the institutions and companies that have made the UIA 2026 Barcelona experience possible, the Congress extends its most sincere gratitude for their commitment to architecture and for helping to bring this space for global dialogue to life.

Convened by

uia

Organised by

CSCAE

COAC arquitectes.cat

Funded by

Gobierno de España — Ministerio de Vivienda y Agenda Urbana

Generalitat de Catalunya

Barcelona

Main Partners

Roca

hp

HOLCIM

Partners

VELUX

Kave Home

Venue Partners

Front Marítim Besòs

DHub Disseny Hub Barcelona

CCIB Centre de Convencions Internacional de Barcelona

COLLAGE CREDITS

BECOMING MORE-THAN-HUMAN
(PP. 12–15)

51N4E, Ringpark Zuid, Antwerp, Belgium, 2020
Image: Team Park Zuid

Petra Blaisse (Inside Outside), Living Soil, 2025.
Image: Inside Outside

Al Borde, *Umbral Crudo – Raw Threshold*, Sharjah Architecture Triennial, UAE, 2023.
Image: Danko Stjepanovic, courtesy of Sharjah Architecture Triennial

Bureau Bas Smets, Brussels Memorial 22/03, Brussels, Belgium, 2017.
Image: © Michiel De Cleene

Bureau Bas Smets, *Building Biospheres*, Venice Architecture Biennale, Italy, 2025.
Image: © Michiel De Cleene

DESIGN EARTH, *After Oil*, Kuwait Pavilion, Venice Architecture Biennale, Italy, 2016.
Image: DESIGN EARTH

junya.ishigami+associates, KAIT Workshop, Kanagawa Institute of Technology, Atsugi, Japan, 2008.
Image: © junya.ishigami+associates

junya.ishigami+associates, Art Biotop Water Garden, Nasu, Tochigi, Japan, 2018.
Image: © junya.ishigami+associates

junya.ishigami+associates, Zaishui Art Museum, Rizhao, China, 2023.
Image: © Arch-Exist

mosbach paysagistes, Lost In Transition, Ulsan, South Korea, 2020.
Image: Catherine Mosbach

Boonserm Premthada / Bangkok Project Studio, Elephant World, Brick Observation Tower, Surin, Thailand, 2020.
Image: MoMa, New York, © Spaceshift Studio

Boonserm Premthada / Bangkok Project Studio, Elephant World, Cultural Courtyard, Surin, Thailand, 2020.
Image: Spaceshift Studio

Shaā/SOC, SOIL Map, from *Terra Forma: A Book of Speculative Maps*, MIT Press, 2022.
Image: Aït-Touati, Arènes, Grégoire

Simulaa, House for Lichen, Central Victoria, Australia, 2023–.
Image: Simulaa

Simulaa, House for Lichen, Central Victoria, Australia, 2023-.
Image: Simulaa

Simulaa, *Strata Signals*, 'Deep Time Real Time' exhibition, RMIT Design Hub Gallery, Melbourne, Australia, 2025.
Image: Tom Ross

TAKK (Mireia Luzárraga and Alejandro Muiño), Co-habitation Dome, Vierzon, France, 2022.
Image: José Hevia

TAKK (Mireia Luzárraga and Alejandro Muiño), Picnic, Logroño, Spain, 2017
Image: © TAKK, Mireia Luzárraga and Alejandro Muiño

Turenscape, Tianjin Qiaoyuan Wetland Park, Tianjin, China, 2008.
Image: Turenscape

Charles Waldheim, *Jujube Town_Species-Town Vignette*, China, 2022.
Image: Harvard GSD Office for Urbanization

Charles Waldheim, *Rapeseed Town_Landscape Portrait*, China, 2022.
Image: Harvard GSD Office for Urbanization

BECOMING CIRCULAR
(PP. 48–51)

Lionel Devlieger, Michaël Ghyoot, Adam Przywara, Karen Steukers, Arne Vande Capelle, Louise Vanhee, Chronograms of Architecture: Circular Design Principles, Between Theory and Practice, Department of Architecture and Urban Planning, Ghent University, Belgium, 2025.
Image: Circular Design Principles: Between Theory and Practice" was initially commissioned as part of Chronograms of Architecture, a collaboration between e-flux Architecture and the Jencks Foundation at the Cosmic House. Graphic design: Moulay Guissé, Stijn Colon, Robbe Van der Mynsbrugge, Louise Vanhee.

Lara Almarcegui, *Construction Materials*, Spanish Pavilion, Venice Architecture Biennale, Italy, 2013.
Image: Ugo Carmeni

Lara Almarcegui, *Rubble Construction*, Secession, Vienna, Austria, 2010.
Image: Wolfgang Thaler

Anupama Kundoo architects, Volontariat Homes for Homeless Children, Pondicherry, India, 2008.
Image: Anupama Kundoo architects

Carles Gabriel Oliver Barceló, 6 social housing units at 21 Ses Monges St., Santa Eugènia, Mallorca, Spain, 2023.
Image: Milena Villalba

BURR, EIR_Coco, Madrid, Spain, 2024.
Image: Maru Serrano

Curro Claret, T300, 'More than this' exhibition, Sala Vinçon, Barcelona, Spain, 2014.
Image: Juan Lemus

Flores & Prats, Sala Beckett, Barcelona, Spain, 2017.
Image: Adrià Goula

Maxence Grangeot/Structural Xploration Lab (SXL), EPFL, Re:bble In Situ, reuse of concrete rubble from demolition into cyclopean masonry walls assembled on site, Lausanne, Switzerland, 2023.
Image: Maxence Grangeot, EPFL, 2023

Maxence Grangeot/Structural Xploration Lab (SXL), EPFL, Re:bble Pavilion, public exhibition of prefabricated load-bearing walls from demolition rubble and saw-cut concrete slabs, Lausanne, Switzerland, 2025.
Image: Maxence Grangeot, EPFL, 2025

Maxence Grangeot/Structural Xploration Lab (SXL), EPFL, Re:bble Tower, research demonstrator of load-bearing walls from concrete rubble over two storeys, Fribourg, Switzerland, 2025.
Image: Maxence Grangeot, EPFL, 2025

H arquitectes, Social Housing 2104, Palma de Mallorca, Spain, 2025.
Image: Adrià Goula

HOLES (Mio Tsuneyama and Fuminori Nousaku), *Urban Fungus: Architecture is a Complex Mesh*, conceptual drawing, 2024.
Image: Jumpei Suzuki, Thomas Adank

Natura Futura, Las Tejedoras community centre, Chongón, Ecuador, 2025.
Image: Jag Studio

Nicolas Dorval-Bory Architectes, Logements rue de Tolbiac, Paris, France, 2019–27.
Image: Nicolas Dorval-Bory Architectes

Nicolas Dorval-Bory Architectes, Observatoire Château-Chinon, Château-Chinon, France, 2023–26.
Image: Nicolas Dorval-Bory Architectes

PARABASE, *De residuo a recurso: patrimonio reutilizado*, 17th Spanish Biennial of Architecture and Urbanism (XVII BEAU), Ponferrada, Spain, 2025.
Image: Olivier Campagne

PARABASE, Pirovana, San Bernardino, Switzerland, 2025.
Image: Olivier Campagne

Rotor, Dismantling of façade cladding, MULTI project, Brussels, Belgium, 2022.
Image: Rotor

Worofila, 'Jang Ban' exhibition, Dakar, Senegal, 2024.
Image: Sylvain Cherkaoui, © Worofila

BECOMING EMBODIED
(PP. 88–91)

AAU Anastas, *All Purpose*, Venice Architecture Biennale, Italy, 2021.
Image: Francesco Galli

AAU Anastas, *Tiamat*, Triennale di Milano, Italy, 2024.
Image: Alecio Ferrari

BC architects & studies & materials, Lot 8, LUMA Arles, France, 2022.
Image: Laurens Bekemans

BC architects & studies & materials, Assemble and Atelier LUMA, The Hanok, Gwangju, South Korea, 2024.
Image: Sooin Jang

BC architects & studies & materials, Usquare, Brussels, Belgium, 2024.
Image: Emile Deroose

BC architects & studies & materials, Biogeological stratum of Barcelona, Grounded Futures, Barcelona, Spain, 2026.
Image: © BC architects & studies & materials / RWTH Aachen

BC architects & studies & materials, Microalgae mortar prototyping, Grounded Futures, Brussels, Belgium, 2026.
Image: © BC architects & studies & materials

Boltshauser Architekten, Kiln Tower, Cham, Switzerland, 2021.
Image: Kuster Frey

BRUTHER, New Generation Research Center, Caen, France, 2016.
Image: BRUTHER @ Maxime Delvaux

BRUTHER and BAUKUNST, FRAME media house, Brussels, Belgium, 2025.
Image: BRUTHER @ Séverin Malaud

DnA_Design and Architecture, Brown Sugar Factory, Songyang county, China, 2016.
Image: Wang Ziling

gru.a, *The Beach and the Time*, Copacabana, Rio de Janeiro, Brazil, 2018.
Image: gru.a

Langarita-Navarro, *Olimpo Nômade*, Portimão, Portugal, 2022.
Image: Luis Díaz Díaz

Manthey Kula, *Ode to Osaka*, National Museum – Architecture, Oslo, Norway, 2015.
Image: Manthey Kula

Nuno Melo Sousa, Boavista II, Porto, Portugal, 2025.
Image: Francisco Ascensão

Nuno Melo Sousa, Corcet Headquarters, Penafiel, Portugal, 2025.
Image: Francisco Ascensão

Mario Monotti and Anne Holtrop, Green Corner Building, Muharraq, Bahrain, 2019.
Image: Studio Anne Holtrop

TEN, House for Five Women, Gradačac, Bosnia and Herzogovina, 2025.
Image: Maxime Delvaux

BECOMING INTERDEPENDENT
(PP. 126–29)

Elizabeth Añaños, Mayuriaga School, Plan Selva Project, Mayuriaga, Morona District, Peru, 2019.
Image: PRONIED

EMI Architekt*innen, Apartment Building Milchbuck, Zurich, Switzerland, 2025.
Image: Alexander Gebetsroither

Assemble and BC architects & studies & materials, Lot 8, LUMA Arles, France, 2022.
Image: Laurens Bekemans

Assemble, OTOProjects, Café OTO, Dalston, London, UK, 2013.
Image: Assemble

Chair of Architecture and Care, Building Pleasures, ETH Zürich, Switzerland, Spring 2025.
Work by Anaik Jeanjaquet, Lara Zimmerman, Linda Arnaboldi, Line Kurth
Image: Luis Úrculo.

Clauss Kahl Merz Atelier, Lyse-Lotte, Lysbüchel Süd, Basel, Switzerland, 2023.
Image: Willem Pab

Estudio Herreros, Trosten Sauna, Oslo, Norway, 2024.
Image: © Einar Aslaksen

Estudio Teddy Cruz + Fonna Forman, MEXUS: Geographies of Interdependence, 2017.
Image: Estudio Teddy Cruz + Fonna Forman

Heritage Foundation of Pakistan and Yasmeen Lari, conservation and rehabilitation of the Sepulcher of Mirza Jan Baba, Makli Necropolis, Sindh, Pakistan, 205–16.
Image: Heritage Foundation of Pakistan

Andreas Hofer/IBA '27, Backnang West Neighbourhood by Teleinternetcafe, Internationale Bauausstellung, Stuttgart, Germany, 2027.
Image: Teleinternetcafe Architektur und Urbanismus with Treibhaus Landschaftsarchitektur

Andreas Hofer/IBA '27, ZERO. – Sustainable working in the office building of the future by RIEHLE KOETH, Internationale Bauausstellung, Stuttgart, Germany, 2025.
Image: Achim Birnbaum

Lacol, La Balma cooperative housing, Barcelona, Spain, 2022.
Image: Milena Villalba

Lacol, La Morada cooperative housing, Barcelona, Spaint, 2024.
Image: Milena Villalba

Lacol, La Raval cooperative housing, Manresa, Spain, 2024.
Image: Adrià Goula

MAIO, 40 social housing units, Sant Felíu de Llobregat, Spain, 2022–23.
Image: José Hevia

Mariana Mazzucato, *The Public Value of Arts and Culture: Investing in Arts and Culture to Reimagine Economic Growth in the 21st Century*, 2025.
Image:: IIPP

Román Meyer Falcón, La Duna Skatepark, Ciudad Juárez, Chihuahua, Mexico, 2019.
Image: Onnis Luque

Peris + Toral Arquitectes, Modulas Matrix, Cornellà de Llobregat, Spain, 2020.
Image: José Hevia

Peris + Toral Arquitectes, Raw Rooms, Ibiza, Spain, 2022.
Image: José Hevia

Peris + Toral Arquitectes, Social Atrium, Barcelona, Spain, 2022.
Image: José Hevia

Plan Común and 51N4E, FESTIVAL stadium and sports neighbourhood, Dürres, Albania, 2023.
Image: OUT OF RAM

Raumlabor, Floating University Berlin, Berlin, Germany, 2018.
Image: Alexander Stumm

Raumlabor, Pioniererstatzstätten, Haus der Statistik, Berlin, Germany, 2022.
Image: Nils Koenning

Rural Urban Framework, Rethinking the Collective, Shizhong County, Fujian, China, 2019.
Image: Rural Urban Framework

BECOMING HYPER-CONSCIOUS
(PP. 162–65)

Accattone and Studio CUMA/ULB La Cambra Horta, *Dirty Materials* publication, exhibition and pedagogy, Brussels, Belgium, 2024/25.
Image: CUMA architecture faculty La Cambre Horta

Afreetekture and Wits University, *Council of Non-Human Beings* panels, South African Pavilion, Venice Architecture Biennale, Italy, 2023.
Image: Dr Sechaba Maape

Brandlhuber+, Antivilla, Krampnitz, Berlin, Germany, 2015.
Image: Future Documentation

Brandlhuber+, *2G 94 b+*, 2025.
Image: Walther König Publishers

Ibiye Camp, Data: the New Black Gold, Freetown, Sierra Leone, 2019.
Image: Ibiye Camp

Lluís Alexandre Casanovas Blanco, Mondiacult: World Conference on Cultural Policies and Sustainable Development, Barcelona, Spain, 2025.
Image: José Hevia

Center for Spatial Technologies, Networked Homes, Kyiv, Ukraine, 2021.
Image: Center for Spatial Technologies

Center for Spatial Technologies, Russian Attack on Kyiv TV Tower, Kyiv, Ukraine, 2022.
Image: Center for Spatial Technologies

Center for Spatial Technologies, Mariupol Drama Theater, Mariupol, Ukraine, 2024.
Image: Center for Spatial Technologies

Common Accounts, Closer Each Day: The Architecture of Everyday Death, 2016–21.
Image: commissioned by the Canadian Centre for Architecture (CCA)

Common Accounts, Don't Let Me Be Lonely, South Algonquin, Ontario, Canada, 2021.
Image: Christopher Sherman

Cooking Sections, *Becoming Xerophile*, Sharjah Architecture Triennial, UAE, 2019.
Image: Sharjah Architecture Triennial

Javier Fernández Contreras, *A Nocturnal History of Architecture*, 2024.
Image: HEAD – Genève

Forensic Architecture, *The Bombing of Rafah*, 2014.
Image: Forensic Architecture

Forensic Architecture and Studio Folder, Earthworks, 2025–26.
Image: Forensic Architecture

GFA2 (Guillermo Fernández-Abascal), Enaire Foundation, Santander, Spain, 2021.
Image: Luis Díaz Díaz

Hiroyuki Ito Architects, PRISM Inn Ogu Hotel, Tokyo, Japan, 2022.
Image: Masao Nishikawa

HouseEurope!, European Citizens' Initiative – Power to Renovation campaign, Berlin, Germany, 2024.
Image: Still from *To Build Law*, Canadian Centre for Architecture (CCA)

Lev Manovich/ Cultural Analytics Lab, Manga Style Space, 2010.
Image: Lev Manovich

Limbo Accra, Limbo Museum, Accra, Ghana, 2024.
Image: Edem J. Tamakloe

Milliøns, *Bathing, Again*, Friedman Benda Gallery, New York, USA, 2018.
Image: Ned Castle

Milliøns, Jack Erwin Flagship and Event Space, New York, USA. 2018.
Image: Ned Castle

Marina Otero Verzier, *Computational Compost*, Tabakalera International Centre of Contemporary Culture, Donostia/San Sebastián, Spain, 2023.
Image: Tabakalera

PLOT Especial 21: Suelos, Ecologías, Territorios, Comunidades, Buenos Aires, Argentina, 2024.
Image: PLOT

PLOT 76, Buenos Aires, Argentina, 2024.
Image: PLOT

Shaā/SOC, Gaïagraphie, Critical Zone Observatory of Lautaret, TERRA FORMA Equipex project (ANR-21-ESRE-0014), France, 2024.
Image: Alexandra Arènes

Paulo Tavares, An Architectural Botany, 2018–.
Image: Paulo Tavares (in collaboration with William Belée)

Paulo Tavares, Trees, Vines, Palms and Other Architectural Monuments, Brazil, 2017–21.
Image: Paulo Tavares / studio autônoma (in collaboration with Gabriel Menotti)

Urtzi Grau / Fake Industries, Murrin Bridge Preschool and Community Hub, Murrin Bridge, New South Wales, Australia, 2023.
Image: Hamish McIntosh

BECOMING ATTUNED
(PP. 206–09)

Atelier Bow-Wow, *Made in Tokyo*, 2001.
Image: Atelier Bow-Wow

Atelier Bow-Wow, Split Machiya, Shinjuku, Tokyo, Japan, 2010.
Image: Manuel Oka

Atelier Bow-Wow, Small Earth, Kamanuma, Japan, 2023.
Image: Small Earth + Tsukamoto Lab, ITS

Jean Jacques Balzac, *Before After*, Paris, France, 2024.
Image : Jean Jacques Balzac

Jean Jacques Balzac, *Properly trimmed garden*, Paris, France, 2024.
Image: Jean Jacques Balzac

Bangkok Tokyo Architecture, House K, Bangkok, Thailand, 2023.
Image: Soopakorn Srisakul

BeAr, Garai Dantzaleku, Garai, Bizkaia, Spain, 2025.
Image: Luis Díaz Díaz

Alexander Brodsky, Rotunda, Nikola-Lenivets, Russia, 2009.
Image: Yuri Palmin

Matilde Cassani, *Quasi Nessuno*, Principato di Lucedio, Italy, 2023.
Image: Delfino Sisto Legnani

Matilde Cassani, Berthe Morisot bookshop, Palazzo Ducale, Genova, Italy, 2024.
Image: Anna Positano

Experience, Office Building, Villejuif, France, 2025.
Image: Filip Dujardin

Go Hasegawa and Associates, Chapel in Guastalla, Guastalla, Italy, 2017.
Image: Davide Galli

KOSMOS Architects, EMA Space, Moscow, Russia, 2016.
Image: Yuri Palmin

Leopold Banchini Architects, House for Architectural Heritage, Muharraq, Bahrain, 2020.
Image: Dylan Perrenoud

Leopold Banchini Architects, Dar El Farina, Al Haouz, Morocco, 2025.
Image: Rory Gardiner

Maxime Delvaux, *žale cemetery in Ljubljana by Jože Plečnik (1940)*, Ljubljana, Slovenia, 2023.
Image: Maxime Delvaux

MOS, House No. 10, New York, 2015.
Image: Michael Vahrenwald

MOS, House No. 10, Washington DC, USA, 2021.
Image: Michael Vahrenwald

MOS, Greenhouse No. 4, Marta Gallery, Los Angeles, USA, 2025.
Image: Michael Vahrenwald

New South, Muqarnas, Paris, France, ongoing.
Image: Jonathan Letoublon

OFFICE Kersten Geers David Van Severen, OFFICE 229 – Library, Sint-Martens-Latem, Belgium, 2003.
Image: Bas Princen

OFFICE Kersten Geers David Van Severen, OFFICE 130 – Solo House, Matarrana, Spain, 2017.
Image: Bas Princen

OFFICE Kersten Geers David Van Severen, OFFICE 227 – Tondo, Brussels, Belgium, 2020.
Image: Bas Princen

Ted'A arquitectes, Ca na Birgit, Calvià, Mallorca, Spain, 2024.
Image: Luís Díaz Díaz

Ted'A arquitectes, Can Gabriel, Palma, Mallorca, Spain, 2024.
Image: Luís Díaz Díaz

Ted'A arquitectes, Casa en Colonia de Sant Pere, Mallorca, Spain, 2025.
Image: Luís Díaz Díaz

Un Parell d'Arquitectes, Can Sau Emergency Scenery, Olot, Spain, 2019.
Image: José Hevia

Un Parell d'Arquitectes, Good morning, Carme! reactivation of Plaça del Carme, Olot, Spain, 2021.
Image: José Hevia

IMAGE CREDITS

BECOMING MORE-THAN-HUMAN

pp. 18, 21(l&r) Courtesy of Mark Wigley
p. 20(t) Allisa Eckert, Centers for Disease Control and Prevention (CDC), courtesy of Mark Wigley
p. 20(b) Tasha Sturm, courtesy of Mark Wigley
p. 23 (top to bottom): Gregory H. Revera, CC BY-SA 3.0 (https://creativecommons.org/licenses/by-sa/3.0/deed.en) Redrawn by the author, original source unknown; XL.Creations; Boskalis
p. 24(l) (top to bottom): RO&AD Architecten
p. 24(r) (top to bottom): Photo by Rudolphous, CC BY-SA 4.0 (https://creativecommons.org/licenses/by-sa/4.0/); Paul van de Velde, CC BY 2.0 (https://creativecommons.org/licenses/by/2.0/; Hugues Tinguy, CC BY-SA 2.0 FR (https://creativecommons.org/licenses/by-sa/2.0/fr/; Agaath, CC BY-SA 4.0 (https://creativecommons.org/licenses/by-sa/4.0/
p. 25(t), 26(b) RO&AD Architecten
p. 25(b) (left to right): Achim Stump, CC BY-SA 4.0 (https://creativecommons.org/licenses/by-sa/4.0/; Alexander Semenov, CC BY 2.0 (https://creativecommons.org/licenses/by/2.0/); Ecomare, CC BY-SA 4.0 (https://creativecommons.org/licenses/by-sa/4.0/; RO&AD Architecten
p. 26(t) Siebe Swart / H+N+S Landscape Architects
p. 26(c) Rijkswaterstaat/Jurriaan Brobbel. Source: '2016 08 24 Zandmotor (15) overzicht vanuit noord' by Zandmotor, public domain
p. 26(b) RO&AD Architecten
p. 27(t) H+N+S Landscape Architects
p. 27(b) Courtesy of Dirk Sijmons and KK+N+S
p. 28 RO&AD Architecten, sections H+N+S Landscape Architects
pp. 29, 30(t&c) DESIGN EARTH
pp. 30b, 31 Simulaa
pp. 32–36 Eva Franch i Gilabert, Mireia Luzárraga and Alejandro Muiño / Institut Ramon Llull. Audiovisual production: Marc Luguera, Núria Gascon, 15 L

pp. 44–48: (1) Siebe Swart; (2) Ty Cole and SCAPE; (3) aldayjover architecture and landscape; (4) Jaime Navarro; (5) Turenscape; (6) José Hevia; (7) Maxime Delvaux; (8) Catherine Mosbach; (9) Inside Outside; (10) junya.ishigami+associates; (11) Arch-Exist; (12) Gustavo Utrabo; (13) Lars Müller; (14) Alessandro Paderni; (15) ImagenSubliminal (Miguel de Guzmán + Rocío Romero); (16) Petros Pattakos; (17) Simulaa; (18) Michel Desvigne Paysagiste; (19) Harvard GSD Office for Urbanization; (20) Christophe Le Dévéhat; (21) Screenshot of Ocellus XR developed by members of the Urban Systems Lab at The New School; (22) JAG Studio; (23) MoMa, New York, © Spaceshift Studio; (24) Iwan Baan; (25) TAKK; (26) Philippe Rahm architectes (with OMA and Laboratorio Permanente); (27) José Hevia; (28) DESIGN EARTH

BECOMING CIRCULAR

p. 53 Locus
p. 54 Andrehmarouti, CC BY-SA 4.0 (https://creativecommons.org/licenses/by-sa/4.0/deed.en)
p. 55(l) Cherry Aala, Rosa Bianco, Denisa Dulaj, Flavia Leone, Mattia Morgia, Laura Pomella, Daniele Scalia, Giusy Solis, Professor Alessandra Battisti
p. 55(c) Elise Wipff, *4°C Entre Toi Et Moi*
p. 55(r) Sacha De Amorim, *4°C Entre Toi Et Moi*
p. 56 Sana Frini and Philippe Rahm, photo Rafael Gamo
pp. 60–65 Drawings H arquitectes, photos Adrià Goula
pp. 66, 67(t&c) Jumpei Suzuki, Thomas Adank
pp. 67(b), 68(t&c) Nicolas Dorval-Bory Architectes
p. 70(t) BAUKUNST – SXL, photo Simone Marcolin
p. 70(c) BAUKUNST – SXL, photo Maxence Grangeot
pp. 70(b), 71 BAUKUNST – SXL, photos Maxence Grangeot/Structural Xploration Lab (SXL), EPFL
pp. 72–75 BAUKUNST – SXL
pp. 76(l), 78(b), 79(l), 80(l) Transsolar KlimaEngineering, illustration by Edith Maier-Neretin
p. 76(r) Photo Transsolar
p. 78(t) Photo Finbarr Fallon
p. 79(r) Courtesy of NUS School of Design and Environment, Architecture: Serie Architects, Multiply Architects, photo Rory Gardiner
p. 80(r) Photo Anja Thierfelder

pp. 82–87: (1) Javier Callejas; (2) Milena Villalba; (3) Jag Studio; (4) Photo Rafael Gamo; (5) Badara Preira, © Worofila; (6) Enrico Cano; (7) Lv Hengzhong; (8) Sulaco Film / Andreas Gefe / HauserSchwarz; (9) Juan Lemus; (10) Charlotte-Maltherre Barthes; (11) RotorDC; (12) Zirkular; (13) Maxence Grangeot – EPFL, 2023; (14) Hampus Berndtson; (15) BAUKUNST – Olivier Campagne; (16) PARABASE; (17) Philippe Ruault; (18) Ryogo Utatsu; (19) Maru Serrano; (20) Adrià Goula; (21) Oral Göktaş; (22) Transsolar KlimaEngineering; (23) Baukuh, Onsite Studio; (24) Adrià Goula; (25) Filip Dujardin; (26) TAAs – totem arquitectos asociados slp; (27) Nicolas Dorval-Bory Architectes; (28) Wolfgang Thaler; (29) Imani Jacqueline Brown; (30) © Canadian Centre for Architecture (CCA); (31) Verso Books; (32) Ministerio de Vivienda y Agenda Urbana

BECOMING EMBODIED

p. 94 Courtesy of Dr Yasmeen Lari, Heritage Foundation of Pakistan
p. 95 (left to right): BC architects & studies & materials, photo Adrien Deweerdt; BRUTHER © Séverin Malaud; TEN, photo Joel Tettamanti; Photo Francisco Ascensão
pp. 97–98, 100–03 BRUTHER, photos Arnaud Bostelmann
p. 99 BRUTHER, photos Benjamin Frei and Jonathan Troger
p. 104(t&b) TEN, photos Olivier Campagne
p. 104(ct&cb) TEN
p. 105 Nuno Melo Sousa
p. 106(l) BC architects & studies & materials / CEAMSA
pp. 106(c&r), 108–09 BC architects & studies & materials
p. 107 BC architects & studies & materials / RWTH Aachen
pp. 110–111 BC architects & studies & materials / RWTH Aachen
p. 112 Alexandre Humbert / BC architects & studies & materials
pp. 114, 117 City syntax
p. 115 Asif Salman
p. 116 ReWET Consortium

pp. 120–26: (1) Asif Salman; (2) Wang Ziling; (3) Nathanael Bennett; (4) Aulets Architects; (5) Jesús Fernández; (6) Hanno Mackowitz; (7) Edem Tamakloe; (8a&b) Roger Boltshauser; (9) Sooin Jang; (10) Studio Anne Holtrop; (11) Francesco Galli; (12) University of California Press; (13) Maxime Delvaux; (14) Luka Alagiyawanna; (15) Adrià Goula; (16) Manthey Kula; (17) Hisao Suzuki; (18) BRUTHER © Maxime Delvaux; (19) Javier Agustin Rojas; (20) Federico Cairoli; (21) Arrhov Frick; (22) Jun Sato; (23) Maxime Delvaux; (24) Francisco Ascensão; (25) BeL Sozietät für Architektur, Sebsatian Schels; (26) Shigeru Ban Architects Europe; (27) Hiroyuki Hirai; (28) Luis Díaz Díaz; (29) TEN, photo Olivier Campagne; (30) ZAV Architects, photo Parham Taghioff

BECOMING INTERDEPENDENT

pp. 134, 136, 138(tr) MAIO, Care. and Pol Esteve Castelló, photos Pol Esteve Castelló
pp. 135, 137, 138(tl) MAIO, Care and Pol Esteve Castelló, photos Laura Bravo and Pau Gelpí Roig
pp. 138(b), 139(t,ct&cb) Plan Común
p. 139(b) Kuehn Malvezzi, Plan Común and Nicolas Dorval-Bory
pp. 140–41 Photography/videography: Antoine Plouzen Morvan
p. 142 Colectivo C733 + Monserrat Loyola
pp. 143(t), 144–48 Colectivo C733
p. 143(b) Photo Santiago Arau
p. 150 Cedric Price fonds, Collection Canadian Centre for Architecture, Montréal. © Peter Murray
pp. 151, 156 © CCA, photos Michel Legendre
p. 153 © CCA, photo Djibril Drame / Sabali
p. 154 © CCA, photo Matthieu Brouillard

pp. 158–62: (1) Maarten Nauw; (2) Iwan Baan; (3) Estudio Teddy Cruz + Fonna Forman; (4) Rural Urban Framework; (5) Rajesh Vora; (6) Penguin Random House; (7) Laurian Ghinițoiu; (8) © CCA, photo Michel Legendre; (9) Rafael Gamo; (10) Einar Aslaksen; (11) Rafael Gamo; (12) José Luis Pérez De La Torre, Marco Antonio Martínez Villanueva, Sonora Horta López; (13) Penguin Random House; (14) PRONIED; (15) José Hevia; (16) Roland Bernath; (17) Adrià Goula;

(18) Rustler Schriever Architekten and Gornik Denkel Landschaftsarchitekten; (19) Michael Nagl; (20) Heritage Foundation of Pakistan; (21) José Hevia; (22) Editorial Kairos; (23) Assemble; (24) Agustin Pina; (25) Milena Villalba; (26) Christian Kahl; (27) NYC Department of Transportation; (28) Rainer Schlautmann; (29) morinakayasuaki

BECOMING HYPER-CONSCIOUS

p. 173 Rafi Segal and Eyal Weizman
pp. 174–79 © Forensic Architecture
p. 180 Ibiye Camp
p. 181 Photo Geray Mena
p. 182 Common Accounts
pp. 183–88 © CCA
p. 189(tl) b+ and Verlag der Buchhandlung Walther König
p. 189(tr) b&k+ Arno Brandlhuber & Markus Emde, Martin Kraushaar + Marc Frohn
p. 189 Cornelia Müller for Brandlhuber+
p. 192 public domain
p. 195 © Giorgio de Chirico, VEGAP, Madrid, 2026. Photo © 2026 DeAgostini Picture Library/New Picture Library/Scala, Florence

pp. 199–206: (1) University of Minnesota Press; (2) Tabakalera; (3) Lev Manovich; (4) Bloomsbury; (5) Columbia Books on Architecture and the City; (6) Paulo Tavares / studio autônoma (in collaboration with Gabriel Menotti); (7) Ibiye Camp; (8) trescientosmil; (9) Thomas McLucas; (10) Alexandra Arènes; (11) © 2023 Massachusetts Institute of Technology, by permission of The MIT Press; (12) Adrià Goula; (13) Petros Pattakos; (14) Center for Spatial Technologies; (15) © Forensic Architecture; (16) Future Documentations; (17) Maxime Delvaux; (18 a&b) Masao Nishikawa; (19) The Architecture Lobby; (20) Quaderns d'Arquitectura i Urbanisme; (21) Accattone, MBL; (22) *Real Review*; (23) *PLOT*; (24) Dr Sechaba Maape; (25) José Hevia; (26) Sharjah Architecture Triennial; (27) Geray Mena; (28) Timothy Hursley; (29) Philip F. Yuan; (30) MASS Design Group; (31) DC-Lab EPFL Architectur

BECOMING ATTUNED

p. 211 © ALTAN/QUIPOS
p. 212 Atelier Bow-Wow and Tsukamoto Lab/ Institute of Science Tokyo
p. 213 Photo Delfino Sisto Legnani, Marco Cappelletti
pp. 218–20 Filip Dujardin
p. 221 Ratthee Phaisanchotsiri
p. 222(t&c) Bangkok Tokyo Architecture
pp. 222(b), 223(t) BeAr
p. 223(c) BeAr, photo Luis Díaz Díaz.
p. 223(b) BeAr, photo Jorge Isla
pp. 224–31 Atelier Bow-Wow and Tsukamoto Lab / Institute of Science, Tokyo

pp. 239–45: (1) Cristobal Palma; (2) Yuri Palmin; (3) Filip Dujardin; (4) Jean Jacques Balzac; (5) Takashi Homma; (6) Maxime Delvaux; (7) Bêka & Lemoine; (8) Enrique Walker; (9) Atelier Bow-Wow; (10) Ratthee Phaisanchotsiri; (11) Bas Princen; (12) Pezo von Ellrichshausen; (13) MOS, photo Michael Vahrenwald; (14) Hao Chen; (15) Filip Dujardin; (16) José Hevia; (17) Yuri Palmin; (18) Joe Abreu; (19) Francisco Ascensão; (20) Filip Dujardin; (21) Luis Díaz Díaz; (22) Rory Gardiner; (23) Luis Díaz Díaz; (24) Delfino Sisto Legnani; (25) José Hevia; (26) ArtefactoryLab; (27) Jonathan Letoublon

SEVEN VISIONS OF BECOMING

p. 249(t) Ingo Arndt
p. 249(b) Jane Goodall Institute Spain
pp. 250, 251(t) Larry Barham
p 251(b) BrixL, CC BY-SA 4.0 (https://creativecommons.org/licenses/by-sa/4.0/)
p. 256 Víctor Cano-Ciborro, 2025
p. 258 Elena Sáez, 2025
p. 259(l) (right to left): Ray Pérez Contreras, 2025; Daniel López, Carlota González, Gabriela p. 259(t) (left to right): Diego Marrero, Iván Marrero, Daniil Sorokin, 2025; Virginia Pérez and Laura González, 2025; Victorina Otero, Laura Sanz and Alejandro Fuhai Tomé
p. 259(b) (left) Ángel Ripollés, Héctor Garcia and Alejandro Jerez, 2025; (right) Diego Farrais Bello, Genaro Capogrosso and Sara Reale, 2026
p. 260(t) Víctor Cano-Ciborro, 2025
p. 260(b) María Barroso, 2025
p. 261 Sara Cruz, Juan Carlos León, 2025
p. 262 Valentina Labriola, 2026
p. 265 Valentina Labriola, 2025
p. 266 Photos Juan Jose Miranda 2025; Graphic design Darya Benzi Kipen; Drawings student work from Atelier 'Architecture, Society and Territory' (Politecnico di Torino) and 'Senior Design Studio' (Barnard + Columbia Architecture Department), 2025
p. 269(t) Bibliothèque Nationale de France
p. 269(b) Caisse Nationale des Monuments Historiques et des Sites, Paris
pp. 271–73 Joan Martí Elías
p. 276(l) Ignacio Cerda Medina
pp. 276(tr), 277, 278(l), 279 Valentina Morales Puebla
p. 276(br) José Luis Gutiérrez
p. 278(r) Guy Wenborne
pp. 282, 284–86 Carlos Zeballos-Velarde
p. 289(l) The U.S. Geological Survey National Minerals Information Center
pp. 289(r), 290 Photos Blanca Pujals
p. 291 Plataforma Sí a la Tierra Viva
p. 292 NOAA
p. 293 Daniel Dan / Pexels

A SITUATED EVENT

pp. 305, 306 Photos © Manifesta 15 Barcelona Metropolitana / Arnau Rovira
p. 308 Pau Bajet, Mariona Benedito, Maria Giramé, Tomeu Ramis, Carmen Torres and Pau Sarquella

UIA INTERNATIONAL STUDENT COMPETITION

pp. 317–18 Harvey Rupp

ACKNOWLEDGEMENTS

This book is a vast, interconnected collective endeavour, made possible through the help, care and imagination of many. Deep gratitude is extended to everyone who has contributed to this three-year journey culminating in the UIA World Congress of Architects 2026 Barcelona and the book's publication. To those who offered generous conversations and thoughtful feedback, and who helped identify and connect contributors – opening perspectives to other ways of thinking and practising space. To the entire technical team involved locally and internationally, the editorial team, publisher, committees, juries, evaluators and UIA representatives, as well as the public institutions and sponsors who together have made both the Congress and this publication possible. And to all the contributors to this book and the Congress – those who shared their investigations, prototypes and reflections, engaging in a collective discussion that has expanded and deepened architectural potentials beyond what could ever have been foreseen.

Becoming.
Architectures for a planet in transition

A publication of the UIA World Congress of Architects 2026 Barcelona, convened by the International Union of Architects / Union Internationale des Architectes (UIA) and organised by the Higher Council of the Orders of Architects of Spain (CSCAE) and the Architects' Association of Catalonia (COAC)

Editors and Curators of the Congress
Pau Bajet, Mariona Benedito, Maria Giramé, Tomeu Ramis, Pau Sarquella and Carmen Torres

Head of Editorial Coordination (CSCAE)
Daniel Monfort and Javier Rodríguez Ulibarri

Editorial Project Manager and Assistant Curator (CSCAE)
Leonie Alessa Bremser

Editorial Project Manager, Copy-editing and Proofreading (Park Books)
Caroline Ellerby

Book and cover design
Judit Musachs and Studiopol (Pol Pérez)

Image processing, printing and binding
Nova Era Publications

Park Books AG
Niederdorfstrasse 54
8001 Zurich
Switzerland
www.park-books.com
T +41 44 262 16 62
E info@park-books.com

Park Books is being supported by the Federal Office of Culture with a general subsidy for the years 2026–2028.

Distribution in Spain, Mexico and Uruguay
Puente editores
Barcelona, España
info@puenteeditores.com
UDL Libros
r.lozano@udllibros.com

ISBN 979-13-992168-1-3

Distribution in all other countries
Park Books AG
Niederdorfstrasse 54
8001 Zurich
Switzerland
www.park-books.com

ISBN 978-3-03860-495-2

MIX
Paper | Supporting responsible forestry
FSC® C121877

Product safety
Responsible person pursuant to EU Regulation 2023/988 (GPSR):
GVA Gemeinsame Verlagsauslieferung Göttingen GmbH & Co. KG
Post Box 2021
37010 Göttingen
Germany
T +49 551 384 200 0
E info@gva-verlage.de